For

Don Reid
October 1985

# The Miners of Decazeville

Mine entrance at turn-of-the-century Decazeville.
The sign warns of pit gas in the mine.

# The Miners of Decazeville

## A Genealogy of Deindustrialization

Donald Reid

Harvard University Press

Cambridge, Massachusetts, and London, England   1985

Publication of this book has been aided by a grant from the
Andrew W. Mellon Foundation.

This book is printed on acid-free paper, and its binding materials
have been chosen for strength and durability.

Library of Congress Cataloging in Publication Data

Reid, Donald.
    The miners of Decazeville.

    Includes bibliographical references and index.
    1. Coal miners—France—Decazeville—History.
2. Decazeville (France)—Industries—History.
3. Coal mines and mining—France—Decazeville—
History.  I. Title.
HD8039.M62F869  1985      331.7'622334'094474      85-5502
ISBN 0-674-57634-9 (alk. paper)

# Acknowledgments

One of the real pleasures in doing a local study is getting to know people. While it would be impossible to mention all those who shared their experiences with me, I would like to single out André Cayrol and Marceau Coursières, local Resistance leaders, and Lucien Estrella, hunger striker in 1962. I also want to thank the dozens of individuals who allowed me to consult the documents which form the basis of this book, including officials of the Confédération Générale du Travail, the Confédération Française des Travailleurs Chrétiens, and the Force Ouvrière at Decazeville, and of the Confédération Générale du Travail-Fédération du Sous-Sol in Paris; M. Bancarel and the staff of the Société de Secours Miniers at Decazeville; M. Sentex and the staff of the Houillères d'Aquitaine at Decazeville, especially my friend Roger Boutonnet; the clergy of the parishes of Decazeville and Combes, and of the bishopric of Rodez; M. André Delmas and his staff at the Archives Départementales de l'Aveyron; the staffs of the *mairies* of Aubin, Cransac, Decazeville, and Firmy; the staffs of the Ecole des Mines (Paris); of the Comité d'Histoire de la Deuxième Guerre Mondiale; of the Charbonnages de France (Paris); and of the Société des Lettres, Sciences et Arts de l'Aveyron (Rodez). I would also like to thank Abbé Foucras, historian of the Resistance; Michel Brun, guardian of the Fayol papers, Lucien Orsane of the Decazeville Socialist party; René Rouquette, former mayor of Decazeville; the Féligandes and the Huntzigers, descendants of François Cabrol; and the late Mme. Ramadier. I would like to acknowledge as well the blue-coated staff of the Archives Nationales who, as they brought me heavy boxes of documents, reiterated the class basis of academic research, and stood as an emblem reminding me, as a labor historian, that my research could simply be a second, though more subtle, exploitation of Decazeville's miners.

I am grateful to two of the leading historians of French labor, Michelle Perrot and Rolande Trempé, who offered me guidance during the early stages of my research. I would also like to thank the many friends and colleagues who commented on various drafts of this manuscript, including Judith Bennett, Jack Censer, Patrice Higonnet, Christopher Johnson, Richard Kuisel (twice!), Carolyn Lougee, John Merriman, Laurent Thévenot, Steve Vincent, and Martha Zuber. I owe particular thanks to Joan Scott, who made me realize that such an insistently neurotic manuscript would benefit from analysis; and to my colleagues Richard Soloway and George Taylor, who made valuable suggestions at several points in the revision process. My greatest debts are to Nathanael Greene, who introduced me to French History, and to Gordon Wright, whose understanding and perspicacity have affected not just this piece of work, but my whole approach to history.

The Harvard University Society of Fellows provided a stimulating environment for work. I would like to single out for thanks the chairman of the Society, Burton Dreben, and Senior Fellow John Clive. In preparing this book for publication I have benefited greatly from the advice and patience of my editors at Harvard University Press, Elizabeth Suttell and Anita Safran. And I want to thank Rosalie Radcliffe for typing what everyone thought was the final version of the manuscript.

I also want to express appreciation to my parents and to my friends Judith Bennett, Susan Blaustein, Terry Castle, Peter Galison, and Richard Garner, who, if they haven't all read the book, know the movie by heart. Finally, in dedicating this work to Holly Russell, I would like to thank her for making the years in which I wrote it the most pleasant of my life.

# Contents

Introduction   1

1. The Triumph of Industrial Capitalism   9

2. Work in the Mines   24

3. The Company Town and the State   37

4. Community in Crisis   49

5. The Long Depression   72

6. The Second Industrial Revolution   114

7. The Politics of Production   158

8. The Coal Miners' Battle   188

Conclusion   214

Appendix: A Social Portrait of Industrial Workers
in Nineteenth-Century Decazeville   221

Abbreviations Used in Sources and Notes   240

Primary Sources   242

Notes   247

Index   325

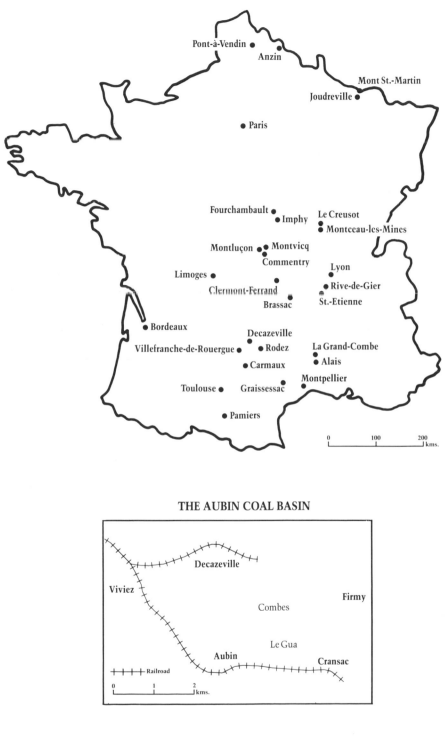

## FRANCE

Pont-à-Vendin ●

Anzin ●

Mont St.-Martin ●

Joudreville ●

Paris ●

Fourchambault ● Le Creusot ●
Imphy ● Montceau-les-Mines ●

Montluçon ● ● Montvicq
Commentry

Limoges ● Lyon ●
Rive-de-Gier ●

Clermont-Ferrand
Brassac St.-Etienne

Bordeaux ●

Decazeville ●

Villefranche-de-Rouergue ● ● Rodez
La Grand-Combe ●
Alais ●

Carmaux ●

Montpellier ●

Toulouse ● Graissessac

Pamiers ●

0        100        200
|—————|—————| kms.

## THE AUBIN COAL BASIN

Decazeville

Viviez

Firmy

Combes

Le Gua

Aubin

Cransac

├┼┼┼┤ Railroad

0        1        2
|————|————| kms.

# Introduction

This book examines how the miners of Decazeville and nearby communities in the Aubin Coal Basin experienced both industrial development and deindustrialization. It traces their story from the final decades of the *ancien régime* until the Fifth Republic. The advantage of this long view is that it allows an examination of the actions of labor, capital, and the state not only in the making of an industrial community, but in the unmaking of it as well.

Decazeville—a town that began with the establishment of large-scale coal mines and metalworks in the Aubin Basin in the 1820s—is now threatened by the closing of these industries. Daily life in Decazeville is no longer structured around shifts at the mine; the soot which every visitor to the town remarks upon may soon be a thing of the past. Events of the last decade show that the deindustrialization of Decazeville is far from unique: I began this study during the 1977 protests at Longwy and elsewhere in the Lorraine against the "restructuring" of the French steel industry and completed it in 1985, during the British miners' strike against pit closings. The lesson of these conflicts is that deindustrialization, like industrialization, is not only an economic phenomenon; it is a social, political, and human one as well.

The term "deindustrialization" describes the decline and disappearance of the nonagricultural sector (or sectors) of a market economy in which nonagricultural production accounts for a significant portion of a region's employment and exports.[1] Deindustrialization is not limited to the era that followed the First Industrial Revolution; historians of early modern Europe have identified several periods of deindustrialization of rural manufacturing.[2] Nor, of course, is it necessarily permanent; new industries may replace the old.[3] In recent

decades, however, the immediate problems raised by deindustrialization in Western Europe and North America have taken on new
urgency because of the size and importance of threatened industrial
regions and the place of industrial workers in the national polity.[4]

Because deindustrialization is both a regional and a national phenomenon, it cannot be analyzed satisfactorily within the confines
of a "community study." This book therefore deals only peripherally
with residents other than miners in the Aubin Basin and leaves large
areas of miners' experiences unexplored.[5] Rather than focusing on
the whole community, I have chosen to study how changes in capitalism and the nation state have affected one group of workers and
how, in turn, these workers, both on their own and in alliance with
other Frenchmen, have shaped the economic, social, and political
history of their nation. This requires a *longue durée* study which
does not separate industrialization and deindustrialization, but sees
the course of industrial development of a particular sector as preparing the conditions for its decline. To the extent that deindustrialization is a dispossession of the working class, it demands an
examination of how that working class came into existence and
what forms of power it developed in its dealings with capital and
the state.

The coal industry provides an excellent case study for several
reasons: its importance in the development of capitalism and the
working class in France, the regional nature of its growth and decline, and the role which the French state played in both the development and the dismantling of coal regions. Coal was one of the
bases of the First Industrial Revolution throughout Europe. France
has relatively small coal deposits in comparison with those of Great
Britain, Belgium, and Germany and always had to import much of
the coal it consumed. This was one factor in orienting the nation's
industrial development in the direction of small-scale, diversified
manufacturing. Ironically, the paucity of big industrial firms gave
coal companies a disproportionate role in the development of large-
scale industrial capitalism in France. Of the 20 most highly capitalized industrial firms in France in 1840, 8 were coal-mining companies and another 3 were integrated coal-mining and metallurgical
enterprises. The largest firm in France, the Anzin Coal Company,
had a capital of 50 million francs, three times that of the runner-
up.[6] Right through World War I, mining and metallurgical companies
remained the largest industrial corporations in France.[7] With nationalization of the coal industry after World War II, it became one
of the prime examples of state-run enterprise in France.

Coal miners, vividly depicted in parliamentary enquiries, popular literature, and their own self-portrayals as representing the essence of the new industrial proletariat, played a key role in the development of the modern working class in France. At their peak, miners composed over 5 percent of the nation's industrial labor force (5.1 percent in 1856; 5.6 percent in 1911).[8] Their power surpassed even their numbers. In the decades before World War I, miners' strikes were among the most dramatic and important in France. Between 1890 and 1914 miners struck at a rate 17.25 times that of the labor force as a whole and several times more often than workers in any other industrial sector.[9] Miners were leading actors in national social conflict and in the development of industrial relations from the Second Empire to the Fifth Republic; at the same time, however, they were members of distinct, relatively isolated communities.

The high costs of labor and shipping in the coal industry encouraged the growth of demographic and economic enclaves in which a large proportion of the population was bound together by a dependence on coal mining. The deindustrialization of these regions was built into the very development of the coal industry: the economics of coal mining is controlled by the depletion of the deposit and the increasing cost of extraction as operations move farther from the surface. Because of the nature of capitalist investment in coal mining, coal communities were frequently either monoindustrial or limited to industries dependent on coal. Although coal mining in the Aubin Basin was of paramount importance to the local economy, it was always secondary in national terms, accounting for less than 4 percent of the national production in the nineteenth century and less than 3 percent in the twentieth century. The decline of coal basins represents one of the most extreme forms of deindustrialization; devastating to a community, but often not to the nation. The isolation of the Aubin coal basin, its coal-based economy, and its long-time secondary status make it a particularly suitable region in which to examine the repercussions of industrialization, economic transformation, and deindustrialization.

In addition, the early intervention of the French state in the coal industry provides an excellent forum for studying the growing involvement of state administrators and legislative bodies in the economy since the early nineteenth century. After creating the conditions for large capital investment in coal mining in the Aubin Basin and elsewhere, the state intervened in mid-nineteenth century to limit the centralization of economic power by placing restrictions on the ability of mining firms to establish regional monopolies. And in part because of the early and active role of the state in monitoring the coal industry, the miners' union evolved a national strategy at the end of the nineteenth century to achieve legislative reform. This served as an important model for later developments in French syndicalism.

This book is ordered chronologically in three sections, each of which analyzes the structures created by the interaction of miners, managers and the state during specific periods. The first section looks briefly at social conditions in the Aubin Basin before the establishment of large industrial enterprises and considers what social, economic, and political changes were necessary preludes to the industrialization of the Basin, which began in the 1820s.

The second part begins with the creation, in the isolated Aubin Basin, of one of the largest industrial enterprises in July Monarchy France and of a community dependent on the firm. It emphasizes the effects of state labor and tariff policies on both the organization of work in the mines and on the enforcement of company authority within the company town. This section concludes with an extended examination of the first "deindustrialization" of Decazeville, from the decline of the iron industry caused by changes in technology and French tariff policies during the Second Empire to the end of the Long Depression in the mid-1890s. This was a period of intense industrial strife. To compensate for the demise of the iron industry, company managers developed new ways to raise productivity and profitability through intervention in miners' lives in and out of the workplace. But miners, who had created a social and cultural community during the half-century of industrialization of the Aubin Basin, challenged company management in several dramatic strikes. Buttressing the informal social bonds of the workplace, miners joined with other elements of the population to develop a local political identity independent of the company. And in the strike of 1886 the miners of Decazeville succeeded in placing their struggle squarely in a national political context.

The last section of the book takes Decazeville from the decades of renewed prosperity in the early twentieth century through the depressed interwar period, to the Coal Battle of the first years of nationalization and the closing of the underground mines at the beginning of the Fifth Republic. Changes in both the recruitment of mine labor and the organization of mining weakened the internal solidarity of the mining community before and during the interwar period. Through the Resistance and the Coal Battle, however, miners established new rights for themselves. In 1961–62 the miners of Decazeville drew on this legacy in turning their strike against the nationalized mining enterprise into a national political movement.

The experiences of Decazeville's miners tell us much about the history of labor in nineteenth and twentieth-century France. Recent work in labor history has focused on the twin themes of workers' defense of control of the labor process and workers' defense of community life.[10] This approach has concentrated on changes in capitalism and forms of production that threatened urban artisans in the 1830s and 1840s and skilled industrial workers in the decades before World War I.[11] The essential argument is that artisans' and skilled industrial workers' control over their work, their shared culture, and their strong community life differentiated them from unskilled and semiskilled workers and gave them the resources to resist energetically new forms of capitalist encroachment. These workers were defeated only when the combined forces of the state and capitalism undercut their social base.[12] This model has been of crucial importance in bringing labor historians to examine the social foundations of collective mobilization and the decisive role of workplace and community culture in orienting social action. Studies of artisans and skilled industrial workers have also pointed to the social roots of early and influential forms of socialist ideology.

Do miners fit the profile developed for nineteenth-century artisans and skilled industrial workers? The miners' attachment to the land, especially in the coalfields of southern and central France, separated them from artisanal and skilled industrial workers, who by the mid-nineteenth century frequently had a clear working-class lineage.[13] The miners did not possess the traditions of the artisanal guild system or the national corporate solidarity of workers in trades where movement from employer to employer across France was common. And unlike artisanal workers, miners rarely ran their own mutual aid societies; these functions were handled by company institutions in which worker representatives cooperated with mine management. Finally, while miners might occasionally rail against the invasion of outsiders into the mines,[14] they had much less opportunity than artisanal and skilled industrial workers to limit entry into their trade and to decide on advancement.[15]

Yet in the control over their work and in the strength of their communities, nineteenth-century miners displayed characteristics associated with artisanal and skilled industrial workers. Like them, miners worked in relatively autonomous crews and formed cohesive occupational communities. Hence, miners present difficulties for those wishing to categorize them. Edward Shorter and Charles Tilly describe coal mining before the widespread introduction of cutting machines as both an "artisanal heavy industry" and a "classic proletarian industry."[16] Elsewhere, Charles Tilly, Louise Tilly, and Richard Tilly note that in France, the "industries breeding extensive organization were older, more artisanal, smaller in scale, with the egregious exception of mining."[17]

Three factors that make the mining industry something of an anomaly in nineteenth-century labor—managerial organization, the role of the state, and regional concentration—also make it a crucial area in which to map an agenda for labor historians who want to follow the history of French workers into the twentieth century.[18] For, unlike many artisanal and skilled industrial trades, mining remained one of the most important industries in France from the mid-nineteenth right through the mid-twentieth century. First, miners worked within different managerial structures than did artisanal workers or most of the skilled elite in the factory. Miners were employed by large, hierarchically ordered firms which constituted some of the earliest examples of modern management in France.[19] In the nineteenth century these firms conceived of labor management as a set of techniques applied to both the workplace and the community. The organization of work and the development of community life in coalfields incorporate a history of cooperation and conflict between labor and managers. The importance of human labor in coal extraction, coupled with the solidarity of underground miners, made it difficult to reduce wages significantly in periods of falling coal prices.[20] Mining firms were forced to restructure management to decrease the production cost of coal relative to the sale price. As a result, the mining industry often provided a catalyst for the development of new managerial strategies, including various forms of paternalism in the nineteenth century, Henri Fayol's business administration at the turn of the century, and state planning after World War II.[21]

The role of the state adds a second dimension to the study of mining. The economic importance of coal and hazards of its extraction encouraged early state interest in mining. Not until well into the twentieth century did the French state begin to play a similar role in industry as a whole. Several recent works have pointed to the importance of state actions in determining the nature and timing of labor conflict in France and elsewhere in Europe.[22] Neither the organization of work nor the development of the working-class community in the Aubin Basin can be understood without considering the part played by the state. Throughout the nineteenth century, state mining engineers forced companies in the Aubin Basin and elsewhere to alter aspects of the organization of work in an effort to promote safe ad productive mining. The state also played a crucial role in supporting and legitimating company-run towns like Decazeville during the first decades of industrialization, and later in creating the conditions for residents to wrest their communities from company control. The Third Republic invested new miner-controlled institutions with powers that allowed unions in Decazeville and elsewhere to maintain a presence in the labor force after changes in the organization of work and the composition of the town's population had sapped miners of earlier sources of strength.[23] In the twentieth century, the state's role in the mining industry has grown significantly, culminating in the nationalization of the mining industry after World War II. Through these years the coal miners' relationship to the state continued to provide an influential model for organized French labor.

The localized impact of mining also provides an opportunity to study worker culture and politics in regional terms. Regional issues have grown in importance with increased international economic interdependence and resulting regional economic disparities. In the century and a half after industrialization, miners in the Aubin Basin created their own culture and political identity. While the state sought to inculcate in all Frenchmen a national culture during the nineteenth century, the presence of northern French managers hired by companies owned by northern French capitalists caused anti-managerial sentiments to be expressed in terms of regional culture. But with the integration of the Aubin Basin into a national and international industrial market over the course of the nineteenth century, firms there lost their leading position in French industry to companies in the north and the east. In confronting the hardships this created, workers in the Aubin Basin came to feel that they did not share the interests of the nearby peasantry with which they shared roots, and began during the Third Republic to embrace national political action. Class consciousness and national consciousness developed together and reinforced one another. Local political and syndical leaders elaborated reformist and radical national strategies to meet the needs of miners in the Aubin Basin. Miners' participation in the Resistance and especially in the "Coal Battle" after

World War II fostered their sense of themselves as the truest of Frenchmen. Faced with deindustrialization, miners in the Aubin Basin demanded a national solution to what they viewed in part as a regional problem created by changes in the international political economy. In counterpoint, the strike of Decazeville's miners against the closing of the mines in the Aubin Basin in 1961–62 was a catalyst for development of the contemporary Occitan movement in south-western France.[24]

Management, the state, and the region represent elements of an agenda for historians of twentieth-century labor. As important factors in the experience of workers in declining sectors of the French and European economy, they also pose questions for contemporary labor movements. In *The Making of the English Working Class*, E. P. Thompson argued that the culture and values of workers in cottage industry and artisanal shops were not lost with the emergence of a new industrial labor force. Instead, they provided a legacy for the first generations of workers during the Industrial Revolution. A crucial issue facing labor today is what it can and should inherit from the experiences of past generations of workers. Assessment of those experiences is a first step in this process.

# 1. The Triumph of Industrial Capitalism

The nocturnal spectacle of tall blue flames shooting into the sky from the burning mountain of Fontaynes vividly impressed late eighteenth-century visitors to the Aubin coal basin. With daybreak the flames seemed to disappear, revealing a forbidding landscape of smoking craters. When it rained, the mountain gave off eerie groans as new fissures were created, while thick clouds of steam that reeked of burning sulfur made the area smell like a forge. Travelers expressed particular concern over the future of the village of Fontaynes, situated only a hundred paces from the conflagration. The residents were accustomed, however, to living on a mountain of coal. They found their smoldering backyard a convenient source of fire to light the hearth and occasionally cooked meals in the outdoor ovens it provided. Underground fires in nearby Cransac sustained mineral springs and fumeroles where hundreds of *curistes* came annually before the Revolution to partake of the waters.[1]

Yet only the intrepid journeyed to Cransac. As the crow flies, it was eighty miles from Toulouse and one hundred miles from Clermont-Ferrand, Limoges, and Montpellier. Until the nineteenth century, the seasonal nature of transport on the Lot River and the dearth of serviceable roads connecting the Basin to the outside world compounded the natural isolation created by hilly terrain and dense forests. These features determined the layout of communities in the Basin. Some were made up of a small cluster of houses around the parish church and a scattering of hamlets, each with a few dozen households at most: Firmy, for example, had 1,610 inhabitants in 1771, 209 of whom resided in the town proper while the rest were spread out among seventy-five hamlets. Aubin, on the other hand, "is neither a village nor a bourg nor a town," the historian Amans-

Alexis Monteils commented in the Year X: "it is a long road built on the side of a hill."[2]

Most inhabitants of the Basin were peasants, but poor soil and primitive farming techniques often prevented them from growing enough grain to meet their needs. Parish priests, the peasants' preferred leaders and most articulate spokesmen, reported in 1771 that a bad harvest might yield only enough to feed the population of the Basin three months of the year.[3] Residents depended on trade to make up the difference. Peasant proprietors raised grapes for wine and devoted their best piece of land to the cultivation of hemp.[4] Yet even in good years coal mining provided an invaluable supplement to the Basin's economy. It prevented some people from dying of hunger, as one priest claimed, and played a role in the lives of everyone in the Basin, whether they dug coal on their own property or "share-crop mined" on their neighbor's, transported coal on land or down the Lot, or simply benefited from low coal prices in supplying their personal needs.

The peasants employed the most rudimentary mining techniques. The abundance of coal just below the surface encouraged them to dig small mines in the hillsides, usually the height of a man and not much more than a meter wide. Because air entered only at the mine opening, tunnels could not be extended very far. The peasants put up wooden braces at the mine entrances, but depended on pillars of coal and schist for interior support. They chipped the coal free with primitive picks, scooped it up in wooden shovels, and carried it out in wicker baskets. Inefficiency and danger characterized these excavations. When a peasant encountered difficulties, he left his pit and opened another. Schists burned in the hundreds of abandoned mines, while the multitude of small shafts spread the fires and caused flooding and cave-ins. The Aubinois "spoil more coal in their foxholes than they extract," a state mine official reported in 1755. Fatal accidents, the parish registers reveal, were not uncommon.[5]

Residents of the Basin believed that landowners had a right to what lay below as well as on the surface of their property. French law, however, gave the state the stewardship of the nation's subsurface and the exclusive right to grant coal-mining concessions. The monarchy, prompted by the desire to limit deforestation, which threatened the nation's economic and naval capabilities, codified the laws governing mining in the edict of 1744. The crown hoped that a reassertion of its rights would lead to increased capital investment in mining and to safer and more productive extraction.

Virtually all of the edict was devoted to the way mining was to be carried out so as not to endanger miners. The monarchy justified the concessionary system in terms of its ability to look after the workers' best interests.[6]

Prerevolutionary concessionaires invariably claimed that they wanted to improve mining in the Basin, often with the aid of foreign supervisory personnel, but they were clearly interested in monopolizing the local coal trade as well. Both projects constituted an attack on the inhabitants' way of life. Mining entrepreneurs, armed with the legal obligation to work their concessions in a safe and orderly fashion, interfered with the individual peasant-miner's right to determine where, when, and how he would mine. As coal merchants, the concessionaires threatened the freedom and livelihood of the community formed by the Basin's peasant-miners, carters, boatmen, and their customers.

Inhabitants of the Basin responded with violence to the nascent capitalist enterprises which attempted to work concessions granted by the crown. In 1692 the Duchess d'Uzès decided to take advantage of the concession granted to her father to exploit all coal mines in France except those of the Nivernais. She dispatched a M. Courtinade to the Aubin coal basin to ensure that no coal was extracted without her authorization. The inhabitants, angered at this interruption of their trade, harassed the Duchess' employees. One infuriated carter decapitated Courtinade and hung his head on a tree as a warning to the other outsiders. The carter went unpunished and the Duchess saw her concession annulled in 1698.[7]

In the 1760s residents of the Basin again put up stiff resistance to efforts by a new company to take advantage of a royal concession to mine in the region. The entrepreneur Tubeuf, who at one point employed 2,500 workers in mines throughout France, managed the operation for the concessionaire.[8] Residents fought Tubeuf's effort to integrate their mining industry into his coal empire. In 1763 they wrecked mine equipment and in the following year carters and boatmen tried to break the company's monopoly of the coal trade. Count de Bournazel, one of the most important nobles in the area, voiced a widespread complaint when he blamed rising coal prices on "the multitude of useless managers and employees who devour and grow fat on their booty." Men armed with sticks and stones pursued Tubeuf for an hour and a half on horseback in 1763, calling him "robber" and "Englishman." This incident prompted the state to garrison thirty soldiers in Aubin to protect company agents. Further disturbances took place in 1766 and 1768. The arrest in March 1769 of two clandestine coal carters precipitated a rebellion that lasted three weeks. After liberating the arrested men, the insurgents destroyed the company's mine installation and attacked its employees, severely injuring one of them. Rioters torched the house of the director, and the Intendant of Montauban blamed the disorders on "the general hatred" of him. Afterward, bands of peasants roamed the countryside carrying an effigy of the director and asking contributions for having delivered the region from his presence. Local authorities claimed to be able to identify only three rioters, a reflection of the united opposition of the community to usurpation of its traditional prerogatives. When the royal prosecutor had the three arrested, a crowd of more than 2,000 armed and angry peasants fought off the *maréchaussée,* injuring several cavaliers and forcing the release of the new prisoners. In the face of this resistance, the state abandoned efforts to punish the rebels. The company, despite an investment of almost 200,000 *livres,* had to abandon its mines. Ten years later, vigilante action quickly squelched another attempt to start up mining operations. The new director had his lodgings repeatedly besieged and burned as he was chased from place to place during his stay of less than a week in the Basin. Heightening his terror was an inability to communicate with the inhabitants, who spoke only *langue d'oc.*[9]

State officials made intermittent efforts to oversee mining in the Basin during the eighteenth century. In 1783 Alexandre Charles Besson, one of the first graduates of the state Ecole des Mines, was sent to survey the mines of Aubin with an eye toward overcoming the inhabitants' hatred of outside mine operators. Knowing of the violent opposition to previous mining companies, he approached the voyage with trepidation: "An unknown stranger," he wrote his superior, "suspect since he comes only to trouble the inhabitants in their work and their possessions, hardly appears suitable to effect such a revolution."[10] As Besson drew nearer, he became more frantic. From Villefranche-de-Rouergue he wrote: "It is distinctly possible I will get myself clubbed in a *pays perdu* without paths or known roads, neither understanding the language nor able to make myself understood and having little money and therefore being deprived of the most important means of aid should something happen."[11] Besson finally arrived in the Aubin Basin the following week. He tipped his guides quite liberally so that they would translate what was being said in the local *patois,* although the scowls of assembled families and their refusals to allow him to inspect their mines made it clear what they thought of him. Relieved when the time came to leave the area, Besson reported that state mine inspectors were as unwelcome as other outsiders.[12] Inhabitants lumped them together with coal mine entrepreneurs as *françimans* who wanted to appropriate their one valuable resource.

The Parlement of Toulouse and the Provincial Assembly of the Haute-Guyenne supported the peasant-miners' resistance to outside companies regulated by officials of the central administration. Yet the issue was not simply the encroachment of central state power. Full exploitation of the Basin's mines would require the state to redefine the relation between property and capitalism. Only the state could carry out the dispossession of local property-owners necessary to allow large-scale mining. In 1782 the Provincial Assembly of the Haute-Guyenne defended the peasant-miners of the Aubin Basin by arguing that the state should abrogate the rights of "speculators" (concessionaires) in favor of "capitalists"· "that is to say those who mined on their own property";[13] the next year the Assembly offered to supervise such mining in the Aubin Basin.[14] Large-scale mining in recalcitrant areas like this one had to await the central state's ability to enforce its conception of mining rights over the claims of both residents of coalfields and regional authorities.

In the century before the Revolution, residents of the Aubin Basin defended the local and regional economy upon which their communities depended against the state's efforts to introduce capitalist enterprises. The inhabitants' uprisings had more in common with seventeenth-century peasant tax revolts than with the protests of miners in the Basin against their employers in the nineteenth century.[15] During the *ancien régime* communities in the Basin were built around the marketplace rather than the workplace, and their values were those of peasants who sold what they produced, rather than of wage-earners whose place in the economy was mediated through a supervisory hierarchy.

Sustained opposition to state-supported mining entrepreneurs was not limited to the Aubin Basin. Property-owners in the coalfields of Languedoc, Auvergne, and the Loire, often more advanced in developing their coal industry than their counterparts in the poor Aubin Basin, were equally hostile to outside operators. The exception was Anzin (Nord), where entrepreneurs discovered and developed the largest and most technologically advanced mines in the country. Having located the mines themselves, the owners of Anzin did not have to fight off local peasant-miners; furthermore, the property structure allowed them to negotiate with large noble landowners rather than stubborn peasant proprietors.[16] By the time of the Revolution Anzin mined close to 300,000 tons of coal annually and had established housing and rudimentary social services for many of its 4,000 employees. The next largest mines, Rive-de-Gier (Loire), extracted about one-third as much coal per year. The mines of the Aubin Basin produced only 5,000 tons of coal annually.[17] Lacking either an interested and wealthy local noble, like the Marquis de Solages at Carmaux (Tarn), or a thriving local bourgeoisie, as in the Loire, the mines of the Aubin Basin remained in the hands of small property-owners into the nineteenth century.

The historian Monteils, an active participant in Aubin politics during the first years of the Revolution, saw the fight against the mining companies as a precursor to the overthrow of royal tyranny. He celebrated the victory of a "handful of vinedressers and coal miners armed only with their anger," who defeated a "despotism that wanted to thrust its iron scepter into the entrails of their generous land." The abolition of mining concessions figured prominently in the local *cahiers de doléances* of the First and Third Estates, and in September 1790 the Aubin district administration of the new department of Aveyron asked that landowners be guaranteed the right to mine on their property and that "concessions be proscribed forever."[18] Other coal-mining areas expressed the same desire. The Constituent Assembly was disposed to abandon the concession system as an affront to the rights of property, but Honoré-Gabriel de Mirabeau countered with an eloquent exposition of the successes achieved at Anzin. These had been possible, he argued, only because the system of mining concessions allowed the firm to exert its prerogatives over individual landowners. The mine legislation which the Assembly passed on 28 July 1791 preserved the principle of concessions, while satisfying in large part the wishes of small property-owners and peasant-miners in southern and central France.[19] The new law gave property-owners priority in obtaining concessions and decreed that concessions previously granted to individuals who did not own the surface property would revert to landowners if they had discovered and exploited mines on their property before the concession had been granted. These proprietors would be left in peace because the law contained no provisions for state supervision of mining.

The peasant-miners' victory was short-lived. Napoléon's mine law of 21 April 1810, the basis of mine legislation until nationalization in 1946, harkened back to the *ancien régime* and was a defeat for individuals who wanted to work deposits on their own property. The law required the state to grant concessions to those best equipped to exploit them without according first preference to landowners. Concessionaires had to indemnify property owners, to pay the state an annual production tax, and to maintain standards in their mines set by the state and monitored by state mining engineers. The prefect was responsible for assuring that concessionaires carried out the engineers' orders. The decree of 3 January 1813 addressed the particular dangers associated with coal mining. In the event of a serious accident, control of operations passed from the operator to the state engineer. Mining firms had to keep necessary medical supplies on hand and to pay for the care of employees injured in work accidents. If a worker was incapacitated or killed, the concessionaire or manager could be brought to court and tried for negligence.[20]

Napoleonic mine legislation established the basis for large capitalist investment in the mining industry. Although peasants in the Basin, who "recalled with enthusiasm" their prerevolutionary triumphs, believed in 1815 that Napoléon's downfall signalled the end of his legislation, the state never allowed them to reestablish their former economy.[21] Furthermore, the Napoleonic mine law laid out clearly the basis for state intervention in the miners' trade. The coal industry enjoyed a special relationship to the state because of the concessionary system and because of the potential importance of coal to national interests. Management of mining was therefore a matter for state supervision. The dangers inherent in mining further authorized the state to specify the companies' responsibilities in the mines and to discipline or replace private management when an accident occurred.

Large-scale exploitation of the natural resources of the Aubin Coal Basin failed during the *ancien régime* because the state was unable to force inhabitants to permit outside investors to reap the Basin's riches in safety. The issue was not feudal restraints on capital; the key factor was the relative vitality of community economies like those of the Aubin Basin in the face of an entrepreneurial capitalism which owed as much to the colonial experience as to the coal mine of the Industrial Revolution. The Napoleonic state prepared the way for a new type of industrial development, however, by reaffirming the monarchy's conception of coal deposits as the special preserve of the state.

The Napoleonic wars and the post-Napoleonic depression weakened the communities of peasant miners which had successfully opposed mining firms before the Revolution. Dearth, disease, and the draft decimated the area. Between 1806 and 1821, Aubin fell in population from 2,954 to 2,364, Cransac from 607 to 489, and Firmy from 1,175 to 1,005: 885 persons emigrated from Aubin alone.[22] A generation of depopulation and economic stagnation made the Basin ripe for outside investors who wanted to adapt the local economy to their needs by creating a town devoted to and dependent on industrialization of the region.

Growing up near Bordeaux, the future Duke Decazes may have heard of "Cahors coal," as coal from the Aubin Basin was called when shipped down the Lot, but his interest in it came much later. When the Ultras pressured Louis XVIII to dismiss the liberal Decazes—his favorite—as prime minister in 1820, the king named him ambassador to Great Britain. There Decazes became intrigued with British ironmasters' use of coke rather than charcoal to smelt iron ore. The technique had received only limited application in France. [23] Stymied in his efforts to bring the British style of liberal politics to France, he turned his attention to introducing the most advanced component of the British model of society to his country. On his return to France, Decazes decided to construct a *forge à l'anglaise*.[23] He chose the Aubin Basin as the site for his ironworks because, as in British metallurgical centers, iron ore and coal were found in close proximity. Taking advantage of the Napoleonic mine legislation, Decazes quickly acquired extensive mining concessions in the Basin.

Decazes' project would have been inconceivable without the establishment of a high tariff on iron in 1822. This incentive led to the creation of "English" forges at Fourchambault, Châtillon, Terrenoire, and Alais as well as in the Aubin Basin. But in contrast to Fourchambault and Châtillon, which depended upon local forges to supply them with pig iron, the industrial complex of Decazeville had to be built from scratch.[24]

The shelter provided by the tariff of 1822 encouraged a group of Parisian bankers to join with Decazes in the establishment of a joint-stock company, the Société Anonyme des Houillères et Fonderies de l'Aveyron, in January 1826. The initial capital of 1,800,000 francs quadrupled by 1832.[25] Renewed demands for funds forced stockholders to plough back returns on their investment for the first decade and a half of the company's existence. Few investors could afford such a policy: for the American economic historian Arthur Louis Dunham, Decazeville was "the toy of a small group of wealthy men."[26] Major stockholders protected their investment by using their influence in the Orleanist state in support of the tariff of 1822.[27]

It has been suggested that one reason for the lack of industrial development in southwestern France during the nineteenth century was the reluctance of prospective investors in the region to take their capital out of land and commerce and put it into potentially risky industrial ventures.[28] The experience of the Houillères et Fonderies bears this out. An analysis of the fifty-four stockholders in 1840 reveals that little of their money came from Aveyron. Fifteen nobles and an almost equal number of bankers and businessmen from Paris and other large cities held most of the stock. Aveyronnais accounted for one-tenth of the stockholders and owned only one-fiftieth of the shares.[29] The outsiders began to exert their influence over local affairs immediately. The first president of the company, the Strasbourgeois Jean-Georges Humann, a political ally of Decazes who had made a fortune through audacious speculation during the Empire, was elected deputy of the district of Villefranche-de-Rouergue in 1828 without ever having left Paris.[30]

In April 1827 the company's board of directors appointed as local director François Gracchus Cabrol, son of the one-time public prosecutor of the Revolutionary Tribunal of Aveyron. As a young man Cabrol had judiciously dropped his middle name in order to adjust to the changing times. A graduate of the Ecole Polytechnique, he served valiantly in the army during the final years of the Napoleonic wars and in the Spanish expedition of 1823. Cabrol's knowledge of British ironmaking and his familiarity with the Aubin Basin gave him solid credentials for the directorship: unlike his successors, he was *rouergat* by birth and spoke the region's *patois* fluently. Cabrol brought to the job great energy and faith in private enterprise, which he did not hesitate to call "the most intelligent force and the most active agent of civilization."[31] Few would disagree with his claim to be "ardent and passionate." "On a hundred occasions," he boasted in 1846, "my *impetuosity* has enabled me to overcome obstacles inseparable from the creation of a vast enterprise."[32]

Cabrol's talents proved invaluable: establishment of an industrial complex in the *pays perdu* of the Aubin Basin was an enormous undertaking. Shortly after his appointment as director Cabrol described his headquarters at the château of Firmy: "Here I am with my papers and belongings pell-mell. I rigged up a drawing board, but as there is no ceiling, dust falls by the handfull. I am sometimes besieged by hens."[33] Yet three years later, in 1830, the board was able to remark with pride: "It is perhaps without parallel in France that a single enterprise has been founded so quickly."[34] By 1833 the three original blast furnaces of La Forézie (Firmy) had been dwarfed by a much larger factory at Lassalle that boasted six blast furnaces as well as puddling and reheating ovens, rolling mills, workshops, and office and administration buildings.[35] Cabrol sought unsuccessfully to convince local peasants to sell his firm the land necessary to build a 3,200-meter canal between the two factories. He foresaw a "Saint-Etienne of the west" springing up along its banks with the establishment of industries requiring iron and coal as raw materials, such as glassmaking, pottery-making, nailmaking, and ironmongery.[36]

The plant at Lassalle was referred to as Decazes-ville from at least January 1831, and a year later the name Decazeville came into regular usage for the village built around it.[37] Residents of surrounding towns scoffed at the new settlement out of fear, Cabrol justly remarked, "that the banner of Decazeville would become brighter than their own."[38] Hundreds of Aubin residents sent a petition to the prefect in October 1832 to oppose the creation of a new commune at the site of the ironworks: "This place was formerly composed of three households. Today it is inhabited by some shopkeepers and winesellers, attracted by the proximity of the foundries. *Ouvriers cosmopolytes* employed temporarily in said factories make up the rest of the population." There was no need, the petitioners continued, to create a new township, particularly one with "the pompous name of Decazeville."[39] Pompous or not, the town's name fit its character, for when Decazeville was made a commune in 1833, its 1,123 inhabitants depended almost exclusively on the new mines and ironworks for their livelihood.[40] Decazeville's neighbors did not remain free of industrial development for long. By the first years of the Second Empire a zinc factory had opened in Viviez, and Campagnac operated mines in Cransac; Gua, a section of Aubin, had almost been named Riantville in honor of the Riant brothers, two of the first investors in the mines and ironworks there.[41] "It is evident," the head of Decazeville's mines commented, "that the Aubin Coal Basin is destined to play the same role in the Midi as Anzin in the north and St. Etienne in the southeast."[42]

From its inception the Houillères et Fonderies portrayed itself as a progressive force doing battle with reactionary groups in the Basin.

When rejecting charges made against it by the Firmy town council in 1838, the company director described a confrontation between liberal economic values and the stultifying vestiges of a bygone era:

> [These complaints] have their source solely in the antipathy [of the company's opponents] toward an establishment which has destroyed their influence over the poor by giving them an education and work, thus making them independent of those who, in their blind passion, would like to destroy an establishment that gives them umbrage.[43]

The growth of the Houillères et Fonderies revealed the sterility of the system which had preceded it:

> [T]he area now taken up by our forces was inaccessible, poor, wild and almost deserted [the company wrote to the prefect in 1844] . . . Where there was a desert before, there now exists a population of five thousand souls, active, working and progressing daily. Products which increase the public wealth by three to four million francs a year surge from tracts of land where coal and iron ore lay dormant for centuries.[44]

The state mining corps agreed that industrialization was in the Basin's best interest: "This new industry would refine the morals, the customs and the life of a population which has lived until now in a state close to poverty," wrote the Conseil Général des Mines in 1828.[45] During the thirties and forties the Houillères et Fonderies developed a close relationship with a number of state mining employees. They cooperated wholeheartedly with the firm in the suppression of illegal mines on its concessions and defended the new company against attacks by irate residents over the price and availability of coal for local sale. On several occasions the Minister of Public Works "lent" the Houillères et Fonderies state engineers to fill positions in the company management;[46] engineers who remained in state service often supplemented their income significantly by serving as consultants to the Houillères et Fonderies and to other firms in the Basin.[47] In addition to providing technical assistance through the mine corps, the state also helped industry in the isolated Aubin Basin reach new markets by building roads and improving the navigability of the Lot River.

The efforts of the July Monarchy to improve France's transportation system aided Decazeville in an even more crucial way. In 1836 the industrial complex at Decazeville produced 6,697 tons of iron and extracted 124,490 tons of coal.[48] Despite these encouraging figures, the firm had trouble finding a market for its iron because impurities in the coal and iron ore made it unsuitable for many types of manufacturing.[49] Poor sales exhausted the firm's working capital and in 1838 the prefect fully expected announcement of the company's liquidation.[50] A dramatic turnabout in the company's fortunes took place shortly thereafter. Government support for the construction of railways created an upsurge in the demand for rails, a product that could be made with Decazeville's inferior iron. By 1840 the Houillères et Fonderies had become the fourth largest industrial firm in France. It ranked second in the production of iron, and seventh in the extraction of coal. Decazeville's new preeminence was reflected in the share of rail production allotted it in agreements among forges; it received 50 percent of the 13,000 ton Paris-Orléans order of 1841 and two years later was given the leading position in the five-company contract with the Compagnie du Nord.[51]

The company's growth was interrupted by the depression at mid-century, but resumed again under the Second Empire. Between 1841 and 1854 the industrial complex at Decazeville expanded from one forge to three, from six blast furnaces to ten, from twenty-six puddling ovens to seventy-seven, from six steam engines providing 500 horsepower to twenty-seven providing 1,600 horsepower. In 1856 production at the forges reached a level unsurpassed during the nineteenth century—33,458 tons of pig iron, 16,304 tons of rails, and 4,175 tons of other iron products.[52] Despite a drop of almost 60 percent in the sale price of rails between 1830 and the late 1850s, the ironworks of Decazeville remained profitable.[53] The firm returned dividends of 8 percent or higher each exercise from 1841–42 to 1855–56 (20 percent in 1847–48) with the exception of the mid-century crisis of 1848–1852.[54]

The new relationship of state and capital which was at the heart of Decazeville's success also affected the Church, the bulwark of prerevolutionary society in the Aubin Basin. Vialarels—part of the future Decazeville—had been a priory before the Revolution. However, the dispersal of popular refractory priests during the Revolution, followed by the demographic crisis of the early nineteenth century, had weakened the Church's position in the Basin. Residents of Vialarels were forced to hire their own priest because the state— exercising its prerogative under the Concordat—decided that the parish was not large enough to warrant the expense. In 1821, after the priest's death, a local noble and future mayor of Vialarels and

Decazeville, M. de Lassalle, wrote to the Bishop of Cahors to urge that a new priest be appointed, adding that if the state was unwilling to pay him, area notables would. With no priestly guidance and under the influence of "the crowd of outsiders" who had invaded the community to work the local mines, "half of the parish miss mass, the farm hands run about all day and abandon their livestock, and the young use Sundays for their scandalous *rendez-vous*." His request remained unanswered until the Houillères et Fonderies stepped in to take on the role the state had spurned.[55]

Like the community leaders it displaced, the company saw the Church as a bulwark against disorder and gave it a prominent place in Decazeville's social life. The firm helped assure that the Church remained the most important social institution in the lives of the first peasants who came to work in the new industries. The original church at Vialarels soon proved inadequate for Decazeville's growing population. By the fifties it could hold only one-tenth of the town's faithful: "In order to hear, most of those attending seated themselves in houses near the church, or better yet, stood at the square and in the public thoroughfare, often in spite of rain, cold or heat."[56] The structure that the Houillères et Fonderies helped to build to replace the old church was designed to reflect the newness of the undertaking at Decazeville. The architect explained to Cabrol that he had placed the baptismal font at the entrance because "one must be baptised to enter the temple. This was *de rigueur* in the primitive Church, and in a completely new town we have envisaged religion free from all the modifications brought by time which may have removed the primitive grandeur from this holy religion."[57] Such symbolism was lost on the passerby, however: one traveler described the church as "a heavy classical building dear to the bourgeois period of King Louis-Philippe."[58] Somewhat later a church was erected in the heart of Gua in Aubin. "This church," noted the Bishop of Rodez, "which is constructed in part of iron, was mostly paid for by the Compagnie d'Orléans [owner of the mines and forges of Aubin]. Its architecture belongs to the modern genre which could be called the industrial genre."[59] Both churches were constructed as monuments to the companies whose industries had transformed the Basin.

Aided by the state and the Church, the Houillères et Fonderies had little trouble establishing hegemony in the Basin. The nonworker residents' dependence on the firm as a client and for employment as sawyers, carters, and boatmen tempered their original opposition to industrialization of the Basin. The commercial capitalism of the eighteenth-century mine entrepreneurs had offered inhabitants nothing in exchange for exploitation of their most valuable resource; the extent of the investments made by industrial capitalist firms, however, gave a new vitality to the Basin. By 1840 the Houillères et Fonderies was defending its projects before the Basin's residents with the argument that the mines and factories "provide them with their living."[60] And when presenting changes that year which he felt were necessary to protect the firm's interests, Cabrol explained: "I should say of the region's inhabitants in general, that those who are attached to the land would like a reform, certainly not for the sake of our interests, but because they think that the fall of the company would mean their ruin."[61]

In any case, the massive influx of immigrants who came to work in the Basin's new industries prevented the issue of traditional rights from forming the basis of political activity as it did in other regions: for example, Rancié (Ariège) where residents defended their communal mining rights, or areas in the Ariège and the Var where wood rights were at issue.[62] When municipal authorities acted to protect local interests it was generally a case of too little too late: in 1853 the Aubin town council approved the mayor's suggestion that the town ask for a mining concession to supply the needs of local consumers at a reasonable price, but nothing came of it.[63]

Industrialization changed the focus of community rights. During the Second Empire mining destroyed the famed mineral waters of Cransac. The town, which had boasted seven or eight *auberges*, four *grands hôtels*, and even a zoo to amuse the almost four thousand visitors who came annually at midcentury, was transformed from a summer resort into a mining town. By 1891 mining had so radically altered Cransac that the town council's protest against encroachment on the remaining springs reflected a set of interests very different from those expressed in lawsuits against the mine operators a few decades earlier. The mayor of Cransac was also director of the local company, Campagnac, and his constituency was composed of his firm's miners. The resolution of the Cransac town council attacked the plans of Campagnac's nearest competitor, the Société des Aciéries de France, to expand its mines in the Parc concession (named after the old resort facilities), and voiced the concern of miners in Cransac that jobs in the new pits would go to workers from outside the Basin.[64] With the establishment of the mines and forges a new local consciousness took root that linked the future of the Basin to industrialization. Company rivalries and hiring practices replaced community mining rights as key issues facing the area. As these disputes unfolded, however, they revealed other conflicts within the companies between people who lived and worked in the Basin and those who profited from their labor.

The dramatic transformation of the Aubin Basin peasant communities to company-dominated industrial towns raises wider issues about the nature of regional economic development. Economic and social historians have recently shown that, well before the spread of the factory system in the late eighteenth and nineteenth centuries, "protoindustrial" domestic manufacturing had incorporated large parts of the rural population in Europe into the capitalist economy. Industrial capitalism therefore did not involve the confrontation of the capitalist town with an isolated precapitalist agricultural hinterland.[65] In fact, protoindustrial areas were among the most likely sites of early industrial development because of their large non-agricultural labor force and the capital generated by protoindustry. The exception to this model were new centers of coal mining and iron production like the Aubin Basin, where the location of natural resources rather than the availability of labor, the agricultural economy, or the accessibility to markets determined investment.[66] Although protoindustry was of secondary importance in the preindustrial Aubin Basin, the area was actively engaged in a small-scale regional economy involving the sale of cash crops and coal and the purchase of food. Yet the Basin would never have developed into a major industrial center without capital from outside of the region, and without the intervention of the national state, in the form of trained technical personnel, tariffs and aid to transportation. The creation of industry in the Aubin Basin was not a specifically regional phenomenon but rather the result of new forms of capital concentration and state-building. These forces made Decazeville not into a Saint-Etienne of the southwest based on a diversified manufacturing structure, but into a town dependent for its existence almost solely on heavy metallurgy and coal mining.

# 2. Work in the Mines

There is an established tradition in French economic history of using comparisons with Great Britain and Germany over the course of the nineteenth century to show that French economic development was retarded. In recent years, however, the trend has been to accept the uniqueness of French society celebrated by Jules Michelet in *The People* in 1846, and to emphasize the role of agriculture and of artisanal and skilled industrial work in the development of a dynamic capitalist economy in nineteenth-century France.[1] The urban artisans worked in small shops and maintained their corporate traditions long after the abolition of guilds in 1791.[2] Outside of the large cities, however, other industries operated with very different forms of management. In coal mines, technical constraints and the concessionary system created a situation in which relatively autonomous crews worked within a hierarchical administrative structure. At Decazeville the economic strategy of the Houillères et Fonderies accentuated this development.

In the decades after the fall of Napoléon, France's modest coal industry developed significantly: production topped one million tons in 1820 and five million tons in 1846. Yet during this same period Great Britain extracted some ten times this amount annually. French mines could not meet the nation's needs and each year France was forced to import a quantity of coal equivalent to one-third to one-half of its own production, primarily from Belgium and Great Britain. These imports increased in the 1830s, when the July Monarchy abandoned the stiff tariff on coal established in 1816. By the last years of the July Monarchy the Loire was responsible for close to one-half of French coal production and the Nord for nearly one-third. Most of the remainder came from small mines in southern and central France, including Grand-Combe (Gard), Montceau-les-Mines (Saône-et-Loire), Commentry (Allier) and Decazeville. The isolation of many basins made transportation of coal costly. This so restricted the adoption of coal in industry that coke did not surpass charcoal in the production of iron until 1864. Before midcentury, coal companies outside of the Nord and the Loire generally depended on a local market, or, like Decazeville, on a nearby industrial consumer.[3]

The Houillères et Fonderies viewed its coal mines as subsidiary to the foundries and forges. The firm used almost all of the coal it extracted in the production of iron. To provide coal for the ironworks, the company often sacrificed upkeep of the mines.[4] The proximity to the surface of a portion of the coal deposits in the Basin allowed the Houillères et Fonderies to mine coal for a relatively small outlay of capital: by the early fifties the firm had sunk close to ten times as much in the ironworks as in the mines.[5] This investment would have been for naught, however, if the firm could not have compensated for the cost of transporting its iron out of the isolated Aubin Basin by paying less for coal than its competitors. Labor was the crucial factor in determining coal costs: it accounted for over 40 percent of the sale price of coal at mid-century, as opposed to 10 to 20 percent of the sale price of iron.[6] Despite a disproportionately large labor force in the mines of the Houillères et Fonderies[7]— explicable by the firm's loose supervision—the factory did receive the inexpensive fuel it required. In 1838 the cost per ton of coal delivered to the factory at Decazeville was among the lowest in the nation: 6 francs in comparison with 7 at Le Creusot and 23 at Fourchambault.[8] In 1845 the production cost of coal in the Aubin Basin was 5.2 francs, the lowest in France: it was 8.7 francs at Le Creusot and 12 francs at Anzin.[9]

The Houillères et Fonderies increased coal production rapidly to satisfy the demands of the ironworks: 41,207 tons in 1830 to 165,460 tons in 1845 to 287,733 tons in 1854–55.[10] In the early years of the Second Empire, production in the Aubin Basin surpassed 5 percent of the national total. The growth of the labor force kept pace with production. The number of miners rose from 122 in 1830 to 693 in 1845 to 1,033 in 1855, 420 of whom worked aboveground in the open-pit mines or in the cleaning and preparation of the coal.[11]

The primacy of the iron industry in the Aubin Basin indirectly shaped the organization of work in the mines. As long as market and tariff conditions made iron Decazeville's major export, coal mining received a minimal degree of supervision. As director, Cabrol's first concerns were the foundries and forges. He devoted his attention to the recruitment and management of the skilled metalworkers, who exercised considerable control over the labor process and the quality of the company's finished product. During the July Monarchy skilled metalworkers commanded daily wages (in the vicinity of 6 francs) at least twice as high as those earned by a well-paid miner and three times those of a well-paid unskilled worker in the mines or factories. The actions of individual skilled metalworkers, rather than of miners and other workers, were the prime source of social conflict in the Aubin Basin before the Second Empire.[12] Yet, despite the attention given skilled metalworkers, industrial development radically changed mining in the Basin as well. Formerly, peasant-miners had not only divided their time between farming and mining, but had carried out their mining like peasants, working alone or in small groups and selling what they extracted on the market. After the Houillères et Fonderies took over mining in the Basin, miners worked within a large organization, even if they often labored under the direction of a contractor *(entrepreneur)*. They carried out specific tasks and were forced to reverse their previous priorities by making farming subservient to mining in their lives.

## Labor Recruitment

The first generation of miners in the Aubin Basin came mostly from the local peasantry.[13] Although the Houillères et Fonderies imported a number of skilled metalworkers from Great Britain, it recruited only a few miners from outside of the region for special jobs like training new miners and boring through rock. Many of Decazeville's miners retained strong ties to the land. Cabrol referred to the harvest season as "the annual tribute which we are obliged to pay to agri-culture."[14] At the end of the Second Empire a state engineer com-plained that

> Many workers in the Aubin Basin have little experience. They are closer to pickers at coal than true miners . . . There is only a small nucleus of true miners in the Aubin Basin. The facility of access to these mines and the advantage of finding oneself occupied all year, or during the rigorous season, brings many miners whom one could call occasional miners but who are in no way trained in this profession, to the mines of Aubin.[15]

In comparison to Anzin, Grand-Combe, and many other major mining firms of the early- to mid-nineteenth century, the Houillères et Fonderies made only minimal efforts to establish a permanent labor force for the mines. Despite disruptions in production, firms in the Basin were slow to abandon the strategy of hiring economical, but often mobile and unskilled labor from the countryside rather than investing heavily in the training and stabilization of a colony of miners. The symbiotic relationship between agriculture and mining that resulted had advantages for both management and workers. The concern that workers who devoted their spare time to farming would not be as productive at the workplace was offset by the fact that miners who worked a piece of land after leaving the mines were less demanding about wages.[16] Fluctuations in the annual number of working days, which were the consequence of the mine's subservience to the needs of the ironworks, encouraged miners to maintain ties to agriculture.[17] Industrial development in the Basin perpetuated the division of property within the region by providing employment for younger sons in the peasant family and a ready market for agricultural produce.[18] The Decazeville tax collector remarked at midcentury: "The small landowners, whom one can almost assimilate to true day-laborers, rush to till the land they own rather haphazardly and then go with their families to work as laborers in the industrial establishment."[19] The reverse occurred as well. Paid by production, first-generation miners often accepted the risks of unsafe mining in order to earn a day's wages without spending an entire day away from their fields and their families.[20]

## Underground Mining

Most coal in the Aubin Basin was extracted from underground pits. Because of the nature of the coal deposits in the Basin, it was often possible to sink shafts into the side of mountains, although vertical shaft mines were dug as well. One of the first steps which the Houillères et Fonderies took was to introduce job specialization, a concept alien to the Basin's peasant-miners. An early local director was dismayed to find that in the Basin "the same workers who dig the coal carry it out on their shoulders by climbing an inclined plane." He arranged a "division of labor" between hewers, who unlodged coal using explosives and picks and put up wooden mine supports in their own galleries, and helpers (*manoeuvres*), who aided the hewers and saw to the removal of coal from the mine in carts on tracks instead of in baskets.[21] Hewers and helpers worked together in small crews which were often bound together by familial ties. The company also employed several other categories of workers, the most important of whom were timbermen *(boiseurs)*, specialized workers who put up mine supports in the large tunnels and were paid about as well as the hewers. Aging hewers were often demoted to helpers or drivers *(conducteurs)*, workers in charge of taking care of the horses used for transport in the mines, or were given positions above-ground. In the absence of extensive rationalization or mechanization, the various categories of mine workers changed relatively little until the end of the nineteenth century.[22]

The hewer was the key figure in the mines. During the first years of operation, the Houillères et Fonderies imported miners from as far away as Great Britain to train local peasants in hewing. Over the course of the nineteenth century the hewer's skills became an issue of crucial importance to management. The simple picking away of coal at the face soon gave way to the use of blasting to loosen the coal. The hewer made a deep lateral cut underneath the seam and then bored a hole near the top of the seam in which he placed blasting powder. The explosion loosened a block of coal. The hewer's skill in this operation determined both the safety of his crew and the amount of coal that remained in the form of the more marketable lump *(gros)* rather than crumbling into fine *(menu)*. One reason for the organization of work by crews was to distribute as widely as possible the limited number of skilled hewers.[23]

The unskilled laborers with whom the hewers worked often disrupted production during the first years of mining. On "Saint Monday," locally recruited helpers would not show up for work. Frustrated hewers, encumbered by piles of coal they had dug, soon joined their coworkers at the local taverns.[24] These problems declined with the development of an informal apprenticeship system. During the nineteenth century the future hewer or timberman entered the mines as a young adolescent. After undertaking a variety of jobs that acquainted him with work above and below ground, he joined a small crew as a helper. An experienced hewer or timberman instructed the *garçon mineur* during breaks and mealtimes. Such instruction was unpaid, so it is not surprising that hewers generally trained their sons or relatives, or the sons of friends and neighbors.[25] Companies profited from this arrangement and did not intervene in it until the end of the century. A worker from the countryside who came to work in the mines as an adult missed this apprenticeship and was therefore more likely to spend his career as an unskilled helper, or to work aboveground in the open-pit mines or preparing fill for underground tunnels, jobs disdained by miners' sons.

Over the course of the nineteenth century, companies established a system whereby one hewer in each crew acted as chief miner *(chef de chantier)*. He had his own lamp and tools, and during the early years of mining even owned the baskets and sacks used to transport coal out of the mines.[26] The chief miner bargained with the engineer, or his subordinate, the master miner, to extract coal at a standard rate per wagon and at a variable rate per meter, determined by conditions in the particular gallery. Although the composition of the crew varied, the chief miner generally took on another hewer and hired a pair of helpers to load the coal, and paid them out of his earnings. The chief miner received a single paysheet from which the company deducted the cost of the explosives, lamp oil, and tool maintenance. At the end of the month the engineer or the master miner often added a bonus to the agreed-upon rate to compensate workers for obstacles they had encountered. The supervisory employee might reduce the rates for advancement in a gallery the following month if he felt that the previous rates had proved too high. Manipulation of the rates was a constant concern of management: as early as 1837 the director at Decazeville had found that locally recruited miners "generally work more at the end of the month than at the beginning", and he set rates accordingly.[27]

The flexibility of this form of remuneration was a response to the difficulties of supervising the mining crew. Whereas a factory hand labored in a setting designed by his employer, a miner continually created the space in which he worked. This gave the mining crew a certain amount of leeway. Perusal of a crew's paysheet, with its compensations for water, fire, bad air, rails laid, schists encountered in a coal seam, and so on, reveals the restricted control management exercised over the miner's physical environment. Nor could management assign a foreman to watch over work in the individual mine galleries as it could on the factory shopfloor. The prevalence of mines that could be entered and exited on foot encouraged miners to set their own hours. Regulations drawn up for one mine in 1830 read: "Work begins at daybreak and ends at night, with the hours of rest to be chosen by the miners."[28] Crews generally left the pits for two hours at mid-day and retained a great deal of control over when they would work. Although the system of small independent crews paid by production created difficulties for management, the consensus in France until the end of the nineteenth century was that such an organization of work was much better than some version of longwall mining, in which a number of hewers would work a vein together. It was thought that in a group of hewers, less diligent workers could "hide" among their more productive comrades. The overall effect would be to reduce productivity to the lowest common denominator.[29]

### Open-Pit Mining

Because many coal deposits in the Aubin Basin were near the surface, firms in Aubin and Decazeville could operate open-pit mines on a scale not found in other parts of France. To excavate an area from the surface required a large initial investment to clear away the surface soil and schist. Once production began, however, the cost per ton was lower than in the underground mines, and a higher percentage of lump coal could be extracted. The profits from operation of open-pit mines made them a necessary element of the mining economy of the Aubin Basin. Because of the high initial investment involved, however, open-pit mines were not well maintained during economic crises. In these periods there was increased pressure for greater production at lower costs from the underground mines.

A particular appeal of open-pit mining for firms in the Basin, as the board of the Houillères et Fonderies explained in 1831, was that "ordinary workers are no less suitable than experienced miners."[30] Two decades later the board's chief executive officer (*administrateur délégué*) recommended development of the open-pit mines because "simple laborers" could work them: "So especially in a time of escalating fuel needs, we will find ourselves safe from the demands and coalitions of miners—exigent workers whose number is quite limited anyways."[31] The board agreed and decided to invest heavily in expansion of the open-pit mines to meet the ironworks' increased demand for coal, and secondarily to provide soil—a by-product of initial open-pit preparations—to fill in old mine tunnels. In 1856, 1,009 of the 2,532 mineworkers in the Aubin Basin worked in open-pit mines. Production in such mines of the Houillères et Fonderies rose from 21,583 tons for 1851–52 to 136,508 tons—half of the company's total production—for 1855–56.[32]

The existence of extensive open-pit mines fragmented the mining population in the Basin. The semiskilled workers in the open-pit mines were less well paid than underground miners and much more mobile. Companies sent newcomers to work in the open-pit mines;

only those who proved themselves there were asked to work underground. Labor in the open-pit mines was less crew-centered than in the underground mines. Instead, there was a division between the open-pit hewers who, with the aid of explosives, extracted the coal, and the myriad of haulers who removed it. Underground miners despised the open-pit mines, where work was done in all weather, and were in fact sent there to work as a punishment.

The Houillères et Fonderies' preoccupation with the ironworks had serious consequences for both the open-pit and the underground mines. A combination of insufficient supervision, minimal investment, and periods of extreme demand for coal led to deterioration of the coal deposits. In the open-pit mines the absence of precautions against landslides cost numerous lives and repeatedly interrupted production. Below ground, the failure to fill in old mine tunnels wreaked havoc: cave-ins, floods, and fires from flammable schists left in abandoned galleries created frequent crises. The difficult work conditions discouraged regular, sustained work by miners. This led to the establishment of a system of harsh, intermittent discipline rather than one form or another of constant surveillance. A visiting army officer left a vivid account of the construction of retaining walls to hold back the fires in Decazeville's mines in the mid-thirties: "The thick torrents of hazardous blinding smoke cannot be tolerated for more than two minutes. Each man brings what he finds at hand—wet hay, stones, boards, etc.—gives a hammer-blow and falls asphyxiated. Another arrives, carries him off, comes back and undergoes the same fate, until they succeed in blocking the principal outlets."[33] Ventilation in mines on fire was provided by dropping bundles of straw down pits while miners held in their mouths a thin leather tube that was connected to fresh air galleries or to the outside. In one case miners rebelled against this practice but were back to work four days later, after having each paid a fine of three francs.[34] The state engineer in charge of containing the underground fires at Firmy in 1838 posted guards to prevent the escape of miners who were working twelve and twenty-four hour shifts in the burning pits.[35] Such forms of coercion were a corollary to the relatively lax day-to-day supervision of mining operations in the Aubin Basin.

## Management

Faced with a refractory and untutored first-generation labor force, the Houillères et Fonderies had to assemble a sufficiently large and disciplined managerial staff of engineers and supervisors to administer the numerous facets of mine operations. This proved impossible as long as engineers demanded autonomy from the director, and split their loyalties between the company and the supervisory personnel. The Houillères et Fonderies sought to subordinate the relations formed between engineers and their men to the overall interests of the company. The case of Michel Delaitre, appointed master miner in 1835 after showing great courage in fighting subterranean fires, illustrates this tension. Several years after the promotion, the director noted that Delaitre had begun the job penniless, but since that time had been able to build and almost finish paying for a house valued at four thousand francs. In response to repeated questioning by the director, the chief mining engineer vigorously denied that Delaitre could be cheating the company. Only Cabrol, intervening as the board's chief executive officer, broke the deadlock. "Cabrol," the director wrote to the board, "remarked to us on the unseemliness of keeping a man who evidently could not justify the acquisition of what he owned except by having defrauded the company." When Delaitre gravely injured a company guard and a worker during a fight, the director had him fired. The mining engineers jumped to the defense of their master miner and backed down only when confronted with the combined opposition of the deputy director and Cabrol. The director drew a lesson for the engineers from Delaitre's dismissal: "No man is indispensable to the firm . . . Anyone in error can be punished immediately."[36]

The local director interpreted such situations as the consequence of a national shortage of mining engineers.[37] Feeling that this was a short-term problem, the board intervened in 1839 to impose a centralized authority over engineers, who had a tendency to treat their pits as fiefdoms. The director feared that competitiveness between engineers would diminish in the more hierarchical administrative structure. "Emulation among our engineers," the board responded, "far from growing weak as you think, will, on the contrary, increase, for they will be paid according to their work and the services which they render."[38] Engineers would no longer seek to exert power over various sectors of the mines, but would vie among themselves to raise production. The engineers' integration into a system based on individual productivity and obedience to company authority was a necessary prerequisite to similar changes later in the lower ranks of supervisory personnel and the miners.[39]

The Houillères et Fonderies had initially shown reluctance to create a supervisory staff below the level of engineer. It recruited these employees from the labor force. Early master miners earned most of their wages extracting coal and could devote little time to overseeing work in the pits. In any case they were often illiterate and could not follow even the simplest mine maps.[40] The firm soon realized the inefficiency of this system and established a small corps of salaried master miners to supervise mining operations. As with the engineers, the company used a variety of incentives and sanctions to ensure that the master miners acted in the company's interests, rather than on behalf of their subordinates.[41]

During the 1830s and 1840s the Houillères et Fonderies established the administrative framework to govern operations in its mines. However, the firm's engineers and master miners were inadequate to recruit and organize miners, to assure that mining on all company concessions was carried out safely and efficiently, and to set production rates. To compensate for shortcomings in its managerial staff, the Houillères et Fonderies was forced to depend on internal contractors, as well as on miners under direct company control. In an early variant of this system, the company contracted with local landowners to mine coal within the company's concessions. A serious accident at Firmy for which the state held the Houillères et Fonderies responsible put an end to this practice.[42] Instead, the firm retained the major elements of mine supervision in its own hands, while turning over most aspects of labor management to contractors. The company paid contractors by production and they, in turn, recruited, supervised, and paid their workers. The use of contractors was widespread in nineteenth-century French industry.[43] In the Aubin Basin it involved an adaptation of the type of labor recruitment used to organize gangs of agricultural labor in the area.[44] Two engineering students who visited the mines of the Aubin Basin in 1854 explained that contractors were a solution to the problem of ensuring a minimum of stability in the labor force:

> The principal reason that [companies] give for the maintenance of the contract system is that the population of the region adapts itself with difficulty to mining. There are no miners properly speaking; everyone has his own field which he tills and does not work elsewhere except when he has nothing to do at his place; it follows from this that those who work at the mine are essentially nomads, and that it is much easier to ask a contractor to recruit them than to go to the trouble oneself.[45]

Contractors often fed and lodged their workers, not infrequently increasing their control over them by keeping them in debt through the payment of advances. This situation placed the contractors in potential conflict with the company management: "these contractors constituted in effect a second power, whose interests were often opposed to those of the company and they had much more authority than company employees over the workers whom they paid."[46]

Contractors bid for the right to work areas that ranged in size from one "room" to whole pits.[47] In the open-pit mines contractors were most important as labor recruiters; in the underground mines they played a major role in the organization of work. Carefully worded contracts permitted the company to limit or to increase production as the requirements of the ironworks demanded.[48] Contractors often underbid one another. A poster announced to miners that eighty yards were being offered in the Paleyrets mine, a mine engineer reported in 1832. "The competition was such that the sum of 60 francs that had seemed low because of the haulage through two hundred meters in a muddy gallery, far from going up, was reduced to 48 francs."[49] Bidding had the added advantage from the company's point of view of removing from it the onus of directly setting rates. On the other hand, as company engineers recognized, it was very difficult to make any adjustments in the way mining was done once work had been turned over to contractors.[50] This created the conditions for fires and cave-ins and led to a general degradation of the deposits entrusted by the state to the company.[51] The two touring students could only lament that as long as Decazeville's ironworks continued to receive coal cheaper than any of its competitors, the company would have little incentive to rectify the "unintelligent direction of the contractors."[52]

## The Mutual Aid Fund

The mutual aid fund was the primary institution linking the company's role as employer to the lives of its employees outside of the workplace. The fund brought workers together in one institution, whether they worked in the factories or mines, under direct company supervision or for a contractor. The Houillères et Fonderies contracted out the medical services it was legally required to offer miners injured in its employ, thus avoiding the cost of constructing an infirmary and providing medical supplies.[53] However, in 1832 the firm did establish a mutual aid fund with an income derived from a 2 percent levy on all wages, from the collection of fines, and from a percentage of the profits of the company store. The fund provided workers and their families with support when they were sick or injured. Unwilling to guarantee housing or heating to lure miners from other coalfields to come to the Aubin Basin, the board of the Houillères et Fonderies hoped that "the advantages [offered by the fund] will procure us quite a few workers."[54] The fund was managed by a board composed of a president, secretary, and a treasurer named by the local director, and nine worker-commissioners chosen by workers grouped in categories based on nationality, occupation, and workplace, thus one English forgeworker and one French forge-worker from Decazeville, one miner from Firmy, and so on. Once a month, the commissioners met to discuss the cases of workers who had asked for assistance. To apply for benefits an individual had to undergo examination by the fund's doctor, who submitted a report to the committee. Those who qualified received a daily financial allotment which varied according to their job. Workers who complained in unseemly terms to the doctor about his description of their condition were fined.[55] Because the engineer and the doctor played parallel roles for the miner, one specifying the conditions for work and the other for recovery from the effects of work, it is not surprising that the company incorporated the doctor into the hierarchy of respect accorded the upper levels of management.

Through the 1850s the Houillères et Fonderies devoted its attention primarily to the iron industry. While the company established a managerial staff in the mines, it left much of the direction of labor to contractors. The nature of coal deposits in the Aubin Basin allowed the firm to invest in open-pit mines which employed unskilled labor, but periodically required large infusions of capital to prepare new areas for excavation.

The firm got most of its coal from underground mines where the crew, composed of a small number of more skilled hewers and helpers, emerged as the primary form of work organization. The crew enjoyed a fair degree of control in its work and bargained with the company over pay either on its own or through a contractor. The autonomy of the crew gave miners a mechanism to control their production, in order to raise their wages during periods of rising coal prices and to protect them during depressions. The miners' success is clear in the near doubling of the hewer's average daily pay between the 1840s and the 1880s.[56] When Decazeville miners struck in the nineteenth century, it was to defend the right of crews to negotiate with individual supervisors against either restrictions on the crew or efforts to impose a general rollback of wages, which seemingly contradicted the system of individual arrangements between crews and supervisors. The form of work organization—the crew—explains why Decazeville miners' strikes were "defensive" during the nineteenth century. Until the end of the century miners depended on the workings of the crew to raise wages; they acted collectively to protect that system.

While employees of the Houillères et Fonderies worked under a variety of conditions in the mines and factories, they all contributed to the company mutual aid fund. It was the primary company institution with which workers had contact outside of the workplace. Its aim of promoting the well-being of the labor force while fostering respect for company authority made it a cornerstone of the company town that the Houillères et Fonderies created at Decazeville.

# 3. The Company Town and the State

As he approached Decazeville one misty night in 1836, an army lieutenant attached to the geological service observed a striking scene:

> Over the completely dark enclosure, a circle of furnaces diffused bluish flames, comparable to the most beautiful Bengal lights, while the clearer and more transparent lights of the blast furnaces played a little in back, clearly sketching their fluctuating contours on the pitch black sky. From time to time human forms appeared like shadows to animate the scene for an instant and on the left the rare lights of the town twinkled like stars.[1]

Industry dominated the new town. Decazeville, wrote one journalist at the end of the nineteenth century, was "one of those artificial towns that industry raised from the soil with its magic wand."[2] A modern social historian uses Decazeville as his textbook example of the town created by the First Industrial Revolution.[3] However, it was not industrial development as such, but the relations between the company and its employees that set the parameters of community life in a company town like Decazeville.

In France the company town developed to meet the requirements of the new coal and iron industries. The so-called English foundries and forges required large amounts of coal. Until completion of the national railway network (which came only after establishment of the new iron industry), France did not possess an inexpensive means of transporting coal long distances. To avoid high shipping costs, new metallurgical companies built their factories in or near coalfields.[4] With the exception of the Loire, Provence, and part of the Nord Basins, the major deposits of coal in France were located some distance from established urban areas. Labor, especially skilled labor, was relatively scarce in large parts of France, where demographic stagnation and the tenacity of small peasant proprietors impeded the formation of a large industrial labor force.[5] Most companies that built mining and metallurgical complexes had to establish new settlements for their workers.[6] These company towns went through three stages. In the first, firms tried to attract, train and hold workers by offering benefits like a mutual aid fund and inexpensive housing. During the second stage, companies encouraged workers to have large families and made sure that the children learned the skills and discipline required for employment by the firm. Incentives and repression, not always clearly differentiated, complemented one another as means of creating obedient, productive workers.[7] With the introduction of shift work in the mines and factories, wives played a crucial role in maintaining a household in which their husbands, sons, and boarders could recuperate.[8] In the final stage of the company town, the firm, faced with a depletion of the natural resources in the area and changes in the national and international market, countered challenges to its authority in the town with threats to close up shop and depart. The large capital investments that made the company vulnerable to labor pressure in its early years had long since been amortized. The residents of the town were now at the mercy of the employer.

This model is an abstraction of experiences throughout France. Particular technological and financial factors affected the workings of individual company towns. Mining firms required fewer highly skilled workers than did ironworks and so pursued somewhat different labor policies.[9] For economic reasons, the means employers devised to control the labor force and to encourage it to reproduce itself were less thoroughly applied in some towns than in others, in such matters as company housing, restrictions on how far from work an employee could live, inter-company agreements not to hire competitors' labor, and the requirement that employers' sons work for the company. These were not unheard of in the Aubin Basin, but they were of less importance there. Because the area was especially susceptible to market downturns, firms limited their efforts to stabilize the labor force.

The second qualification to the model concerns the effects of the different investment and managerial strategies in company towns. The ability and opportunity for residents of the company town to act collectively depended on the relationships among individuals and groups in the community. The nature of company intervention contributed to the delineation of various groups. For instance, whether or not the company was active in commerce helped determine the number of shopkeepers and their political orientation. Company decisions concerning the organization of work—dependence on contractors for example—affected the character and strength of workers' informal organizations in the community.

New company towns lacked the multitiered class structure found in established urban centers. During the 1840s the bourgeois in the more heterogeneous Loire Basin backed miners in their opposition to coal operators.[10] In emerging industrial centers in the Aubin Basin and elsewhere, however, the few artisans and bourgeois offered little resistance to company control. This encouraged firms to look upon management of municipal life as an extension of management of the mines and factories.

Finally, there is the question of the isolation that is built into the model of the company town. The original intention of the company town was to insure that the worker and his progeny settle and accept company discipline rather than risk expulsion from the enterprise. But while contemporary company literature about company towns conveys a sense of self-containment, another, and generally unacknowledged actor in such accounts was the state. During the July Monarchy, industrial firms depended on the state's economic policy (for example, tariff levels and railway construction), its repression of organized labor, and its disinterest in other aspects of labor/management relations.[11] As a corollary, the firm required state recognition of its right to exercise political control over the company town. When the company was challenged by its employees in the economic or the political sphere, its initial reaction was often to assume the posture of a state within a state. Such a response could work only as long as the national state did not undercut either the national political economy or the local political hegemony on which the company town depended.

As company town, Decazeville functioned in a particular demographic, economic, and political context. The population of Decazeville grew from 1,123 in 1833 to 6,323 in 1846 and to 8,842 in 1856. Clearly, most residents of the town at mid-century were not natives: more than four-fifths of the men married in Decazeville between 1837 and 1846 had been born outside of the Basin.[12] These immigrants came to an area that lacked both housing and the commercial infrastructure to meet their needs. But the Houillères et

Fonderies, anxious to see a return on its large investments, minimized its financial contribution to development of the new town of Decazeville. It was encouraged in this direction by the boom-and-bust economy of the iron trade during the first decades of the Industrial Revolution in France, and by Decazeville's location in an area with few large employers to compete for labor before the Second Empire, when industry developed at Aubin, Cransac, and Viviez.

Industrial towns in the Basin suffered from a serious housing shortage. What existed was generally damp, dirty, and unsanitary. Writing in the 1870s, Louis Reybaud complained that Decazeville was a victim of its location: "A product of chance, [the site of Decazeville] was deplorably chosen . . . One is often at the first floor on one side of a house and at the ground floor on the other. Even for the principal routes there is no trace of planning; everything is pell-mell, nowhere is there the hint of an attempt at alignment."[13] Michel Chevalier had come to the same conclusion thirty years earlier. He described the Decazeville of 1843 as a "locality"; he would have called it a town "had the municipal authorities taken the trouble to align the houses and to build roads."[14] Companies in the Basin constructed only a limited number of dwellings for their workers. The Houillères et Fonderies provided the materials for workers to build houses in which they could live rent-free as long as they continued to work for the company, and it urged local landowners to put up new housing and to become landlords.[15] In the mid-fifties the companies in Aubin and Decazeville owned almost two hundred houses of two to four rooms. These offered lodging for only a small percentage of their workers, mostly bachelors. "At Decazeville company houses are occupied," the prefect commented, "but are hardly sought after."[16] Most workers shunned the restrictions of company housing. Single men generally lodged in boardinghouses, not infrequently run by foremen and contractors. Many miners with families lived in the countryside and worked small plots of land in their spare time.

Even before industrialization, the population of the Aubin Basin had been unable to feed itself without importing grain. The influx of workers, first to Decazeville and then elsewhere in the Basin, forced companies to take responsibility for provisioning. In the 1830s the Houillères et Fonderies established a company store composed of a bakery, a butcher's shop, a canteen, a grocery store, and a clothing store.[17] At first the company hoped to lease the store to an independent businessman, but was chastened by its experience with the brother of an interim director who blatantly cheated the firm.[18] The Houillères et Fonderies advanced wages, generally to the limit of a worker's previous month's salary, in tokens redeemable only at the company store.[19] While the offer of credit bound workers to the firm, the store also took company managerial personnel out of retail trade, thus undercutting what director Cabrol called "that strange abuse by which company employees are authorized to conduct their own businesses in order to exploit the workers. If we had wait[ed] any longer, every supervisory employee would have had a store."[20] Cabrol used the store to limit workers' freedom to leave Decazeville, while restricting the power of managerial personnel to the workplace. Both strategies complemented contemporaneous reforms in the mines and factories.

The Houillères et Fonderies intended the company store only as an expedient until the establishment of competitive local commerce. The needs of the rapidly expanding labor force in the fifties overwhelmed the Basin, however, and forced companies to assume temporary control of the food market. The stockholders of the Houillères et Fonderies resolved in 1854 "to take the most careful measures to shelter workers from exaggerated food prices because they would have a dire effect on wages."[21] Companies purchased large amounts of grain to assure a steady supply of bread for their workers.[22] In the mid-fifties the Aubin company established a model bakery and a model butcher's shop with personnel and material sent from Paris. These operated under contract to the company until local butchers and bakers became competitive enough to do away with the need for them several years later.[23]

Companies viewed the construction of a limited amount of housing and participation in local commerce as interim activities to restrict workers and supervisors and to give local residents time to develop moderately priced services. Firms hoped that a healthy local commerce would allow them to devote their full attention to production and would create a tax base that would permit towns to finance their own municipal services. On hearing that Decazeville had approved a toll on foodstuffs in 1855, the board of the Houillères et Fonderies responded exuberantly: "Now nothing will stop the town council and its mayor from executing the good things they are planning in the way of communal services."[24]

Tolls on foodstuffs were only one way for the workers at Decazeville to finance the operation of their town. More important were their contributions to the company mutual aid fund. In addition to providing for the care of sick and injured workers, the fund supported important aspects of community life, including the costs of educating the children of company employees. The fund also allocated severance pay for the most senior workers laid off in 1849.[25] During the Second Empire it provided the money to purchase grain and used profits from this trade to help defray the costs of constructing the town church.[26]

The Houillères et Fonderies' dependence on private and public forms of enforced taxation of workers to finance municipal services at Decazeville reveals its fundamental goal of making its employees pay for the creation of the new industrial town. This, rather than paternalism or the autocratic domination of all aspects of community life, characterized the first decades of the company town at Decazeville. Even in the prosperous 1840s and 1850s, when industry in the Basin was able to benefit from its position in the national market as one of the earliest and largest French iron producers, the Houillères et Fonderies devoted fewer resources than did its competitors, such as Grand-Combe and Le Creusot, to the creation of a well-endowed *ville-usine*.[27] The firm sought instead to exploit its political power to bolster its position in the workplace.

In contrast to its desire to see an economically independent, self-financing municipality take shape at Decazeville, the Houillères et Fonderies kept a tight grip on the town's political life well into the Second Empire. When requesting that Decazeville be made a commune in 1832, Cabrol argued that the company required this additional statutory authority to supplement its control over the labor force: "As fights are numerous in a population composed of workers, it is necessary to have a municipal authority on the spot that can stop serious disorders and that can often forestall the unfortunate incidents that develop while one goes off looking for the mayor [of another town] or his adjunct."[28] After a period during which local notables served as mayors of Decazeville, Cabrol assumed the post in 1844. Municipal authority was embodied in the managerial personnel and company guards. The police were perceived as agents of the national state and therefore of secondary importance: Decazeville did not hire a police commissioner until 1852, and as late as 1873 the town council threatened to stop paying half of his salary because most of his time was taken up by administrative matters.[29]

Until the Third Republic, national politics in Decazeville naturally centered on issues of concern to the company: workers in the Aubin Basin had little contact with the seditious doctrines developed by urban artisans. Because the Decazeville ironworks depended on the shelter provided by the tariff of 1822, both Decazes and Cabrol were ardent protectionists.[30] In 1846 Cabrol ran for a seat in the Chamber against Michel Chevalier, a leading proponent of free trade. Cabrol argued that France's high tariffs on iron protected an industry that supported whole regions: "The total value of the goods produced [at Decazeville] now stands at about five million francs, the better part of which is given in wages which, when exchanged for foodstuffs and consumer goods, pass into the hands of the farmers and shop-keepers of Aveyron."[31] Chevalier's free-trade theories conflicted with the interests of the area he sought to represent: "Your economic doctrine," Cabrol wrote to his opponent, "does not apply in the least to our department, while in this debate it is only the interest of our department that really matters."[32] Cabrol was particularly incensed by the unwillingness of free traders like Chevalier to take regional handicaps into account:

If an enterprise prospers, it is, if one believes the [free traders], an odious monopoly. On the contrary, if it suffers, due to local difficulties or those inherent in anything new, what is the good, they say, of industries in conditions inferior to foreign rivals that have every advantage—abundant raw materials, economic transportation, etc.?

According to the *économistes* then, there should not be a national industry when a similar foreign industry enjoys better production conditions.[33]

Cabrol's election was a victory for the new town and cause for a memorable celebration marked by a two-kilometer-long torchlight parade and a feast attended by all the company's workers.[34]

During the July Monarchy the Houillères et Fonderies' relationship to the state buttressed its political position in Decazeville. Visits by national leaders like Duke de Montpensier, son of King Louis-Philippe, who came to Decazeville in July 1843 to examine the ironworks' potential for military production, enhanced the prestige of the company. The king's son arrived at a time of industrial crisis—the only rails manufactured that month were those produced in his honor—but no pains were spared to make his sojourn memorable. Cabrol had a triumphal arch of two thousand tons of rails constructed in the square in front of the forge and decorated it with signs painted in gold proclaiming his devotion ("Long live the King. National industry owes him its prosperity") and celebrating the queen

("Long live the Queen. She is the model of all virtues"). At the center stood a meter-high Gallic cock and the national flag. According to a contemporary account the celebration was a great success: wherever the duke went, cheering crowds in which "perfect docility was mixed with enthusiasm" greeted him.[35]

The Revolution of 1848 threatened the Houillères et Fonderies' ties to the state and, indirectly, its hold over the town. On 5 March 1848, while the staunch Orleanist Cabrol was in Paris, Cadiat, a company engineer in the machines workshop, proclaimed the republic to the forgeworkers whom he had assembled in the schoolhouse. "If you exert yourself for [the Republic], she will look after you and your well-being," he told them. Cadiat was in contact with the provisional government and had himself appointed mayor of Decazeville: in the context of the Second Republic, what would have been a managerial problem became a political one.[36] Cadiat instructed the foremen under his direction to propagandize for the new government among their workers. The message they spread, however, was apparently not one of conciliation. Some workshops had been shut down in February, and foremen passed the word that large industries were in the hands of "industrial aristocrats" who were planning to close the factories in order to provoke a civil war. With the assistance of the provisional government's local appointees, the republicans even managed to get a Decazeville worker included on the republican slate: this, a friend of Cabrol wrote him, "seems to me to have been done with the sole aim of embarrassing you."[37]

Cabrol had been shocked by what he had seen of the February Revolution in Paris, and on his return to Decazeville late the next month he had Cadiat and his supporters, including the Protestant minister who served the British forgeworkers, run out of town. The commissioner of the provisional government rescinded Cadiat's appointment as mayor and, in Cabrol's words, became "meek as a lamb." He sent a plenipotentiary to Decazeville to inform Cabrol that the authorities wanted nothing better than to live in harmony with the company. Cabrol replied that the commissioner was to keep out of Decazeville: "I am more master here than any commissioner of the provisional government and more than the provisional government itself in Paris." To prove his point Cabrol set up a six-hundred man national guard unit commanded by the head of the coal mines and staffed with officers drawn from the company's managerial personnel.[38] The firm printed its own currency and enforced its usage in Decazeville.[39]

Ironically, the establishment of the Second Republic permitted Cabrol and the Houillères et Fonderies to increase their control over the labor force. Cabrol's first speech to Decazeville's workers echoed that of Cadiat a few weeks earlier, but in Cabrol's version the company replaced the nation as the entity to which workers owed allegiance and for which workers should make sacrifices in times of economic hardship. When Cabrol finished speaking, the population paraded under the leadership of the managerial personnel to the director's house to absolve itself of participation, however limited, in the revolutionary republic, and to demonstrate its appreciation of the company's efforts to maintain production.[40] The dormant rhetoric of paternalism surfaced when republicanism threatened company hegemony. The board reported to the stockholders' general assembly: "Thanks to [Cabrol's] firmness and to the confidence which he has inspired in the many workers who see in him a father as much as a chief, he has been able to maintain order and calm among them and to foil attempted wrongdoing with exceptional energy."[41]

The Houillères et Fonderies exploited the troubled history of the Second Republic to argue that radical politics threatened the economic basis of the town's existence. In a period of crisis the workers' only salvation was to identify themselves as employees of the company and to repudiate membership in a national working class. In mid-1849 the depressed market for rails forced the company to lay off some workers and to reduce the wages of the rest. At a meeting of forgeworkers Cabrol outlined the causes of the economic crisis:

> The first, I told them, evidently results from the February Revolution . . . I made the workers see that they themselves had contributed much to the aggravation of the situation. But then, wishing to rehabilitate them, I told them that they had been seduced and fooled by the lies of anarchists, and that they were beginning to understand this; that on 13 June [1849] the majority of Parisian workers had spurned the chief rioters.

Cabrol recognized the ties between workers in Decazeville and workers in the rest of the nation, symbolized by Paris, and used his insight both to chastise Decazeville's workers and to suggest that events elsewhere had confirmed the bankruptcy of independent working-class action. Cabrol's primary goal, however, was to reinforce the employees' commitment to the company. Citing the need to reduce production costs, he asked, "Do you want Decazeville to live or to die?" He presented the crowd with a plan to cut wages, supervisors' salaries, and shareholders' profits: "There can be no doubt as to the response of workers who care about the preservation of Decazeville. As I am only concerned with them, here is the plan which I have decided on. I leave those who do not accept it perfectly free to quit the company's service."[42]

In the company-dominated communities of the Basin, the largely first-generation immigrant workers lacked the organization necessary to oppose their employers or to intervene effectively in national politics on their own. They possessed neither the ideology nor the associational life of the politically active urban artisanry. The local prosecutor reported in 1850 that there were no secret societies in Decazeville: the only voluntary association of note was the apolitical Circle of Commerce and Industry frequented by company managerial personnel.[43] Aubin sheltered a small but vocal group of republicans, but they were drawn from the town's professionals. When the news of Louis Napoléon's December 1851 coup d'état reached the Aubin Basin, the local republican leader, a former mining engineer, was unable to convince many miners to turn the celebration of their patron Sainte Barbe, which fell on that day, into a protest march on the prefecture in Rodez. His cronies were even less successful. They burst into a bar frequented by miners and proclaimed, "If you are really with us raise your hand." This provoked laughter, while some miners pointed out that money and shoes would be required to walk the forty-odd kilometers to Rodez.[44] In its birth and in its death the Second Republic was clearly dearer to dissident engineers, who saw in it a vindication of their opposition to the authoritarianism of industrial capitalism, than to workers in the Basin, who had difficulty recognizing themselves in republican rhetoric.

Cabrol himself was one of the most ardent opponents of Louis Napoléon in the department. In November 1848 he wrote to Duke Decazes that the election of Louis Napoléon would "likely present yet another great obstacle to the establishment of a republican monarchy, the only form of government which suits a people like ours."[45] Cabrol condemned the coup d'état as the disastrous outcome of the excesses of the Second Republic: "the regime of the sword is based only on fear, arbitrary violence and such; it can produce nothing good in the future." However Cabrol decided not to use his influence in Decazeville to oppose the plebiscite called to ratify the coup. Instead, he took comfort that the failure of uprisings against the coup revealed the Montagnards' demise:

Certainly no one is a greater adversary of demagogic doctrines than myself and if in these recent events there is something that satisfies me, it is the evident proof in my eyes that these doctrines are not as deeply rooted as had been thought, and that the part of the population which is exempt, which is healthy in this regard, is an immense majority of the country.[46]

During the first decades of industrialization, national political events affected the Basin's workers only inasmuch as they involved their employers. The political consciousness of workers in the Basin grew out of their perceptions of local firms' relations with one another.[47] The first threat to the power of the Houillères et Fonderies in the Basin came from the growth of a rival mining and metallurgical company at Aubin during the Second Empire. Cabrol took the competition personally and even fought a duel with one of the heads of the neighboring firm in 1852.[48] He was convinced that Duke de Morny, a major investor in the new enterprise, was using his political clout in the Imperial government to aid Aubin at Decazeville's expense. This upset the collaboration between state and capital that had contributed to the economic success of the Houillères et Fonderies during the July Monarchy.[49] In the mid-fifties Grand Central, owner of the Montauban-Rodez railroad, bought the Aubin industrial complex. Much to the dismay of the Houillères et Fonderies, Grand Central put a line through Aubin rather than through the larger town of Decazeville, which did not receive a branch line until 1861.[50] Furthermore, Aubin was able to sell rails to Grand Central at prices up to 25 percent higher than market rates and to use the profit from the mark-up to lure workers away from Decazeville.[51] In 1857 the Compagnie d'Orléans purchased Aubin and turned to its new acquisition for rails, thus depriving Decazeville of one of its major clients.

The clash between Decazeville and Aubin took on a more political character than had any event since the establishment of the Houillères et Fonderies. In 1854 the prefect described the effect on the workers of the intense competition between the two companies: "The populations of Decazeville and Aubin [participate in this struggle between the companies], profiting from it [to demand higher wages] and attaching to it an almost political significance."[52] In the 1850s the workers of Decazeville developed their political identity by showing support at election time for their company director's opposition to the Second Empire. In 1853 the Houillères et Fonderies refused to endorse the government candidate for deputy, Auguste Chevalier, brother of Michel. "A nest of ardent opposition, inspired and maintained by the Decazeville company, systematically rivals that of Aubin," the prefect reported.[53] Although Decazeville's police commissioner campaigned actively for Chevalier, less than one percent of Decazeville's electorate cast their ballots for him; 20 percent voted for his opponent Rolland and the rest abstained. In contrast, 58 percent of Aubin's registered voters chose Chevalier; only four voters broke stride and selected Rolland.[54] In 1857 the sub-prefect severely reprimanded Cabrol when over 90 percent of Decazeville's voters abstained from the legislative elections. In the sub-prefect's opinion, Cabrol harbored "an extreme bitterness toward the Emperor's government." He was "a strange man who sat on a nest egg of one million francs acquired with great difficulty, but who plays at revolution like a dreamer or a starving man."[55] Cabrol, however, was looking for more from the state than the assurance of public order which the Second Empire offered. Government intervention in favor of a local competitor posed the first serious challenge to the relation of state and capital on which the Houillères et Fonderies was based. The future of the firm would depend on its ability to limit further threats to its economic situation.

Although all company towns came into existence to meet the labor requirements of new industries in isolated areas, they differed widely in character. At Decazeville the company's primary contribution to inhabitants was always jobs; workers financed indirectly and directly development of much of the town's infrastructure and social services. Managerial control over the labor force at Decazeville was based not only on the delivery of social services, but also on the firm's exercise of political power through its relationship to the national state.[56] Company actions and inter-company conflict created a political universe that was at once local and national. Only threats to the political and economic system on which Decazeville depended brought the town's workers into national politics and eventually encouraged certain elements in Decazeville's population to question company hegemony.

# 4. Community in Crisis

Beginning in 1859 Napoléon III took steps to liberalize and modernize the economy and government of France. The Second Empire signed free trade treaties with Great Britain and other European nations. It legalized strikes and announced toleration of unions, outlawed since the Le Chapelier law of 1791. Napoléon III balanced his concessions to labor by ending previous restrictions on the formation of joint-stock companies. The right of public assembly was extended and the legislature was given somewhat greater responsibilities. A major aim of the liberal Empire was to endow France with a more open economy and society. This in turn changed the state's role in social conflicts. While not forsaking the outright repression of sedition, the state took steps toward a policy of monitoring and controlling sanctioned activities. In labor relations, the opening of France to foreign goods and the legalization of strikes created conditions for the strike wave of 1867–1870, the first involving large numbers of miners and factory workers. State intervention in these conflicts varied from pressure to replace managerial personnel to the shooting of strikers at Ricamarie and Aubin in 1869. Not labor unrest, but military defeat at the hands of the Prussians in 1870 brought an end to the Second Empire. The young Third Republic earned its spurs by crushing the Paris Commune in 1871. The republic was soon recognized as the least divisive form of government, and in 1875 parliament approved a republican constitution. The triumph of republicanism in the nation was a slower process, however, and was far from complete by 1875 in areas like the Aubin Basin.

## The Aubin Basin Turns to Coal

Midway into the Second Empire the economy of the Aubin Basin underwent a fundamental transformation: coal replaced iron as the region's primary export. This was the first precursor of the deindustrialization of Decazeville. From an industrial center based on the transformation of raw materials, Decazeville became for several decades primarily a supplier of raw materials for use elsewhere. The Houillères et Fonderies survived only a few years in this new economic environment before going into receivership in 1865. The population of Decazeville fell 18 percent between 1861 and 1866. After this crisis the town never regained its dynamism as an urban center. The geographer M. R. Guglielmo commented in the mid-1950s that "it was as if [Decazeville] congealed the way it was in 1865–1870, never again to know anything but minor growth and transformations and an internal redistribution of its contents."[1]

The iron industry in the Basin suffered from the twin blows of changes in technology and in state economic policy. The introduction of the Bessemer process for making steel revolutionized the metallurgical industry. Unfortunately, the iron ore found near the Aubin Basin proved unsuitable for Bessemer production, while the reduction in coal consumption allowed by the new technique reduced Decazeville's comparative advantage with respect to other metallurgical producers. In the 1870s development of the Gilchrist-Thomas process, which permitted the use of iron ore high in phosphorus, further aggravated Decazeville's situation because it led to the creation of a vast new metallurgical center in the Lorraine.

The Second Empire's decision to open up France to foreign competition undercut Decazeville's iron market. Several accords with Great Britain, culminating in the free-trade treaty signed by Richard Cobden and Cabrol's old nemesis Michel Chevalier in 1860, significantly reduced tariffs on British metallurgical goods. To make matters worse, state support of railway building in the southwest declined at the same time. In the late 1870s, when the state next stepped in to promote massive railway construction through the Freycinet plan, Decazeville was no longer a competitive rail producer. Its share of French metallurgical production fell from 4 percent in 1860 to 1.5 percent in 1869 and to 1 percent in 1880.[2]

To the extent that the Second Empire had considered the economic consequences of its free trade policies on the Aubin Basin, it favored a shift from the production of coal for use in the nearby foundries and forges to the sale of coal on the open market. In 1861 the state lent the Houillères et Fonderies 1,500,000 francs to expand its open-pit mines and to build new coke ovens, in the vain hope that the Aubin Basin would capture the Bordeaux coal market from the British.[3] Although this effort failed, firms in the Basin did turn to the sale of coal as their main source of income. From the 1860s until the 1890s the Houillères et Fonderies and its successor, the Société Nouvelle des Houillères et Fonderies de l'Aveyron, marketed the higher grades of coal and kept the ironworks in operation only to use the low-grade coal which could not be transported profitably elsewhere for sale.[4] Companies in the Aubin Basin faced a handicap in the restricted coal market of largely unindustrialized southwestern France. Coal from the Basin was generally less desirable than that of its competitors: the high percentage of volatile materials limited its domestic and industrial uses. Well into the twentieth century the pit-head price of coal from the Aubin Basin remained below the national average, and was significantly lower than the price at the nearby mines of Carmaux: coal from the Aubin Basin sold at 48 percent of that from Carmaux in 1853; 63 percent in 1876; and 75 percent in 1909.[5]

While French coal consumption grew during the Second Empire (290 percent), so did competition between mining firms. To block possible monopolies, the Second Empire prevented companies in the Aubin Basin and elsewhere from taking advantage of potential economies of scale by placing restrictions on mergers and by limiting the size of coal concessions.[6] The expansion of the rail system during the Second Empire opened up new markets, but intensified competition as well. The relatively high freight charges allowed by the state hurt the more isolated coal basins.[7] While Anzin had to contend with competition from the newly discovered Pas-de-Calais coalfield—the cause of the strike Emile Zola depicted in *Germinal*—firms in the Aubin Basin vied for sales with mines throughout southern France, including Carmaux, Commentry, Grand-Combe, and Graissessac. Although Decazeville limited this competition by negotiating a division of the market with other companies,[8] it had no defense against the increase in British coal imports prompted by a 78 percent fall in the tariff in coal between the beginning of the Second Empire and 1863.[9]

In spite of these difficulties, firms in the Aubin Basin were able to take advantage of the strong demand for coal in France during the Second Empire: production in the Basin shot from a low of

291,834 tons in 1858 to 503,385 tons four years later. The Basin exported 25,000 tons of coal in 1858; this figure increased almost tenfold by 1867.[10] Companies in the Basin were ill-prepared to establish the more orderly and safer methods of coal extraction required to sustain this higher production. Careful supervision of mining, which companies had earlier seen as a financial burden, came to be understood as a necessary element in the efficient use of capital. Because the mines of Decazeville had enjoyed a guaranteed market until the middle of the Second Empire, reforms in mine organization took place later there than in coalfields which had long depended on sales in the open market.[11] But the administration of work in the mines did not change solely as the result of new market conditions. The state mining corps also played an important role in this process by delineating more clearly the individual and collective responsibilities of managerial personnel for the safe operation of the mines under their control.

The gradual development of an indigenous working population during the first decades of industrialization allowed firms to consider bypassing contractors, but also created the basis for resistance to more intensive forms of labor exploitation. Workers with ties to the community were less likely to choose the employees' most basic form of protest: quitting. While miners in the larger Nord and Loire coalfields had struck during the July Monarchy,[12] their counterparts in the Aubin Basin did not collectively oppose their employers until the final years of the Second Empire. The collapse of the Houillères et Fonderies after 1860 resulted in a mistrust of capitalist enterprise and entrepreneurs that allowed community leaders who were independent of the company to achieve prominence. Forms of work organization and labor management suitable to the earlier conditions of the mining economy in the Basin failed in the late 1860s. Miners in Decazeville and Aubin took advantage of legalization of the right to strike in 1864 to protest what they interpreted as unjust attempts to increase the amount of work expected from them.

The institution of the strike plays a central role in both miners' communities and in popular perceptions of miners. The cause of miners' renowned combativity is to be found not in the physical difficulty of their work, but in the clash of their occupational community and the coercive managerial strategies used to promote productivity. Throughout much of the nineteenth century craft structures protected important sectors of the artisanal/skilled labor force in France. French miners, unlike their counterparts in Germany, did not inherit a formal craft structure and had to develop new organizational and ideological defenses. "In a sense," Joan Scott has written, "the strike provided for the miners what the structure of their craft provided the glassworkers."[13]

Although the state dispatched troops to put down labor disorders, it also saw in strikes a means to diagnose managerial failure. State administrators availed themselves of strikes to encourage mining companies to reform the highest reaches of management, at the same time that state mining engineers were using regulation of mine safety to advocate changes in the powers and duties of engineers and master miners. Through tariff reform the Second Empire helped to undercut the political economy on which Decazeville's iron industry had depended. The state's attitude to safety and to strikes contributed in turn to shaping Decazeville's response to the emergence of a new economic situation that favored development of the Basin's coal deposits.

### The Redistribution of Authority in the Mines

In the late 1850s changes in the coal market, the labor supply, and state intervention in mining prompted companies in the Basin to question contractors' ability to carry out both the technical and the personnel aspects of labor management.[14] The elimination of contractors offered firms several technical advantages. They would be able to get rid of intermediaries and to employ a higher percentage of their miners at production rates and under direct company control. This was important because the sale of coal on the open market required not only increased production, but also more attention to the quality of the product. Management saw the replacement of contractors with company supervisors as a means of obtaining a greater proportion of high-priced lump coal.[15]

Contractors also lost some of their allure as labor recruiters. Population figures and indices of geographic origins, occupational endogamy, and sociability for Decazeville in the 1860s reveal the presence of a larger, more rooted, and more closely knit working-class community than had existed a generation earlier.[16] This reduced the need and desirability of using contractors to find and organize workers. In this new environment, miners began to challenge the authority of the contractors who hired them, both in and out of the work place. Many brought contractors to court for failure to pay agreed-upon wages. In 1867 the justice of the peace of Aubin chronicled the breakdown of the contract system in the Aubin Basin: as the contractor "usually has no set contract with the company, he eludes all contracts of this nature with the workers whom he employs . . . If the contractor is poorly paid, he pays poorly or does not pay his workers at all."[17]

Contracting was a legacy not only of the Basin's earlier demographic and economic structure, in which labor was scarce and the extraction of coal secondary, but also of the period before development of competitive local commerce. In the 1860s miners, supported by local shopkeepers, protested the contractors' practice of selling them wine and foodstuffs, or requiring them to buy these goods from designated vendors. The contractors "do not sell at a higher price than the shopkeepers," the attorney general reported, "but it is felt that they encourage the workers to buy more; in this way the workers receive a significant portion and sometimes all of their wages in kind, wages which they could put to much better use."[18] The workers' grievance was not so much the price of food as the perversion of the wage system, which restricted their freedom to participate in the social community created by the spread of local commerce.

The state authorities also turned against contracting. Second Empire officials identified contractors as a threat to public order and an impediment to economic efficiency, the regime's primary concerns. On occasion contractors disappeared with the money given them to pay their workers, leaving government officials the task of calming the disgruntled workers.[19] As late as 1874 the sub-prefect complained of the situation at the mines of Campagnac (Cransac):

> The system of extraction by contractors who have four or five workers under their direction does not permit [the company] to exercise rigorous supervision or to be informed of the morality of each of its men. The director appears young to me and I have been told that he does not have all the authority necessary to direct such an extensive operation.[20]

State mining engineers criticized contracting from a technical standpoint. In the thirties and forties state engineers had frequently tangled with companies over administrative matters such as the failure to file subterranean maps at the prefecture, and the assessment of the annual tax due the state on the value of the coal extracted. But only the determination of the causes of accidents gave state engineers an opportunity to make detailed evaluations of a company's supervision of its mines. Until the middle of the Second Empire the nature of work organization in the mines shaped the attitude of management, state engineers, and workers toward safety.[21] Responsibility for mine operations, although legally in the concessionaire's hands, was shared by the company and the contractor or chief miner. In a variant on contracting, companies hired members of the state mining corps to provide technical assistance and managerial personnel in periods of crisis. The labor force, on the other hand, was composed of peasants' sons, forced off the land by the need to earn a living. They were not, in the parlance of state engineers, "professional miners," ironically because they worked solely with their wages in mind, often ignoring the precautions that a more skilled miner would have taken. State mining officials, like the companies, tended to view these miners as individuals working freely for their own advantage and therefore as largely responsible for accidents which befell them.

After the midcentury state engineers sought to make companies more accountable for what went on in their mines, directing their complaints first to the highest reaches of management. Late in 1856 the board of the Houillères et Fonderies strongly advised that another engineer be hired to replace one who had left, in the hope that this would diminish the chances of a serious accident at Decazeville: "This measure has become quite urgent as the result of the decision of the [state mining] administration, already applied to M. Chagot, director of the Mines of Blanzy [Montceau-les-Mines], to prosecute in mining accidents which involve death or even serious injuries."[22] After an accident the same year which took three lives, the Conseil Général des Mines criticized the management of Campagnac for failing to direct its contractors carefully enough:

> The concessionary company itself should be blamed for the way that it operates its mines, it hands their direction over to young engineers, recent graduates, very zealous and undoubtedly very capable, but who still lack experience. It pays them parsimoniously. Overworked and continually occupied, they cannot give to each particular task all the attention it requires.[23]

An 1866 report by the state chief engineer on the mines of the same company illustrates the shift from the view that accidents were the result of miners' carelessness to the position that mining operations required stricter supervision:

> Accidents have been frequent for some time at Campagnac. All of them have been considered the result of workers' imprudence or fortuitous circumstances and none have given rise to judicial

proceedings. It must be admitted, however, that some of them could have been avoided if a more active supervision of the workers and their work were exercised.[24]

The 1860s witnessed challenges to the use of contractors from all sides. However, companies were still reluctant to abandon a system that relieved them of the difficult tasks of recruiting, disciplining, and supervising miners. In any case, the strike of 1867 at Decazeville revealed that any significant change in the organization of work in the mines, including the abolition of contractors, would require both a restructuring of authority at all levels of management and a new conceptualization of the type of control that firms could exercise over their employees.

## The Strike of 1867

"One is deeply shocked," a touring engineering student remarked after visiting Decazeville in 1862, "by the general disorder, which seems to reach up to the administration."[25] The board of the Houillères et Fonderies proved powerless to halt the company's decline. Cabrol had earlier won for the local director a degree of autonomy from the board in order to deal with the particular problems arising from management of a staff of highly skilled metalworkers.[26] This *politique de présence dans l'usine*, to use Jean Vial's phrase, was a common practice in nineteenth-century metallurgy, but not in coal-mining firms, where the board of directors generally made the major decisions.[27] Certainly Cabrol himself was unsuited to run a coal-mining firm. He readily admitted to an ignorance of the finer points of coal mining, an activity he had viewed only in terms of the needs of the ironworks.[28] The board, accustomed to letting Cabrol run things during the prosperous forties and fifties, was ill-prepared to take up the slack when Cabrol resigned as director in 1860, and coal mining replaced the production of iron as the company's major activity. From his new vantage point on the board, Cabrol criticized the board's lack of involvement in the firm's affairs and blamed it for the decline of the ironworks:

> The almost complete self-effacement of the board [gives it] the moral responsibility for the sad situation [of the Houillères et Fonderies and] its consequences redound on us . . . In reality what role does the board play? What useful action can it take in monthly or bimonthly meetings of a half-hour or quite rarely

of an hour—never fully attended—devoted ordinarily to the rapid reading of letters full of figures none of which remain or could remain in your mind? Doesn't each of us recognize almost without exception, either openly or to himself, that in the way it functions, the board is an almost worthless cog? ... The administration of our Company is therefore in a state of deep atony at Paris and in complete disorder at Decazeville.[29]

During the company's final years the board limited itself to harassing the management at Decazeville. The engineer who replaced Cabrol resigned in 1863 over what an observer at Campagnac called *les tracasseries de M.M. les administrateurs.*[30] The need to redistribute authority in the new mining economy affected other firms in the Basin as well. The Campagnac board, for instance, recognized that in theory the local director was the "deus ex machina" of the enterprise, but did not hesitate to deprecate him behind his back.[31]

The problem of determining the proper degree of managerial independence was endemic to coal-mining companies across the nation. Large mining firms had sometimes begun without any real local executives. Although the original board of directors of the Compagnie des Mines de la Loire contained no engineers, it tried in the 1840s to operate the mines without a director. Only reluctantly, and under pressure from the state, did it finally agree to choose a director and to give him a measure of independence.[32] Through most of the nineteenth century it was common for the board of directors to usurp the powers of the operational management during periods of falling profits.[33]

The strike of 1867 at Decazeville (and the more famous strike at Aubin in 1869)[34] should be seen in the context of this crisis of managerial authority. In company-dominated communities like Decazeville and Aubin, managerial ineptness and injustice provided an opportunity and a justification for workers to strike. After the severe crisis of the previous decade, marked by wage reductions, lay-offs, and changes in work organization, miners protested against a management that promised further disruption and hardship. The atmosphere of instability that management seemed to create at Decazeville in the 1860s clashed with the development of a sense of independent community life fostered by the diminution of company authority during the economic crisis. The miners' decision to employ the recently legalized strike revealed their consciousness of themselves not solely as displaced peasants, but as workers dependent on their employers, whose actions took on greater importance for this very reason.

The collapse of local industry in the early 1860s forced the town of Decazeville to act independently of the company for the first time in its history. The Houillères et Fonderies abandoned participation in local commerce. Late in 1861 it terminated the company bakery and turned the trade over completely to local bakers.[35] More important, the company lost its political hold over the town. In 1863 the government candidate for deputy, Auguste Chevalier, brother of Michel, won equal levels of support in Aubin and Decazeville: in marked contrast to the elections of the previous decades, 80 percent of the Decazeville electorate went to the polls; 85 percent of these voters cast their ballots for Chevalier.[36] Cabrol's tactics of electoral opposition to the Second Empire had failed; with Cabrol gone, Decazeville's voters pursued a more politic policy toward the government. They also looked outside of the company for municipal leadership. The town, governed by a non-company mayor for the first time since 1844, identified native Decazevillois and repatriated outsiders, distributed relief funds, and ran public works projects for the unemployed.[37] In handling the crisis, Decazeville came to consciousness of itself as separate from the company that had founded it.

The attitude of the receivership that took over operation of the mines and forges in 1865 heightened the town's awareness of its identity. The new management did not conceal that its sole goal was to turn a monthly profit sufficient to satisfy its investors.[38] The residents displayed their deep distrust of the receivership by voting two-to-one in the municipal elections of 1865 for an independent list against one headed by B. Rouquayrol, chief mining engineer during the last year of the Houillères et Fonderies, and head of the receivership's operations at Decazeville. "By this vote," the new mayor of Decazeville proclaimed, "the town sought to show that it desired a town council independent of the company [receivership]."[39] Local political leaders lobbied vigorously in government circles to have the receivership replaced by a firm interested in the long-term prosperity of the industrial complex of Decazeville.[40]

In January 1867 the receivership lowered rates and wages in the mine by 10 percent. Although the state's chief mining engineer described the miners as "tormented by the desire to make use of their new liberties" to strike, they did not protest for fear that this would lead to the closing of the mines and factories.[41] Only Rouquayrol's decision to cut wages again at the end of September 1867 ended the workers' quiescence. Rouquayrol also took the opportunity to announce that fixed times for entrance and departure from the mine would be rigorously observed: infractions would be punished by the loss of a half-day's wages. The next day, the first of October, miners who arrived late to work found the Bourran pit entrance barred by a locked iron gate.

Angered by these changes, 300 miners assembled at town hall to demand that wage reductions made since the beginning of the year be rescinded. At the mayor's suggestion they chose delegates to meet with Rouquayrol, and the mayor accompanied these delegates to the director's office. The crowd waiting at the windows and doors of the director's building grew impatient when it learned that Rouquayrol was refusing their demands, and forced him to go to town hall to defend his position before the mayor. There the crowd swelled to 1,500 and the concerted efforts of the mayor, the justice of the peace of Aubin, and the local *gendarmerie* were required to enable Rouquayrol to leave safely at the end of the afternoon. That evening miners tore down the grill at Bourran, broke into the factory, and made workers shut down the two blast furnaces in operation. About nine o'clock a crowd invaded the director's garden and encircled his house. The assemblage shouted threats and threw objects at the building, but did little damage. Once again the mayor and the justice of the peace persuaded the rioters to disperse. The next day the subprefect and the district attorney arrived at Decazeville and negotiated a settlement between the strike delegates and the receivership.[42] The brief work stoppage revealed the fundamental elements of the new social geography of the town. The workers looked to the independent mayor for advice and wanted to confront Rouquayrol at the town hall. Conversely, the strikers' attack on Rouquayrol's house expressed their complete identification of the individual director with the interests of the receivership.

The strikers' demands constituted a comprehensive critique of the receivership's approach to labor management. The miners called for dismantling of the iron gate at Bourran, rescission of the wage reductions made since the beginning of the year, reform of the mutual aid fund, and dismissal of individual managerial personnel. They considered the grill both unfair and dangerous and demanded its permanent removal to allow free access to the mine at all times. The grill was unfair because the company paid miners by production and not by hours of presence; coupled with the reduction in the rate paid per wagon of coal extracted, the effort to ensure a full working day was a crude means to get miners to produce more coal for the same wages. The locked gate was also dangerous, because in the event of an accident those inside the mine would be unable to escape. Like state engineers, miners were coming to recognize safety as an issue in labor relations. Government officials suggested that had the iron gate not been erected, there might not have been a strike.[43]

Because Decazeville's miners were beginning to see themselves as full-time industrial workers with only their labor power to provide for their livelihood, they also demanded reform of the medical system administered by the company's mutual aid fund. Control of miners' mutual aid funds had been a serious bone of contention in the Loire Basin for some time. In 1852 Napoléon III gave some satisfaction to the miners of Rive-de-Gier after they asked him for a closer accounting of the money in their company mutual aid fund.[44] In 1866 the prefect of the Loire gave miners in his department the right to organize their own mutual aid fund.[45] By 1869 half of the 10,000 miners in the Loire Basin had joined. That year the fund took a leading role in a miners' strike in the Loire in which one of the demands was the centralization and standardization of company-run mutual aid funds. The following year control of company mutual aid funds was a major issue in forgeworkers' strikes at Fourchambault and Le Creusot.[46]

Companies feared that employee management of the funds would place a potential "war chest," along the British model, in workers' hands. However, strikers at Decazeville were more concerned with control over the functioning than the finances of the fund. They asked for the immediate dismissal of the company doctor, whose power over workers' lives placed him in an analogous position to the engineers: this particular doctor was severe and formal, as well as notoriously deaf (il y a aucune manière de ce faire antendre [sic]) and did not keep regular office hours. The company doctor's job was both to attend to injured workers and to decide when they were ready to return to work. The demand to fire the doctor, like the demand to remove the grill, was intended to subvert the receivership's effort to wrest more work from miners at the expense of their health and liberty.

Rouquayrol granted partial satisfaction to each of these demands: he returned wages to their previous level, took down the grill, and made arrangements for the two sides to discuss reform of the mutual aid fund.[47] But the receivership refused the strikers' final demand—

dismissal of the director Rouquayrol and the engineer Colamet—for fear that such a step would weaken the firm's authority in the work place. Yet this was the central issue of the strike. The district attorney pointed out that the very manner in which Rouquayrol carried out his reforms revealed the absence of trust and understanding between workers and their employers. Instead of following the custom at Decazeville of having foremen warn workers of planned changes in the rules and of projected wage cuts, and of posting such modifications fifteen or twenty days in advance, Rouquayrol had the new working conditions implemented almost immediately. This "offended tradition which is, as it were, the only law of these workers."

Were strikers at Decazeville therefore "traditionalists" in the sense that the term is employed in modernization theory?[48] The answer is no, for tradition in the mines was not the product of a backward consciousness, but of a work culture built around the independence of the crew, which had been created and reaffirmed during the few decades following industrialization of the Basin. If many of the striking miners saw some of their demands as a way to allow them to farm on a part-time basis, this was a rational, not an atavistic, choice in a region where the very future of industry was questionable. And in a managerial system where the individual will of the director was presented as the guiding force of operations, discontented workers followed the same policy which a board of directors would have taken if an accustomed level of profitability had disappeared: they asked for dismissal of the director.

Rouquayrol's competence was an issue for workers not just on the job, but as residents of the town of Decazeville as well. Over and above specific demands, the strike raised the issue of the future of industry in Decazeville. Both the workers and the local municipal elite viewed Rouquayrol and the receivership as threats to the town's economic security and wanted to see the establishment of a new company committed to the development of Decazeville. Rumors were rife that several creditors were seeking to extend the receivership, which the workers and other inhabitants of Decazeville associated with insecurity and hardship, for five years. Public opinion in Decazeville held that Rouquayrol had tried to foment trouble in order to scare off potential buyers. After the strike town residents circulated a petition addressed to the prefect urging the government to take all possible steps to assure that the sale of the mines and forges not be delayed for any reason.[49]

The concessions won by the strikers masked a greater triumph over the previously unassailable authority of the director. Rouquayrol understood this and resigned only a week after posting the wage reductions. In a letter to the receiver, he declared that "the management finds itself dishonored by my person, and I judge that it is impossible to retain the functions with which I am charged." Rouquayrol's decision to resign, and the terms in which he couched his resignation, reflected his conception of the director's relations with the labor force: the director should hold absolute power over his workers. On the other side, workers focused their antagonisms on the person of the director as embodiment of the totality of company activities. Consequently, Rouquayrol's resignation was more significant than restoration of the former wage scale. Workers and supervisors discussed wages each month; management, however, had rarely been challenged.[50]

The receivership, only interested in turning a profit, had left management of the mines and forges completely up to Rouquayrol. His resignation revealed the chaotic managerial structure at Decazeville. Rouquayrol's subordinates disassociated themselves from him and refused to take his place.[51] The receivership's only alternative was to ask the state mining engineer Jausions, who had frequently worked as a consultant for local companies, to manage the mines and forges at Decazeville.[52] During the strike Jausions had been quite concerned about the danger of a breakdown in the discipline necessary for the labor force to keep fires in the mines from raging out of control. In his annual report in 1867, he commented on "the quite exceptional gravity of [strikes] for mines like those of the Aubin Basin, where fires exist. If [the fires] cease to be continually watched and fought, they could wreak real havoc and could even compromise the source of employment of the workers who had stopped work."[53] The state engineer justified his assumption of leadership on technical grounds: the nature of coal mining in the Basin was such that a work stoppage or lack of supervision could turn against the workers. The prefect convinced the Minister of Public Works to let Jausions stay at Decazeville until the receivership ended: "This young engineer is the only one with sufficient authority to maintain calm in a working population still animated by bad attitudes, and to protect the interests of the bankrupt company's creditors."[54] State engineers' efforts to increase company responsibility for safe mining thus culminated in the state's decision to allow one of its engineers to take over management of the mines of Decazeville.[55]

The question of whether to prosecute workers accused of strike-related offenses forced the government to reflect on its role in labor/management relations. The Minister of Public Works and the Minister of Interior favored prosecution, but the Minister of Justice, who opposed the idea, prevailed. Like the local authorities, he chose to assign to the management responsibility for the disorders that had taken place. In his opinion, the receivership was at fault for having allowed a situation to develop that was likely to lead to a riot: "Prosecution would make the administrative and judicial authorities lose all the benefits of their very energetic and successful intervention in the affair in favor of a company management which has much for which to reproach itself."[56] However, the government's decision not to bring strikers to trial should not be construed as support for the workers. It was considered the most expeditious means to return order to a labor force that had been improperly managed. In the Second Empire the state promoted the modernization of the mining industry in various indirect ways, including the expansion of the rail system, the reduction of tariffs, and stricter supervision of mine conditions. The Decazeville strike of 1867 reveals that one consequence of the legalization of strikes in 1864 was that a strike, like a mine accident, could reveal faulty management practices and put the state in a position to intervene to remedy the situation.

The receivership clearly illustrated the naked quest for short-term profit and its threat to communities in peripheral economic areas like the Aubin Basin during periods of crisis. The strikers' demands were those of workers who judged management not on traditionalist grounds, but on criteria derived from their experiences at work. They turned for guidance to the mayor, who represented the community that had begun to take form independently of the company. This community demanded state intervention not only to settle immediate grievances, but in order to assure the long-term economic survival of industry in the town. The state sympathized with these calls for reform of industry in the Basin and expedited sale of the receivership.

## Managerial Reform

The Société Nouvelle, led by a group of financiers with ties to the Le Creusot ironworks, bought the industrial complex of Decazeville in January 1868. The board of directors of the new company concentrated power in its own hands. The board ran the general assemblies, which were limited to stockholders with a minimum of twenty stocks, valued at 500 francs apiece. Board members kept dividends low while awarding themselves substantial fees for their work as administrators. They drew the lesson from the strike of the previous year that they would have to take a more active role in management. The board abolished the position of director and concentrated power in the hands of its designated representative, the chief executive officer.[57] It decided that the post of chief mining engineer would "necessarily be much more modest" and withdrew many of his and his subordinates' discretionary powers to hire and grant raises and advances. By concentrating authority in its chief executive officer, the board limited opportunities for the creation of individual power bases within the firm.

The board chose as its first chief executive officer Alfred Deseilligny, who was married to his cousin, the daughter of Eugène Schneider, owner of Le Creusot. Deseilligny had managed the mines and factories of Le Creusot from 1850 to 1866 and served as mayor of the town of Le Creusot from 1855 to 1866.[58] He used his preeminent position on the board to limit its interference in the operation of the industrial complex and to provide mining operations at Decazeville with a strong centralized management for the first time. Under his direction the firm limited fires in the mine by constructing two large ventilators at Bourran (Decazeville) and by making the filling in of old mine galleries a standard practice. The company expanded the open-pit mines and built new coal-sorting and cleaning facilities, new coke ovens, and a briquette factory to use the otherwise wasted coal dust.[59] The Société Nouvelle profited from the booming market for coal during the first years of the Third Republic.[60] Its annual payroll in 1868 amounted to 2,800,000 francs; in 1872 the figure stood at close to five million francs and climbed to 5,550,000 francs in 1875.[61] For a brief while the management of Decazeville even looked beyond protectionism: Deseilligny supported free trade in the hope that it would spur rail traffic and have the indirect effect of increasing the railways' need for coal.[62]

Under Deseilligny the Société Nouvelle restructured the labor force by bringing in more women and by putting into effect a managerial system that permitted the abolition of contracting. The new company exploited the large female labor force in the Basin more efficiently and extensively than had been done in the past. Women never worked underground in the mines of the Aubin Basin, as they had earlier in the century in the northern coal mines. In the early 1870s, however, the Société Nouvelle hired many single and widowed women to staff the new coal-sorting and cleaning installations. These women labored under conditions of strict supervision and discipline that differed significantly from the work environment of male miners. Their travail in the preparation of coal was an important element in the adaptation of Decazeville's mining industry to the competitive market. The low wages paid women workers were intended only to supplement—one might say subsidize—those of male workers, and women's sporadic protests over wages were fruitless.[63] The availability of inexpensive female workers encouraged companies in the Basin to take advantage of their services rather than to mechanize operations fully: in 1889 there were 499 women employed at installations in the Aubin Basin, but none at nearby Carmaux.[64] Women continued to work in the preparation of coal in the Basin until nationalization of the mines after World War II.

As part of his reform program, Deseilligny also ended contracting in the mines. Engineers took full control of hiring, a job they had previously shared with the contractors. Master miners and the greatly increased staff of *chefs de poste* assumed the supervisory aspects of the contractor's job.[65] Under the new system, management monitored promotion to hewer more closely than in the past; this increased its ability to maintain discipline among young mineworkers. In 1883, when the abolition of contractors was complete in the major mining firms in Decazeville, Aubin, and Cransac, there was approximately one supervisor for every eighteen mineworkers in the Aubin Basin. Two-thirds of these were *chefs de poste* and another 20 percent were master miners.[66]

Deseilligny carried out these reforms in the paternalist style which had made Le Creusot arguably the most influential managerial model in French industry. Deseilligny believed that the modern industrial enterprise required a labor force that had received both moral and technical education. First, a worker had to learn to prepare himself to work well. More work could be expected of a man who followed a good diet, but it was not always easy to convince a worker from the countryside to eat well.[67] The correlation of proper diet with production gave a moral value to the piece-rate wage. Dissolute workers expended energy unproductively and incurred unnecessary expenses that could have been used for better nourishment: "The budget of vice is added to that of the family. Discontent, demands and strikes almost always follow. All that is needed is for a few workers to be afflicted with these bad moral habits to alter the spirit of a whole workshop."[68] A moral education limited such abuses and provided a common ground for discussion between management and labor. Deseilligny claimed he felt more confident dealing with an educated working class with which he could talk over matters rationally, even though it would "be led more often to discuss the rates offered them," than with an uneducated mass that fluctuated between passivity and violence.[69]

Miners had previously required limited formal training. Now, Deseilligny argued, they needed a firm grounding in writing and mathematics—as much for reasons of morale, however, as of technology. Deseilligny told a scientific congress in 1874 that science had recently changed several aspects of mining at Decazeville: fossils helped to determine the location of coal deposits, explosives were used with greater frequency, and an elaborate coal-sorting and washing system had been constructed at Lacaze: "And note, gentlemen, that this process has ended up modifying the miner's working conditions. It is not only a laborious and robust worker who is necessary, but an educated man, prepared by schooling to operate and direct this scientific machinery, whose mechanisms are at once powerful and delicate."[70] But, in fact, miners had little control over this new equipment. Engineers located coal deposits, specially trained *boute-feux* soon took over the handling of explosives, and unskilled women sorted and washed coal. Deseilligny responded that the manual worker would find the real value of education not in his job, but in the opportunity it gave him to advance into management:

> What is most disheartening for a worker is the belief that he is eternally condemned to the present task, that a better future is closed to him. He then curses his fate and the society that he holds responsible for it. But when from the heart of an intelligent and educated population there come from time to time supervisory personnel, sometimes even—rarely, it is true, but these examples are beneficial—heads of industry, then a hope is born which supports and moralizes all those who feel capable of being selected in their turn for this promotion. But this hope exists only in an educated population.[71]

In return for the miners' acceptance of more direct supervision, the company offered them the opportunity to enter the managerial hierarchy created by the abolition of contractors. Deseilligny sought to encourage the workers who made up new working-class communities like Decazeville by holding out the slim chance for individuals to advance within the firm. In this sense he was clearly a man of the Third Republic, if not an ardent republican. His conception of education and social mobility offered a version of *solidarisme* within the confines of the company town.[72]

Deseilligny complemented reforms in the workplace with a new approach to politics. He took advantage of the liberalization and democratization of French society at the end of the Second Empire and the beginning of the Third Republic to strengthen the company's position in Decazeville. Although officials of the Houillères et Fonderies had played a major role in the political life of the Basin, Deseilligny made a radical break with previous practice by publicly appealing to the area's workers in his campaign for deputy in May 1869. Deseilligny was an industrial hero like Cabrol, but, more than his predecessor, he recognized the importance of cultivating popular political support. After the 1867 strike, the mayor of Decazeville claimed that only Deseilligny's candidacy would prevent the town's workers from voting republican.[73] At a time when an increasing number of miners and forgeworkers came from an industrial working-class background, Deseilligny capitalized on their identification with industrial life. He explained to the sub-prefect that he had not made any reference to the Emperor in his *profession de foi* because he was running as "the head of the largest industry in the Aveyron"; his "industrial point of view" transcended the political opinions of his backers.[74] In 1867 Decazeville had defended itself against the incompetence of the receivership. Deseilligny sought to repair the breach that had developed between the company and the community since 1860. By organizing workers to support him politically, he supplemented the closer control of labor in the workplace with new bonds of allegiance in the community.

Deseilligny's opponent was Alfred Cibiel, scion of one of Villefranche-de-Rouergue's leading families. Although both candidates supported the government, they took very different approaches to politics. Cibiel was also a member of the board of directors of the Société Nouvelle. But, Deseilligny charged, his opponent's interest in Decazeville was purely financial, while he had devoted himself to regenerating the town's industry.[75] Deseilligny relied on the votes of the Basin's workers; the opposing candidate drew his strength from Villefranche-de-Rouergue and rural areas in the district. For Cibiel, the Basin's workers formed "a sort of band of strangers to the region [who sought] to snatch away the election," by employing intimidation and threats to win over rural voters. Cibiel's supporters were aghast at Deseilligny's direct appeal to labor and charged that it made him "not the head [of the mines and forges of Decazeville], but the courtesan and slave of his personnel." To be sure, the workers who campaigned for Deseilligny maintained strong family ties in the countryside and were far from "a band of strangers" to the villages they visited; yet Cibiel's backers were correct in pointing to the novelty of the mass mobilization of workers. Cibiel depended on the traditional power bases in the district and, although born in Rouen, he touted himself as an *enfant du pays*. His supporters' methods, like the *charivari* organized against a Deseilligny man in Villefranche-de-Rouergue, were traditional as well. The clash of the two cultures was explosive: the sub-prefect and assorted "old-timers" in the area remarked that no event since the Revolution of 1789 had so agitated the region.[76]

Although every industrial firm in the Basin except the mines and forges of Aubin (which saw Deseilligny as a threat to its hold over its workers) put some pressure on its employees to vote for Deseilligny, workers' support for him appears to have been genuine.[77] Promises of jobs and economic growth struck a receptive chord in the Basin's working-class population. His supporters chanted enthusiastically in *patois* the refrain: "Bibo lou po, bibo lou bi / Bibo moussu Deseilligny!" ("Long live bread, long live wine / Long live Monsieur Deseilligny!"). Bread and wine were political issues to men who had experienced hard times for more than a decade. The ideology of nineteenth-century industrialization taught workers to pin hope and blame on individual leaders: support for Deseilligny was the counterpart to the attacks on Rouquayrol during the strike of 1867.

Deseilligny's tactics earned him a narrow victory over Cibiel: he was elected deputy in 1869 by 18,414 votes to 18,037. In the canton of Aubin, however, Deseilligny captured more than 85 percent of the vote. In Decazeville he beat Cibiel by a margin of 2,445 to 29; in Firmy the results were equally decisive, 801 to 7. The election of 1869 marks a transitional stage in the development of the political consciousness of the Basin's workers. While the workers revealed their rural roots by campaigning in the countryside, the election itself pitted an outsider from the industrial center of Le Creusot against a self-proclaimed *enfant du pays*. By identifying so unanimously with Deseilligny, the Basin's workers expressed themselves politically as a group more strongly than ever before. His success helps explain why Decazeville remained immune from the national strike wave of 1869–70, which affected mining and metallurgical enterprises across the country, including Aubin.[78]

Rouquayrol's experience during the strike of 1867 had revealed to management the danger of isolation from state and municipal authority. Deseilligny took immediate steps to rectify this situation. After his election, he was named to several ministerial posts in the Third Republic. During the Franco-Prussian War he profited from his position as Minister of Industry to obtain military contracts for the idled factories of Decazeville; after the iron crisis of 1873 he used his political influence to obtain rail orders for Decazeville from western France.[79]

Deseilligny became mayor of Decazeville in 1871, in the midst of a municipal economic crisis precipitated by the abolition of tolls on foodstuffs entering town. The new mayor handled the situation by arranging to have the company keep the town solvent.[80] In succeeding years Decazeville took on some of the characteristics of the classic *ville-usine* exemplified by Le Creusot. In the early seventies the town obtained several sorely needed municipal services as by-products of improvements in the industrial complex. When the Société Nouvelle built pumping facilities to provide the factories and mines with much needed fresh water from the Lot, Decazeville received this service as well. In addition, the Société Nouvelle saw to the installation of gas lights on its premises and in the town. At the coal-sorting and washing facilities the lights allowed work to continue after dusk; in Decazeville, Mayor Deseilligny told the town council, the lights would help maintain public order on pay days.[81] The Société Nouvelle provided a hospital for its workers, a humanitarian gesture that also allowed the firm to monitor more closely when injured workers were ready to return to work.[82] The company built a limited amount of housing, which reflected the influence of developments at Le Creusot and, indirectly, the change from a dependence on contractors to direct dealings with individual chief miners. Cabrol had constructed adjoining lodgings for workers, but as the industrial observer Louis Reybaud commented in 1875, that plan "is now condemned; it does not isolate households enough and leads to too much promiscuity. It has been clearly shown that it is not good for workers to live too close to one another."[83] The Société Nouvelle's greater reliance on managerial personnel led to a concern for their housing needs as well. The stockholders' general assembly agreed in 1880 "to devote a certain sum each year to the construction of managerial employees' houses suitably arranged and grouped around the director's house."[84] Companies also looked for other, less costly ways to mark the return of order and prosperity to the Basin. The workers' feast-days, Sainte Barbe for miners and Saint Eloi for forge-workers, were a favorite vehicle. In the seventies and eighties firms turned these into paid holidays and elaborate ceremonial occasions to celebrate the community of shared interests between management and labor.[85]

Examination of Decazeville's miners in the decade and a half after 1860 shows first that the organization of work was not simply the product of technology or a struggle between management and labor; in the mining industry the state intervened directly and indirectly in the reorganization of the labor process. State officials criticized both small-scale contracting and the upper reaches of management in their investigations of accidents and strikes. Second, the strike of 1867 demonstrates that workers were not traditionalists, acting solely out of fear of the consequences change might bring. Miners actively shaped the structure of their craft. They accepted the dismissal of contractors, but opposed the new forms of exploitation that took the place of contracting. Third, the temporary resolution of labor conflict at Decazeville during the first years of the Société Nouvelle reveals that the kind of management generally subsumed under the term "paternalism" was not only a means to attract and discipline labor outside of the work place, but could also be an integral part of changes in the administration of the labor process itself.[86] Deseilligny introduced a new style of labor management based both on cooptation of the community identity Decazeville had developed in the mid-1860s and on integration of workers into an expanded managerial structure. Ironically, this effort to produce a community loyal to the company helped to lay the basis for later forms of labor solidarity directed against management.

The apparent harmony in Decazeville during the first years of the Third Republic should not obscure the town's declining position within the French economy. The iron industry almost died in the 1860s. And despite an increase in average annual coal production in the Aubin Basin from 389,266 tons in 1856–1860 to 660,263 tons in 1871–1875, the Basin's share of national coal production fell during this period from 5.1 to 4.2 percent. The relative decline of the area's mining industry contributed to a two-stage pattern of development, strongly correlated with national and international business cycles. In the first stage the operator sought to counter unfavorable market conditions through changes in the organization of work in the mines which increased productivity without significant new investment. Miners drew on bonds of solidarity in the workplace and the community to fight this increased exploitation of their labor and the implicit divestment in local industry. In the second stage, a new firm took advantage of an improving business climate to invest in Decazeville's industry, and used its leverage to change the organization of work and the structure and composition of the labor force. The town's political life alternated between opposition to coercive local managers and acceptance of their investment-oriented successors. While this model fits the changes from the Houillères et Fonderies to the Société Nouvelle, it requires further consideration of relations among social groups in the town and in the French nation to explain the course of events in Decazeville after Descilligny's death in 1875.

# 5. The Long Depression

While the Constitution of 1875 gave the Third Republic its political structure, the republicans' triumph over Marshall MacMahon's effort to exercise the power of the presidency in the *seize mai* crisis of 1877 marked its coming of age. Over the next decade moderate republicans expanded the railway system, launched a series of colonial adventures, and promoted public education with the aim of creating an economically and politically stable parliamentary republic. They were stymied, however, by the persistent strength of groups on both the right and the left whose discontent with the Third Republic was exacerbated by the effects of the worldwide Long Depression of 1873 to 1895. The situation reached a head in the support given by workers, peasants, Jacobin republicans, and monarchists to General Georges Boulanger's assault on the parliamentary republic at the end of the 1880s.

The Long Depression posed a challenge to the fundamentally *laissez-faire* economies of France and other western European nations. A generation of economic distress spurred governments to establish institutional mechanisms to investigate and alleviate social problems. Workers organized not only to oppose their employers, but increasingly to exert their influence on the parliamentary bodies charged with making social policy. New categories of workers—skilled factory workers and miners—replaced urban artisans at the forefront of the labor movement. Through a series of the longest and most bitter strikes in French history, miners made their grievances known not only to the owners, but to the state and the public as well. This nationwide politicization of social and economic life in the final decades of the nineteenth century challenged the artificial isolation and political foundations of company towns like Decazeville.

## The Long Depression and Community Life

The Long Depression had particularly severe effects in secondary industrial areas like the Aubin Basin. It stymied the efforts of metallurgical centers in southern France to recover from the tariff policies of the Second Empire and to fend off competition from new steelworks in the Lorraine. The labor force in Decazeville's factories fell one-third between 1870 and 1886, and the ironworks of Aubin closed in the mid-1880s.[1] The price of coal declined after the boom of the early 1870s; to make matters worse, in the early eighties production dropped at the open-pit mine of Lavaysse, the Société Nouvelle's most profitable operation. The company complained bitterly that state solicitude for the railways hurt isolated mines like Decazeville: high rail freight charges made it difficult for the Aubin Basin to vie with Great Britain for markets in southwestern France.[2] Dividend payments reflected the company's falling fortunes. Until 1877 the Société Nouvelle awarded dividends ranging from 5 to 8 percent. None were distributed in 1878; then dividends fell to between 2.5 and 5 percent in the next six years. From 1886 until 1892, dividends were given only once: 1 percent in 1889. The experience of the Société Nouvelle was not unique. The Long Depression accelerated the shift in economic power from southern to northern French industry. "Overall," writes Michelle Perrot of the worst years of the slump, "it [was] less a matter of a global decline than of a profound change in structure, of a modification of geographic concentration to the profit of the North and to the detriment of old industrial regions south of the Loire. The crisis of 1883–1886 [was] a turning point in the history of the underdevelopment of southern France."[3]

In an effort to limit the impact of the Long Depression, the board of the Société Nouvelle assumed many of the powers Deseilligny had exercised in its name before his death in 1875. Yet the board itself was split on the question of national economic policy. Leading free traders Léon Say and company vice-president Fernand Raoul-Duval (who in 1876 tried to have tariffs on imported coal terminated) faced prominent protectionists Arthur Joly de Bammeville and Paul Schneider, vice-president and secretary respectively of the principal

protectionist organization, the Association de l'Industrie Française.[4]
What they could all agree on was the need to exercise strict control
over the labor force. The emergence of the board as the dominant
force in the firm encouraged the short-term planning that was particularly devastating to a peripheral economic region like the Aubin
Basin. The board's usurpation of authority from management during
a period of crisis turned the paternalist ethos developed by Deseilligny into a web of hypocrisy and deceit in the workers' eyes.

The depression threatened the community of locally recruited
workers who had shared in the prosperity of the Société Nouvelle's
early years. In 1876 three-quarters of the active male population of
Decazeville were industrial workers: miners (19.4 percent); forgeworkers (26.2 percent); *manoeuvres* (29.3 percent). In 1882 almost
half of the total population of Decazeville had been born in the town;
another quarter had been born within ten kilometers of the town.[5]
(Many miners who worked for Decazeville companies lived in surrounding communities, especially around the pits at Combes in
Aubin.) The dramatic increase in marriages by Decazeville miners
under the age of twenty-five—two-fifths of those married for the
first time between 1881 and 1885—suggests that growing numbers
of men had become dependent on the steady income provided by a
job in the mines rather than on the hope of inheriting land at their
father's death.[6] The Société de la Vieille Montagne, a zinc manufacturing company in Viviez, a town adjoining Decazeville, noted
in the early seventies that its workers rarely became landowners
because "of the difficulty of finding land in our mountainous country
and the very high price of land which they could buy."[7] Nor could
most workers afford to buy a home: in the last decades of the century
a three-room house in Decazeville sold for about two thousand francs,
significantly more than a hewer's annual wages.[8] As the opportunity
to acquire land or housing declined, workers came face to face with
their proletarian status: in 1886 ninety-two percent of working-class
families in Decazeville left nothing to their descendants.[9] While
such statistics point to the existence of an autonomous worker community in Decazeville, tabulation of the occupations of wedding
witnesses shows, however, that industrial workers in Decazeville
maintained important social ties with other groups in town.[10]

Demographic, social, and economic factors shaped the development of community life in Decazeville. A further element was the
persistence of regional culture. If the ability to sign the marriage
certificate is a good indicator of literacy,[11] most of Decazeville's

workers knew some French by the early 1880s.[12] But the constant arrival of rural immigrants from the surrounding area ensured that the regional culture thrived in the town. One observer wrote that it served as an integrating factor for the disparate individuals drawn by the promise of employment in Decazeville's mines and forges: "Now everyone speaks the same *patois* and professes the same sneering and slightly contemptuous indifference toward the 'françimans.'"[13] A Parisian correspondent reported from Decazeville in 1886, "Twenty years ago, they tell me, the inhabitants of Aveyron only understood and spoke their *patois*. Now they are just as much at ease with French, but they still prefer their *patois*."[14]

As the Long Depression persisted, the Société Nouvelle sought to shore up its sagging finances through more intensive exploitation of labor at Decazeville. To use the explicitly economic terminology of contemporary sociology, workers at Decazeville mobilized their "resources"—occupational, class, and inter-class bonds and a strong regional culture—against the projects of capital.[15] The battle itself was waged between the institutional structures of labor and capital: the crews and community on the one hand, and company management on the other. Yet these conflicts were not fought in isolation. Miners' struggles against the effects of the economic crisis combined with republican efforts to assert control over local and national government to create the conditions for strikes of national import. Late nineteenth-century miners' strikes attracted national attention because they galvanized a wide range of national economic, political, and social concerns. The resolution of these strikes helped shape the future of labor relations in France.

## The Struggle for Control of the Community

Until his death in 1875 Deseilligny made skillful use of electoral politics to solidify the position of the Société Nouvelle. However, the deepening of the depression in the late seventies and the national victory of the republicans in the *seize mai* elections nurtured a republican movement in Decazeville that threatened the basis of the company town. Republicanism provided the ideological framework for Decazeville to break the isolation it experienced as a company town and to participate for the first time in a national political movement.

Republicanism in Decazeville drew support from a popular challenge to the company's use of the Church to legitimate its authority

on ideological, noneconomic grounds.[16] This was an issue of particular importance in the chronically depressed Aubin Basin. The
Houillères et Fonderies had built a church and brought in religious
personnel to run the local schools. The Church in turn had given
its full support to the new enterprise.[17] For rural immigrants to the
Basin the Church was the most important element of continuity
between agrarian society and life in an industrial town. As workers
came to see themselves as members of an urban industrial community, however, they broke with past religious traditions on which
the Church depended to sustain its position. Shifts, Sunday maintenance work, and the rigors of industrial life encouraged breaches
in the private and public behavior prescribed by the Church.[18] The
rituals of greatest appeal to workers often drew on a rich local religious folklore that lay outside of direct clerical control.[19] Surveys
taken during the seventies and eighties revealed that the percentage
of males over thirteen who took communion on Easter had fallen
to 49 percent in the canton of Decazeville (which included several
rural communities) and to 26 percent in the more industrial canton
of Aubin; the figures for women stood at 62 percent and 66 percent
respectively. For comparison, the percentages for men and women
in one nearby agricultural canton, Montbazens, were 88 percent and
99 percent, and in another, Rieupeyroux, 99 percent for both sexes.[20]

The election in 1878 of a republican ticket led by the doctor Jules
Cayrade and the businessman Alexandre Bos over a company-backed
slate affirmed the existence in Decazeville of a lay republican community of workers, small shopkeepers, and professionals. Three years
later the same voters elected Cayrade to the Chamber. In both cases
Cayrade's candidacy was a challenge to the company-based populism
developed by Deseilligny: in fact, Cayrade had first achieved noto-
riety in the unpopular role of Deseilligny's early opponent in both
the company and the town. Workers had strongly disapproved of
Cayrade's appointment as company doctor in 1868. He soon resigned
his job, but on election day in 1869 workers threatened both Cayrade
and Bos because of their support for Cibiel.[21] During the first years
of the Third Republic Cayrade became a republican and in the late
1870s forged a coalition of republican businessmen and workers who
opposed Deseilligny's successors at Decazeville. Although no workers sat in the town's first republican town council, they recognized
it as their government.

Decazeville's republicans, like republicans throughout France,
sought to reduce the Church's role in education. During the Second

Empire Decazeville had virtually abandoned lay education and, with company cooperation, contracted with religious orders to run its school system.[22] The decision of the company's mutual aid fund in 1877 to save money by ending payment for the education of employees' children opened up new opportunities for the republican municipality.[23] The republican town council sought funds for the construction of lay schools and arranged lay classes for students who did not live near a lay school.[24] Given the value that both managers like Deseilligny and the leaders of the young Republic placed on education, such measures were significant steps in the development of a community independent of company control.

It was not school reform, however, but a strike that drew the new town government into conflict with the company. The strike of 1878 differed from the one eleven years earlier in that the board of the Société Nouvelle, which had assumed many of the powers held by its first chief executive officer Deseilligny, carefully prepared for it. The board's active role during the strike convinced government officials that the company held a tight rein over all levels of management and won the Société Nouvelle the support from the state its predecessor had lacked in 1867.

The Société Nouvelle dismissed the last contractors in 1876. Faced with declining coal and iron prices, the firm decided to reduce wages by 10 percent. The board directed every facet of the operation from Paris. The miners struck, as expected, on 14 March 1878, the day the reductions were posted. The forgeworkers reluctantly followed. Representatives of the striking miners made demands similar to those posed in 1867: reorganization of the mutual aid fund, restoration of the old wage rates, discharge of four engineers and two master-miners, and a promise that no strikers would be dismissed. Workers tied the defense of wages to an effort to prevent managerial encroachment on their positions in the mutual aid fund and in individual crews. In 1867 strikers had won greater control over the mutual aid fund, but their success was short-lived. One of the Société Nouvelle's first actions had been to take away the right the strikers had obtained for the fund to name its own medical staff.[25] The economic depression of the late seventies reduced the fund's revenues and forced the company to assume some of the financial burdens the fund had previously shouldered. The Société Nouvelle took advantage of this situation to reassert its power in this one company-wide labor institution. It revised the statutes to give the chief executive officer and the engineers greater control over operations.

The fund lost its guise of independence and turned over its property to the company.[26]

As in 1867, the prime issue for striking miners was management's introduction of a flat reduction in pay which undercut the crews' ability to use their control over the labor process to defend their wages in negotiations with individual supervisors. The workers' delegates argued that they were not to blame for the company's critical financial situation: this should be attributed to "squanderers and to the excessive number of supervisory employees"; "the company doesn't run any better since the suppression of the contractors," they added.[27] The board refused to consider the strikers' demands and rejected the conciliatory gestures suggested by its chief executive officer Jules Petitjean. It decided instead to meet in permanent session in Paris,[28] and sent two of its members to Decazeville to ensure that the local leadership did not buckle.[29] The board played its trump card and informed the prefect and later the workers that the company would go into liquidation rather than continue to operate under the old conditions.[30] The prefect dispatched seven hundred soldiers to Decazeville, and reiterated the board's message that the strikers were endangering the future of their town.[31] In 1867 the state had identified management as a threat to the coal deposits, which formed part of the national patrimony; eleven years later, it applied the same criteria to support the company's position.

Mayor Cayrade, in contrast to the prefect, had approved of the decision to strike and met frequently with the strike delegates: police reports labeled him *très ami des ouvriers*. Cayrade was concerned with maintaining public order and used his influence to convince strikers not to stage open meetings or marches, and to observe an eight o'clock curfew. These steps kept strikers out of public view and allowed Cayrade and his republican colleagues to take a leading role in the strike. Many sympathetic merchants extended unlimited credit to the strikers.[32] Cayrade ordered the town council to meet in permanent session at the outbreak of the strike: it was a counterpart to the board of directors sitting in permanent session in Paris. He earned the workers' respect by refusing to allow the soldiers to set up camp in the center of Decazeville; they had to bivouac in hastily constructed barracks on the outskirts of town or lodge with the managerial personnel. And as the town would not pay for the troops' stay at Decazeville, the company was forced to foot the bill.[33]

The strikers received virtually no support from outside of the

Basin and had to return to work after a few weeks in early April 1878. Yet their isolation from other groups in the nation was not as great as that of Decazeville's miners eleven years earlier, at the beginning of the largely apolitical national strike wave of the final years of the Second Empire. The Decazeville strike of 1878 was one of a number of miners' strikes with republican overtones that took place after the crisis of *seize mai* had secured control of the government for republicans.[34] Under Cayrade's leadership, strikers identified their local community with the idea of the Republic in their struggle against the company. Yet state officials combated the strike from the beginning. The workers contrasted the support shown by local elected representatives, including the deputy, with the hostility of the prefect, the state engineer, and the judiciary. Such conflicts between elected officials and state administrators were endemic to peripheral economic areas like the Aubin Basin, where communities frequently clashed with interest groups protected by the state. In the company town, the company had claimed to represent the worker to the state, or when state and capital were in conflict, to represent his interests better than the state. The strike of 1878 was the origin of a new and recurring belief at Decazeville that republican values extended to the workplace and that the workers' community embodied these values better than the republican state apparatus.

Defeat of the strikers emboldened the board to put aside the concern for Decazeville's future that Deseilligny had shown and to concentrate instead on securing profits despite the depressed iron and coal prices. Since the strength of the strike movement had come from its support within the community, the board drew the lesson that labor management in the future would require control of municipal politics and local commerce as well as of work in the mines and factories. It placed responsibility for these tasks squarely on the engineers' shoulders, but neither increased the number of managerial personnel nor upgraded the company's machinery. This was as true in the factory as in the mines. Mine engineers pleaded without success for investments in several pits;[35] the mine engineer at Firmy complained that "there is barely one supervisory employee for every one hundred workers."[36] At the ironworks Decazeville's engineers carried out important research but "almost none of it produced any results," a later director remarked, "because of the indifference of the board of directors toward the factory"; when engineers asked for increased managerial supervision to ensure better puddling, the board reduced the number of foremen on the job.[37]

This made the engineers scapegoats for the workers' grievances, but left them little latitude to take independent action at Decazeville. Whereas Deseilligny had run the board during his tenure as chief executive officer, the board dictated policy to his successor Petitjean. Petitjean summed up the dilemma of Decazeville's local management in his criticism of the board's proposal to cut forge-workers' wages by 34 percent: "we will obey the board because we are soldiers, although public opinion will be absolutely against us."[38] While the workers disliked Petitjean, they really hated the highest managerial personnel with whom they came into regular contact: Camille Blazy, chief mining engineer, and Jules Watrin, chief engineer at the forges and assistant director. Watrin was the model "soldier": "In moneysaving matters M. Watrin followed orders given by the board," Petitjean explained. "[H]e was of a mathematical exactitude in everything. If he received an order from his superiors, he executed it."[39] The state mining engineer Joseph Paul Laur characterized Watrin as having "one passion: the prosperity of his factory. He was above all a man of duty. Inflexible for himself, he was equally so for others."[40]

The board's demands forced Watrin to play off the paternalist ethos against the hierarchical managerial structure. Jules Grès, a forge foreman, reported that Watrin "was friendly to the principal workers and if he wanted some information, he would sometimes address himself to a roller or to another worker before asking us."[41] Another supervisory employee at the forge, Pierre Galtié, complained that Watrin's attitude was a ruse to exploit the workers: "[he] was very haughty toward us. He would try to destroy our prestige before a worker. In front of a worker he was very flattering; he cajoled him and it was proverbial that he had two hands, one of the lamb and one of the tiger, which is to say that with one hand he caressed and with the other he clawed."[42] Workers came to agree that Watrin used what he learned from them to reduce wages more effectively.[43] His moral righteousness only made such hypocrisy more detestable.

Watrin was a bachelor from Metz and a devout Catholic. His austerity and ignorance of the area's mores and *patois* created further barriers between him and the southern workers under his command. The *Journal de l'Aveyron* described him as "very meticulous, very economical . . . but ignorant of the language and the customs of Aveyron."[44] Watrin had run-ins with his subordinates who, he complained, demanded various prerogatives "according to the custom of the region."[45] The Société Nouvelle valued Watrin for these qualities and, shortly after hiring him, looked for "someone from the center or from the north, not a southerner" to fill a position as mining engineer. One letter of recommendation the company received from a coal-mining firm in Saint-Etienne addressed this issue: "I believe that, *as to character,* [the candidate] is a little southern, but I think that he knows how to control himself."[46] The southerner's reputed passionate nature was considered unsuitable for the maintenance of order. At a time when southern industry was losing out to competition in northern France, the Société Nouvelle imported an engineer from the north to inculcate Decazeville's workers with the "northern" cultural attitude toward work necessary to make profits for predominantly northern French stockholders.[47]

Watrin took an active interest in his workers' lives. He belonged to the tradition of "social engineers" that thrived in the late nineteenth and early twentieth centuries.[48] "As to his relations with the workers," Petitjean explained, "he was kind and knew almost all of them. He called them by name and frequently spoke with them."[49] Watrin's openness and willingness to do favors for individuals weakened workers' efforts to oppose the company. Yet those very workers who were indebted to Watrin for their jobs or for various forms of relief came to resent the personal control that he assumed over their lives.[50]

As individuals many workers were beholden to Watrin; as a group they viewed his apparent interest in their welfare with trepidation. Workers claimed that Watrin "had their family life closely watched":

> "[Watrin] counted our morsels," said a miner who had a wife and three children at his charge. He explained that the assistant director made inquiries about their purchases at the market and about the nature and amount of their expenses. And he who "ate too well" ran the strong risk of seeing his wages cut, for "a worker should not buy game for himself. . . ."[51]

Perusal of a report written by Watrin following a trip to Longwy in 1885 would have confirmed the workers' worst suspicions. The Lorraine factory owners' use of company stores had particularly impressed Watrin:

> The manufacturer becomes merchant. He does not lose in his commercial operations, but he does not try to make a profit. His goal is to prevent business from establishing itself around

his factory or to destroy it when it already exists there. Here is how the system works: as soon as a worker is hired, one makes it easy for him to buy his food and his clothes, which are sold at the factory. The cost is deducted from his daily wages. It is a rule that the factory is never open about this. A worker can thus draw his wages as he earns them, but until payday these wages can be spent only in company stores and can be used only for the workers' needs. As advances are never made, local business becomes impossible or at least very difficult.

Watrin continued enthusiastically: "as a result of the crisis [the Aciéries de Mont St. Martin] has made incredible progress in [reducing] production costs in the last two or three years. It was able to cut most through the establishment of company stores. By a variety of means it hoped to free itself from the servitude of commerce." Mont St. Martin disbursed three-quarters of its workers' wages in goods.[52]

The company-operated store institutionalized the correlation between consumption and production which Deseilligny had made the cornerstone of an effective labor policy. While providing a safeguard against strikes, the company store also pushed out small merchants of the sort who threatened to stir up discontent among workers. In 1878 the Société Nouvelle had sought to limit expenditures and to undermine Decazeville's republican administration by reducing financial support for the town. This had forced the municipality to reintroduce the unpopular toll on foodstuffs entering the town.[53] A company-controlled commercial establishment had the advantage of allowing the company to act more directly on individual workers' consumption patterns than by subsidizing tolls, without channeling aid through a hostile municipal government.

During the late seventies and early eighties residents of the Basin started several cooperative bakeries. The largest of these, Decazeville's La Fraternelle, was founded by a group of managerial personnel, workers and non-workers of various political persuasions. La Fraternelle prospered by systematizing the offer of credit which had always been the backbone of commerce in a working-class community. The cooperative had to depend on the Société Nouvelle's offer to deduct debts of workers in arrears from their monthly pay, however, and soon fell under the company's domination. Watrin and his associates saw that the largely working-class membership of the cooperative made it the perfect instrument to limit local commerce: of the 520 members in February 1886, 77 percent were company workers and 9 percent were company supervisory personnel; 16 percent of the company's employees were members and 3.4 percent of the monthly payroll was spent at the cooperative. The cooperative soon outgrew its first quarters and leased a new building from the company. Company engineers took control of the cooperative's board of directors: the head mining engineer Blazy became president and another mining engineer, Martin, assumed the vice-presidency. When asked about the cooperative in 1886, a cafe owner who had served as its first vice-president reported:

> For close to three years I have not been an active member of this group. I withdrew little by little when I realized that the Decazeville company apparently wanted to take over direction of our group. I recognized this when a company engineer was chosen president. It was then that I also realized that M. Watrin was intervening indirectly in the management of the group, a fact we learned from M. Blazy.[54]

Company intervention in the town's retail trade was not a new idea, but the rationale for it had changed since the early years of the Houillères et Fonderies. When Cabrol set up a company store, one of his primary aims had been to bar company managerial employees from commerce. He had felt that the company suffered when supervisors dealt with workers as both producers and consumers. This had been Deseilligny's policy as well.[55] Watrin broke with this tradition. He reintroduced supervisory personnel—in their capacity as members of the managerial hierarchy—into the economic life of the community in order to tighten the company's hold over workers.

The success of the bakery prompted La Fraternelle to open a butcher's shop in 1885.[56] The cooperative also approved establishing a general store and made arrangements with the Société Nouvelle to house the new business in a company warehouse. As of the scheduled opening date in late January 1886, the cooperative had not decided what the general store would stock, although clothes, shoes, and various foodstuffs were under consideration. Many worker members disapproved of La Fraternelle's entry into new markets and the company's role in promoting it. The miner Jean-Louis Soubrié acknowledged the high quality of the cooperative's bread, but objected to an expansion of the enterprise "because then one would never have any money": "I know some people who have to resell

the meat and bread at a loss to pay their rent."[57] When Blazy told
workers that the new store would stock dry grapes to make *piquette,*
they jumped to the conclusion that soon they would not earn enough
to afford wine.[58]

Decazeville's grocers and tradesmen voiced strong opposition to
the plans to open a general store. When the cooperative was independent of the company, the workers' participation in it had marked
a breach with small businessmen who were their political allies. As
the shopkeepers' standard bearer, Cayrade had frowned on the creation of La Fraternelle from the beginning. However, once the cooperative became a company institution, many workers joined small
merchants in criticizing it. Late in 1885 Mayor Cayrade met with
Petitjean in an effort to halt the opening of the general store. Referring to the infamous Bande Noire affair, the mayor warned that
the coal company at Montceau-les-Mines "had paid dearly, very
dearly, for its conflict with the town."[59] Cayrade followed up this
discussion with a letter to the president of the Société Nouvelle in
which he explained his opposition to the creation of a general store:

> I understand the intervention of a company when it creates an
> enterprise in an area bereft of resources and which could not
> satisfy the needs of the workers it attracts, but in the present
> case such intervention is in no way justified. Cooperatives should
> stay out of company hands. Whatever you may say and do, "La
> Fraternelle," directed by the chief mine engineer and supported
> by the board of directors [of the Société Nouvelle], will never
> be considered a spontaneous creation of the workers. To the
> more impartial it will appear to be an abuse of power and an
> outrage committed against the workers' liberty.

Cayrade also doubted that the general store would make life cheaper
for the worker. On the contrary, he suspected that the use of tokens
permitting members of the cooperative bakery to charge purchases
against their future pay would encourage workers to squander their
earnings. The mayor went on to explain the social role played by
the small shopkeepers whom he was trying to protect: "The small
businesses of Decazeville, and certainly those which concern me
above all, are run by [the families of] workers who find in the small
profit they draw from them the means to support themselves. These
individuals are going to be hurt the most." Cayrade argued that only
under constraint would workers patronize a store run by the hated
Blazy, "for one can hardly separate the worker from the shopkeeper,

because a large number [of the workers] have a son, a brother, an uncle, or a cousin who is a businessman in the town."[60] The mayor estimated that the opening of the general store would force at least a quarter of Decazeville's shopkeepers to close their doors: the general store "would ruin Decazeville without profiting the workers. They would not save as promised, and would be denied, by the suppression of small retail business, one means of earning their livelihood, a kind of pension when the company could no longer employ them."[61] Although the company refused to back down, pointing to the small percentage of total sales in the community that went to the cooperative, Cayrade was able to prevent the general store from opening in January 1886 as Blazy had planned.[62]

Between 1878 and 1886 the Société Nouvelle tried to exercise two forms of community regulation: sociological and political. The proponent of the first approach, Watrin, observed workers on the job and intervened in their family and community life to create the conditions for labor to satisfy the company's need for lower production costs. The second approach, through politics, would have a less direct effect on wages. For most of Decazeville's history the mayor had been drawn from the company's managerial personnel. The Société Nouvelle smarted under Cayrade's republican administration. In the words of a police informant: "The company formerly controlled the whole town administration, while now it has been evicted from any share. Consequently, not a day passes when a conflict does not erupt between the municipality, which is moderately republican, and the company, which is absolutely reactionary."[63] Yet not all managerial personnel favored participation in local politics. Watrin, from his "sociological" perspective, viewed electoral politics as an inefficient form of labor management. He told Jean-François Rouzet, head of the company's iron warehouse: "When one is a member of the managerial personnel, one should devote oneself only to one's work and not to politics." Rouzet added that "Watrin always tried to remain aloof from political questions."[64] Others in management, however, hoped to reestablish the harmonious political climate that had existed during Deseilligny's tenure. Although the company repeatedly proclaimed its electoral neutrality,[65] it took advantage of its position in the community to undermine support for Cayrade and other republicans. Just as low-level managerial employees could apportion work more efficiently, they could also try to get out the vote for company candidates.

The company's political approach blossomed during the election for deputy in 1885, which pitted the Orleanist Cibiel, Deseilligny's unsuccessful opponent in 1869, against Mandagot, a republican from Montbazens.[66] There was special pressure on workers to vote for Cibiel because he was a major stockholder in the Société Nouvelle. It was widely believed that employees who worked in the republican campaign would be punished or fired.[67] Cibiel hired Eugène Delon, a Decazeville landowner, to win over the workers to his side. Delon paid workers to campaign for Cibiel and had the word spread through Fontvergnes, a working-class section of Decazeville, that if Cibiel were elected, the Société Nouvelle would spend 1,200,000 francs to prepare an open-pit mine at Fontvergnes. This would bring prosperity to Fontvergnes and steady jobs for its workers in a time of economic crisis. Such promises lent support to the workers' view that the company could improve their situation if it wished, and that its decisions on such matters were politically motivated: one miner alleged that "before elections the foremen would recommend to workers that they vote the company's way, saying that otherwise hardship would come."[68] Delon's efforts on Cibiel's behalf failed locally; although the conservative list swept the department, it received only one-quarter of the votes cast in Decazeville.[69]

Until the 1860s the Houillères et Fonderies had largely monopolized public expressions of political power at Decazeville. In its conception of the company town, the firm intervened in commerce to make up for the absence of local business rather than to crush it. The constitution of a core community of residents, the economic crisis of the Second Empire, and the establishment of the Third Republic in the 1870s disrupted the company town at Decazeville by creating the conditions for the emergence of economic and political arenas independent of and opposed to managerial control. The Long Depression transformed the company town from a necessary adjunct to industry into a mechanism for the efficient exploitation of labor. This change accompanied the shift from a form of work organization in which contractors—often shopkeepers on the side— played an important role to more direct company supervision of the labor process. The close relationship between developments in the workplace and the town explains why the Decazeville miners' union devoted its efforts both to labor issues and to local politics in the final decades of the nineteenth century.

**The Union**

The alliance of republican small businessmen and workers at Decazeville that withstood the attacks of the Société Nouvelle was an
example of the coalition that the Opportunist leader René Waldeck-
Rousseau was attempting to build on the national level. He viewed
the formal legalization of trade unions in 1884 as an essential element in the development of working-class support for a stable moderate republic. Because of the size of the mining population and the
importance of the coal industry to the economy, miners' unions
would clearly have the opportunity to play an important role in this
integration of organized labor into republican politics. Georges Stell
made this clear in his 1882 *cahiers de doléances* for French miners,
which the nation's first miners' union at Saint-Etienne ordered re-
printed and sent to miners across the nation: "the interests of French
miners represent and summarize those of our nation's workers. . . . The miners have the right to speak in the name of the proletariat."[70] This position had special relevance for miners in central
and southern France. The *cahiers* went on to argue that these miners
did not receive the same level of benefits which companies in the
Nord and Pas-de-Calais gave their miners.[71] Miners' unions were
intended in part as a vehicle to enable miners in less favored basins
to seek through parliamentary action and accords with employers
the gains that northern miners had already received. The miners'
unions therefore had a number of potential missions beyond the
defense of their constituents' particular interests. They were called
upon to act as bulwarks of the Republic, to win passage of special
legislation for workers, to represent the aspirations of the proletariat
as a whole, and to combat the effects of regional differences in the
remuneration of miners. While the effort to obtain particular advantages for the miners' corporation dominated the activities of the
national miners' federation, miners' unions in the Aubin Basin frequently pursued one or more other goals in the decades before World
War I.

It was in hopes of organizing miners to work for legislative reforms
that Michel Rondet, leader of the Loire miners' union, made a speaking tour of the Aubin Basin in March 1884. In public meetings that
drew as many as 200 workers, Rondet outlined the four demands
contained in his 1881 "Call to Miners": recognition of mine-safety
delegates elected by their fellow miners to ensure safe operation of

the mines; establishment of a mutual aid and pension fund controlled by miners; the eight-hour day; and formation of *conseils de prud'hommes*, composed of equal numbers of miners' and owners' representatives, to settle grievances between labor and management. Such corporative, reformist demands characterized the miners' union from its origins. Rondet's goal was to convince miners across the nation to pursue the strategy developed by miners in the Loire Basin during the Second Empire: trying to achieve reform by invoking the state's special relationship to the mining industry. He spoke in moderate terms to miners in the Aubin Basin: he called revolution an impossibility given the size and military strength of the forces of repression, and he condemned strikes as counterproductive. He asked his listeners not to imitate the anarchists who took two steps backward with each step forward, and praised the current government and its ministers.[72]

After Rondet's visit, miners established a union at Decazeville in the spring of 1884. The new organization recruited only a small minority of the labor force: at the beginning of 1886 it enrolled 175 members, predominantly hewers and timbermen, and possessed a treasury of just 100 francs. The union was staunchly republican. In preparation for the 1885 elections it devoted whole meetings to prorepublican readings and speeches.

In dealings with the Société Nouvelle, the union was primarily concerned with protecting the rights of miners as a group and as individuals. In this sense it served as a complement to the small crew. While reaffirming its support on the national level for the measures in Rondet's "Call," the union attacked the company mutual aid fund, one of the foundations of labor management at Decazeville and an issue in the strikes of 1867 and 1878. Transformation of the fund was a necessary step toward the union's goal of recognition as the miners' spokesman. With the appearance of unions, mining firms began to see the workers elected by their peers to the fund board of directors as a natural foil to independent worker organization. C. Ledoux, one-time director of Anzin, praised fund commissioners as "the true miners' delegates, who function naturally and without legislative apparatus" (in contrast to the mine-safety delegates proposed by Rondet).[73] Companies in the Aubin Basin often attempted to use the fund commissioners to get across their position to miners.[74] When 13 candidates ran for two openings on the Decazeville fund's administrative board in 1887, the police commented: "The small favors granted to the commissioners by the company [explain] their eagerness to declare their candidacy."[75] Union leaders were more blunt: the commissioners "must remain blind, deaf, and mute, under pain of being fired."[76] The union reacted to company domination of the fund by running candidates for the fund's board of directors, and demanding changes in the regulations under which the fund operated, including the eligibility of workers to its presidency and vice-presidency.[77] The union supplemented company benefits programs by organizing collections for injured and sick members and the widows and children of deceased members; it also ran its own mutual aid fund' which in turn paid half of the union secretary's salary.[78]

The union defended the rights of accident victims as well. Companies used the mutual aid funds to minimize the effects of their growing liability for accidents in the mines. The Société Nouvelle put pressure on accident victims and their families to settle out of court and then transferred the costs to the fund.[79] A visitor to Decazeville sympathetic to the company noted in 1886, "Thanks to the mutual aid fund, differences over the responsibility for accidents are amicably arranged and in the best interests of the company." The union responded by helping injured miners sue the Société Nouvelle for compensation.[80]

The union shied away from more direct confrontations with the company, however, out of weakness and a belief that organized labor could achieve more through legislative action than strikes. At its origin, the Decazeville miners' union was primarily concerned with the creation and reform of institutions in which miners could exercise power; the setting of wages was an issue for the crews and management to settle. In fact, when asked by judicial authorities in 1886, "Don't you concern yourself with the question of wages as well?" Jean-Pierre Blanc, the union leader could answer, "Never has such a question arisen in the union."[81] The union had roots in the development of republican social policy. It sought legislation which would answer miners' criticism of the company's autocratic and demeaning delivery of social services. Only changes in the organization of work—and the discontent these generated among the rank-and-file—brought the issue of wages to the fore in the union.

Developments in Decazeville during the early 1880s were part of a nationwide change in the structure of the coal industry. The depression weakened the ability of mines in southern France to compete with the richer mines of the north. Long-established northern mines, including Anzin, were in turn challenged by the rapid expansion of new coalfields in the Pas-de-Calais.[82] Although Cayrade threatened the firm with the example of the disorders at Montceau-les-Mines in 1882, the crucial event of the period for mine operators was the Anzin strike of February–April 1884. The long, bitter strike in the nation's leading mining firm provided Emile Zola with material for *Germinal,* which appeared the following year. The novel reinforced impressions created by extensive newspaper reporting during the strike and helped to make the miners' relations with their employers a subject of national debate. The Anzin strike raised crucial issues for managers in heavy industry and for republican social reformers. It elicited a serious discussion among "social engineers" as to whether harmonious, paternalist labor relations were possible in a joint-stock company, where ownership was separate from management. Although contributors to the debate failed to reach a consensus, they posed clearly the question of whether the growing concentration of capital coupled with the consolidation of a democratic republic did not require the development of a new system of labor management.[83]

The Anzin strike was a turning point for republicans as well. A minority of republican deputies, led by Georges Clemenceau, felt that the Republic had to do more for workers than enact educational reforms. For Clemenceau parliamentary investigation of labor conflicts, like the strike in the mines of the Gard in 1882, and especially the 1884 Anzin miners' strike, expanded the prerogatives of the Chamber along British lines and therefore strengthened the republic.[84] Clemenceau and his allies looked to the coalfields and saw in the miners' struggles against their employers archetypal republican battles. Clemenceau's report to the Chamber of Deputies on the Anzin strike in 1884 is one of the first full statements of republican opposition to the creation of a state within a state in company towns. He argued convincingly that creating loyal company employees conflicted with the Republic's goal of creating citizens.[85]

The strike at Decazeville in 1886 resembled, but did not replicate that at Anzin two years earlier. It took place under conditions created by previous conflicts and therefore developed differently. Company efforts to combat the effects of the industrial depression at Decazeville reinforced the anticompany republican alliance of workers and members of the middle class. However, the intervention of leading socialists in the strike eventually revealed the weaknesses of this alliance in both Decazeville and in the nation.

## The Strike of 1886

Since switching to production of coal as their primary business, firms at Decazeville had depended heavily on the sale of the more highly priced lump coal. In the early 1880s the Lavaysse open-pit mine had yielded up to 40 percent lump coal, and had accounted for 70 percent of the lump coal mined at Decazeville. Until 1883 Lavaysse produced an average of 100,000 tons of coal annually, but no new areas had been prepared for open-pit mining. Rather than investing in such work, which would pay off only several years later, the company allowed production at Lavaysse to drop to 40,000 thousand tons per year.[86]

The Société Nouvelle turned to the underground mines to make up for its loss of profitable lump coal and to find a way to take advantage of the unskilled, inexpensive labor it had previously employed in the open-pit mines. Until the middle of the Second Empire the prosperity of Decazeville's iron industry had allowed the use of contractors in the mines. During the 1870s and early 1880s the company's ability to extract one-quarter of its coal at a significant profit from the open-pit mines had helped keep the enterprise profitable. With the depletion of this sector, the Société Nouvelle looked to reduce its expenses by intervening in the organization and remuneration of the crew, the fundamental unit in underground mining.

The miners' reactions to the elimination of the contractor had been mixed. While contractors were often popular among their workers, they were also perceived in times of crisis as exploiters of the miners' labor. The chief miner's position was different. Respect for him within the crew was based on his skill, strength, and ability to organize work. He did not attain his position solely through the goodwill of his superiors, as supervisors appeared to have, but by mastering his profession, a path open to all. Crew members accepted his leadership and did not consider him an exploiter. For this reason, the company's challenge to the chief miner's position in the crew was an issue that clearly pitted miners against management.

The Société Nouvelle's attack on the organization of work in the mines took several forms. The management weakened the crew by assigning to it mobile, untrained helpers from the countryside at lower daily wages than those chief miners usually gave their helpers. The presence of these less well-paid workers was used to justify the offer of lower production rates. This was a clear violation of the chief miner's right to choose and pay his own helpers.[87] Some observers claimed that if the hewer felt so strongly about choosing his own helper, "it is evidently to pay him less: it is a petty exploitation of the worker by the worker."[88] In this case the charge was inaccurate; what was really at stake was the hewers' role in the recruitment and training of new miners. In a period of economic hardship miners wanted to preserve the existing apprenticeship system embodied in the crew. For, if the crew was a means of teaching skills, it was also a means of restricting the spread of skills. The uncontrolled influx of *campagnards* to work in the mines would contribute to the lowering of the average daily wage in the short term and to the demise of the crew as a form of quasi-craft organization in the long run.

In addition to threatening the hewers' control of the apprenticeship system, the Société Nouvelle also disrupted the careers of miners who no longer worked in crews due to age and infirmity. The company traditionally employed these men in maintenance work, including timbering. In the early 1880s the company began to make use of manifestly inadequate pensions to retire less productive older workers.[89] It turned over a portion of the work they had done to the crews.[90] Taken together, the changes introduced by the Société Nouvelle in the 1880s challenged the authority of the chief miner and reduced the income of helpers and older workers, whose wages were an integral part of the miners' household economy.[91]

The most direct effect of the reduced production in the open-pit mine on the crews of underground miners was the company's decision to replace the flat rate paid per wagon of coal (1.15 francs) with rates based on incentives to produce more of the difficult-to-mine lump coal (2 francs per wagon) and less of the hard-to-market fine coal (.85 francs). While introducing this change in 1885, management postponed setting the rates to be paid per meter dug until the end of the month in order to see how much lump coal miners would extract. As a consequence miners worked without knowing the rate at which they would be paid.[92] This enabled the Société Nouvelle's commercial agent Jules Gastambide to tell a reporter from *Le Matin* at the end of January 1886: "Despite the crisis which is shaking the mining industry, we have not, officially at least, reduced the rates; we have *tightened* them a little, that's all."[93]

These changes in the organization of work and the mode of remuneration created a tense atmosphere in the mines: supervisors reported to Blazy about small groups of miners which furtively dispersed when management representatives approached. On 26 January 1886 miners at Decazeville struck to protest what they considered irregularities in their pay.[94] The miners who initiated the walkout did not belong to the union. Shortly before the strike they revealed their plans to Mayor Cayrade—who recommended against it—but not to the union. Union secretary Blanc claimed that he knew nothing of it beforehand. When he heard that the miners were leaving the pits, he went to Cayrade and told him that he thought the strike came at an inopportune time.

> I believe that they were wrong to go out on strike, especially now. There is much misery in the area, it is true, but it is the same in all the coal basins . . . It would be better to wait to obtain the laws on mine-safety delegates and on the mutual aid and pension funds. Then the situation would improve and we could get something without striking.

As union leader, Blanc placed his faith in national legislative reform rather than in individual strikes over wages. He and the mayor agreed to work together to calm the workers.[95]

The strikers initially sought out Watrin, acting head in Petitjean's absence, and forcibly escorted him from his office to the town hall to discuss their grievances: the miners chose Watrin as their target because Blazy always blamed wage reductions on pressure from his superiors. At the town hall Cayrade persuaded the strikers to name delegates and to draw up a list of grievances. Blanc and fellow union leader Jean-Baptiste Carrié were among the first delegates selected. Carrié remarked to Blanc that in choosing them the strikers seemed to be pursuing the path of moderation.[96] The pair shaped the maze of complaints about irregularities in the previous month's pay and dissatisfactions with the management into negotiable proposals. Blanc told strikers that their demand for the resignation of Blazy would never be granted. Counting on the widespread belief that Watrin was disliked by his superiors, Blanc convinced the strikers to ask for the resignation of Watrin instead.[97] In addition, the striking miners demanded that workers fired after the strike of 1878 be rehired and that no sanctions be taken against delegates in the current strike. Further demands were: negotiation of rates with master miners rather than engineers; guaranteed minimum wages for hewers, timbermen, and helpers; the right for hewers to choose their own helpers; bringing the wood closer to where the timbering was done; and payment of wages every two weeks instead of monthly to reduce miners' dependence on company credit. The core of these demands was a defense of the crew. Miners sought to limit the power that Watrin and the distant despotic mine engineers wielded over their lives. They preferred to negotiate with the master miners, who were former miners and presumably more susceptible to pressure from workers. Guaranteed minimum wages would raise the overall pay-scale, while reducing the incentives for introducing inexpensive rural labor and limiting the potential for unjust evaluations of miners' work by supervisory personnel. Confirmation of the hewer's right to choose his coworkers would reassert his control of the organization of labor at the pit face. The demand for depots of wood closer to the working area was a particular necessity for the safety of the crews since the retirement of older maintenance workers.

Cayrade presided over negotiations, the orderliness of which contrasted with the turmoil outside of the town hall. Watrin claimed that he lacked the authority to discuss the strikers' demands and announced that the chief executive officer Petitjean would arrive the following day with full powers to negotiate with the miners. Watrin's assertion that he could do nothing did not sit well with workers who experienced his power in the community daily. A warehouse worker who had been recently dismissed by the company told him: "You say that you don't have the power to deal alone; but you certainly had the power to have me fired." Watrin seemed to confirm this point by chiding personally one strike delegate, a member of the board of the company mutual aid fund: "Look, Entraygues, what do you have to reproach me with? You who have come many times to call on me, have I ever refused to do right by you?"[98]

As the afternoon progressed, state officials converged on Decazeville. With negotiations at a deadlock the state mining engineer suggested to the delegates that they join him in an inspection of the mines to ensure that the work stoppage had not allowed the fires to get out of control. Although everyone at the meeting tried to convince Watrin not to come along, he insisted that as acting director he should accompany the group. The strike delegates pledged to try to protect him, but could not stop the crowd of some 1,500 from pressing in on the small party of officials and company engineers. Unable to make it to the pits, they took refuge in the second story of an abandoned company building. Angry workers and townspeople calling for the resignation of "the Prussian" laid siege to the structure. Cayrade could not gain control of the crowd, but decided not to call on the *gendarmerie* for fear that its presence would lead to a massacre. Some rioters broke down the doors and others mounted a ladder to get to the second floor. Once in the building, they sought out Watrin. Despite strenuous efforts by the delegates to protect the assistant director, the invaders savagely clubbed him and threw him out of a window to the crowd below. As dusk set in, the throng dispersed and Watrin was taken to a nearby house. He never regained consciousness and died that night.

The murder stunned both workers and management. The following day the sub-prefect had little trouble getting the company to agree to the following conditions: payment every two weeks; bargaining at the existing rates between the miners and the master miners; a commitment to study the issue of timbering. With these assurances the strikers returned to work, although rumors were rife that the company would not uphold its end of the bargain.[99] In any case the workers' greatest victory was not put into the accord: they expected that Blazy's hasty departure during the strike would be permanent, and that therefore the events of the twenty-sixth had rid them of their two most hated engineers.

Bolstered by the arrival of 1,530 soldiers and *gendarmes*—close to the number of adult male miners employed by the Société Nouvelle—[100] and the arrest of a number of men and women accused of Watrin's murder, the board took measures to restore the company's authority in Decazeville.[101] It decided to retreat on the politically sensitive and secondary means of controlling wages through the cooperative, but to pursue efforts to restructure rates. On 15 February the board ordered management to stop withholding sums owed to La Fraternelle from workers' wages. A week later it instructed managerial personnel—and Blazy in particular—to resign from the cooperative's board of directors.[102] As a matter of principle, however, the board retained Blazy as chief mining engineer. The board spurned the conciliatory gestures made by the state. It told stockholders in February that a government reduction in rail freight charges to Bordeaux, made after Watrin's death, was insufficient to allow Decazeville's coal to challenge that of Great Britain in the Bordeaux region.[103] A month after Watrin's murder, the Société Nouvelle announced it would pay for timbering done by the crews, but cut ten centimes off each wagon of coal. The prefect was shocked by the company's temerity; the miners, who calculated that their total pay would be reduced, went on strike immediately. The strikers' demands resembled those they had formulated in January: the dismissal of Blazy, rate-setting by master miners, a minimum wage for helpers, and higher pay for workers involved in filling old mine galleries. They offered to accept a lower rate per wagon of lump coal than that set by the company in exchange for higher rates for fine and for timbering.[104]

As soon as it received word of the strike, the board ordered Petitjean to inform miners that to be rehired they would have to receive individual permission from the board. The prefect refused to allow the posting of such an inflammatory notice. In retaliation, Léon Say, prominent liberal economist, former minister, and president of the Société Nouvelle, threatened the Minister of Interior with grave potential consequences: "Beside the fact that the meddling of a representative of [public] authority in private affairs might engage the pecuniary responsibility of the state, a prolongation of the current troubles could also result, a prolongation that could have as a consequence the liquidation of the enterprise."[105] The board was undaunted by the Minister of Public Works' suggestion a few days later, after he had met with a delegation of Radicals, that the Société Nouvelle was risking abrogation of its mining concession by pursuing a strategy that seemed designed to make the return to work more difficult.[106]

The board played an active role throughout the strike. Watrin's death had shattered the engineers' morale. Blazy had initially wanted to quit and the engineer Martin suffered a breakdown and had to be given a year's leave of absence. Board members strengthened Petitjean's resolve during the first weeks of the strike and took his place temporarily when he went to Paris for consultation.[107] The board practiced a *politique du pire*. At the end of March it precipitated a strike of Firmy's miners rather than grant concessions amounting to a few hundred francs per month.[108] With no more coal leaving the pits, the company had to shut down the ironworks soon afterward, forcing the forgeworkers to join the strike. Under Say's direction the Société Nouvelle pursued the classic strike strategy of fending off state interference in the name of private property, while seeking to starve the workers into submission.

When the board left Petitjean to his own devices, he tried unsuccessfully to use company institutions to influence the strikers. In mid-March, for instance, he took advantage of a meeting of the mutual aid fund—"our almost intimate conversations," he termed it—to present the company's opinion of the strikers' grievances: "I think that you know me better than do those who insult me, since I have lived in your midst for twelve years. I have shared your work and your dangers more than my age allows. Each morning, between eight and ten, you see me receive your wives and your children. I always try to aid [your families] and to grant satisfaction to [your demands]." Petitjean then went on to promote the theory that the company contribution to the mutual aid fund was a form of profit-sharing. He argued that the total company contribution to the mutual aid fund, pensions, and other employee welfare programs in the previous year was equivalent to the distribution of a dividend of 3.15 percent on the company's capital of 6,500,000 francs. He concluded: "You see very well that since you and your families receive this privileged dividend, you are treated better than the stockholders who received nothing, despite all the efforts we are making." Petitjean's demonstration that the company was more generous to its employees than to its stockholders persuaded few strikers to return to work.[109]

Petitjean's disquisition was not an offer to negotiate. Throughout the spring of 1886 the Société Nouvelle refused to bargain with the strikers. The firm's only offer was to have state mining engineers "verify"—after the miners had returned to work—that the rate paid per ton of coal extracted was the same under the rates proposed in February as under those in effect before. The strikers refused. They saw no reason to acquiesce in the company's attempt to use the technical prestige of the state engineers to ratify its rationalization of rates.

The strikers' chances depended on two factors: their opportunity to participate in other aspects of the Aubin Basin's local economy, and, more important, their ability to elicit outside intervention in the conflict. Miners in the Aubin Basin, although they were full-time industrial workers, did not lose touch with agriculture. As the strike dragged on, many workers tilled their small plots or worked the land of peasants in the area. What in the past had provided a defense against low pay, layoffs, and short work weeks became a strike tactic in 1886. The location of the mines in the countryside furnished resources unavailable to strikers in more urban areas. For this reason, the length of some mining strikes was not necessarily a sign of proletarian combativeness; it could indicate a certain distance from the model of the urban worker. At Decazeville, however, striking miners' opportunities to engage in farming were clearly secondary to their need for national support.

The murder of Watrin, ironically, brought workers and republican municipal officials in Decazeville together; the transition from spon-

taneous violence to organized working-class resistance later separated them. Conservative deputies in the Chamber blamed Cayrade
for his failure to call in the *gendarmes* on the afternoon of Watrin's
murder. Cayrade and his assistant mayor Bos later told investigators
that they were unable to recognize any of the murderers, for they
were used to seeing workers in garb other than the dirty work clothes
the strikers had been wearing. The local officials' reticence was in
stark contrast to the state officials' lack of hesitation in picking out
a number of assailants from among a crowd of strangers.[110]

Yet Cayrade and the moderate republicanism he embodied lost
their influence over Decazeville's miners during the course of the
strike. Strikers went beyond their middle-class allies in town by
calling for creation of a worker-owned cooperative bakery and by
staging well-attended civil burials which challenged the Church's
previously uncontested monopoly of such public demonstrations.[111]
Although the union had not planned the initial January walkout, it
was the union, not the town council as in 1878, that provided leadership to the strikers. In response to demands made by the strikers,
the union took on new issues, including work organization and
wages. Over the course of the strike, union membership grew considerably; by 24 May 1886 it stood at 807, well over half of the male
labor force in the mines. Union-organized strike committees, staffed
by hewers and timbermen, called almost daily meetings, and saw
to the collection and distribution of strike funds.[112] Strike delegates
refused to allow the mayor to represent them in negotiations to
settle the strike. A disappointed Cayrade deplored the presence of
outside propagandists and predicted their influence would grow as
the strike dragged on: "It is therefore of the greatest importance for
all France," he concluded, "that this affair end as soon as possible."[113]

For three and one-half months Decazeville's strikers were exposed
to some of the most influential left-wing leaders in France, many
of whom took up residence in the town. These individuals—*représentants en mission* of the social revolution—presented an alternative to Cayrade's moderate, locally based republicanism. They
showed how issues raised in the strike were part of larger problems
facing workers throughout the country. The assistance that these
national figures provided was essential to the strikers, bereft as they
were of experience and financial resources. While deputies and cor-
respondents made daily speeches, *Le Cri du peuple, L'Intransigeant,*
and other Parisian newspapers organized subscriptions that netted
200,000 to 300,000 francs for the strikers. In addition, more than

twenty town councils across the nation sent funds to the miners. No other strike during the period generated such mass support.[114] Contributions from men and women across France, not aid from other miners, enabled the strikers at Decazeville to persevere.[115]

Late nineteenth-century miners' strikes, and none more so than the Decazeville strike of 1886, became intimately bound with the press that covered them. Newspapers made the strikes national events and gave the miner a public image as the determined, resolute proletarian. The 60,000 readers of *Le Cri du peuple*, many of whom contributed to the paper's strike fund, avidly followed events in the isolated mining town of Decazeville. Each day the paper published the passionate statements of support which accompanied donations to the fund.[116] The government revealed its concern over the effects of the extensive press coverage of the Decazeville strike by bringing two left-wing Parisian reporters to trial for alleged inaccuracies in their articles, which supposedly increased the miners' will to resist.[117]

The newspapermen and politicians urged strikers to interpret their conflict with the Société Nouvelle in terms of the state's role in the coal business. When the Société Nouvelle threatened to liquidate operations at Decazeville, left-wing leaders encouraged strikers to respond with a reinterpretation of the 1810 mine law. By refusing to negotiate, the company prolonged the strike. Because of the strike, it could no longer protect the mines from fire; therefore the state should rescind the firm's mining concessions.[118] This argument undercut the position taken by state authorities in past strikes at Decazeville: that miners should return to work to save their mines. The implication of the strikers' view was that a mining company which could not sustain a satisfactory relationship with its labor force should not be sanctioned by the Republic.

National spokesmen showed the strikers new possibilities for state action. In early March the local union leader Carrié spoke in favor of dividing up the mine concessions of the Société Nouvelle among a number of smaller companies, a plan that he expected would ensure full employment and higher wages. Emile Basly, a Socialist deputy and former miner who had first achieved national prominence as leader of the Anzin strike of 1884, followed Carrié to the podium. The creation of smaller firms, he told the strikers, would only reduce the competitiveness of the Basin's coal. Basly called instead for nationalization of the mines.[119] His message encountered a receptive audience. The attorney general reported later in the month:

"The workers continue to put their faith in the belief that the state will appropriate the mines and they will then be run under the supervision of unionized miners."[120]

The strike made the residents of Decazeville acutely aware of the potential impact of public policy decisions on their future. The four sessions of the Chamber devoted to the murder of Watrin and to the strike brought the town to national prominence and developed its residents' perception of themselves as a community within the national context. For the first time, Decazeville's workers had reason to pay close attention to the workings of the legislature: "Without witnessing it," wrote a reporter in early March, "one could not believe with what passion people here comment on the attitude of parliament toward the miners. They repeat publicly that the Chamber of Deputies will take the strikers' side and will find a solution to the current conflict favorable to them."[121] This expectation became a crucial factor in strike tactics and strategy. It helps explain the surprisingly orderly and steadfast demeanor of striking miners at Decazeville in 1886 and throughout France before World War I. In late May union leaders spurred on strikers after the failure of negotiations by reminding them of the growing support for their cause in the Chamber: "Citizens Carrié and Bouyssi showed the value of resisting until the Chamber reconvenes. They ask workers to stay calm so as not to lose the sympathy of republican France, sympathy that they have gained since the [company's] refusal to negotiate."[122]

In the company town, workers had been encouraged to see themselves as employees first and as members of the working class and the French nation second. The lengthy strike of 1886 developed both their class and national consciousness. Articles in the national left-wing press, avidly read by the strikers, and the nationwide contributions to the strike fund gave miners in Decazeville a new view of their place in the nation. Social conflict was in fact a prime way in which workers "became Frenchmen."[123] Cultural change in the French provinces was not simply the result of an ever greater cultural hegemony exercised by Paris over the hinterlands. Strikers at Decazeville appropriated symbols of the national republic in a fundamentally political effort to rally support against their employers. The strikers paraded about with the tricolor flag and sang the Marseillaise, while branding the most hated of their opponents foreigners; they had called Watrin a "Prussian" and referred to miners who returned to work during the strike as "kroumirs," after the North

African tribesmen French soldiers had fought a few years earlier.[124] Yet the strikers saw no contradiction between their regional culture and their patriotic affirmations. Local militants who spoke and led songs in *patois* frequently accompanied national political leaders to the rostrum. As long as the community remained the focal point of the miners' struggle, issues of economic and political power transcended a concern with regional particularism.

The Decazeville strike of 1886 cannot be understood solely in terms of the accelerated entry of the town's labor force into the national polity. The strike also shaped national politics by creating the conditions for development of an autonomous Socialist movement. This in turn forced republicans of various stripes to come up with a response to the call by a new generation of Socialists—influenced as much by Marxism as by the tradition of the Second Republic—for the overthrow of capitalism and the establishment of collective ownership of the means of production.

In 1884 Clemenceau and other Radicals had championed the miners at Anzin. However, after the conservative revival in the elections of 1885 created a political stalemate in the Chamber, the Radicals became hesitant to take steps which might topple the moderate government of Charles Freycinet and allow the formation of a conservative government. The Decazeville strike put the Radicals in an awkward position. Despite the popular Minister of War Boulanger's fanciful evocation before the Chamber of soldiers sharing their rations with Decazeville's strikers, the continued presence of army troops in the town made clear the government's commitment to protect the company's investment.[125] Although the Radicals tried to elicit government intervention in early March 1886, they were soon eclipsed by the Socialists, who played the leading role in Decazeville and in the nation in rallying support for the strikers.

The strike was an important ideological and organizational step in the development of the Socialist movement in France. Marxists, in particular, perceived the strike as crucial for enlisting popular support against the financial bourgeoisie which controlled French economic life. Paul Lafargue, Karl Marx's son-in-law and a leader of the French Marxists, wrote in *Le Cri du peuple:*

> The Decazeville strike is the most important event of the fifteen years of the vile capitalist Republic . . .
> This strike, like a flash of lightning, has illuminated the social situation by revealing to all the role of finance. The petty

bourgeoisie has seen who the real enemies are: the Says, the Rothschilds and the other cosmopolitan rascals who hold the instruments of labor and the social capital want to turn the entire nation into proletarians to exploit.[126]

In Paris the Decazeville strike provided a rallying point for the various Socialist groups. As Marx's daughter Laura Lafargue wrote to Friedrich Engels in late May 1886, the strike had "worked wonders for us in Paris, over and above what partial alleviation it may bring to the sufferings of the miners."[127] The passions stirred by the Decazeville strike found an outlet in the ballot box. When Parisian Socialists ran one of the journalists arrested for his coverage of the strike in by-elections in the spring of 1886, he garnered more than 100,000 votes, close to 40 percent of those cast.[128]

The strike galvanized Socialists in the Chamber as well. In the *scrutin de liste* elections of 1885 Socialist deputies had been elected on Radical slates. The Decazeville strike acted as a catalyst to separate them from the Radicals, who remained loyal to the Freycinet government. Through their work in aiding the Decazeville strikers the Socialist deputies came to form an independent group for the first time, much to Engels' satisfaction: "To me, this appearance of a workers' party in the Palais-Bourbon is *the* great event of the year."[129]

The Socialists' success over the course of the strike had a major impact on republican politics. Two strategies emerged: cooperatives and labor legislation, the first associated with Francis Laur, the second with Waldeck-Rousseau. Company antipathy for the Socialist leadership of the strike combined with a paralysis on the part of the government throughout most of the strike to create an opening for the maverick deputy from the Loire, Francis Laur. Laur espoused the republicanism of Jules Michelet's *The People.* As a youth, he had followed the advice of his mentor Georges Sand and trained to be an engineer at the Saint-Etienne School of Mines rather than go to Paris to become a writer. He was a strong supporter and friend of Léon Gambetta.[130] Laur responded to the impasse at Decazeville in terms of the organization of labor in cooperatives, a once influential tradition of republican social thought that was losing ground at the end of the nineteenth century.

Laur was the only republican deputy to win the strikers' confidence. In May they gave him a mandate to represent them in talks with the company. Both the Minister of Public Works and prominent members of the board of directors recommended to the board that it accept Laur's mediation proposal. "We should make people stop talking about us," Petitjean urged, "for they are talking of us and they are talking too much."[131] Despite these pleas, the board rejected Laur's offer. The spurned Laur responded by framing the strike in terms of the Second Republic. He claimed that the company was consciously pursuing the same policy as the Constituent Assembly had in 1848 in hope of "provoking new June days." He drew a connection between the strike and the contemporary debate in the Chamber over whether to allow princes from former ruling houses to live in France. Referring to the political sympathies of several members of the board, he told the miners, "The company embodies the Orleanists; you embody the Republic. Your strike is the struggle of universal suffrage against the monarchy."[132] Like Lafargue, Laur saw the financial capitalism of Léon Say and his ilk as the real enemy. Laur's response, however, was republican fraternity, not socialist revolution. First, he proposed that he and other deputies could make a lecture tour through the nation to raise the money needed to pay miners the additional ten centimes per wagon which the company refused them.[133]

The heart of Laur's solution to the strike, however, was his response to the question of who should own the mines, posed earlier in the strike by Carrié and Basly. Laur was a strong proponent of the *mine aux mineurs*, a mine owned not by private capital or the state, but by miners. The *mine aux mineurs* had precedents in several areas of France, including the famous iron-ore mines of Rancié. Laur's adaptation of the socialism of mid-nineteenth century urban artisans to the mines struck a receptive chord among miners who were fighting the efforts of capitalist firms to weaken labor's control over work during the Long Depression. With the approval of Decazeville's miners, Laur asked the government to concede small unexploited deposits in the area to miners who might be laid off after the strike. He proposed that sympathetic newspapers establish a fund to support such ventures. "With patience," Laur concluded, "miners will eventually have the capital to allow them to deal with the companies as equals."[134] For Laur the creation of worker-owned and operated enterprises in the mines and elsewhere would complete the social program inaugurated by the Third Republic's educational legislation.[135]

There is also a kind of *experimental* education from which even the untutored worker can profit. This is the education which results from the enlargement of the intellectual horizons through

participation in social affairs, the technical, financial and administrative aspects of management, which manual wage labor
paid by the day totally prohibits in today's society.[136]

Precisely this aspect made *mines aux mineurs* more efficient than
capitalist enterprises, because they did not have to pay the salaries
of engineers and directors.[137] In his book on a *mine aux mineurs* in
Rive-de-Gier (Loire), for which he was a technical consultant, Laur
brought the spirit of Michelet to the mines:

> The Revolution would begin again [with the *mines aux mi-
> neurs*]. Why does France now have its peasants, small propri-
> etors, a satisfied class whatever one says, and for whom the
> social question is resolved? It is because the large landhold-
> ings . . . have been little by little bought up and divided by the
> peasants. These *specialists* [the peasants] have the lowest ag-
> ricultural production costs . . . We believe that the miner is called
> upon to play the same role for the underground; he will little
> by little become the peasant of the mine to the greatest profit
> of all.[138]

An effort to set up a *mine aux mineurs* in Aveyron after the strike
failed; coal companies had already acquired the rights to the profitable coal deposits.[139] What is significant about Laur's proposals is
that they mark perhaps the fullest and last articulation of a solution
to labor problems in the mines in the Second Republic's terms of
fraternity and cooperation.[140]

The strike at Decazeville prompted influential leaders of the Third
Republic to suggest a different solution to labor conflict. The Opportunists, who had blamed the Société Nouvelle at the beginning
of the strike, disassociated themselves from the miners when Socialists took leadership of the movement. A group of Opportunists
then turned to elements of the right and to the Radicals. Under
Waldeck-Rousseau's leadership, they went beyond the legalization
of unions and proposed that a broad spectrum of republicans, from
conservatives to Radicals, put aside their internecine political quarrels and work for passage of moderate reforms to respond to the
"social problem."[141] Republican social policy at the turn of the century followed along the lines set out by Waldeck-Rousseau. Instead
of workers' cooperatives, it stressed the state's role in the institutionalization and formalization of workers' power to compensate for
the autonomy workers might lose through changes in the organi-

zation of work and the market. The republican alliance around Wal-deck-Rousseau and like-minded reformers provided the votes for passage of labor legislation that especially benefited miners in the 1890s.

Although the proposals of Socialists and republicans were important contributions to social thought, they played only an indirect role in resolving the strike. The deadlock ended only when the conflict turned from a local incident in an isolated part of France into an issue of concern to the national state. Spirited condemnations of the Société Nouvelle by deputies who had visited Decazeville created pressure on the state to intervene. In early June the Minister of Public Works, responding to the most recent round of criticism in the Chamber of company policy and government inaction, called in three leaders of the board of directors and asked them to make some concession, "no matter how small," to get the strikers to return to work.[142] These board members—who, some accounts say, threatened to resign if the board did not agree—persuaded the rest of the board to accept a settlement Petitjean had devised. The firm agreed to place timber closer to mining areas and to raise the rate per wagon of lump coal from 1.90 francs to 2 francs. Basly, "tired of this interminable strike," convinced the strikers to accept the settlement even though it did not guarantee that all workers would be rehired.[143] Petitjean greeted the end of the 108-day strike with relief; without the concession on rates, he wrote, the conflict would have turned into a "political strike" that could have "led to all sorts of theories troublesome to the concessionaires."[144]

The resolution of the strike came with the delineation of worker and company spheres of control in the administration of labor. While the Société Nouvelle retained the right to hire and fire all workers and managerial personnel, including Blazy, it was forced in return to recognize the right of the chief miner to select his helpers from among the company personnel and to pay them as he wished. Although the company cashier would disburse wages, the chief miner would be given a collective paysheet rather than individual ones for each member of his crew. Chief miners shared the fruits of victory by raising the daily pay of their helpers fifty centimes, an arrangement they had apparently made during the strike; many chief miners took on their helpers as hewers.[145]

The trial of the ten individuals charged with Watrin's murder, held shortly after the miners returned to work, provided a coda to the strike. The fact that several of the accused had been dependent on personal favors from Watrin for their jobs and sustenance testified to the company's violation of individuals' independence and self-respect in the community. Early on, the prosecution had to abandon its original plan of showing that the workers had plotted to kill their engineer and to turn instead to an examination of the workers' grievances. As a result, the Société Nouvelle was implicitly put on trial.[146] Even the public prosecutor, while making it clear that the trial concerned criminal rather than political issues, said that he believed labor did not get a large enough share of the profits from industry.[147] The defense put forward Watrin's personality, the operation of the company-controlled cooperative store, the financial situation of the Société Nouvelle, and the system of wage payment as the rationale for the brutal slaying. The court's verdict reflected the ambiguities of the case: six of the accused were acquitted and the other four received a total of twenty-six years in prison.

While the Decazeville strike played an important role in making the "social question" a subject of national debate, it proved to be a Pyrrhic victory for the town's workers. The Société Nouvelle soon reintroduced its previous policies, but now to a community weakened by the strike and lacking the leadership of some 120 union militants who were not rehired. The population of Decazeville fell by close to one-fifth between 1886 and 1891, and the miners' union—split for a year between moderates and a minority of radicals known as "Les Incorrigibles"—returned to its pre-strike size.[148] The final challenge to the managerial strategy pursued by the Société Nouvelle came not from striking workers and national Socialist militants, but from the moderate republican state and a dynamic capitalist competitor.

## The Demise of the Société Nouvelle

The board's conduct of the strike added to the already serious economic problems confronting the Société Nouvelle. The company estimated that it lost 590,524 francs in sales during the strike.[149] Despite a rise in coal production and serious neglect of mine maintenance during the firm's final years, losses on the forges ate up profits from coal sales.[150] Yet coal mining would have been untenable without the forges to use the low-grade coal. Petitjean fell victim to his intermediary position between the board and Decazeville, and resigned in 1887, a broken man frustrated because his advice to the board had been repeatedly ignored.[151] The board replaced him with its secretary Jules Gastambide, a man nicknamed *pisse-vinaigre* by the workers, and so obtuse to their ways that he told reporters after the *watrinade* that it had been the result of the miners' reading of *Germinal*.[152]

Gastambide responded to the continuing economic crisis with a political interpretation of the company town. The rationale of the company town had been to establish the conditions for regular and economical production. Gastambide reversed this logic and ran the mines and ironworks with the aim of increasing the company's political power within the town. In a perverse way, the company town reached its fulfillment under Gastambide, while industry suffered the consequences. The state chief mining engineer reported in 1889 that fires were so poorly controlled in the major underground mines of Bourran "that if the operator calculated the time the miners lose [as a result of intolerable temperatures and abysmal working conditions], it would come up with a very significant portion of the time its personnel spend at work."[153] Under Gastambide's direction, the company courted rural voters by switching some of its provisioning to more expensive nearby sources and hiring large numbers of unemployed local rural workers.[154] In 1892, shortly after the Société Anonyme de Commentry-Fourchambault purchased the Société Nouvelle, an engineer at the ironworks told the general director of the new firm that Gastambide had tried to bolster his electoral support by instructing engineers to increase production so as to employ as many workers as possible: "the municipal elections in 1888 and the legislative elections of 1889 took up all [Gastambide's] attention and influenced all measures taken [at the ironworks] during those eighteen months."[155]

Gastambide faced an obstacle largely absent from the company towns of his models, Cabrol and Deseilligny. His efforts to wrest control of Decazeville from moderate republicans and their allies in the miners' union were checked repeatedly by the state, which saw his activities as a threat to public order in Decazeville and as part of a larger nationwide challenge to republican authority. The prefect annulled Gastambide's victory over the republican ticket in the municipal elections of May 1888 in response to allegations that the company had used its supervisory personnel to intimidate workers at the polls. Gastambide's slate won again using the same strategy more tactfully in September 1888, and he ran for deputy against the Aubin republican Emile Maruéjouls the following year. Although Gastambide subsidized a *boulangiste* newspaper, *Le Pays noir*, he eschewed affiliation with the Boulangist national committee in his campaign. Nevertheless, the prefect considered him a Boulangist candidate and suspended him as mayor shortly before the election over a technicality. In his campaign, Gastambide appealed to the local chauvinism of the company town by pitting the workers of Decazeville against those of surrounding communities. Although he won Decazeville, he lost the election to his republican opponent.[156]

Gastambide's political exploits were the backbone of a comprehensive effort by the company to regain control of community life. Watrin had hoped to create a closed economic community that would eliminate small commerce in the interest of economic efficiency; his successor neglected this approach in favor of harassing local tradesmen and the cooperative in order to destroy opposition to his authoritarian politics. Within days after his defeat in the election of 1889, Gastambide took revenge on the town's shopkeepers. He instructed the master miners and foremen to inform workers that some twenty of the town's republican merchants, landlords, and barkeepers had been placed on a blacklist: workers who patronized them would be punished. Gastambide had *Le Pays noir* announce that the workers of Decazeville had decided on the boycott "spontaneously and unanimously." The local management even named a committee of four workers to visit the board of directors in Paris to corroborate this story. The boycott lasted over a month amidst protestations by Gastambide and the board that the company placed no restrictions on workers' patronage of business. The government was incredulous. Under instructions from Paris, the prefect used his power to suspend Gastambide as mayor once again in order to put an end to the boycott.[157] However, this did not stop Gastambide from devoting the company's resources to the destruction of the cooperative bakery started after the strike because it harbored active republicans on its staff.[158]

Gastambide's most insidious tactic was to try to build political support within the town by setting himself up as the sole defender of the ironworks. His backers claimed that after the strike of 1886, Gastambide "was the only member of the board of directors to plead the cause of the forges. It is only thanks to him that, despite the industrial crisis in France, the forges have regained the activity they had at the time of M. Deseilligny, with whom [Gastambide] worked as a partner."[159] In the summer of 1890, the board asked Gastambide and his immediate subordinate Jules Héliot if forgeworkers should be laid off and production decreased at the ironworks. Gastambide said no, but Héliot approved of the proposal. These discussions were leaked to the public, creating an uproar that ended only with Héliot's departure at the end of the summer. Gastambide was no stranger to the removal of his second-in-command and tried to turn it to political advantage. The director of Campagnac (Cransac) described the situation in scathing terms: "From what they say, Gastambide is in the process of spreading revolution among his own workers and is turning them against their own director, M. Héliot."[160]

Gastambide's political posturing could not hide the damage his policies were doing to Decazeville. "A profound anemia paralyzes every organ of every service," the general assembly of the Société Nouvelle was told in 1891, "and death will come of its own accord if we do not have recourse to energetic medication."[161] The conflicts that developed between the republican state and the Decazeville management, and between the needs of the company town and those of the workplace, divided the board of directors. Serious debates arose as to whether the company town could be reestablished in the political context of the Third Republic and whether it offered a solution to Decazeville's economic problems. Some of the board's charter members quit to protest Gastambide's political activities and managerial ineptitude. In explaining his decision to resign, Paul Schneider, a member of the board of the Société Nouvelle since its founding, argued that "it is always in the interest of a mining company, dependent on the Minister of Public Works, and therefore on the administration, to stay out of politics."[162] If company control of local politics had once limited government interference in relations between mining firms and their employees, it now encouraged such intervention.

The company town fell victim to the republican state, which took on many of the duties that firms in towns like Decazeville had previously handled. This happened first in economically weaker industrial centers and only later and less completely so in more prosperous communities like Montceau-les-Mines and Le Creusot. State aid gave lay schools a foothold in company towns; by the late eighties the state was taking steps to protect public education in Decazeville against company-backed parochial schools.[163] Bitter strikes in the town forced a transfer of police power from the company to the republican state. Until the Third Republic, company guards not only protected the company's property, but played a significant role in maintaining order in the community as well. In the early 1870s company guards were often former workers and the town's police commissioner was an employee of the company-controlled municipality. This changed in 1878, when the town government escaped from the company's political control. After the strike that year the board of directors decided that in the future company guards would be chosen from among former *gendarmes* from outside the area.[164] Following the strike of 1886, the Société Nouvelle persuaded the town to share in the expense of building a headquarters for a brigade of *gendarmerie* next to the company offices.[165] The process was completed in the late eighties, when a *commissaire spécial*, a national police official who reported on political affairs to the Minister of Interior, was assigned to Decazeville. *Commissaires spéciaux* were attached to railway lines and represented a new way in which the railroad integrated Decazeville into the national polity. As a representative of the state, the *commissaire spécial* at Decazeville criticized company efforts to subvert the republic, while devoting most of his time to the supervision of local unions and Socialist organizations.[166]

The republican state sought to appropriate some of the allegiance that the paternalist policies of Cabrol and Deseilligny had once elicited from workers. The government made immediate political capital of the pit gas explosion at Cransac on 3 November 1888, which took the lives of forty-nine miners.[167] The first state aid was distributed personally by the prefect, the department's sub-prefects and a Commandant Chaneau, sent by President Carnot himself to express his condolences. The prefect reported to the Minister of Interior:

> We went to each victim's family, covering the hamlets and villages of three communes. In all the Coal Basin this intervention of the Head of State . . . more than the money distributed, produced an impression, the memory of which will long remain alive . . . From a political point of view the effect produced is and will remain considerable. Our visit to each family was for those unfortunates a clear proof of the solicitude of the Head of State and of the government, the first represented by Commandant Chaneau and the second by the prefect accompanied by all the sub-prefects.[168]

Six years later the miners of Cransac contributed money to have a large wreath sent for the funeral of the assassinated Carnot, a wreath which was later placed on his crypt at the Panthéon.[169]

To counter the effects of the Long Depression, the Société Nouvelle launched an attack in the late 1870s on the institutional cornerstones of workers' life at the mines and forges, and in the town. In 1878 it took advantage of the direct control it achieved over work in the mines after eliminating the last contractors to effect an across-the-board reduction in wages. The firm's defeat of the miners' strike which ensued encouraged it to attempt to restructure the crew, the basis of the organization of work in the mines, a few years later. The Société Nouvelle's intervention in the labor process in the mines was intimately tied to its campaign to regulate the political and economic life of Decazeville. As workers lost their ties with rural life, they began to forsake the Church, which was perceived to be the company's ally, for the Republic. The election of a republican municipal government in 1878 was a victory for the workers and town residents who opposed the control exercised by the Church and the company in their community. The town's support of striking miners in 1878 seemed to sound the death knell for the company town, which, with brief interruptions, had provided the framework for industrial life since the founding of Decazeville. While the *ville-usine* had originally been created to provide services for workers attracted to the new industrial center, it soon became an essential component of managerial strategies to discipline the labor force. The Société Nouvelle felt that industry in a peripheral economic region like the Aubin Basin was especially dependent on the maintenance of company hegemony within the town. The firm vigorously combated efforts by Decazeville's middle class to expand its economic and political power by providing political guidance to the town's workers.

The struggle for control of Decazeville's political and economic institutions set the stage for the lengthy strike of 1886, which directed national attention to Decazeville's miners for the first time. The strike brought into clear focus the effect of Decazeville's declining position in French industry on managerial practice. It temporarily transformed the union from an association that used political and institutional channels to oppose company authority, into the leading force among miners. Widespread support for the strike developed the miners' national political identity. Intervention in the strike by left-wing deputies and Parisian journalists challenged the company's hold over Decazeville, but also threatened the town's republican alliance of workers and middle-class citizens. By making the strike a national affair, these politicians eventually brought the state to take action in a conflict which, because of its location in the isolated, economically depressed Aubin Basin, might otherwise have been left to run its course.

The strike at Decazeville was one of a number of long conflicts in coal-mining regions throughout France that reshaped the popular image of the working class.[170] Emile Zola's *Germinal* in 1885 and its real-life embodiment at Decazeville the following year highlighted new forms of labor conflict far from the old urban centers of Paris and Lyon.[171] Engels celebrated this development: in March 1886 he wrote to Laura Lafargue that it was "a very good thing" the Decazeville strike was taking place "not in Paris but in one of the darkest and most reactionary and clerical corners of the provinces."[172] Miners' strikes were the subject of intense debate in the Chamber of Deputies. The miner became, in Jacques Julliard's words, *"l'Ouvrier par excellence*, the symbol of the world of labor struggling for its emancipation."[173]

Strikes in Decazeville and elsewhere raised important political questions. Socialists saw these strikes as significant steps toward the creation of a national working-class movement. This spectre forced republicans to consider various solutions to conflicts in the mines. For Francis Laur, the answer was an adaptation of the co-operative movement which had been a pillar of Second Republic ideology. For others, the Third Republic would have to develop institutional means to allow miners a certain independence with respect to their employers.

Nowhere did this appear more true than at Decazeville, where the board's obstinate disregard for economic, political, and social constraints on its action during the strike of 1886 took the Société Nouvelle to the edge of bankruptcy. In the years after the strike the firm continued seeking to control the community, giving this goal priority over management of the mines and factories. It played on Decazeville's vulnerability by making the threat to close down the ironworks an element of day-to-day local politics for the first time. Only the republican state, fortified by its campaign against General Boulanger, could hold such practices in check. It began to intervene politically in peripheral economic areas like the Aubin Basin, where private economic power found few constraints on its efforts to intimidate communities that sought to exercise republican liberties.

For the miners of the Aubin Basin this conflict took place in a particularly unfavorable economic situation. In the 1880s not only did the iron industry atrophy, but also the Basin's share of national coal production dropped to 3 percent. The economic decline of the Société Nouvelle, the emergence of a strong national republican political structure, and the failure of efforts to fuse the company town and the workplace prepared the way for the transformation of Decazeville in the decades before the war.

# 6. The Second Industrial Revolution

The Long Depression ended in the mid-1890s. The Second Industrial Revolution of the succeeding decades consolidated the geographic and sectoral realignments made by French industry during the Depression. Northern and eastern France retained their dominant position in the economy; steel and chemicals grew more rapidly than the stalwarts of the First Industrial Revolution: textiles, iron, and coal. The Second Industrial Revolution also brought a certain decline of the family firm and the rationalization and bureaucratization of managerial structures at all levels, from the shop floor to the board room.[1]

The Long Depression had helped generate widespread popular support for General Boulanger's campaign against the parliamentary republic at the end of the 1880s. After disposing of Boulanger in 1889, the Third Republic buttressed its social support and ideological appeal. Its first step was passage in 1892 of the Méline Tariff, which guaranteed protection from foreign competition for important sectors of French business and agriculture, largely at the expense of workers, who ended up paying more for food as a result.[2] The governing coalition of Waldeck-Rousseau Moderates, Radicals, and Socialists which emerged from the Dreyfus Affair at the turn of the century added ideological coherence and—by the very fact of weathering the Affair—a new degree of political stability to the Republic. Although the decade before the war saw a movement toward conservatism and nationalism, culminating in government repression of labor movements in 1906–1910 and the successful campaign for three-year military service, the parliamentary republic remained largely unchallenged.

The two decades before the war were a crucial period for organized labor, in the face of renewed vitality of French business and the new-found stability of the Third Republic after the Dreyfus Affair. Although the Third Republic provided a bulwark against reactionary and clerical forces in French society, it lagged behind Great Britain and Germany in legislating social reform. The Confédération Générale du Travail (CGT), founded in 1895, drew its most ardent support from the small sector of craftsmen and skilled industrial workers; 90 percent of French workers were unorganized in the first decade of the twentieth century. While many workers voted for Radicals and Socialists, CGT spokesmen expressed mistrust and antipathy for politicians of all stripes. Their response to changes in the French economy was to look forward to a general strike which would lead to the destruction of capitalism and the state and to creation of a decentralized society based on workers' control of their workplace and community life. As has often been pointed out, such views were embraced by only a small minority of workers.[3] Because of the state's relationship to the mining industry, miners' unions generally pursued a different strategy, one based on trying to achieve collective bargaining and legislative reform. The miners, rather than the revolutionary syndicalists, provided a model closer to that which French labor would follow in the twentieth century.

## The New Owners

In 1892 the Société Anonyme de Commentry-Fourchambault purchased the ailing Société Nouvelle. Comambault was a large iron, steel, and coal conglomerate which prospered by making investments and divestments in its numerous holdings throughout the declining industrial areas of central and southwestern France. Whereas the previous firms at Decazeville had operated only in the Aubin Basin, Commentry-Fourchambault (et Decazeville after 1899) at one time owned mines or factories in Commentry, Fourchambault, Brassac, Imphy, Montvicq, Montluçon, Pamiers, Cransac, Decazeville, and before World War I, co-owned Batère, as well as Pont-à-Vendin and Joudreville in the Lorraine. Comambault deftly rearranged assets among its various holdings. Thus when the firm took over Decazeville it brought 250 workers and one million francs in machinery from Fourchambault to Decazeville.[4] It limited competition through negotiation of commercial agreements with other firms in the Aubin Basin.[5]

Over the course of the nineteenth century, industrial enterprises in peripheral economic areas came to rely on relations with larger corporate structures for capital and for implementation of contemporary managerial strategies. This was already apparent in the ties that several investors in the Société Nouvelle had with Le Creusot, and in Deseilligny's reorganization of management at Decazeville along the lines he had developed at Le Creusot. Yet as a lone industrial complex, Decazeville continued to find itself short of capital. Made flagship of the conglomerate Comambault, however, Decazeville blossomed in the industrial boom that followed the end of the Long Depression. Comambault expanded Decazeville's mining operations and rebuilt the metallurgical industry around the production of steel rather than iron. In the years before the war coal production surpassed 400,000 tons per year, peaking at 503,520 tons in 1913; steel manufacture reached a record high of 75,729 tons in 1911–12. The firm turned a profit of well over one million francs annually at Decazeville.[6] On the eve of the war the mines and factories in the Basin employed over 11,000 workers, almost twice as many as in the depressed period of the late 1880s.[7] Such prosperity, far from being uniform throughout the nation, helped complete the restructuring of the industrial economy of southern France which had begun in the Second Empire. While firms in the Tarn and the Aubin Basin prospered, and industry in the Loire diversified, the coal mines and metallurgical factories of the Gard and the Hérault declined in the decades before the war.[8]

Comambault invested in all areas of production at Decazeville. It checked the underground fires that had raged out of control during the last years of the Société Nouvelle's tenure: by 1896 the number of miners who had to work naked because of the heat had dropped from 30 to 7 percent.[9] The firm renovated the open-pit mines, where production rose from less than one-eighth of Decazeville's total in the early nineties to about one-fifth during the decade and a half before the war.[10] It kept "ahead" in the preparation of the open-pit mines so as to be able to push production when the price of coal rose. The open-pit mines gave Comambault an advantage over its competitors, whose underground mines required more scarce hewers or more work from their current labor force to boost production quickly.[11] The company experimented with the use of jackhammers powered by compressed air in the underground mines and steam shovels in the open-pit mines, although neither technique received widespread application until after World War I. It also redesigned the washing and sorting installations and changed remuneration of the largely female labor force in these jobs from a day-wage to a piece-rate. This allowed the firm to cut the costs of supervision and to reduce the number of workers.[12]

Comambault's most important investment, however, was in the metallurgical factory. After some hesitation, the firm decided to construct a large, modern facility to produce steel at Decazeville. The metallurgical crisis of the 1880s had decimated competitors in southwestern France. Comambault figured that the new plant would require relatively fewer skilled workers and more unskilled workers than the iron-producing forges it would replace. The less expensive labor of southwestern France would allow Decazeville to compete with metallurgical plants in the Lorraine. As in the past, the factory would provide a ready market for the town's coal. Savings on coke made from this coal would offset the advantages which plants in the Lorraine derived from cheaper iron ore.[13]

Comambault's strategy in both the mines and factories of Decazeville was to increase production to take advantage of the booming market in the decades after the Long Depression. Between 1894 and 1902, the company labor force rose from 3,600 to 4,700. This exhausted the local labor market, and in succeeding years stockholders were told repeatedly that an insufficient labor supply at Decazeville limited production.[14] Shortage of workers preoccupied management throughout the decade before World War I.

**Labor Recruitment**

In the second half of the nineteenth century towns in the Aubin Basin had supplied the majority of workers required by industry at Decazeville. The remainder of the labor force came from nearby agricultural communities. The Long Depression permanently disrupted this equilibrium. Since 1886 there has been a steady decline in the population of Aveyron to this day. Many younger sons left family farms for urban centers to the south or for Paris rather than go to the stagnant industrial towns of the Aubin Basin. After the 1886 strike a number of the Basin's unemployed miners and metalworkers crossed the Atlantic to settle in California and South America. (Old-timers in Decazeville still refer to one section of town as La Californie.) The population of Decazeville fell almost 20 percent between 1886 and 1891. There is evidence that economic crises in industrial towns of the Aubin Basin and elsewhere led miners and factory workers to limit the size of their families; this reduced the number of potential workers in the next generation.[15]

When prosperity returned to French industry at the turn of the century, the shortage of labor was more severe in the Aubin Basin than in most other industrial areas. Large mining firms in the Nord and the Pas-de-Calais had gone to great lengths in the second half of the nineteenth century to create a self-renewing labor force—*la race minière*—by providing housing and welfare services to encourage miners to have large families. The social infrastructure in the Aubin Basin was much more rudimentary. This was a historical legacy of the troubled economic record of firms in the Basin. There were no large housing developments like the *corons* of the northern mining towns, and Comambault had no intention of making the necessary long-term investment to construct them. Population growth far outstripped the construction of new housing in the years before the war; household size grew and the number of inhabitants per dwelling rose.[16]

In the past the primary problem for firms in the Basin had been recruitment of enough hewers, timbermen, and skilled metalworkers. As late as the mid-1890s, firms in the Aubin Basin complained that they had to keep hewers past the age when they would have been shifted to low-paying maintenance jobs in the Pas-de-Calais.[17] The first years of the new century marked a decisive turning point, however. With the development of the open-pit mines and the switch from iron to steel, Comambault's major effort went to assembling a large body of low-paid unskilled workers.

The wide range of skills required of a hewer or a timberman in the nineteenth century were acquired during the years he spent as an adolescent in the mines. It was difficult to impart these things to men who entered the mines as adults, and costly to lure trained miners from other firms. While Comambault had success in the 1890s recruiting labor for the underground mines from nearby rural areas with a tradition of sending workers to the Basin, by the turn of the century it had virtually exhausted this source. In early February 1900 the Decazeville management reported that to increase the labor force by 279 men it had been necessary to hire 1,267 individuals. The greatest turnover was in the underground mines: to raise this labor force by three, the mine had to hire 434 workers![18] And because Comambault was particularly keen on keeping wage rates down, it could not afford to hire away miners from neighboring firms. It even signed an accord with other companies in the Basin forbidding this practice.[19] Rather than recruit outsiders for the underground mines, Comambault kept production fairly constant and relied on the rootedness of the hewers and timbermen—when compared to other industrial workers at Decazeville—to maintain the skilled labor force it needed. The number of underground workers grew by fewer than 100 between 1901–02 and 1910–11; the number of hewers, timbermen, and their helpers rose by only 50 to a total of 1,204, compared to an increase of 150 in the decade before 1901–02.[20]

For the large numbers of unskilled workers it required, Comambault again turned first to the countryside. The Decazeville mine union leader Victor Mazars contended that it was in the nature of the mining industry to require constant infusions of rural labor: in mining communities "the lack of air, the poor food and the excesses of the cabaret weaken a whole generation and lead after two or three generations to the birth of just a group of *avortons*. The special mining population would soon disappear if it was not continually renewed, made younger and fortified by the arrival of robust peasants who weaken in their turn."[21] But rural labor proved more difficult to attract to Decazeville than in the past. The Méline Tariff reduced the flow of peasants from the land. In the years before World War I, company recruiters found that conditions for agricultural workers had improved greatly; it was harder to persuade them to give industry a try.[22] Most of those who did come to Decazeville were loath to stay because of the poor housing and low wages.[23] The dramatic rise in the price of consumer goods in the years before the war was particularly hard on new migrants working as unskilled workers in the factory and the open-pit mines.[24]

For a while Comambault resorted to the use of contractors who assembled "nomads" to work the open-pit mines, but this supply proved insufficient. In the years before the war the firm broke with past practice and began to recruit unskilled laborers from northern Spain. This labor market, long exploited by French grape growers, was a natural extension of the Basin's traditional source of rural labor; in fact, miners in the Basin were often able to converse with the new Spanish workers in their *patois* because it was similar to dialects spoken in northern Spain. The first large contingents of Spaniards arrived in 1909; by the end of April 1914, one in eight industrial workers in the Basin was foreign, with 6.8 percent and 21.6 percent respectively at the mines and factories of Comambault, and 18.9 percent at the mines of Aubin.[25] The population of Decazeville grew 60 percent between 1891 and 1911. In importing large numbers of immigrant workers, companies accepted a degree of labor turnover that would have been intolerable a generation earlier: in 1912 the management at Decazeville reported that only one of seven Spanish workers stayed a year.[26] On the other hand, the Spaniards made noticeably fewer demands on the town's limited infrastructure than French workers. They lived apart from the rest of the population in overcrowded, unfurnished rooms in the oldest and most dilapidated sections of Decazeville. To save money the Spaniards went without toiletries and linen, and ate cheaply on rice, vegetables, stockfish, and an occasional boiled rabbit.[27]

Threatened since the Second Empire by the internationalization of the market for coal and iron, industry in the Basin internationalized its labor market to take advantage of the prosperous economy of the early twentieth century. Comambault and other firms in the Aubin Basin used immigrant labor before many of their competitors; Carmaux, for instance, although closer to Spain, did not hire immigrant workers before the war.[28] One reason for Decazeville's precocious exploitation of this new labor market was the historical legacy of the Basin's uneven development and peripheral position in the national economy. Living conditions in the Basin were worse than in most other industrial centers, and it was difficult for firms there to attract French labor from other parts of the country. The second reason was Comambault's industrial strategy at Decazeville. The greatest expansion in the job market occurred not in skilled metallurgy or in the underground mines, but in the less skilled and less well-paid jobs in the factory and open-pit mines, for which it was increasingly difficult to find French labor.

The presence of immigrant workers, lacking political and full syndical rights and sometimes even the means to communicate with their French colleagues, challenged the community of workers that had developed in Decazeville at the end of the nineteenth century. French underground miners—who had traditionally been sent to the open-pit mines as a punishment—saw the expansion of these pits and the arrival of Spanish labor to work them as a proletarianization of their profession.[29] In 1914 the local Socialist newspaper *L'Eclaireur* described with a mixture of irony and bitterness the daily arrival of "veritable *smalahs*, entire caravans of Spaniards" in Decazeville: "This element will soon dominate. There is talk, it appears, of changing street names and bestowing on them Moorish names."[30]

The infusion of outside labor affected not only the nature of the work done in the mines and factories of Decazeville, but also bonds among workers and therefore indirectly the syndical and political life of the town. The new workers' jobs, origins, and mobility gave them fewer incentives than the preceding generation of unskilled workers to accept the leadership of skilled factory workers or hewers and timbermen. This lack of interest, added to the long-standing division in the town between labor in the factories and the mines, restricted the possibilities for organized labor to challenge the new owners.

## Managerial Reform

Changes in the corporate structure, economic base, and type of labor at Decazeville demanded a new approach to management. At the end of the Second Empire, Alfred Deseilligny had reformed the management of Decazeville along the lines of organization at Le Creusot, the leading industrial complex in France. When Comambault purchased the Société Nouvelle in 1892, Decazeville received another infusion of managerial expertise. The general director of Comambault, Henri Fayol, went on to become the most important theorist of industrial administration in twentieth-century France.[31] He often cited his work at Decazeville as the practical application of his system. Fayol changed management at Decazeville in two basic ways. First, Fayol saw that in a multi-plant firm, like Comambault, coordinated action was crucial. In order to facilitate this, he made sure that the central management in Paris was given full authority in company operations: the central office was made largely independent of the board of directors and put in clear control of the local management of individual enterprises. This ended the quarrels between the board and the local management that had plagued the Société Nouvelle, and marked the definitive transfer of decision-making from capital to management and from Decazeville to Paris. When the board of Comambault met at the beginning of the 1902 strike, it rejected the interventionist strategy pursued by its predecessors sixteen years earlier: "in these circumstances, it is of the greatest interest to make known without delay that the board is in strong agreement with the central management [in Paris] and the local management [in Decazeville] and that it encourages them in the efforts necessary to defend the company's interests."[32]

The second major change that Comambault effected under Fayol's leadership was to break fundamentally with previous systems of paternalism. In its first years at Decazeville the firm ended the kind of intense personal relationships between engineers and workers that had developed under the Société Nouvelle. It transferred or released the most hated engineers, including Blazy.[33] Unlike its predecessors, Comambault did not seek to turn the ties formed between supervisors and their subordinates into a form of political allegiance to the company as a whole, or try to exploit these ties in an effort to dissipate opposition to company policies. The new firm even abandoned the ostentatious celebration of workers' feastdays as a means of expressing symbolic hegemony over what was an increasingly heterogeneous population.[34]

Instead of fostering relationships between labor and management based on paternalism or politics, Fayol emphasized management's role as the administrator and coordinator of production at all levels of the enterprise. This brought to fruition two long-term developments in the organization of work in the underground mines at Decazeville: the stricter delineation of the responsibilities of supervisory personnel, motivated by developments within the firm and in state administration of the mines, and the individualization of production. The company hired a few additional supervisory personnel and placed greater emphasis on their training. While one supervisor for every 19.5 miners had sufficed in 1883, the proportion fluctuated from one per 15.3 in 1897 to one per 16.4 in 1913.[35] Although Comambault continued to recruit most of its underground supervisors from the pool of experienced miners, it increasingly looked to the town's schools, and especially the parochial schools, for other supervisors. Of the six new men hired in 1896–97, for instance, five were taken directly from the Ecole des Frères and only one from the mines.[36] Supervisors recruited from school were given supplemental technical instruction.[37] Thus, despite an increase in the number of supervisory personnel, Deseilligny's vision of social harmony based on advancement from the ranks was even less plausible under Comambault than it had been under the Société Nouvelle. Not surprisingly, it was now toward these lower supervisory ranks, rather than the engineers, that miners directed their antagonism. After 1886 striking miners at Decazeville never again asked for removal of an engineer. Comambault tried to limit the friction between lower supervisory personnel and workers by ensuring that the engineer monitored their relations. In 1893 the new management at Decazeville issued a note to this effect: "We reiterate that the *chefs de poste*, master miners, foremen and other managerial personnel in *direct* contact with the workers, can inflict no punishments without first referring to their superiors" (my emphasis).[38]

Comambault's reform of management at Decazeville was in keeping with initiatives taken by state engineers in the last decades of the nineteenth century. In its campaign to increase companies' concern for mine safety during the Second Empire, the state mine corps had initially attributed accidents that were the firm's fault to the firm's engineers; as master miners and *chefs de poste* replaced contractors, they too started to receive a share of the blame. State officials began to cite them for accidents that previously would have been called fortuitous or ascribed to the workers' negligence. The state more and more took the economics of coal mining into account by arguing that the degree of responsibility assigned to an individual in the event of an accident should be commensurate with his position, his wages, and whether he was paid by piece-rate.[39] This gave accident victims and their families somewhat greater opportunities to sue their employers for negligence, and spurred companies to ensure stricter discipline in the mines. Daily enforcement of rules and regulations supplemented and in part replaced the intermittent institution of severe measures during emergencies which had formerly characterized the companies' approach to safety. During the first decades of the Third Republic, the state, which had previously promoted efficiency in mining by demanding that coal beds be protected from fire, floods, and other mishaps, succeeded in directing companies' attention to the larger question of the administration of mine labor.

State intervention during the Second Empire and early Third Republic had focused on redefinition of the powers and authority of managerial personnel. In the final decades of the century the state's attention shifted to a bureaucratization of safety procedures and an attendant rationalization of the work organization in the mines which paralleled that proposed by Fayol. For instance, one source of fire in the mines had been the miner's habit of relighting his lamp underground instead of sending it to the surface to be relit. Prodded by state engineers, companies introduced a safety lamp that could not be opened by miners—the first piece of standard mining equipment in the Aubin Basin that was not owned and maintained by the miner. The safety lamp permitted a new form of company intervention in the way a miner did his work. A company employee issued the lamps at the beginning of the shift and collected them when miners left work, thus enabling the company to monitor the arrival and depar-

ture of workers, and to deny access to those whom it wished to keep
out of the mine.[40]

Company control of explosives followed a similar pattern. Miners
had originally bought powder from the company and stored it at
home. State engineers worried about the dangers involved in this
practice, while employers came to feel that miners did not produce
as much lump coal as they might because they used more dynamite
than necessary in their efforts to increase production. Both parties
were shocked by strikers' use of dynamite against the houses of
miners who returned to work during the strike of 1886.[41] In the late
1880s and early 1890s the state and the company cooperated in the
creation of *boute-feux*, specially trained personnel who supervised
the laying and detonating of explosives.[42] Widespread use of *boute-
feux* reduced the chief miner's autonomy and removed one of the
most craft-oriented aspects of mining from his control. Other aspects
of mine supervision were bureaucratized as well: companies established special registers to record observations concerning not only
lamps and powder, but pit gas, elevator cables, and interior transports
as well.[43] In keeping with this new emphasis on safety measures in
the decades before the war, the company meted out relatively more
punishments for the violation of impersonal safety regulations, and
fewer for conflicts with supervisors.[44] Comambault's willingness to
monitor working conditions won it the support of the state mine
corps. The firm reported in 1897–98 that relations with the state
engineers were good: "little by little we are escaping their tute-
lage."[45]

In reforming management of the underground mines, Comambault went beyond devoting more attention to supervisors and bu-
reaucratizing safety measures, to intervene in the organization of
work itself. Mine managers had long recognized the advantages of
cohesive, worker-organized crews. Fayol himself, when a mining
engineer at Commentry, had written that "the organization by crews
free to form themselves as they wish stimulates workers. There is
a continual process of elimination; the good or strong workers reject
the bad or the weak."[46] Consequently, "workers associated by choice
remain together a long time. They motivate each other and work
hard."[47] Only at the end of the century, as the supply of rural labor
dried up, did firms attempt to change the attributes of the crew.

In the 1880s the Société Nouvelle had tried to take away the power
of the chief miner to hire and pay his helpers, so that it could bring
in less expensive rural labor. The miners had opposed this measure

as a means to reduce production rates and, in a depressed market, as a threat to the employment of their sons. After the strike of 1886 the Société Nouvelle agreed to leave the designation of helpers and their wages to the chief miner. Other firms in the Aubin Basin, however, experienced numerous fights in the late 1880s and early 1890s between established helpers and recent immigrants who were willing to work for less.[48]

Under Comambault the crew remained the primary unit of production in the mines. Within the crew, however, the firm limited the hewer's role in the organization of work, while emphasizing his role as producer. The company's immediate aim—like that of the Société Nouvelle a decade earlier—was to introduce large numbers of rural recruits into the mines; its long-term goal was to change the organization and remuneration of mining. Comambault took advantage of a provision in the 1894 national miners' pension fund legislation, specifying the need for individual deductions, to replace the single paysheet per crew with individual paysheets.[49] It presented this new accounting procedure as its rationale for terminating the chief miner's right to choose his helpers and to set their pay. In the future, company supervisors promised only to take into account the chief miner's advice on the organization and remuneration of the crew. The chief miners complained that the new system contravened the settlement ending the strike of 1886 and undercut their authority: "they could [no longer] give orders" to their helpers.[50] The union reported: "The individual paysheet is the source of numerous complaints because the chief miner does not dare to order his helper, given that he doesn't set the daily pay. He cannot raise it or lower it; if they cannot work together because their personalities are not compatible, one of them has to file a grievance against the other."[51] Under the new system, in a six-month period beginning in September 1895 Comambault recruited enough rural workers to increase the underground labor force by 20 percent. These new recruits were paid 75 centimes less per day than internally recruited helpers.[52] But with the reduced flow of rural workers to the Basin after the turn of the century, this aspect of the change in the crew declined in relative importance; Comambault preferred to send its inexpensive rural labor to the open-pit mines and factories.

The second result of the reduction of the chief miner's authority within the crew was the opportunity the company gained to tie wages more closely to production. The mode of payment in use until the end of the nineteenth century involved an implicit recognition that each crew faced a specific situation in its individual work area and had to be remunerated accordingly. Comambault took a different approach. It eliminated payment per meter of advancement and for filling in old mine galleries and timbering, so that the hewer's wages would rest solely on the number of wagons of coal he extracted.[53] It was able to introduce this new uniformity in part because its investments in the underground mines, especially in the control of fires, had reduced the disparities in working environments for which miners had previously received compensation. The firm shifted the variable element in wage-setting from the conditions of production to production itself. It abandoned the uniform price per wagon for various grades of coal, and instead had supervisory personnel set rates in each individual work area.[54] This flexibility had the effect of introducing a *de facto* average daily wage for hewers.[55] The new mode of payment was especially adapted to areas where one hewer was assigned to work a large mine face with the aid of several helpers.[56] This reduced the cooperation that had previously characterized the crew. The hewer devoted himself more singlemindedly to extracting coal and less to directing helpers. The advantage of this system, as the state engineer pointed out, was that the productivity of the hewer, freed from some of his previous responsibility to organize production, could be expected to increase.[57]

As a result of these changes, management could differentiate for the first time between the wages paid the hewer and his helpers, instead of dealing with the crew as a unit. Unofficially (and later officially) it pegged the wages of helpers and timbermen to those of the hewers. Previously, the crew had organized production under the guidance of the chief miner, and workers in the crew had shared in a mutually agreed-upon fashion in the remuneration for production. In the new system, the chief miner lost some of the power and authority he had derived from his relationship with other workers in the crew. Management reallocated certain functions formerly exercised by the hewer, including the placement and detonation of explosives, and organized production so as to serve the hewer, by assigning to other workers jobs requiring more strength than skill, which he had previously helped to do.[58]

Specialization of the hewer's job affected the training of young miners. The state indirectly increased the time an adolescent spent as a helper. Compulsory military service interrupted the young miner's career. Furthermore, legislation passed in 1893 restricted the hours that a youth below age eighteen could work underground.[59] As young miners learned their trade by working alongside experienced miners, these restrictions threatened the existing means of apprenticeship within the mining community. In addition to these new legal impediments in the miner's career, the hewer's role as producer altered his relationship to his helpers and restricted the educational aspects of work in the crew. Comambault responded to these developments by monitoring advancement of young miners more closely. The company replaced the catch-all designation of *manoeuvres* for helpers with the categories *aide-picqueurs* and *aide-boiseurs*. These titles formalized an extended period of apprenticeship and increased the power which naming hewers and timbermen gave the company over young mineworkers. Whereas in the past an adolescent might expect to be named hewer by age twenty-one, after the turn of the century no one under eighteen could become an *aide* and no one under twenty-five could be named a hewer.[60]

Young miners grew frustrated at the length of time it took for them to advance from *aide* to hewer or timberman. With the size of the labor force in the underground mines relatively constant, opportunities for advancement decreased. From the company's perspective, the presence of a stable population of *aides* with years of experience in the mines permitted it to pay less for labor by men in their prime. In the long term, however, this blockage raised the average age of a native French underground miner at Decazeville by five years, to close to forty, between 1901 and 1913.[61] In an industry as dependent on the physical expenditure of energy as mining, this eventually reduced possibilities for raising productivity in the underground mines and further increased the importance of other elements of the industrial complex in Decazeville's economy.

In the short run, however, Comambault's effort to tailor wages to production paid off handsomely. During the firm's first six years at Decazeville the hewer's average production rose almost 25 percent with respect to wages. As the underground hewer became more strictly a producer and less an organizer of labor within the crew, however, his pay rose with respect to other mineworkers. In the mid-eighties timbermen had received slightly higher wages on the average than hewers; by the outbreak of the war hewers were 20 percent better paid.[62] Comambault also increased the differential between the wages of underground and open-pit hewers. Between 1884–85 and 1901–02, the average daily wage of the underground hewer rose 15.2 percent to 4.80 francs, while that of the hewer working aboveground fell 10.7 percent to 3.43 francs.[63] Efficient exploitation of the labor force was the key to success in marketing the inferior coal of the Aubin Basin: although the percentage of the sale price of the coal from Decazeville needed to cover labor costs was 10 percent more than at Carmaux in the early 1890s, the wages paid a hewer were 25 percent less.[64] By 1898–99 Comambault had reached a plateau in terms of the reduction of production costs through improvements in the mine installation and increased labor productivity: further gains in productivity would be eaten up by wage increases.[65] The firm was therefore in an excellent position to profit from the rise in coal prices at the turn of the century.

Comambault's investment policy made industry at Decazeville less subject to immediate fluctuations in the market and prepared it to compete in the improved coal and steel markets of the decade and a half before World War I. The firm, reacting in part to continued pressure from the state, reorganized management at all levels. The clear distinction between the representatives of capital on the board of directors and the central management reduced dissension within the company. The technology of the new steelworks introduced greater separation between skilled and unskilled workers than had existed in the ironworks.[66] The restructuring of the crew had a similar—though less dramatic—effect in the underground mines. It allowed a dilution of the locally recruited labor force of the 1890s; in the decade and a half before the war it loosened the bonds between hewers and helpers. Although miners remained the strongest occupational community in Decazeville, they lost some of their power within the economic and political life of the town after the turn of the century. The influx of workers from elsewhere, the decrease in the relative importance of the underground mines in Decazeville's economy, and new forms of work organization limited the ability of Decazeville's miners to challenge their employer and helped orient their union toward a national political strategy.

## The Union: Protecting the Miner

The union was the miners' prime means of responding to the changes introduced by Comambault. Through the union the hewers wielded a different form of power than they exercised as leaders of crews. Although the Decazeville union was neither large, nor wealthy, nor well represented in the open-pit mines, it succeeded in establishing itself as the most important spokesman for the Basin's miners. The union's strategy reflected its origin in the 1880s, when it was a means of winning republican support for the institutionalization of workers' power. While Comambault and other mining firms succeeded in reducing the autonomy of the crew, miners were able to obtain some indirect compensation in the form of state-authorized and worker-administered institutions to foster their safety and well-being. Because of the miners' aim of achieving special treatment from the state, miners' unions rarely endorsed anti-statist CGT doctrine. The Decazeville union was an exception. Unable to institute regular negotiations with management or to gain control of town hall, it briefly espoused a variant of revolutionary syndicalism. In the decade before the war, however, the Decazeville union became a firm partisan of national action by miners to elicit concessions from the owners and parliament.

Membership in the Decazeville miners' union fluctuated between 200 and 550 active members from the end of the strike of 1886 to the outbreak of World War I; it never exceeded one-sixth of the total labor force in the mines. The union at Aubin and Cransac, virtually inactive until the turn of the century, did enroll close to 100 percent of the miners employed by the Aciéries de France during a strike against the firm in 1913, but union leaders encouraged the bulk of the union membership to leave the area until the conflict ended and to let union militants run the strike.[67]

Unions in the Aubin Basin were not rich. The Decazeville union was unable to pay all, or sometimes even part, of the salary of its general secretary, Victor Mazars, who held the post from 1892 until after World War I. He was forced to hold a variety of jobs to make ends meet after being fired for unauthorized absences from the mines to campaign for the Socialist candidate in the legislative elections of 1893. In 1902 Mazars was a wine salesman, sold watches for a workers' cooperative in the Doubs, represented firms dealing in foodstuffs, oils, and soaps, sold insurance, served as local correspondent for the Bordeaux newspaper *La France*, and was mine-safety delegate for the district of Combes.[68]

The union held its greatest appeal to the relatively stable elite of the mining profession, the hewers and the timbermen. They dominated union ranks. Hewers and timbermen emphasized the prestige of their positions with respect to that of the *manoeuvre*. A candidate for mine-safety delegate in 1892 wrote in a broadside:

Name a competent delegate, that is to say someone who knows the work.
It is necessary to know its dangers. This is not true of a

*manoeuvre*, like one of my opponents about whom, I am told, they say in the mines that he would not be a *délégué mineur*, but a *délégué manoeuvre* if elected since he has only worked as *manoeuvre* and not even a long time at that.[69]

Protection of the interests of the hewers, timbermen, and their sons was one of the union's prime goals in the first decade Comambault was at Decazeville. These skilled workers viewed changes in the organization of work as threats to their power and to their sons' advancement. Through a union-sponsored committee they demanded in 1900 that the right to select helpers be returned to the chief miners; that the collective paysheet be restored; that miners' sons receive preference in hiring; and that *aides* be promoted by seniority. Two years later striking miners asked that *aides* be promoted within specified lengths of time. Although Comambault reiterated its general policy of hiring miners' sons, it refused to make any commitments about promotion.[70] The union reluctantly accepted company control over hiring and promotions, and did not raise the issue again.

Even when the union moved to issues of general concern to miners, it had difficulty winning the support of aboveground personnel. Few of the women in the sorting and washing installations, or the men in the open-pit mines, especially the foreigners, joined the union. Both groups viewed their positions as temporary and saw little reason to struggle for reforms such as higher pensions that benefited only lifetime miners. In any case, most of the legislation covered only underground miners. Although the Decazeville union fought to have open-pit miners included in special legislation like the eight-hour day, its lack of success reinforced the division between underground and open-pit miners.[71]

The Decazeville miners' union led a dual existence: it was an institution with a limited membership, but also the self-proclaimed representative of the miners as a whole. In 1895, which was a low point in terms of union membership, the prefect remarked that "The influence of the leadership of the [miners' union] is considerable and has an impact on those who do not belong to the union as well as on those who do."[72] Comambault itself recognized that the majority of the miners followed the union and that membership would have been significantly higher but for the monthly dues of two francs.[73] Union victories in elections for mine-safety delegates and for boards of directors of mutual aid and pension funds confirmed the unorganized workers' sympathy for the union and gave the union an institutional base of support.[74] Minority unionism found its justification in syndicalist principles. "It is true," Mazars explained in 1909, "that union members do not make up half of the labor force in our coal basin, but it should be recognized that activist and conscious minorities often lay down the law to majorities."[75] The same principle governed the internal life of the union: "Democracy . . . is the demonstration of unconscious majorities which, by the game of universal suffrage and by virtue of the dogma of popular sovereignty, form a bloc to stifle conscious minorities . . . The decisions of the [union's] general assembly are sovereign and valid no matter how many members are present."[76]

The union drew a firm line between members and other workers. The union's general assembly frequently denied admission to candidates and expelled refractory members. The union also tried to protect the status of their members in the labor force. In 1909 miners who were planning to leave the Basin to work on construction projects in Paris applied for membership in the Aubin union to obtain the union card they would need to be hired at their new jobs. The union called such a practice "of a nature to do great harm to unionized comrades" and agreed to allow it only by special vote of the general assembly.[77] The following year the governing council of the Aubin union reaffirmed its desire for a separate identity. The sick funds collected among union members should be reserved for union comrades, and "it should be so for all information held by the organization; it is absolutely necessary to know . . . to whom to speak confidentially so as not to be duped all of the time. This logical reflection was accepted unanimously and all the members present took an oath of honor not to depart from this rule."[78] The admonition not to speak of union matters to outsiders complemented rules of behavior governing relations among union members. Serious disagreements occasionally resulted from the choice of candidates for various offices. To end these crises the Decazeville miners' union resolved unanimously in 1910 that a union member who opposed a candidate chosen by the union for any office would be expelled from the union and not permitted to rejoin it for at least five years.[79] Public disclosure of discord within the union was promptly reprimanded. The opening page of one set of mine union statutes warned that "any member of the union found guilty of criticizing another member outside of the union [meeting] will be publicly censured the first time and expelled if he does so again."[80] The minutes of union meetings reveal that bad-mouthing union members and officials outside of union gatherings—particularly in bars—was severely punished.[81]

Mazars and the other leaders of the Decazeville miners' union thought that changes in capitalism and management required miners to go beyond organization or institutionalization of existing forms of solidarity. Several projects that had enjoyed great popularity among union members after the 1886 strike had to be reconsidered. In the early nineties the union repudiated the idea that it should act as a mutual aid fund and a funeral society: "the union has learned to purify itself of this stumbling block [mutualism] which it has recognized as dangerous to the forward progress of syndicalism whose mission is workers' emancipation."[82] It left the organization of relief funds to groups independent of the union, reserving the right to condemn those which "served the capitalists in the exploitation of all of humanity" by allowing nonunion workers to join.[83] The union also laid to rest the goal of the worker-owned and operated *mine aux mineurs* promoted during and after the strike of 1886 by deputy Laur. In the Loire, Napoléon III's breakup of the Compagnic dcs Mines de la Loire had left a number of small mining firms that collapsed during the crisis of the 1880s. There such ventures—including the one with which Laur was associated—enjoyed some success in stemming the decline of the Loire coalfield.[84] No such opportunities existed in the Aubin Basin. The poor quality of the concessions which the state offered miners doomed the *mine aux mineurs* attempted in the Aveyron, and reinforced the union's view that such self-help initiatives outside of the national capitalist economy were fruitless. Late in 1912 Mazars reflected on the past history of the Decazeville miners' union. Unions, he wrote, had once "cherished the dream of emancipating themselves through cooperation," but this had only resulted in an "adaptation of the union to the capitalist milieu"; "with the aid of experience, [unions] have now separated themselves [from cooperation] and it is resistance to capitalist exploitation that preoccupies them."[85]

The miners' union defined its role as neither the organizer of mutual aid nor the propagandist for producer-owned mines. Instead, the union sought to profit from the passage of republican legislation both to protect miners against the physical effects of exploitation in the mines and to develop new enclaves of miners' power at a time when the crew was under attack. The establishment in 1890 of mine-safety delegates, elected by the miners and paid by the company, the reform of miners' mutual aid and pension funds in 1894, and the approval of principles governing compensation for industrial accidents in 1898 helped the Decazeville miners' union to secure a position in the labor force far beyond its limited membership.

The idea of mine-safety delegates originated not only in republican legislators' desire for safer mines, but in their realization that mining companies were denying workers their rights as citizens. A Decazeville union leader pointed out that as long as the company director was mayor, he would only belatedly carry out his legal duty of informing the state mining corps of accidents. The state was hampered in carrying out full investigations of accidents, and therefore the possibility for the injured miner and his family to sue the company for negligence was limited.[86]

Miners usually voted for mine-safety delegates endorsed by the union. In return for union support delegates took on the role of the first full-time paid union officials. Although unions saw the delegates as a new source of authority in the mines and as a possible liaison with management, company supervisors viewed them askance: "Rather than seeing the mine-safety delegates as assistants, they look upon them as rivals," long-time delegate Mazars lamented.[87] Although the delegates were most competent to assess matters like insufficient timbering, they were reluctant to do so for fear of exposing individual miners to punishment.[88] Instead, they used their position to develop critiques of the company's handling of safety measures. This required a familiarity with labor and mining law. At the national congress of miners' unions in 1920 Mazars berated delegates for not knowing the law well enough and explained that this had been the key to his success as a delegate and union leader in a region with a relatively weak union movement.[89]

Miners and other industrial workers throughout France had contested company control of mutual aid and pension funds since the Second Empire. Administration of these funds offered mining firms several benefits. It allowed them to monitor the recovery of sick and injured miners and inhibited older miners, who hoped to receive a pension, from striking or leaving the firm's employ. Moreover, company management of these funds served the negative function of preventing the funds from becoming a workers' bastion. Finally, the operation of the funds was a means for the company to create a workers' elite and to establish special ties with it. That Comambault saw definite advantages in having control of the fund was clear from its refusal to change the rules governing the metalworkers' fund after legislation passed in 1894 took the miners' fund out of company control.[90]

The 1894 law gave elected miners' representatives the right to control the mutual aid funds and placed pensions under state jurisdiction. Conditions for the granting of pensions were made uniform, and the restrictions on a miner's mobility, which company funds had previously entailed, ended. The reorganization of the fund also gave workers a new defense against productivity demands in the mines. In the two decades before the war the percentage of workers receiving compensation for a minor injury in a year more than doubled to over one-third.[91] The explanation is not necessarily that more workers were illicitly taking off time from work; with miners in charge of the fund and with passage of the accident compensation law of 1898, the appraisal of what constituted an injury changed.

The union quickly took control of the new fund. It won landslide victories in elections to determine the structure of the fund at Decazeville and the composition of its governing board.[92] Mazars concluded that "these elections proved that despite the small number of union members, the comrades were on our side."[93] Under the new legislation the presidency and other positions on the board were no longer reserved for the owners: instead, the board elected officers from within its own ranks. The fund moved from a company building to the center of town. As Mazars liked to put it, the legislation put an end to the days when a "company jailer" ushered the worker or a member of his family into the fund offices. Rather than speaking to a pompous company supervisor, the worker could "talk with a comrade who served as accountant, who reserves the same greeting for the worker's overalls as for the engineer's jacket. This is a change which has not gone unnoticed in the miners' profession."[94]

During the early years of worker administration of the fund, board meetings occasionally produced conflicts between representatives of the miners and the outnumbered managerial personnel. At first the owners' representatives hesitated to cooperate with the miners on the board. They often abstained to express their disapproval of the workers' actions. At Aubin, managerial representatives walked out over ratification of the statutes. Two months later they returned to contest one article of these statutes. The workers pointed out that the state mining engineer Deverdière had approved it. The workers recorded the owners' response in the minutes: *"Ils ont répondu qu'est-ce que ça peut nous faire que Monsieur Deverdière l'ait voulu."* When the miners refused to strike this slighting reference to the state engineer from the minutes at the next meeting, the managerial representatives walked out again.[95] An incident like this one revealed the miners' determination not to hand over control of the funds to the companies, as the latter had expected. Instead, the workers' representatives turned the funds into strongholds of organized labor.

The fund also provided miners with an opportunity to challenge the position of middle-class professionals in the town. The miners' primary goal was to reform the medical services. Even the Decazeville *commissaire spécial* admitted that under the company-run mutual aid fund the doctors, who received a fixed sum for the services they performed for the fund, would see regular paying patients before workers, while the company pharmacy had supplied drugs of inferior quality.[96] The original statutes for the new fund presented by the workers of Aubin included rewards for doctors whose patients were treated best and punishments for doctors who abused the system of higher rates for night visits. This arrangement, the Aubin management remarked, "seemed contrary to the dignity" of the doctors who "are answerable only to their consciences."[97] The miners answered "that this is exactly as if you were to say that French workers will no longer accept work at a piece-rate . . . We think that here as elsewhere, it is permissible to reward commitment and knowledge simultaneously." In any case, the miners' representatives argued that the suggested provisions were "not of great severity, since the board will not have the right to fire [the doctors]. One should not find [the rules] surprising in today's society where not a single organization exists without discipline."[98] The Aubin miners sought to reduce the distance between themselves and professionals by applying to doctors the standards applied to themselves daily in the workplace. The doctors bitterly opposed such schemes, however,[99] as did the pharmacists when funds in the Basin sought to exercise control over the filling of prescriptions.[100]

The mutual aid fund handled only illness and minor injuries. By the end of the nineteenth century the issue of compensation for more serious accidents was becoming very complicated. As firms were expected to take on greater responsibility for what went on in the workplace, they were frequently assigned blame for accidents that would have been attributed to the worker in the past. By the mid-nineties, in some cases responsibility was even allocated proportionately to the company and to the victim. For instance, when Eugène Petit was injured in 1897 in an accident involving the wagons used to transport coal, the courts attributed three-quarters of the responsibility to Comambault and one-quarter to Petit.[101]

The industrial accidents law of 1898 limited such situations by introducing the concept of professional risk: the potential for accident inherent in a job independent of worker or employer responsibility. The legislation had certain advantages for both workers and employers. It assured the injured worker some form of accident compensation, while limiting the occasions in which an accident victim would take his employer to court.[102] The Decazeville union remained active in accident compensation cases, however, to prevent the defense of workers' rights from becoming solely a matter for lawyers. Even though the law ensured legal assistance to accident victims and to their families, the union continued to play an important intermediary position between the accident victim and the various professionals with whom he had to deal. At the turn of the century Mazars told a union meeting that the union's quarters "have resembled in some ways a legal office to which come accident victims, both union and non-union members. Information has been given to both, and thanks to this service, many accident victims have later joined the union."[103] In a report on an accident compensation case that was drawing to a successful close, he compared the roles of the union secretary and the lawyer in defending a worker's rights:

> The citizen Mazars seized this opportunity to show the assembly that all unionized miners had an interest in having for a secretary a comrade from the mines who was independent of the company, paid according to his work, his social situation and the status of the union treasury. For a lawyer coming down from the upper ranks of society who has never known the inside of a mine it is impossible to recognize any of the possible technical causes of an accident. Often if the worker-victim does not win his case, it is not the lawyer's fault but because . . . a knowledgeable person serving as an intermediary between the lawyer and his client is missing.[104]

At the union's general assembly in 1900 Mazars repeated his message that the stronger the union, the more successful the suits brought against the company would be, and even suggested that union leaders could take the place of lawyers:

> If the union was firmly constituted, its board would be a sort of Committee for the Defense of Accident Victims. It would

collect all the legal publications, jurisprudence and other compendiums relating to accident legislation. There one could find all the [necessary] information without resorting to legal experts.

Instead of a lawyer, to whom accident victims and their families turn most often, the secretary or another union representative would assist the injured worker or the widow of a dead worker in the investigation and in court.[105]

Many accident victims requested that the union secretary accompany them to court. In 1911 the Decazeville union decided that "when a union member is victim of an accident, the general secretary M. Mazars will serve as counsel throughout the proceedings provided by the law of 1898."[106] Having a comrade alongside who was articulate and comfortable dealing with the authorities was of great importance to many accident victims. On the board of the mutual aid fund and in accident litigation the union dealt in the workers' name with a variety of professionals: state and company engineers, lawyers, doctors, and pharmacists. In so doing the union established a degree of independent leadership for workers in turn-of-the-century Decazeville.

Sickness, accident, and injury were significant aspects of the miner's life. Miners had previously experienced them in the context of company-controlled social welfare institutions. The legislation of the 1890s gave a new meaning to these fundamental determinants of their lives. The union's work in the mutual aid fund and in defending accident victims and their families was an important force in the creation of institutional solidarity among miners. Accidents that claimed many victims had always created a united front among miners. But the frequent smaller accidents that sooner or later befell many miners could not have had the same effect on a labor force divided up among hundreds of crews. Institution of the mine-safety delegate, which soon became a union fiefdom, and the publicizing of company negligence in accident cases, reinforced for miners a conflict-based interpretation of their working conditions.[107]

In the crew the hewer was responsible for organizing all aspects of work, including safety conditions. By the nature of his job, the timberman was even more concerned with safety. The union developed out of the organization of work by crews. The natural leaders in this system, the hewers and timbermen, provided the leadership of the union. Through the union hewers and timbermen countered their loss of authority in the work place. After a brief flirtation with various forms of mutualism, the union established its position within the mining population by controlling the institutions set up for miners by the republican state in the 1890s.

## May Day

The greatest contemporary effort by workers to improve working conditions was the movement for the eight-hour day with no reduction in pay. Beginning in 1890 workers around the world participated in May day demonstrations in support of the eight-hour day. This demand reflected a fundamental change taking place in the mines of the Aubin Basin. In the late nineteenth century miners at Decazeville generally worked a nine and one-half or ten hour day; approximately eight and one-half hours were spent at the coal face.[108] The length of the working day varied among pits, however, and when a firm reduced rates, it might suggest that miners could make up the difference by working extra hours.[109] But at the end of the century miners began to enforce a uniform working day to discourage changes in production rates. Firms lamented that miners were no longer willing to work more than the minimum required.[110] Having lost control over important aspects of the organization of work, miners turned away from production rates as their primary concern and toward a reduction in hours and eventually to minimum wages by category of worker.

Participation in May day activities was one expression of this movement. Because of opposition by Comambault, however, early May day events were poorly attended. Hence, during the 1890s, the national significance of May day demonstrations in the Basin was secondary to their role of separating the miners' union from the rest of the labor force. (The metalworkers' union refused to participate at all.)[111] In 1891 union members in Combes, between Aubin and Decazeville, established a May day itinerary for themselves: they met at one bar at 9 A.M., had vermouth at another at 2 P.M., and a drink at a third bar at 5 P.M.[112] In so doing, they were not merely celebrating: they were organizing an eight-hour demonstration of *camaraderie* for their peers. Later, at Decazeville, striking miners from the daytime shift established the tradition of meeting in their work clothes to have breakfast at 5 A.M. at the Place Decazes as they would on a normal work day: "Here is a valuable means of propaganda because those who are refractory to May day can join this national demonstration, either from *a feeling of fear* [of their comrades] or through a sense of duty."[113]

May day lost much of its immediate significance for miners after parliament voted the eight-hour day for underground miners in 1905.[114] Beginning in 1906, the year that the May day demonstration reached its peak in France, Comambault and other firms in the Basin decided that a one-day protest aimed at the nation's legislative bodies rather than at individual firms presented little danger. They adopted a policy of neither forbidding nor authorizing miners to strike on May day.[115] Miners in the Basin had some difficulty accepting that once the May day strike was no longer primarily directed at forcing the majority of recalcitrant miners to join, it should not be used to win concessions from the company. Early in 1907 Mazars reviewed the previous May day in the Basin: "The union campaign in favor of the eight-hour day and the May day demonstration was not completely understood by the miners, even those within the union, for the principal demand, a reduction in the hours of work, was overshadowed by the demand for a wage increase."[116] The union leadership was forced to educate the miners of Decazeville on the benefits of national labor solidarity and the need to subordinate immediate local demands to long-term national goals.

After 1906 the May day strike became an opportunity for miners to express their solidarity in a relatively passive fashion, in contrast to the activism of the small corps of May day strikers in the nineties. As the May day strike began to assume a universal character in the mines, attracting over four-fifths of all miners, participation in union demonstrations fell: the number of participants in the processions at Decazeville dropped from 300 to 350 to between 50 and 90 in the final years before the war.[117] The special police commissioner at Decazeville remarked that "the worker is increasingly losing interest in outside demonstrations." Two weeks before May day of 1913 the sub-prefect suggested that fishing be tolerated out of season for one day because many strikers would do this rather than attend union meetings.[118]

The history of May day demonstrations encapsulates developments in the labor movement at Decazeville before 1914. In the decade and a half before 1906, May day was primarily the affair of a core of union militants; the majority of miners did not participate. In the years before World War I, however, the majority of miners took advantage of company toleration to strike, although relatively few demonstrated publicly. During the earlier period, the active union minority asserted its position in the new miners' institutions and, as we shall see, in local politics. In the decade before the war the union retained its minority, vanguard position, but abandoned efforts to control local political life or to lead the miners in radical action. It sought instead to mobilize miners to participate in brief strikes—for which May day was the prototype—to put pressure on the legislature.

## The Union: Developing a National Strategy

The union could defend the miner in the mutual aid fund and in court; however, it could not force Comambault to the bargaining table. In the decade and a half before the war the firm allocated a number of cost-of-living increases for all workers, but it never negotiated these directly with the union. Instead, the company patterned these wage hikes on those offered in other basins in order to maintain its competitive edge in labor costs. The union, frustrated by its inability to establish direct relations with management at Decazeville, became a strong partisan of action by the national miners' federation.

The Decazeville miners' union attempted repeatedly to establish regular negotiations with the owners. As a prerequisite it asserted *de facto* control over the mine labor force: the 1886 strike was the last in the Basin not called by the union. The union sought to use this position to establish an alternative to the strike. In June 1890 the leader of the Decazeville miners' union declared that he "had always fought the strike as being a bad means of achieving anything because it is always harmful to both workers and owners."[119] As long as the crew acted as a unit relatively independent of the company, the union generally restricted itself to supporting the strikers' demands for higher production rates. When pay shifted from the crew to individual workers, however, the union saw an opportunity to negotiate minimum and/or average wages by category of mineworker. But unions in the Aubin Basin were thwarted in this goal. They never succeeded in establishing an equivalent to the *conventions*, pioneering collective bargaining agreements, signed periodically by owners and union representatives in the Nord/Pas-de-Calais beginning in 1891, and later in the Loire.[120] Government intervention in turn-of-the-century labor conflicts at Le Creusot and Montceau-les-Mines, which resulted in formal consultations between representatives of workers and management, raised the hopes of the

Decazeville unions that Comambault would establish a similar system.[121] Both the miners' and metalworkers' unions at Decazeville agreed in 1902: "This, in our opinion, is the best means to ward off conflicts, regrettable on all counts, conflicts whose origin usually goes back to a misunderstanding that it would have been easy to smooth over if, before letting it fester, the two sides had frankly presented their positions."[122] But even the state engineer's suggestion that worker-management councils would give Comambault an opportunity to explain the difficult conditions under which industry operated in the Aubin Basin fell on deaf ears.[123] Operators in the Basin, who depended on maintaining low labor costs with respect to other basins, refused to go beyond unofficial contacts. In this situation one of the appeals of the reformed mutual aid fund for the union was the opportunity it gave union leaders to deal with management in a situation in which they could not be ignored. Yet Comambault was always careful to differentiate between miners as fund administrators, and as union delegates. In 1900 for instance, the Decazeville director took aside Philippe Bos, a union leader and fund president, and presented the company's stand on the union's most recent demands, addressing Bos explicitly in his second capacity as the fund's president.[124]

The key to Comambault's avoidance of direct negotiations with the union was cultivating good relations with the state. In 1900 the miners' union tried to take advantage of the apparent willingness of the Waldeck-Rousseau government to intervene in labor disputes. Comambault responded by granting a twenty-centime raise: this would, it correctly surmised, "put the companies in the [Aubin Basin] in a excellent position *vis à vis* the government." Not only did the government not intervene; it dismissed the union's claim to represent the whole work force.[125]

The raise, approximately 4 percent of a hewer's average pay in 1900, was the first of a series of cost-of-living and family supplements given by companies in the Basin during the years before the war. If Comambault originally referred to the raise in terms of profit-sharing,[126] it soon switched to the much safer explanation that the raises were intended to counter increases in the cost of living. While the nation as a whole experienced a sharp rise in the price of certain consumer goods before the war, the situation was particularly severe in the rapidly expanding towns of the Aubin Basin. In Decazeville, the payment of cost-of-living increases was therefore in part a way for Comambault to compensate for its decision not to make major investments in the town's infrastructure despite the rise in population.

Companies in the Aubin Basin did not negotiate these raises directly with the miners' union. On the contrary, during the first decade of the twentieth century Comambault took to publishing statistics to show that it increased wages "without waiting for the workers' demands."[127] Firms in the Aubin Basin pegged these raises to similar wage adjustments made in other mining centers in such a way as to institutionalize the secondary position of their miners in the national wage market. A further effect of these periodic increases was to shift the debate over wages to issues of consumption. Yet, unlike the former company-controlled cooperatives, cost-of-living increases were not perceived as intrusive by workers. Wage hikes presented in terms of the cost-of-living had the effect of turning the unions from the assertion that workers deserved a greater share of the profits of production to an assessment of the minimum compensation a worker required to continue producing. When the Aubin union requested a cost-of-living increase in 1910, it argued that because of the high price of food miners were malnourished, and it was hard for them to do a full day's work. "Be assured, Monsieur le Directeur," wrote the union, "that your sacrifice will be accorded the unanimous and unfailing recognition of all recipients."[128] The Socialist town council of Aubin pursued the same train of thought: "if the worker does not have the money to feed himself decently, it is absolutely impossible for him to do enough work. From this it appears that a wage increase is necessary, in the companies' interest as well."[129] The company granted the request in the terms in which it had been asked: it specified that any worker who missed more than five days of work per month without a valid excuse would not receive the allocation.[130]

The overall effect of changes in the organization of work, the recruitment of labor, and the mode of remuneration was to shift the locus of conflict between miners and management from the local to the national scene. The union at Decazeville sought to compensate for its weak position with respect to the company and for Decazeville's secondary position within the national coal market by promoting action by the national miners' federation. Decazeville's position as only one of a number of industrial complexes operated by Comambault reinforced the local union's view that permanent improvements in the miners' situation required a national effort. In 1911 Mazars, following the example of CGT leader Alphonse Merrheim's pathbreaking investigation of the finances of the French steel industry, made a study of the financial structure of Comambault. He showed how its recent agreement with the Société des Mines de Lens in the Pas-de-Calais to develop an industrial center at Pont-à-Vendin (Pas-de-Calais) could harm the long-term interests of Decazeville's workers.[131] Furthermore, the union recognized that a strike in an individual industrial complex would be less effective against a conglomerate like Comambault than it had been against previous employers at Decazeville. The potential effects of a miners' strike at Decazeville were further reduced in 1907, when Comambault took out strike insurance with the national coal mine owners' association, the Comité Central des Houillères Françaises (CCHF) for 7,000 francs per year.[132]

This combination of factors inclined the Decazeville miners' union toward national action and made it critical of unions in the prosperous basins for ignoring the interests of the miners' corporation as a whole. The coal industry was particularly prone to such regional divisions because labor costs were high and the location and quality of deposits were determining factors in production costs. By the turn of the century Basly, deputy from the Pas-de-Calais coalfield, had developed a tacit strategy of cooperation in his area between the mining industry and organized labor.[133] Periodic renewal of the *conventions* between the majority union and the *patronat* in the Nord/Pas-de-Calais limited the options of miners in poorer areas like the Aubin Basin, and made efforts to pressure parliament the only form of national action which could possibly unite miners.[134] Right up through the war the Decazeville miners' union opposed labor-management conciliation committees favored by unions elsewhere because it saw them as weakening its position; if in other basins such committees could settle differences arising from the interpretation of contracts arranged between unions and management, in Decazeville they could potentially displace the union altogether.[135]

In Georges Stell's *Cahiers de doléances,* which the Loire miners' union had made its own in the early 1880s, one reason given for the formation of unions had been to win for all miners the benefits companies in the Nord and the Pas-de-Calais accorded their miners. In order to prevent unions in these favored basins from ignoring the concerns of unions in southern and central France, the latter needed to be able to wield the authority of the national federation. At the 1894 congress, the southern and central unions assured themselves control by means of a rule that gave delegates from the Nord and

the Pas-de-Calais only one-half of the votes to which they would
have been entitled with strict proportional representation. The Aubin
Basin received the third largest number of mandates (15.2 percent),
trailing only the Pas-de-Calais and the Loire![136]

Unions in the large northern coalfields refused to tolerate such a
system. Conflicts within the federation came to a head after the
turn of the century. In 1901 miners voted in favor of a general strike
in three national referendums, but the unions in the Nord/Pas-de-
Calais wavered. The Decazeville and Montceau-les-Mines unions
seceded in frustration at the March 1902 meeting. The head of the
Decazeville union, Victor Mazars, blamed the split on those who
favored the "defense of the republic" while forgetting the *belle max-
ime,* borrowed from the *allemaniste* socialists, that "the workers'
emancipation can only be the work of the workers themselves."[137]
When the national general strike was finally called in October 1902
to demand from parliament a pension of two francs per day after
twenty-five years of work, an eight-hour day, and a minimum wage
set by region, it failed because unions in the Nord and Pas-de-Calais
withdrew to negotiate a separate agreement. After the strike—which
led to 140 firings at Decazeville[138]—the Decazeville union joined in
1903 with that of Montceau-les-Mines and the radical minority *jeune
syndicat* of the Pas-de-Calais to form the new Union Fédérale, affiliated to the CGT. These dissident miners' unions thus registered
their disagreement with the general approach of the miners' federation, which had not joined the CGT at its formation in 1895, and
which repudiated the CGT's revolutionary rhetoric and antiparlia-
mentarianism.[139]

If the ideological rigor of the Decazeville union's stance was com-
mendable, the practical effects were nil. The local union could ac-
complish little for its membership outside of the national federation.
The Union Fédérale reunited with the federation in 1906; two years
later the federation joined the CGT.[140] Like the CGT as a whole,
the Decazeville miners' union underwent a *rectification du tir,* a
movement toward a more reform-minded position, in the years before the war. Miners' unions returned to the efforts begun at the
turn of the century to force parliament to raise pensions. This issue
was especially important to career miners in the Aubin Basin because, as a result of special arrangements offered by companies in
the more prosperous basins, regional disparities in pensions were
greater than in wages. In 1911 a miner in the Pas-de-Calais who
retired after thirty years received an annual pension 36 percent higher

than that of a miner in the Aubin Basin, which had the lowest pensions in the nation.[141]

The national general strike of 1902, and even more so the strikes of 1912 and 1914, differed significantly from earlier walkouts in the Basin. The Decazeville union found itself explaining issues to miners—a thing it never had to do when demands concerned an unpopular engineer or wages. Mazars noted before the 1911 national miners' federation congress: "The numerous meetings which will be held [in the Basin] from now until the congress will have the sole aim of instructing the miners about their duties if they want to profit from . . . the national movement."[142] Local issues were shunted aside in favor of national demands. In 1911 the Decazeville union rejected a local grievance on the advice of the national mine union leader, "Comrade Bartuel, who says that it would be stupid to let the prey go for the shadow by making such a demand."[143] A few days later Mazars wrote that "a wage demand concerning the workers of one company should never be made without consultation with the federation or its national council, which is in charge of seeing that the decisions of the national congress are carried out."[144]

The prewar national general strikes were characterized by a passivity that was antithetical to the spirit of the earlier local strikes. The Decazeville *commissaire spécial* commented that the twenty-four hour strike of 11 March 1912 was "nothing more than an active referendum by which the miners mean to show their rulers that they are ready to act together if their demands are not satisfied."[145] For the leader of the Aubin miners' union, the strike was a time for others to act: he "recommend[ed] that all comrades remain calm on that day, that they imitate the English who all go to the countryside and breathe a little fresh air while the owners and rulers debate in the corridors."[146]

Success in mobilizing the mass of non-unionized miners for these national strikes seemed to the Decazeville union to vindicate its claim to speak for the collectivity of miners. Assessing the strike of 23 February 1914–2 March 1914, Mazars wrote: "we have often said quality is worth more than quantity; our method of action is not always inspired by the vulgar idea of democracy, for never has the Decazeville miners' union encompassed the whole work force."[147] He pointed with pride to the arrangement the union had made to supervise the mines during the strike: "This proves that the strike is made solely against the government."[148] Mazars ignored Comambault's careful avoidance of direct dealings with the union over

this matter.[149] Instead, he interpreted it as a new step in labor relations: "Was such an agreement forcing the company to deal with
the union to save the mine ever seen in 1868 [*sic*], in 1878, in 1886
or in 1902? Of this the miners can be proud."[150]

Elsewhere Mazars sought to explain how strikes had changed between 1886 and the prewar years. The development of unions allowed for a strategy based on the attainment of limited reforms to
supersede the apocalyptic visions of earlier strikes:

> In a strike of unorganized workers, revolutionary method and
> consciousness play a greater role, and the economic import of
> the conflict is not limited to just the issues in contention; the
> strike also appears as an episode in the social war. *Decazeville
> in 1886.*
>
> It is necessary to see that the workers' view of the value of
> the strike, as a means of achieving revolution, has changed
> considerably under the influence of syndicalism. The strike is
> no longer regarded as a fatal and inevitable *evil*, an abscess
> which in bursting would brutally display the antagonism be-
> tween capital and labor, but without possible immediate profit
> for the latter. [The strike] has undergone a modification parallel
> to that which the idea of revolution has undergone.[151]

The Decazeville miners' union carved out an institutional presence for itself in the 1890s, but the local situation limited miners'
hopes for establishing direct dealings with management. This weakness was at the heart of the Decazeville union's efforts to profit from
participation in the national labor movement. Yet Mazars realized
that there were dangers in a strategy too dependent on winning
reforms from the state. He commented in 1913:

> [T]he miners believe too much in the *Providence-Etat.*
>
> We know quite well that we are heading more steadily toward
> nationalization of the mines; but nothing tells us that the na-
> tionalization that is dreamed of will not be a lure.
>
> Who says that the state-boss will not be as bad [*aussi mufle*]
> and more detestable than the stockholders? We could just as
> well ask those who are looking forward to this nationalization
> if they do not fear, with the state as boss, being ordered about
> one day at the bottom of the pits by retired army officers, old
> warrant officers, colonial soldiers, by the cast-offs of state bu-

reaucracy, who would not be worth much more than [the Decazeville mine director] *Miquel and the others?*

Mazars was far more certain that miners would benefit from an
agreement between the national miners' federation and the CCHF
that would do away with payment by production—the real basis of
exploitation—and set hourly wages for various categories of workers.[152] It was the ability to exercise power through the state, not the
centralization of authority in the state, that offered the most to
miners in an area like the Aubin Basin.

Mazars' reflection on the potential hazards of nationalization of
the mines for the workers brought together the two forces that had
shaped the miners' union since its origin: changes in the organization of work and developments in state policy toward labor. As
management reduced the autonomy of the crew, hewers and timbermen turned more and more to the union as their means of organization and defense. The union took advantage of the opportunities
offered by the labor legislation of the 1890s to establish an institutional presence in the mining population and a certain autonomy
with respect to both management and town professionals. However,
this *ouvrieriste* self-affirmation had its limitations. The union was
stymied in its aim to take over from the crew as the miners' bargaining agent. Company refusal to negotiate directly encouraged the
union to look to national syndical action to win concessions for
miners. The Decazeville union initially embraced a radical stance
in the national federation, but moderated its position in the decade
before the war as it came to place its hope in legislative reform and
national collective bargaining. On the local level, the unions were
uncontested after the turn of the century in their control of the
institutions established to protect the miners' well-being, and therefore found it less necessary to make militant statements of their
class independence.

Political life in Decazeville was influenced by these reorientations
of union activity in the early nineties and again a decade later. The
union had supported moderate republicans in the 1880s: in 1888,
for instance, the union president ran on the republican slate for the
municipal council against Gastambide; a year later the union proclaimed, "The workers owe to the Republic the right to band together, to unionize and to federate; in a word, the right to demand
their rights; this cannot be contested by anyone, no more than can
the unions' republicanism."[153] In the 1890s, however, the miners'

union broke with their local middle-class republican allies, espoused an *ouvrieriste* socialism, and sought to institute syndical control over local politics. A few years into the new century, the miners' union changed course. Mine union leaders found that they could not attract the votes of the waves of new immigrants who were arriving in the town to work in the factories and open-pit mines. After 1906 the union lost leadership of the Socialist party in the Basin to left-leaning professionals. In keeping with the strategy of putting pressure on parliament through corporate strikes, the union supported the election of middle-class Socialist deputies who would promote the miners' interests in Paris.

## Politics

Comambault complemented changes in the administration of the workplace and the composition of the labor force with a new approach to municipal life. When the company came to Decazeville in 1892, it had resolved to play a much smaller role in the political and commercial life of the town than had its predecessors, which had considered control of town institutions a vital element in the management of labor. But Comambault believed that struggles with local residents and the republican state for control of the town had negative effects that outweighed any benefits. While many major industrial firms in company towns sought to control labor unrest at the end of the nineteenth century by promoting an active, quasi-independent, politically neutral associational life, Comambault eschewed even such ostensibly nonrepressive forms of company paternalism.[154] Comambault's abstention from municipal matters revealed a reluctance to become deeply embroiled in the affairs of any one of its enterprises, and a desire to avoid enmeshing itself in the management of local affairs in what was, in the long run, a declining region.

The new firm's lack of involvement contributed to the dissolution of the republican alliance between Decazeville's middle class and workers, which had developed in opposition to the policies of the Société Nouvelle. Unlike its predecessor, Comambault viewed intervention in local commerce as antithetical to its goal of creating "an economical and provident" labor force. During its first years at Decazeville, the firm phased out seizures on the pay of indebted workers, long a form of security for shopkeepers in the Basin, and refused to make any advances on wages, even the traditional loan to enable a miner to buy a pig in January.[155] Full responsibility for the allocation of credit shifted from the company to the local merchant. This exacerbated the effects of a change in the status of local tradesmen. In the mid-eighties many *commerçants* had been former workers and had sent their sons to work in the mines and factories. By the early twentieth century, however, one can identify a growing number of tradesmen who were significantly better off than the workers who were their clients. A clearly middle-class section of town took shape, sheltered from the smoke and grime of the factories.[156]

In 1878 shopkeepers had strongly supported the miners' strike; in 1886 they petitioned the government to intervene to end the strike against the company's wishes. In the strike of 1902, however, businesses refused to extend credit to strikers and a committee of leading merchants came out in favor of ending the walkout on the company's terms.[157] Angry workers responded by organizing a consumer cooperative, this time not in opposition to the company's role in the economy of the community, but against the town's merchants. Although this particular cooperative failed, others were founded at the end of the first decade of the century by various groups, including both the miners' and the metalworkers' unions, and became quite successful. By 1913 there were sixteen consumer cooperatives in the Basin: 4,089 members did well over one million francs in business at them. Socialist support of the cooperatives as a means of controlling the spiraling cost of consumer goods in the years before the war exacerbated differences between workers and businessmen in Decazeville.[158]

In the realm of politics, Comambault discreetly supported republicans such as the deputy Maruéjouls, with whom it enjoyed a good working relationship. It could accept Maruéjouls' support of moderate social reforms, including his active role in the passage of the industrial accidents law of 1898, as a way of reducing conflict with labor. The company particularly appreciated both his efforts on behalf of the mining industry in the Mines Commission and as Minister of Public Works (1902–1905), and his solicitude for the economy of the region. In 1893 the general management of Comambault privately informed the local director at Decazeville that "it keenly desired the victory of M. Maruéjouls, who had never hesitated to help out every time the occasion presented itself."[159] The next year the firm gave Maruéjouls 20,000 francs to start a paper that would defend the economic interests of southwestern France.[160]

Comambault took a relatively liberal view of workers' political activities, perhaps because of its experience at Commentry, which had elected France's first Socialist municipality in 1881. Despite the firm's republican sympathies, it remained publicly neutral during elections, and forbade the director and the two chief engineers to seek office. Comambault abandoned this stance only in order to defeat Gastambide in the municipal elections of 1892. Even after the stockholders of the Société Nouvelle had approved the sale of their firm, Gastambide decided to head a slate of candidates for the town council. He made the firm's demise the central issue of the campaign. Under Comambault, Gastambide claimed, the ironworks would close and Decazeville would lose the autonomy and personal attention it had received from previous owners. Gastambide's self-image as the local manager (of a defunct firm) standing up to distant insensitive owners completed his disassociation of industrial paternalism and the interests of capital.

Gastambide's crusade for an independent Decazeville rang false to the town's republicans. They viewed the sale of the Société Nouvelle as a means of destroying Gastambide's power within the community, and sought to form an electoral coalition with Comambault to ensure the defeat of the previous *patron*. Like their counterparts in the national government, Decazeville's moderate republicans had nothing against large capitalist firms, as long as they did not interfere in public life. In fact, Decazeville's republican middle class accepted the town's dependence on outside capital and had no qualms about pursuing an alliance with a firm that did not attack its political and commercial prerogatives. The republicans allotted eight positions on their ticket to company engineers and doctors. This arrangement threatened to shatter the unity that the town's left had always found in opposing the company. Left-wing republicans and union leaders considered running a separate slate in protest, but finally threw their support to the moderate republicans in order to assure Gastambide's defeat.[161]

The municipal elections of 1892 were the last in Decazeville's history in which no Socialists ran for office. The broad coalition that had rallied to defeat Gastambide disintegrated shortly afterwards. During the nineties unions played the leading role in building support for socialism in the Basin.[162] The miners' union overcame the traditional estrangement between miners and metalworkers and cooperated with the metalworkers' union in the decade after 1892, going so far as to launch a sympathy walkout for striking metalworkers in 1902. In 1893 the Decazeville miners' and metalworkers' unions persuaded Albert Duc-Quercy, a Socialist journalist who had been arrested during the strike of 1886, to oppose the incumbent Maruéjouls.[163] Comambault warned workers to follow its example and not to mix business and politics; the company fired the leaders of both unions two days before the election for taking unauthorized days off to work in Duc-Quercy's campaign.[164]

Across the nation, voters elected 37 Socialists to the Chamber in 1893. In the Aveyron, however, Maruéjouls defeated Duc-Quercy on the strength of his showing in rural areas. The totals for the whole electoral district—55 percent of the vote for Maruéjouls and 45 percent for Duc-Quercy—tell only part of the story. Duc-Quercy received over 80 percent of the ballots cast in Decazeville.[165] Industrial life had given the town's workers a political outlook radically different from that of the surrounding countryside, where most of them had their roots. Already in 1887 a vocal minority of Decazeville's workers had protested the republican candidate's support of grain tariffs, which raised the cost of bread. They argued that the workers had their own interests, separate from those of the peasantry.[166] In his campaign Maruéjouls stressed his rural ties. "The status of agricultural landowner and the facility with which he spoke to the rural inhabitants in *patois* won him a very sympathetic welcome" in the countryside, the Decazeville police commissioner explained.[167] But the workers, who faced a company with a center of power far from the Basin, were much more open to a national figure like Duc-Quercy. After the election, local Socialist leaders informed Maruéjouls that he did not represent the Basin's workers. A few months later the Decazeville miners' union asked him to resign from the Mines Commission in the Chamber.[168]

Soon after the defeat of Duc-Quercy, Decazeville's working-class leaders affiliated with the most radical of the nation's five Socialist parties, Jean Allemane's Parti Ouvrier Socialiste Révolutionnaire (POSR). Skilled artisanal workers in small Parisian workshops provided the core of *allemaniste* support. The seeming anomaly of the POSR in Decazeville is explicable by the leading role which the miners' union—composed of hewers and timbermen trying to protect their status—played in Decazeville politics in the 1890s. The POSR was strictly a working-class party that advocated the general strike to bring about revolution. It rejected bourgeois parliamentary democracy in favor of direct working-class control of municipalities.[169] The POSR, Mazars explained, "draws its strength from workers' unions, as do other parties with the socialist label, but, contrary to the others, has at its root the aim of grouping workers in unions." Mazars celebrated the primacy of syndicalism in the POSR and the *ouvrierisme* of its slogan: "the emancipation of workers by the workers themselves."[170]

In 1896 Mazars ran on a slate for town council which included the cream of Decazeville's working-class leadership: the head of the metalworkers' union, four mine-safety delegates, and three union men on the board of the miners' mutual aid fund. The narrow defeat of this ticket reinforced the allemanistes' *ouvrieriste* message. Later that year Mazars "told union members to be increasingly wary of politicians who wear a false mask and come to try to sow discord in the heart of the union."[171] In 1898 the Basin's Socialists put up Allemane for deputy. As a candidate he refused to temper his revolutionary beliefs to suit the conservative countryside: "We can permit no concessions to obtain votes that would be worthless in the eyes of sincere militants, since they would be the result of statements that partially concealed our way of thinking."[172] Under Allemane's leadership the Basin's working class turned in on itself: he took 57 percent of the vote in Decazeville, but less than 30 percent in the district.

*Allemanisme* suited Socialists in Decazeville for a number of reasons. The primacy it accorded the union fit with the role of the miners' union in providing Socialist leadership; the rejection of parliamentary politics reduced the importance of not having elected a Socialist deputy; and the refusal to compromise to gain rural votes appealed to urban workers who had long seen their interests sacrificed to the countryside. The *allemaniste* view of worker-run municipalities as the political counterpart to unions fueled efforts by Decazeville's workers to win control of their town from the moderate republicans to whom they had previously entrusted it. Decazeville's Socialists decided to assure victory in 1900 by including several of the town's leading Radicals on their ticket. The Radical/Socialist slate won handily, but the Socialists soon found to their dismay that their republican allies were unwilling to undertake expensive public works projects and had no intention of allowing town hall to be used as a forum for anticlericalism.[173] The miners' union concluded at the end of March 1901:

> We had once thought . . . that the capture of the town hall was a great step in advance, but it isn't at all.

All this proves is that the workers of Decazeville made the mistake of many others. Not making their first priority the defense of their class interests in the economic realm, they renounced the principles of class struggle, going into politics where they have nothing to gain except to become suckers.[174]

In the aftermath of the turn-of-the-century Radical/Socialist alliance in Decazeville and in the nation, marked by the participation of the Socialist Alexandre Millerand in the government, the majority of the town's Socialists joined Mazars in his return to a more *ouvrieriste* stance.[175] In 1902, after the demise of the POSR, Mazars himself ran for deputy as a follower of the Marxist Jules Guesde. He received over one-half of the votes in Decazeville, but was soundly defeated in the district as a whole.[176] Later in 1902 a long, unsuccessful metalworkers' strike put an end to the metalworkers' union for several years, and two briefer, but equally unsuccessful miners' strikes (one in support of the metalworkers, and one part of an abortive national miners' movement) sharply reduced support for the miners' union.[177] In 1906 Duc-Quercy "overcame [his] disgust" at the disorganization of worker politics at Decazeville and consented to run for deputy.[178] He took less than one-eighth of the total vote and failed to surpass 26 percent in any of the industrial towns in the district. The peasant-worker conflict surfaced again as a conservative Action Libérale opponent of Maruéjouls and Duc-Quercy pursued the "Boulangist" strategy of parading carts of peasants armed with pitchforks through the streets of Decazeville.[179]

This debacle revealed to organized labor in Decazeville the need to consider a change in political strategy. Massive immigration into the town, and the rapid expansion of the unskilled and semiskilled labor force in the factories and open-pit mines undercut the ability of the leadership of the miners' union to command the political allegiance of the town's workers. While the newcomers took up residence in Decazeville and swelled its electoral rolls, a number of underground miners and loyal union members continued to live in Combes and other communities outside the town limits. Many of Decazeville's new residents were too afraid of playing into the hands of the "reactionaries" to deny their vote to Maruéjouls.[180] Although the metalworkers' union revived before the war, it was fairly inactive and displayed little interest in cooperating with the miners' union.[181] Local factors were not the sole cause of the collapse of Decazeville's *ouvrieriste* politics however. Union radicalism in Decazeville had been posited on the support of a stronger socialist and syndicalist movement than existed in turn-of-the-century France. Without sustained outside assistance, a class-based movement in an isolated area like the Aubin Basin had limited potential.

The various strands of French socialism united in 1905, but it took well over a year for competing factions of the party in the Basin to put aside their differences. While the *allemanisme* and *guesdisme* professed by militants in the miners' union had been *ouvrieriste* in character, the national unified party espoused a less class-based approach to politics. In Decazeville discouraged union leaders formed an alliance with a new generation of bourgeois Socialists like those who controlled the national party after unification. The severe defeat of Socialists in the 1906 legislative elections in the Aubin Basin coincided with the CGT's decision to ban union participation in politics at the Congress of Amiens. Union officials in the Aubin Basin surrendered their positions of leadership in the party to professionals such as the pharmacists Jules Cabrol in Aubin and Auguste Douzeich in Decazeville, and the lawyer Paul Ramadier in Decazeville, who aided both the miners' and the metalworkers' unions in accident cases.[182]

The new generation of Socialist leadership shared more with the popular republican deputy Maruéjouls than with union leaders like Mazars. Ramadier rallied Decazeville's Socialists around support of consumers' cooperatives, anticlericalism, and cooperation with Radicals. His moderate positions formed the basis of a broad-based alliance of workers and elements of the middle class and peasantry, like the one that the republicans Cayrade and Maruéjouls had developed earlier. Cabrol adopted a similar approach. After the death of Maruéjouls, he won for Socialists in the Basin their first seat in the Chamber in 1908 and remained in office until 1919. Cabrol sat on the Mines Commission in the Chamber, and was a "miners' deputy," along the model of Basly and Arthur Lamendin in the Pas-de-Calais, Emile Bouvari in the Saône-et-Loire, and Jean Jaurès in the Tarn. These deputies' support of legislation to aid miners meshed with the Decazeville union's turn toward a strategy of national strike movements to influence parliament.

In 1892 Comambault faced a situation not unlike that which the Société Nouvelle had confronted a generation earlier. In both cases the previous operators had encountered stiff resistance from miners and the community when they tried to change the organization of work in the mines and raised the threat of divestment. The new owners then took advantage of improved market conditions to make new investments in local industry and to change the organization of work and the composition of the labor force. In the Decazeville of Deseilligny this change had seemed to take place in a political vacuum. A quarter-century later, however, the state played a much more visible role, setting the parameters for political life in the town and orienting miners' responses to the changes introduced by management.

In the two decades before 1914 Comambault transformed Decazeville. The new owner rebuilt the metallurgical plant and renovated the open-pit mines. Large numbers of unskilled workers came to staff these facilities. The firm also introduced changes in the organization and remuneration of underground miners, which reduced the hewer's authority within the crew. In the years between 1893 and 1906 the miners' union responded to these changes with a class-based strategy. While opposing the diminution of the hewers' authority, it took advantage of special miners' legislation to establish a new base of power. Whereas the power miners could mobilize through crews was private, in the sense that the activity of the crew was largely free from external supervision, the mine-safety delegate and the mutual aid fund were elected, state-sanctioned institutions. And while the strength of the crew was its ability to limit the application of managerial power, the influence of the new institutions depended on the union's ability to articulate new forms of power. Although these institutions could not directly elicit concessions from management, they did give the union an opportunity to lead the largely unorganized labor force. Despite this, Comambault refused to negotiate with the union as the representative of the miners. Stymied in this effort, the union pursued a radical course in the national miners' federation. In municipal politics, it abandoned the republican alliance with the town's middle class in favor of an *ouvrieriste* socialism and cooperation with the metalworkers' union.

After 1906 the union retained its strong position in the special miners' institutions, but changed its syndical and political strategies. It moderated its tone in the national federation and strongly supported the prewar general strikes to achieve parliamentary reforms. In the Basin the miners' union found that its *ouvrieriste* stance had less appeal to the droves of new unskilled workers than the reformism of the progressive republican Maruéjouls. Although the metalworkers' union revived in the years before the war, it showed little desire to restore the turn-of-the-century class-based alliance with the miners. The miners' union passed leadership of the Socialist party in the Basin on to a new generation of bourgeois Socialists, who in turn supported efforts to win special miners' legislation.

Nothing captures the transformation of union life between the two periods better than a comparison of Sainte-Barbe day in 1893 and 1911. In 1893 the union took advantage of Comambault's withdrawal from Sainte-Barbe festivities to organize a march and banquet for workers' groups in town. Some hundred and fifty workers consumed a meal of Proletarian bouillon, Federal boiled beef, Stuffed fatted young fowl *à la Syndicale,* Possibilist rabbit stew, Socialist giblets, Revolutionary mutton legs (with beans), Capitalist turkeys (with olives), and International desserts.[183] An effort to hold a similar dinner in 1911 failed when a majority within the union voted to spend Sainte-Barbe with their families instead.[184]

Both the miners' union's class-conscious stance in the 1890s and its participation in national movements to elicit legislative reform in the prewar years reinforced the Decazeville workers' identification of their cause with a national political culture. Support of national strategies, whether radical or reformist, to benefit workers in a relatively disadvantaged industrial region forced Decazeville's miners to reflect on the significance of their place in French society. While the use of *patois* provided a bond among inhabitants of the Basin, miners came to recognize French as the language of national social and political change. Some left-wing leaders associated *patois,* rhetorically at least, with political backwardness. In 1892, for instance, a union leader wrote an article in which all of the characters spoke French except for the oafish anti-union master miner, who made his comments in *patois.*[185] When Jaurès came to the Aubin Basin in 1910, "he closed his speech with a few phrases in *patois* which astonished and delighted the audience of workers":

> But Jaurès said that the various *patois,* monuments to the past, were condemned to disappear, like the civilization which they conveyed. Science and sociology, whose progress have been immense and whose fields of endeavor are international, necessarily speak another language. A new social state is spreading through the entire world which demands one language, one expression of a single thought in France. It requires a unified France which can be a living cell of humanity, a brotherly collaboration of all nations on earth.[186]

The triumph of a national political culture in the Basin was the fruit not only of the establishment of the Third Republic and the demise of the company town, but of Decazeville's new position in the economy as well. Workers, especially those in an economically disadvantaged region like the Aubin Basin, Jaurès suggested, would find the allies they required only in the movement that was attempting to bring a socialist state into being.

# 7. The Politics of Production

The devastating economic, demographic, and psychological costs of World War I abruptly ended the Belle Epoque. The war forced the French state to intervene in an unprecedented manner to allocate the nation's human and material resources. But when the war ended, the state withdrew from this directing role. Without conscripted labor and a guaranteed state market, heavy industry in France turned to immigrant workers and to new methods of organizing work in its effort to reestablish prewar levels of profitability. This was especially true in the mining industry. The Great Depression came late to France, but lasted longer than in most of its neighbors because of the nation's less developed industrial structure and the government's conservative financial policies. Under Clemenceau's leadership the Third Republic had shown its mettle by organizing France for victory in World War I. But the Republic proved much less successful in developing the means to deal successfully with the Great Depression and the rise of fascism in Europe in the 1930s.

The brief period of labor militancy after the war gave rise not to a strong union movement, but to one divided along political lines. The CGT fully repudiated the revolutionary syndicalism of its early years and devoted its energies instead to working through the republican state to win a place for unions in the economic structure. The CGT drew its strongest support from civil servants and looked to the Socialists for aid in achieving labor reforms. The minority Confédération Générale du Travail Unitaire (CGTU) recruited supporters from skilled industrial workers and to some extent from workers in new mass production industries. It too repudiated revolutionary syndicalism, and instead accepted the new Communist party's goal of international revolution along the Soviet model.

The formation by Radicals, Socialists, and Communists of a Popular Front in 1934 to oppose fascism and the depression led to the reunification of the CGT. In the long run, however, the election of the Popular Front to office in 1936 heightened divisions within French society. These fissures became fully evident in 1940 after the fall of France to the Germans and the creation of the Vichy regime. Vichy's dependence on the Nazis and its persecution of the political and syndical left temporarily clarified the political scene in France. In 1944, however, the combined triumph of the disproportionately Communist Resistance and Charles de Gaulle's Free French created the impetus for an effort to make the state a force of renewal and regeneration different from that proposed by Vichy. State planners drew on experiences in World War I, the Popular Front, and even the Vichy period to create the basis for new economic development in France.[1] World War I, the Great Depression, the Occupation, and the Liberation transformed Decazeville's relationship to the national state. Politics and union activities in the Aubin Basin became increasingly framed in national and international terms. By 1948 the future of industry in the Basin lay in state hands.

### State Intervention: An Overview

German occupation of the industrial regions of northern and eastern France at the beginning of World War I temporarily produced a situation that made Decazeville's location economically advantageous for the first time in its history. With the state controlling prices, wages, and labor mobility, the mines and factories of the Aubin Basin worked to capacity.[2] Coal production reached a record of 610,510 tons at Decazeville in 1918. After the war, however, large profits gave way to hard times. The return to a free market in labor and goods accentuated the effects of the national postwar industrial depression on industry in southern France.[3] Mines and factories in northern France were rebuilt quickly and the return of Alsace and Lorraine to France greatly increased the industrial capacity of eastern France; reparations payments brought quantities of German coal and steel into the French market. Meanwhile Decazeville lost two major clients for its lower grades of coal. The steelworks at Decazeville, literally worn out by war production and unable to compete with steel from Lorraine, closed in the 1920s. The zinc industry in Viviez, having long since exhausted the local zinc ore deposits, switched between the wars from coal to electricity as its source of power.

State policy with respect to railway freight rates hampered the efforts of mines in the Basin to find new markets. In the 1920s the state pursued a policy of adjusting rail rates to actual shipping costs. The result was to lower the cost of longer hauls and thus increase the national market for the mines of the north and the east. This, Comambault explained, "destroyed the equilibrium which had formerly existed between the various basins. The [state-run mines of the] Saar sell coal in Rodez and even in Toulouse." Decazeville was denied other markets because of the decision of state enterprises, like the Tulle arsenal, not to purchase the highly volatile coal of Decazeville.[4]

Despite these problems Decazeville was able to weather the postwar depression and to return to the 1913 production level of approximately one-half million tons in the late 1920s. The key to the firm's success was the development of subsidiary industries in Decazeville to produce benzols, coke, tar, ammonium sulfate, and electric power from its coal: in 1926–27 Decazeville sold three-fifths of its coal on the market and two-fifths to its local subsidiaries.[5] This period of prosperity was brief. The industrial depression of the 1930s was particularly devastating at Decazeville because its coal was poorly suited to domestic use. Between 1929–30 and 1933–34 the amount of coal extracted at Decazeville fell from 540,000 to 346,177 tons; the work week was cut by an average of one day and the mine personnel dropped from 3,829 to 2,336.[6] The Aubin Basin's share of national production went from almost 2.5 percent in 1913 to half that amount in the 1930s.

The depression and the national labor agreements signed under the Popular Front in the spring of 1936 forced mining firms in less profitable coalfields, like the Aubin Basin, to turn to the state to remain in business. The state's role in the coal industry grew even further during the Occupation. The Vichy regime controlled all facets of mining and forcibly integrated Decazeville's mines into an international political economy created to feed the German war machine. The nationalization of the coal industry at the Liberation, and the ensuing "battle" to produce coal to rebuild France, completed the cycle of state intervention in mining that had begun in World War I.

## The Recruitment and Management of Miners

Like all French mining firms, Comambault faced a severe labor shortage after World War I. More workers were required to achieve prewar production levels. Implementation in 1919 of the eight-hour day, based on arrival and departure from the mine rather than time at the pitface, reduced the time the miner spent working by more than an hour. The shorter shift also required a higher percentage of timbermen and other maintenance workers: at Aubin the proportion of hewers and helpers in the underground force fell by one-sixth between 1913 and 1922.[7]

New French labor was hard to come by. The war had depleted the reservoir of rural recruits on whom mining firms had long depended. In addition, the war and the new employment opportunities that accompanied economic growth in the 1920s contributed to a break-down in the insularity of the company-dominated mining community. Many sons of miners trained to become mine electricians and mechanics; others left mining altogether. One element of Comambault's solution was to accept a considerable degree of mobility on the part of workers. Rather than investing heavily in the construction of housing to keep workers at Decazeville, it offered the miner who was productive and cooperative the liberty to absent himself for a day, a week, or even a month with the relative assurance of a job on his return.[8] The nature of mining operations at Decazeville allowed the firm this flexibility. The underground mines constituted the domain of the more specialized and more stable personnel; a less skilled and more mobile population worked the open-pit mines, where the opportunities for adjusting production schedules were greater. Temporary replacements for the underground mines were drawn from the pool of open-pit mineworkers. Occasionally these individuals were kept on and trained to become permanent members of the underground labor force.[9] In the years of short work weeks after the war and again during the depression, both miners and companies found advantage in the opportunity for many workers to cultivate their own plots or to hire themselves out as agricultural laborers.[10] In some cases Comambault was able to play on the desire of workers, especially foreigners and first-generation rural migrants, to avoid a commitment to a lifetime in the mines, in order to assure their good behavior at work. Such an informal, paternalistic approach to labor relations persisted longest in industrial firms like the mines of Decazeville, where the economic situation did not allow for more costly efforts to maintain a permanent labor supply.

These approaches to labor recruitment were secondary, however, to the extensive use all French coal companies made of immigrant workers during the interwar period.[11] Before 1914, immigrant miners in the Basin had come almost exclusively from Spain and had been employed mainly in the open-pit mines. This changed during the war: in addition to mobilized miners from the Nord and the Pas-de-Calais, the state allocated colonial labor, contingents of Chinese workers under military control, captured Russian soldiers, and large numbers of German prisoners of war—early in 1919 the mines of Decazeville employed more than 700 German soldiers.[12] When these workers left, firms in the Aubin Basin and elsewhere in France turned to central and eastern Europe for both experienced miners and single young men willing to train as hewers and timbermen. By the end of 1926, 55.3 percent of the underground miners in the mines of Aubin were foreigners; 91.6 percent of the immigrant miners worked underground; 64.9 percent of the foreigners were Poles, 24.8 percent were Spaniards, and 7.0 percent were Czechs.[13] In Decazeville immigrant miners made up over one-third of the labor force in the mines in the 1920s. They were even more important for production than their numbers would indicate: in 1925 almost half of the miners at Banel (Decazeville) were foreign, but almost three-quarters of the hewers were foreigners.[14] Before the war the presence of an established native labor force had slowed down advancement in the mines of Decazeville. However, the prewar specialization of the miner's work had actually reduced the amount of time required to train new miners. This was crucial to the recruitment of immigrant non-miners in the 1920s because they usually began work in the mines as adults and therefore missed the long adolescent apprenticeship, and because they generally signed short-term contracts and required constant replacement.[15]

Since authorization of the state mining engineer was needed to import new groups of immigrant workers, state supervision of mining in the interwar years extended from overseeing the work to the composition of the labor force itself. This was especially crucial in the Aubin Basin which, because of its marginal economic situation, could not offer the wages or social services necessary to attract the best immigrant labor, and therefore faced new obstacles to its competitiveness.[16]

Before the war immigrant labor had supplemented the native French labor force and allowed Comambault to profit from the strong demand for coal and steel. After the war immigrant labor became crucial to the maintenance of industry in Decazeville. In 1935, in the midst of the depression, the Decazeville management reported that it had reduced the proportion of immigrant miners in the labor force to 23.5 percent, but could go no further: "after the massive compression of our personnel carried out in the last years, the foreign workers we have kept are for the most part excellent specialists, and in particular very good hewers. It is difficult to replace these workers with Frenchmen, given the repugnance which the latter show, despite the crisis, for the difficult underground work."[17] Further layoffs of immigrant workers would have forced the dismissal of Frenchmen employed aboveground.

Although the influx of foreign workers had been facilitated by the prewar changes in the organization of work, further specialization in the Aubin Basin after the war was restricted in comparison to other coalfields. In 1919 Comambault decided to provide hewers' tools and to pay for their repair and sharpening in hopes of raising productivity.[18] The firm began to make use of jackhammers and air drills in the 1920s, but the irregular nature of coal deposits restricted the introduction of cutting machines. For the same reason, long-wall mining received more limited application at Decazeville than at many other French mines.[19] Long-wall mining, in which groups of hewers attacked a mine face together (although they were often paid individually and retained some form of crew structure), decreased the hewer's control of the pace of production and increased the danger of roof falls. While changes in transport and production required more mechanics and electricians, rationalization in the sense that F. W. Taylor conceived it was ill-suited to the underground mines of the Aubin Basin, where mining crews frequently worked in isolated, separate areas, free from constant supervision.[20] The director of the Aubin mines reported that in 1929, despite the limited specialization of mining work, the hewer still performed much the same tasks as his nineteenth-century predecessor: "the productivity of a hewer [in the Aubin Basin could not] be compared to that obtained in other mines because of the complexity of the labor asked of this category of workers (hewing, propping, loading, often haulage for some distance manually, preparation of the mine-fill)."[21] Even after the adoption of long-wall mining in some Basin mines in the early 1930s, the crew remained a fundamental form of work organization. "The mines of Decazeville," the management explained to the board of directors of Comambault at the end of 1943,

> have always had and will always have a very hard life, because the deposit is of mediocre quality. Doubled over, and in jagged fragments, it only rarely lends itself to the establishment of

large production areas that are easy to organize and to supervise. It requires, on the contrary, the use of small rooms of two or three workers spread about. These are of an artisanal nature and, as a result, the influence of the quality and the good will of labor is preponderant.[22]

Inflation during the war had led the state to approve relatively uniform cost-of-living increases for all French miners. These had reduced the monetary incentives for hewers; at Decazeville, for instance, hewers saw their wages fall from 177 percent to 118 percent of those of their helpers between 1913 and mid-1921.[23] In postwar wage accords—based in large part on settlements reached elsewhere—Comambault was never able to reestablish in full the prewar financial inducements for hewers to produce. This was particularly serious for less mechanized mines like those of the Aubin Basin where, as the Decazeville management pointed out, the effort of the individual worker was of such importance.

In the early-to-mid twenties Comambault's major concern was to find enough workers to staff its mines; beginning in the late twenties, the firm responded to changes in the market by devoting itself to the reduction of production expenses. Limited in its ability to pursue the primary means of cutting labor costs by fundamentally altering either the organization of work or production rates, Comambault extended Fayol's managerial strategy of trying to change the administration of labor, and especially the relations that master miners and *chefs de poste* had with the miners under their command. The lower supervisory personnel had always depended primarily on personal authority in dealing with their subordinates. The inefficiencies of this system increased as the labor force, but not the managerial staff, grew more international in composition.[24]

Before the war Comambault had established the supremacy of the central management in Paris over both the board and the local management in Decazeville. In the interwar years the central management set up a special Bureau d'Etudes to explore how, without an increase in the proportion of managerial personnel to workers,[25] supervisors could carry out their work more efficiently. The master miners and *chefs de poste* initially feared and resented company efforts to give their supervision a more technical foundation. The director of the Aubin mines explained that in 1929, the "supervisory personnel was made up of men who were devoted, but who were all aged, who were anchored tenaciously in a routine and for whom any idea of modernization was considered a dangerous innovation."[26] The Bureau d'Etudes at Decazeville sought to create a new attitude in the future by establishing classes for prospective *chefs de poste* and master miners. At the same time Comambault set stricter rules to govern how supervisors should carry out their jobs. It also increased the importance of production bonuses and introduced a degree of specialization of supervisory personnel, such as extraction, timbering, transportation, and filling-in.[27]

The Bureau d'Etudes looked into aspects of mining peripheral to production as well. Taking paid days off for health reasons was the miners' primary means of compensating for increased production demands and stricter supervision; reducing this benefit would lower production costs without significantly altering the labor process. The Bureau carried out its own safety inspections and made a statistical analysis of all accidents to suggest ways to operate the mines more safely and to weed out miners who were frequently injured. It devoted special efforts to convincing supervisory personnel of the pecuniary importance of accident prevention. Foremen who failed to limit the number of accidents among their workers saw their bonuses "amputated." As a result of the Bureau's efforts, the number of injuries per miner fell by one-half between 1929–30 and 1933–34. By actively involving supervisory personnel in the prevention and treatment of accidents, the company also raised the percentage of accident victims who chose to be treated by company physicians from one-third in 1932–33 to one-half the following year. This reduced the number of workers who took time off for accidents and lowered medical costs for the company.[28] Furthermore, the company safety inspections and the restricted access to non-company doctors posed an indirect threat to the power and influence of the mine-safety delegates and the mutual aid fund, union bastions since the 1890s.

Comambault's efforts to raise productivity and to reduce paid absences depended on the actions of the subaltern supervisory personnel. The victory of the Popular Front in 1936 was a tremendous shock to mining firms throughout France because it threatened the very roots of the managerial hierarchy. "By sapping the principle of authority and destroying the spirit of work [the Popular Front] produced a decline from which no industry escaped," the Decazeville management commented a few years later. "The mines, where the dominant element in the production price [labor] was deeply affected, declined more than other enterprises."[29] The company complained that master miners became demoralized and unable to enforce discipline in the mines. The union responded that workers would refuse to accept a return to the "partiality and brutality" that had characterized relations between miners and their immediate supervisors in the past. The introduction of collective bargaining in 1936 ironically aggravated the situation. "Relations improved considerably" between workers and their employers, the union explained, but this brought out more sharply the conflicts between miners and the lower ranks of management.[30] One response of Comambault was to redouble efforts to ground supervisors' authority on a technical rather than a personal basis. In 1938 it introduced the timing of various tasks, which had the particular advantage of contrasting with the "old methods" of alleged "partiality and brutality" displayed by many *agents de maîtrise*. Timing was the culmination of the earlier efforts by the Bureau d'Etudes to introduce a greater degree of uniformity and coordination into the management of mining. Although it was intended to reduce the miners' freedom to work as they pleased, the effect was to limit the autonomy of the managerial staff as well. The false impartiality of timing elicited a spirited protest from, of all people, the company engineers: "[they] admit with difficulty that their work alone is not enough to decide cases of insufficient productivity. [Spending] every day in the mine they know in detail all the *chantiers* . . . and the worth of the workers themselves. They considered the measures an indication of a lack of confidence in their value and in their professional conscientiousness."[31] In the late 1930s Comambault began to introduce restrictions on the engineers' prerogatives similar to those previously placed on the lower supervisory personnel. In both cases the firm's goal was to give the initiative to the upper levels of management while basing the exercise of power in the mines on less controvertible grounds than the individual supervisor's personal authority and aptitudes.

Comambault complemented the rationalization of supervisory techniques with a reevaluation of the profitability of both the underground and open-pit mines. The extensive use of immigrant workers on short-term contracts during the interwar years made it easier for companies to justify the disruptions in miners' lives necessary to consolidate operations in the underground mines.[32] The scarcity of native French labor and the tight coal market also encouraged Comambault to mechanize the open-pit mines. The Aubin Basin was the coalfield in France most suited to open-pit mining; Comambault hoped that mechanization would enable the Basin to overcome its liabilities in the national coal market. In the early thirties it purchased eighteen electric shovels, and replaced the steam locomotives and horses in the open-pit mines with fifty-six diesel tractors. From less than one-fifth of Decazeville's annual tonnage after the war, open-pit production jumped to well over one-third in 1934–35. Production per open-pit worker rose 262 percent between 1927 and 1938.[33] For the first time in Decazeville's history mechanization, rather than more intensive exploitation of the existing form of work organization, was the major factor in increasing miners' productivity. The effects of the Popular Front victory on labor discipline led Comambault to seek further expansion and mechanization of the open-pit mines. Only the outbreak of war forced it to put aside these plans.

During the interwar years Comambault developed the programs it had introduced in the mines of Decazeville in the prewar period. Before 1914 the firm had employed Spanish workers in the factories and open-pit mines; in the 1920s Eastern European workers became the crucial element in the underground mine labor force. While making further efforts to mechanize and rationalize labor in the underground mines, Comambault devoted special attention to reorganization and specialization of the supervisory staff. The economic depression of the 1930s also encouraged Comambault to begin mechanizing the open-pit mines. The native underground mine labor force at Decazeville found its means of dealing with the company sapped by large numbers of foreign workers whose cultural background and transience separated them from the French population, especially in the 1920s; by a new rigor in supervision; and by the growing importance of the mechanized open-pit mines in the town's economy. These changes forced miners' political and syndical organizations to pursue national strategies to prevent conditions in their basin from falling further behind those in other French coalfields.

## Political and Syndical Action before the Popular Front

The growth in state intervention in economic life, which began during World War I, raised new issues for syndicalists and Socialists in the Basin. In 1917 the government, which controlled the length of the work day, the labor supply, and the allocation of industrial production for the war effort, established "mixed commissions" composed of union and employer representatives to set minimum wages by region, industry, and job. In theory the mixed commissions satisfied a long-standing desire of unions in the Basin to negotiate openly and as equals with management. Yet because the two sides were never able to agree, the government decided on the minimum wage in the end. It invariably set this wage low to encourage production and lent its disciplinary authority to company supervisors on matters like absenteeism.[34] Although miners in the Basin did not strike during the war, they participated actively in postwar national strike movements. Victorious in June 1919, the miners suffered a terrible reverse in the general strike called by their national federation in May 1920 to support striking railway workers and to demand nationalization of public services. Mining companies across the nation, acting with the state's approval, cracked down: firms in the Basin fired sixty strikers, including a number of union leaders. The return to a free market involved destruction of the union movement which had developed during and after the war.[35]

The disastrous strike of May 1920 helped to precipitate a split in the French labor movement in December 1920 between the reformist Socialists and the radical Communists, and in December 1921 between their syndical counterparts, the CGT *confédérés* and the *unitaires* of the CGTU.[36] Despite the schism, Ramadier held Decazeville's Socialist party together by reviving the national, turn-of-the-century, anticlerical Radical/Socialist alliance. Ramadier became the town's first Socialist mayor in 1919 and the first Socialist deputy from the town in 1928. He was a gifted administrator and under his tenure the town expanded significantly the municipal services which it offered. The Socialist town council saw protection of the consumer as one of its primary responsibilities. The town aided cooperatives and replaced the toll on goods entering town, finally substituting higher property taxes for this bane of nineteenth-century municipal administrators.[37]

Ramadier rejected the revolutionary syndicalism of the prewar period as a romantic illusion, and the Communist movement of the interwar years as an insidious threat to the republic. He temporarily left the Socialists in the early thirties for the Neo-Socialist party, in which he hoped to be able to pursue his support of state economic planning. Like his predecessors as Decazeville's mayor and deputy, Cabrol and Deseilligny, Ramadier used his position in parliament to defend the interests of the Aubin Basin and of the French coal industry. He argued in favor of duties to protect French coal, a recalculation of rail rates to establish a privileged market around each coal basin, and higher wages for miners to encourage Frenchmen to continue to enter the profession.[38] Ramadier's triumph came in 1936, when he led a Popular Front slate to victory in the Decazeville municipal elections and was named under-secretary of the Ministry of Public Works in charge of mines in the first Popular Front government—the first of a number of cabinet posts he was to hold. As under-secretary he oversaw reform of the French coal industry. To compensate poorer coal companies, like those of the Aubin Basin, for the extraordinary costs imposed on them by the Popular Front labor legislation and wage settlements, the state decided to set prices for coal and to subsidize mines that were operating at a deficit.

Although the Communists had difficulty cracking the Socialist stronghold of Decazeville in the 1920s,[39] both the CGT and the CGTU developed a following among miners in the Basin. The *confédérés'* national predominance in the labor movement and inside the mining profession was replicated at Decazeville, where they commanded the allegiance of between one-third and two-fifths of the labor force. The *unitaires* controlled somewhat less than half of that number. However the CGTU did well in the corporate elections for mine-safety delegates, mutual aid fund administrators, and national miners' pension fund administrators, approaching parity with the *confédérés* for these positions in the Basin after the mid-twenties. The large contingent of immigrant miners was an impediment to both unions, for these workers could neither vote in corporate elections nor hold union office, and feared expulsion if they publicly opposed their employers.

Before World War I union leaders in the Basin had relinquished the leading role they had originally played in the socialist movement. The *confédérés* continued this policy, while supporting Ramadier's moderate socialism and pursuing the prewar union's efforts to serve as an intermediary between workers and social welfare institutions. Instead of supplying services itself, the union ensured that the state or the company followed through on its obligations to the worker. This service was keenly appreciated by miners, especially after the managerial crackdown on benefits. Injured nonunionized workers frequently asked the union secretary to help them get a *bon de blessure* which a supervisor had refused them. (The Aubin *confédéré* union council decided that this service should be rendered only if the worker agreed to join the union and to pay six months dues.[40])

The CGT's long-term goal was establishment of a nationalized mining industry managed by representatives of workers, consumers, and the state.[41] In the interim, the *confédérés* mounted a rearguard action against the relative decline during the interwar years in miners' wages with respect to those in other industries. Following the precedent set by state control of labor relations during the war, the CCHF, the owners' association, and the CGT bargained nationally over base wage rates per category of miner. Such a system embodied only part of Mazars' prewar hope for a new system of labor relations in the mines, however, because it did not do away with payment by production. Yet it marked an important development in the situation of miners in the Aubin Basin. Until 1886, wages had been an issue for the crews, not the union; and until World War I wages were still established outside of a formal national framework. After 1914, however, wages were increasingly decided by union bargaining on the national level. The prefect reported on this development during a period of extended negotiations in July 1925: "the miners of the Aveyron Basin are growing quite uninterested in the matter . . . They know that the key to events is in Paris and that negotiations . . . cannot be undertaken fruitfully except between the CCHF and the miners' federation."[42] These national negotiations did not fundamentally alter the labor economics of the less favored coalfields, however, because individual basins were left to work out their own accords. Although companies in the Aubin Basin would meet with the local *confédéré* unions, they refused to negotiate until agreements had been reached in the larger and more prosperous Nord/Pas-de-Calais and Loire basins. They then offered somewhat less to their miners on the grounds that the Aubin Basin suffered from worse market conditions.

Local CGT leaders vigorously attacked the institutionalization of the secondary status of miners in less favored coalfields, and demanded that the national federation do all in its power to end it. The leader of the Aubin union, Paul Oustry, argued with growing insistence that the failure to work out national accords with the operators threatened the very existence of the *confédérés* in areas like the Aubin Basin. Early in 1925 he wrote to the national union secretary:

> If, contrary to our expectations, the regions which were lucky enough to be able to reach an agreement with their companies disassociate themselves from us, it is probable, if not certain, that the *confédéré* union will come to an end in our region. I

do not know if one could find comrades so hardened as to face up to the justifiable discontent that would rise from the mass, and to the *"unitaires,"* who would not fail to take advantage of the discontent with us and with our Fédération.[43]

Oustry repeatedly warned the national federation that its failure to look after the interests of miners in the Aubin Basin would force his union to cooperate with the *unitaires:* he wrote to the secretary of the national federation in September 1925 that he had read that unions in the Nord had decided to meet with mining companies to discuss wages:

> Our owners are in no way disposed to give us satisfaction unless constrained to by force. We alone cannot constrain them. If, as in the past, the same tactical error occurs, and the regions negotiate separately with the representatives of their basins, some accepting to sign an agreement, caring very little about what is done in other regions, I am telling you that as far as I am concerned I will find myself obliged to denounce the method used until now that makes for rich relations and poor relations at the heart of the Fédération.
>
> Furthermore, I am informing you that if satisfaction is not given to all miners as a whole, and that if the Fédération Unitaire, organizing the justifiable discontent that will not fail to arise in the slighted basins, takes action, I will, without accepting all its demagogy, follow it.[44]

The next year Oustry insisted that "we will never accept a raise less than that given in other basins": "It is no longer possible for us to accept always being treated like pariahs."[45] The marginalization of the Basin's miners led local *confédérés* to threaten their national federation with the spectre of cooperation with the renegade *unitaires.* Their inferior position also created a particular longing for syndical reunification, which would give them enough clout to be treated on an equal footing with their peers across the nation.[46]

Unfortunately, the *unitaires'* radical strategies made it very difficult for the *confédérés* to envisage cooperation with them. The *unitaires* analyzed the difficulties of the mining industry in the Aubin Basin as part of a worldwide capitalist crisis. They did not look to the Third Republic to improve the situation of labor, but worked instead for national and international revolution to sweep away the institutions of the existing economic and political order.

While the *confédérés* were primarily concerned with taking advantage of the potential for government-sanctioned cooperation of labor and capital suggested by the wartime experience, the *unitaires* concentrated on recent changes in labor recruitment and mining management. They saw the internationalization of the labor market as particularly significant and devoted considerable effort to organizing immigrant workers.[47] They were also much harsher critics than the *confédérés* of the effects on miners of company efforts to rationalize mining operations. The *unitaires'* pointed attack on *capitalist* rationalization suggested, however, that in another political economy technological change and greater discipline would be to the workers' advantage.

In the 1920s the CGT elaborated the prewar strategy of using the threat of peaceful general strikes of limited duration to bring pressure to bear on the CCHF, and indirectly on the state.[48] The *unitaires* criticized the limitations of this tactic. In April 1933, during one of the few strikes called by both unions, the Decazeville *unitaire* leader Albert Tournier criticized the *confédérés:* "one does not strike by going fishing, working one's garden, or sitting in the cafes, but by battling in the roads, by forming strike pickets, by coming in numbers to meetings."[49] The *unitaires'* demands for job control and wages fixed by occupation rather than production were more radical than those posed by the *confédérés*. Furthermore, the *unitaires* formulated their demands "not by region, but nationally."[50] "As long as the *patronat* wants to discuss by region," Tournier added, "you will be dupes. Defeat with dignity is better than accepting humiliation."[51] In fact, the *unitaire* militants did not figure to win many of the strikes they launched, but wanted to use these struggles as lessons to educate both the organized and unorganized miners who participated.

The *unitaires'* educational project was nowhere more clear than in the stringent criticism to which they subjected themselves after their strikes.[52] Whereas the CGT strikes were intended to influence the government, the *unitaires* sought to create the conditions for workers to come to understand the political basis of the exploitation they experienced in the workplace and to commit themselves to working against it. The national CGTU federation continually pushed its adherents in the Basin. Although they worked selflessly to comply, they had great difficulty mobilizing miners in the chronically depressed Aubin region. When the national leadership called a twenty-four hour general strike to express support for Sacco and Vanzetti in August 1927, the Decazeville *unitaires* passed a resolution asking its confederation to give local unions more advance notice "and not to forget that orders are easier to give than to execute, especially when one has nothing, absolutely nothing, on hand to do the least thing to apply them with even a minimum of success."[53] This scenario was repeated on several occasions during the twenties and thirties.[54] Self-criticism plays an essential role in all Communist organizations, but was particularly harsh among *unitaires* in the Aubin Basin, where the effort to organize a revolutionary movement proved very difficult. For if the Basin's secondary position in the French economy generated considerable discontent, it also made workers reluctant to undertake the radical actions proposed by the *unitaires*. While the Aubin Basin CGT repeatedly chided and cajoled its national leadership to support equitable treatment of all miners, the local CGTU was subject to frequent chastisements from its national federation. This highlighted the difference between the *confédérés'* reformism, which often required local unions to generate action on the national level, and the *unitaires'* strategy, directed from above, to overturn the existing political economy.

Unification of the *confédérés* and the *unitaires* in the CGT in the fall of 1935 revitalized the labor movement on the national level. This created the basis for miners in the Basin to share in the gains of workers throughout the country the following year. Mazars' successor and long-time Decazeville *confédéré* leader Albert Rieux described the emotion he experienced at the unification congress: "This joint meeting of delegates will remain unforgettable for me. The *unitaire* delegates sought out the *confédéré* delegates from their region in the hall. They exchanged handshakes and some even embraced. Others wept with joy."[55] The reunited union grew quickly to encompass 2,100 of Decazeville's miners within a year, including a sizable contingent of immigrant miners, who unionized freely for the first time. The union was strong enough in the spring of 1936 to negotiate significant wage increases and improvements in working conditions. This agreement was in turn cited as a model for miners' unions throughout the nation. Following strikes in the Nord/Pas-de-Calais and other basins in June 1936, the CGT worked out a more comprehensive contract under the auspices of the Ministry of Public Works. This accord set a minimum base rate for all miners, regardless of their production. The miners in the Aubin Basin, although they had not struck, shared in the benefits of the new agreement.[56]

**From the Popular Front to the Strike of 1948**

Miners saw in the Popular Front a liberation from unemployment, underemployment, and the low wages and harsh discipline that had characterized the Depression years. The events of the spring of 1936 also opened a new period in the history of the managerial staff and in the level of state involvement in the coal industry. The managerial personnel perceived the triumphs of the Popular Front as a threat and responded by following the miners' example and unionizing. The supervisory and technical staff below the level of engineer had gained a new identity through the training programs established since the war, and four-fifths unionized late in 1936 to protect their positions and prerogatives against the organized workers. The following year the engineers launched their own unions.[57]

The new freedom experienced by the miners contributed to a significant increase in absenteeism and to an 18 percent drop in the daily production of a hewer in the underground mines of the Aubin Basin between May 1936 and September 1937 (after having risen 22 percent at Decazeville and 32 percent at Aubin between 1930 and 1935).[58] In 1937 the state responded by bringing together the companies and the unions of miners, supervisory personnel, and engineers in a commission headed by the Inspector General of the Mines.[59] In the nineteenth century the state mining corps had concerned itself largely with conditions in the mines; in the 1920s it had turned to monitoring the labor supply. The next step was consideration of the issue of productivity itself.

Although the commission had no power, it provided a forum for firms to try to convince miners' unions that their cooperation in raising productivity was needed to maintain the current level of mining in the Basin. The commission put the miners' unions on the defensive after their stunning successes of the year before. The discussions made the miners' unions "very nervous," the state chief engineer reported, because they feared being forced into disciplining individual workers.[60] While Comambault claimed to have never entertained "the idle hope of counting on union delegates to reestablish order," it did follow the state engineers' example and send the mine-safety delegates it considered "most intelligent" to visit unproductive crews in order to foster awareness of the issue of productivity. When the union ventured to criticize these tactics and to protest the introduction of stopwatch-men, Comambault threatened to close down certain pits unless productivity rose. This impressed the state mine corps and Ramadier, who urged the union to get miners to work harder.

Matters reached a head at Decazeville in mid-May 1938 when several hewers, under pressure to increase production, complained of their helpers, who were then punished. The state chief engineer refused the union's request that he intervene in the matter on the grounds that such a step would interfere with management's efforts to raise productivity. A strike was narrowly averted when the departmental Commission de Conciliation, set up under the Popular Front legislation, stepped in and got the punishments reduced.[61] Yet such breaches of the solidarity of the crew, still the fundamental unit in mining, served their purpose. The next year the Decazeville management reported that "productivity [had] increased as the result of measures taken by the government to reestablish the authority of the supervisory personnel."[62] The state cooperated with the companies to handle the crisis of authority that accompanied the Popular Front. And despite union resistance, the state engineers joined with company officials in suggesting that unions' new strength made them in part responsible for assuring miners' productivity. Nationwide, this same period saw the withdrawal of a number of the gains made during the Popular Front, including the forty-hour week. (Ramadier resigned as Minister of Labor in 1938 over this measure.)

Obliterating the legacy of the Popular Front was a prime concern of the Vichy regime, established after the fall of France in 1940. The new government stepped up the repression of Communists (which the Third Republic had initiated in the fall of 1939 after the signing of the Nazi-Soviet Non-Aggression Pact) and severely limited syndical rights.[63] With strong support from Vichy, Comambault established an apprenticeship program at Decazeville. The new institution had two goals, in addition to providing technical training for young workers. The first was to form career miners at Decazeville. Between the wars Comambault had depended on immigrant labor and mechanization of the open-pit mines. The exigencies of a wartime economy closed off these options after 1940, and forced Comambault to reassess the future of its native French labor force at Decazeville. Wartime restrictions on labor mobility and—after 1943—the dreaded conscription of young Frenchmen who were not employed in certain key industries, including mining, to work in Germany (Service du Travail Obligatoire, STO), gave Comambault unprecedented leverage in the recruitment of adolescents into mining.[64] Youths who sought to leave the mine apprenticeship program after age sixteen were barred from future employment in the firm, as were adolescents who, after being turned down for the much more popular machine shop apprenticeship program, refused to enter the mine pre-apprenticeship.[65] This left them open for conscription by STO. Comambault had a second goal as well—to create a labor force free of the anti-managerial spirit that had characterized the Popular Front period—and suggested that the solution to class conflict could be found within the firm itself: "Today intellectual capital has intervened in social life. Between capital-labor and capital-money, the engineers serve as mediators."[66] But only a new generation of workers, free from the influence of past experiences, could see this. The apprenticeship program took the instruction of young miners out of the hands of their fellow workers, who presumably passed on undesirable values along with technical advice.[67] Upon graduation, the apprentice miners were given their own section of the mine to work "to shield them from the influence of other workers."[68]

Yet, if the Vichy period initially seemed a propitious time to break the spirit of the Popular Front in the labor force, economic and political conditions in and out of the mines—malnutrition, the absenteeism of miners cultivating their plots or seeking contraband food in the countryside, an eight-fold increase in the number of injured under treatment,[69] an influx of young non-miners seeking to evade STO, shortages of material and rolling stock, workers' discontent with the Vichy regime—came to present far more serious problems for Comambault than it had faced in 1936.[70]

Vichy's subservience to the German war economy, culminating in the STO, led to the clear expression within the mining population of a widely based opposition to both the state and the private firm. By 1943 Resistance movements had developed throughout the Basin. While a small local of the Catholic Confédération Française des Travailleurs Chrétiens (CFTC), which had been founded in the Basin after the Popular Front, and an officially recognized union led by former confédérés pressed Vichy authorities to improve miners' living conditions,[71] an illegal union active in the Resistance developed alongside them.[72] The underground Communist party played a leading role in the Resistance in the Basin. The Nazi-Soviet pact had split the union movement in the Basin and isolated the former unitaires and Communists.[73] Their position within the Resistance movement allowed them to shed the image of traitors and to assume the mantle of the truest patriots.[74]

While the Resistance drew most of its support from workers and young men evading the STO, it also attracted sympathizers from other social classes in the area. By August 1944 units, averaging thirty-five men apiece, existed in every town in the Basin. Larger military groups were quartered in the surrounding countryside: the biggest of these, composed in large part of Spanish Civil War veterans, had 420 members in August 1944. At that time the unified Resistance army, the Forces Françaises de l'Intérieur, enrolled 2,783 *maquis* in northern Aveyron, more than half of whom operated out of the Basin and its immediate environs. Had weapons been more plentiful, the local commander estimated, the figure would have been three to four times higher.[75] The Resistance used explosives stolen from the Basin's industrial firms to wreak havoc in the mines, factories, communication systems, power plants, and power lines; it also executed several of the area's leading collaborators.[76]

The Resistance movement was so successful in the Basin because it drew on fundamental aspects of the miners' lives. By raising the issue of the use to be made of the coal, Resistance groups operating in and around the mines integrated and legitimated as part of a political struggle against the Nazis the miners' long-standing fight against injustice in the mines. While Comambault used the Occupation to continue the rationalization it had begun before the war, the miners, in sabotaging the mines and stealing explosives and fuel, turned the tools of their trade from productive to political ends. Resistance efforts to impede economic collaboration with the Germans implied that in the long run control of the mines by miners rather than by private firms would be in the nation's best interest. The war experience also reduced the divisiveness that ethnic and occupational diversity had created during the interwar years. Common participation in the political struggle against fascism helped French and immigrant workers to overcome the cultural barriers which had separated them before the Popular Front and the Resistance. Many immigrant workers, especially the Spanish Civil War refugees hired out of French concentration camps, established themselves in the Decazeville community through their Resistance activities.[77] In a period of extreme scarcity, the legal union bargained to have all categories of miners receive the benefits accorded underground miners. In addition, the participation of individual supervisors in the Resistance prepared the way for a new relationship between labor and management[78]; this was very different from the situation in the German-occupied Nord/Pas-de-Calais, where the absence of managerial personnel in the Resistance exacerbated conflicts between miners and supervisors after the Liberation.[79] The strength of the Resistance in isolated areas of France like the Aubin Basin, and the important role that workers and foreigners, marginal social groups during the Third Republic, played in the movement, gave the miners of Decazeville a new importance in the nation.

The Resistance prepared worker organizations to assume briefly an unprecedented degree of control over their community and their work. In June 1944 the Decazeville Liberation Committee took over provisioning of the Aubin Basin at the request of the Vichy prefecture.[80] Resistance forces occupied the individual towns on 14 July and dismissed the Vichy-appointed municipal governments.[81] Following the departure of the Germans in August 1944, the CGT, Communist-dominated after the purge of union officials who had not cooperated with the illegal union, took responsibility for keeping the mines in operation. Union leaders called for the dismissal of those managerial personnel who were technically incompetent or who had compromised themselves during the Occupation.[82] Some miners took the punishment of supervisors into their own hands. These local initiatives soon gave way to reassertion of control by national authorities, however. In the fall of 1944 Gaullist authorities curbed Resistance control of both the town and the workplace. They first stripped the Resistance forces of their police powers; late in 1944 the Gaullist Provisional Government requisitioned the mines of the Aubin Basin and placed them under the direction of a labor-management committee.[83] The CGT took a leading role in the new organization of the mines and exercised control over hiring and the distribution of clothes and shoes to miners.[84] By May 1945 membership in the Decazeville miners' union had swelled to 3,200, out of a total labor force of less than four thousand.[85]

The Fourth Republic nationalized the mining industry in 1946 and set up the Charbonnages de France to administer it. In June 1946 the Charbonnages created the Houillères du Bassin d'Aquitaine, composed of the mines of the Aveyron and the Tarn (Carmaux and Albi). A new administrative structure replaced the labor-management committee. At the top a board of directors made up of six representatives for the Charbonnages, six for the consumers, and seven for the personnel was selected to govern each basin. At a lower level the CGT consolidated its position within the new industrial structure. As a result of the proliferation of committees generated by postwar labor reforms, nearly 200 union militants held office by the spring of 1947.[86] While the organizational form of the Charbonnages resembled the plans proposed by the *confédérés* and Neo-Socialists in the early thirties, its implementation after the overthrow of the Vichy state also placed nationalization within the *unitaire* tradition.

In the immediate postwar period, nationalization had both a political and an economic rationale: to punish collaboration with Occupation forces, especially in the Nord/Pas-de-Calais, where miners refused to work under their old supervisors,[87] and to resuscitate the French mining industry, suffering from a chronic underinvestment that had grown worse during the Vichy period.[88] State planners saw control of energy industries, especially coal, as the way to raise production and productivity to the levels necessary to spur development of the whole French economy. This would require significant investment in the mines and higher wages and better benefits to attract new workers.

The national CGT miners' federation saw the revitalization of the coal industry as an opportunity for miners to regain the relative advance in benefits and wages they had enjoyed before World War I, and lost between then and the Popular Front. Between 1914 and 1937, the Communist Minister of Industrial Production Marcel Paul told the federation's congress in February 1946, large portions of the special legislation initially accorded miners had been extended to the rest of the industrial labor force, including the eight-hour day, a national pension plan, and elected delegates. At the same time, miners' wages had fallen from 140 percent to 88 percent of those of an unskilled Parisian metalworker.[89] Later that year miners' demands for better compensation and working conditions were granted in the Miner's Statute, which guaranteed miners high indexed wages and pensions, a variety of benefits, and protection from abusive treatment by their superiors; in addition, miners' silicosis—a much greater problem since the introduction of jackhammers and cutting machines—was recognized for compensation as an occupational illness.

For miners in the Aubin Basin the Miner's Statute held out the promise of an end to the regional disparities in benefits and wages they had so resented during the interwar years. Historically, companies in the Aubin Basin had lagged behind other firms, even in southwestern France, in the provision of social services. The Charbonnages sought to make up for the deficiencies of employers in less favored coal fields such as the Aubin Basin. In 1946 companies housed 38 percent of the personnel at Carmaux and Albi compared to only 10 percent in Aubin and Decazeville; in less than a decade the percentage in the Aubin Basin rose to 22 percent of the miners and 38 percent of the supervisors.[90] On the issue of wages the national CGT federation led the fight for equal treatment of miners in all basins. In June 1947 the Decazeville CGT union council congratulated its northern comrades for opposing separate settlements by basin in the first movement of protest against the nationalized mines: "This proves that syndicalism has taken a great step, for, it must be said, the large basins have always wanted supremacy over the small basins in terms of wages. Now, however, they are supporters of equality."[91]

Nationalization of the mines raised the issue of the miners' place in French society. After the Liberation the Communist party and the CGT urged miners to assume leadership in a battle of all workers to raise production in order to defeat the Nazis and then to rebuild France.[92] This was a major element in the Communists' effort to secure their position in the government and obtain for their working-class constituency a strong voice in shaping the political economy of postwar France. The Coal Battle, like the illegal union during the Occupation, defined production in political terms. By promoting production in the national interest, the CGT showed coal miners to be integral members of French society, rather than the marginal, if essential, producers of the era before nationalization. The issue of the intensity of work was no longer limited to the hermetic world of the mines, but was to be understood as a national social issue. The Houillères du Bassin d'Aquitaine captured this aspect of nationalization in summarizing its first full year of operations, 1947: while noting a decline in productivity with respect to the prewar period, it concluded that "the activity of the underground personnel remains quite probably superior to that of the average Frenchmen."[93] It was no longer just as miners, but as Frenchmen as well, that miners would analyze the justice of their cause.

The Coal Battle placed the union in the unaccustomed role of promoting production. It put political priority over the miners' long-standing craft-based demand to control the pace of their work. Minister of Industrial Production Paul and Minister of the Mines Auguste Lecœur, both Communists and CGT militants, attempted to generate support for the Coal Battle among miners by appointing union leaders to key administrative posts in nationalized industry. When increased wages and return of the eight-hour day failed to boost production enough, union leaders turned to exhorting workers.[94] In a celebrated speech at Waziers, Communist party leader Maurice Thorez told miners that "to produce coal is the highest form of class consciousness." Party writers transformed the rebel of *Germinal* into another model proletarian, the heroic producer.[95] A Communist mine-safety delegate at Decazeville explained that a union member "was disciplined, respected the hours of work, accomplished his task correctly and observed respectful relations with management." He did not take off unnecessary days for injuries.[96] "There is no need for class struggle now," he concluded early in 1945.[97] The union secretary Tournier added, "Today the class struggle does not express itself in the battle of the strike; it expresses itself in the battle of labor."[98]

The Coal Battle suggested the possibility of a new relationship between miners and their supervisors. While the CGT maintained its ideological consistency by blaming impediments to production on individual unnamed supervisors "devoted to the trusts," it created unions for engineers and supervisory personnel after the Liberation.[99] The latter union boasted 400 members by the summer of 1945 and in the fall of that year asked for the same control over hiring exercised by the miners' union.[100] More generally, the supervisors' union tried to assure that the supervisors shared in the benefits accorded the miners as part of the Coal Battle.[101] CGT unionization of supervisory personnel was the culmination of a long series of developments, beginning with reductions in discretionary authority in the nineteenth century and including the creation of independent unions in the late 1930s. A primary aim of the miners' union at the start had been to protect the position of the miner in the workplace; the same was true for the unions of supervisory personnel. As long as the CGT preached production, the goals of the miners and their supervisors could be reconciled. The miners' union accepted the dictum of Decazeville's new director that "it is necessary for the chief to exercise a firm and just command, to command with the workers and not in spite of them."[102] In April 1947 CGT union delegates from the miners' union and the *maîtrise* union gave a *vin d'honneur* for a departing CGT engineer; a few months later the miners' union announced that the *maîtrise* should not relax discipline out of fear of union intervention.[103]

The Coal Battle and the form of labor relations it fostered were a temporary phenomenon of the political economy of postwar France. The signing of accords in 1946 committing France to political and economic cooperation with the United States ended the first phase

of the battle for production.[104] Soon after, the Communist ministers
Paul and Lecœur left office. Lecœur's replacement, the Socialist Robert Lacoste, reduced CGT representation on the Charbonnages board.[105]
The rift between the Socialists and the Communists culminated in
May 1947, when the Prime Minister, Decazeville's mayor Ramadier,
expelled the Communists from the government for their opposition
to his plans to reduce inflation. This threw into doubt the strategy
of a battle for production to build a new France in which the Communists would share power. Production had never been an end in
itself for the CGT; exclusion of the Communists from state power
forced the union to rethink its position. On the other hand, many
miners began to doubt the national loyalities of the Communist
leadership. A significant minority of anti-Communist workers in
Decazeville defected from the CGT to the newly created dissident
Force Ouvrière (FO), which was particularly strong among surface
workers.[106] In elections for the board of the mutual aid fund in the
summer of 1947 the CGT received just over 60 percent of the votes;
the FO and the CFTC shared the rest.[107]

While the CGT's subservience to the Communists split the miners' union, the CGT's second thoughts about promoting production
threatened the basis of its support among the supervisory personnel.
The day after the CGT's miners' unions approved a strike in November 1947 over the firing of a union leader who had been an
administrator in the northern coal basin, the CGT engineers in the
Basin voted to call on the miners to reconsider their decision, la-
beling it "an action undertaken prematurely that risks provoking a
real catastrophe for the chemical and metallurgical establishments"
in Decazeville. The engineers posted their resolution at the pit heads.[108]
The CGT supervisors voted overwhelmingly against the strike and
split after it ended.[109]

The brief strike in November 1947 was a prelude to the lengthy
and bitter nationwide miners' strike of the following year. The CGT,
FO, and CFTC in the Basin launched the strike together on 4 October
1948 in protest against Lacoste's plan to reduce labor costs through
layoffs, changes in the Miner's Statute, and restrictions on miners'
wages and benefits. The three unions opposed the government's
policy, which they viewed as an effort to stem the inflationary cycle
on the backs of the miners, but disagreed sharply over tactics. The
CGT took the most radical stance. It went beyond its partners'
emphasis on the bread-and-butter demands to draw connections between the strike and the miners' role in fighting an unjust regime

during the Resistance.[110] A national CGT decision to refuse to assure safety in the mines and to confront troops sent to the coalfields alienated not only the FO and the CFTC, but members of the local CGT as well.[111] For many miners this decision was the ultimate politicization—and abandonment—of an important element of a craft ideology built around the miner's relationship to his work. The CGT in the Aubin Basin even worked out an agreement to provide safety crews, but had to renege a few days later when the national federation explained that this was not a matter for local unions to decide.[112] State police occupied the pitheads.

The strike, and the decision to neglect safety measures in particular, severely strained relations between the CGT miners' union and the already weakened CGT supervisors' and engineers' unions. While 85 percent of the workers had favored calling the strike, only 59 percent of the supervisory and office staff, and 38 percent of the engineers had supported the decision.[113] On 31 October underground supervisors from all unions met and voted to accept the government's call to work in areas where fires had broken out. Although the CGT miners' union agreed privately to allow the necessary supervisors to enter the mines to carry out this work, it publicly condemned them.[114] Support for the strike among the supervisors dissipated when large numbers of miners began returning to work in early November. On 8 November Louis Marty, head of the CGT supervisors' union, announced that only twenty men were still on strike and that they had decided to return to work together. He explained that during the strike he had had a very difficult time convincing members to stay in the union and that the CGT should recognize that a five-week strike of the supervisors was an unprecedented accomplishment. The national union was unmoved however, and ordered Marty to go back out on strike, even if he was alone.[115]

The strike ended in defeat on 28 November. Unions in the Aubin Basin, like those throughout France, had launched the strike for reasons stemming from both the international politics of the Cold War and their declining position in the French economy. Worsening relations between the Soviets and the West prompted the CGT to stop supporting the national government, while miners, freed from the CGT's Coal Battle, attacked the disproportionate sacrifices demanded of them by the national policy of economic reconstruction. The violence and bitterness of the strike of 1948 not only hardened the splits in the labor movement and significantly reduced union membership, but also broke the brief alliance within the CGT of miners and supervisory personnel.

In retrospect, miners across the nation considered the defeat in 1948 the beginning of their decline from their brief tenure as France's model workers. All nationalized industries experienced a breach between organized labor and management, but in no sector was it deeper than in mining. A study of one mining community in the Pas-de-Calais concluded that "the strikes of 1947 and especially 1948 put an end to the great illusion of national integration, under the leadership of a worker and miner *avant-garde,* with an unprecedented brutality."[116] "After 1948," reported sociologists who spoke with miners in the Aubin Basin and other southern coal fields a decade after, "the miners felt that the policies of the Charbonnages de France, its fundamental orientation, was escaping them."[117] "Even if they recognize the benefits, they do not give a lot of importance to a nationalization which did not bring them collectively, and not just on the individual level, a permanent social change."[118]

After the strike the state substituted bargaining for the miners' previously guaranteed high minimum wages. It revoked CGT mine-safety delegates and CGT members of the Charbonnages' board of directors for supporting the suspension of safety measures during the strike. The CGT refused to replace its representatives. The Houillères du Bassin d'Aquitaine reached the same impasse.[119] In 1953 the state changed the composition of the board of directors to reflect the new position of the coal industry in the national political economy. "Consumers" still held one-third of the seats on the board, but were redefined to include "personalities designated for their competence in industrial and financial matters." The largest coal importer and a former director of the Blanzy mines were among those chosen. The president of the board was in the future to be appointed by the state rather than elected by the board. Finally, the government appointed commissioners to the board and the basins and empowered them with a limited veto and with the job of overseeing the mines' finances.[120] Taken together, these measures marked a reversal in the state institutionalization of miners' power which had begun before the turn of the century with the creation of mine-safety delegates and the reform of mutual aid funds, and had culminated in the initial administrative structure of the nationalized mines. This change was the prelude to a new generation of conflicts between miners and the state.

The Coal Battle of the postwar years has often been portrayed by critics of the CGT and the Communist party as a betrayal of the workers' true interests. Miners clearly resented the extra labor demanded of them. The productionist ideology had a profound appeal to workers throughout France, however, and especially to miners in a marginal economic area like the Aubin Basin. It lauded labor rather than profit, and suggested that the issue of production could erase regional disparities in the treatment of miners and serve as the basis of an alliance of all the producers in the mine, from the helper to the engineer. Furthermore, by identifying the international trusts as the enemy, the Coal Battle made the miner the most loyal of Frenchmen. The Cold War and the strike of 1948 destroyed the basis of the Coal Battle, but not the miners' faith in the value of their work which the Battle had celebrated.

Before 1914 Comambault had innovated in a number of areas of production at Decazeville. It built steelworks, imported foreign workers, placed new emphasis on the training of supervisors, introduced a degree of specialization into underground mining, and expanded the open-pit mines. The decision to close the steelworks encouraged the firm to pursue the other strategies vigorously between the wars. In coalfields throughout France rationalization of the miners' trade undercut artisanal elements of mining, and helped create conditions for the massive influx of foreigners into the underground mines. These developments generated the need for a national syndical response.

The CGT and the CGTU proposed radically different strategies for workers in the Aubin Basin. The *confédérés* elaborated the prewar approach of trying to negotiate with employers while depending on the miners' corporation as a whole to put pressure on the state. They cooperated with Ramadier, who used his position to aid the Basin's troubled coal industry. As only the CGT was recognized by the companies and the state as a reasonable interlocutor, it acted as an intermediary for workers in their dealings with officials inside and outside of the company. On the national level, the *confédérés* participated in the loose bargaining structure implemented after the war. They strove to win the same wages for miners in the Aubin Basin as those allotted miners elsewhere in France. However, the kind of national labor solidarity required to achieve parity in the treatment of all miners proved frustratingly difficult for the *confédérés* to achieve in the competitive coal market of the interwar period.

The CGTU vehemently rejected this reformism which, it felt, had been proved bankrupt by the experiences of the war and the immediate postwar period. Rather than seek concessions from the republican state, the *unitaires* pursued tactics which aimed to transcend the particular economic situation of the Aubin Basin. Loyal to the Communist party and to the Soviet Union, its partisans brought an internationalization of the labor movement to the Basin, and devoted more efforts than the *confédérés* to criticizing changes in the labor process and to organizing immigrant workers. The debilitating schism in French labor ended in 1935 with the unification of the two national federations. For the miners of the Aubin Basin, the Popular Front epitomized the benefits of participation in national political and syndical movements: although they did not strike in the spring of 1936, they received the wage increases given miners across the country.

The triumph of the Popular Front was short-lived. Even before the outbreak of war the state used the new position it had assumed in industrial relations to try to make the reluctant unions take on some responsibility for the productivity of their members. The repression of the Communist party in 1939 and the defeat of France in 1940 raised more sharply the issue of unions' relationship to the state. A legal miners' union in the Aubin Basin took advantage of the Vichy regime's control of the coal industry to bargain for wage and rationing concessions for miners. In 1943 an illegal union, with ties to the legal union, came into existence. It opposed the Vichy state's organization of the French economy to aid the Germans, and participated actively in the extensive Resistance efforts to disrupt industry in the Aubin Basin.

Under Vichy mining enterprises, including Comambault, had sought to use the social climate created by the Occupation to rationalize operations and to create a new labor force. These firms were swept away with the requisition and subsequent nationalization of the mines that followed the collapse of the Vichy regime. Within the new political economy of the post-Liberation period, the CGT, following the Communists' lead, turned from the rhetoric of the Resistance to that of the "battle" for coal production to win the war and to rebuild France. The years 1944–1948 saw the miners emerge from the isolation of their mining towns to become the national industrial heroes of France. This exceptional situation was the product of the particular constellation of politics and economics of the early years of the Fourth Republic, with the state willing to make generous concessions to miners to encourage production, and the

Communists eager to devote themselves to the reconstruction of a France in which they would play a major role. This era ended definitively with an epic strike in the fall of 1948, brought on by the Cold War and a shift in national economic policy.

Nationalization increased the distance between the centralized management in Paris and employees in the mines of Decazeville. No longer tied to a private firm, many among the managerial personnel acted in the spirit of the Liberation and the Coal Battle by unionizing in cooperation with rather than against the miners' union, as they had done in the aftermath of the Popular Front. However, this did not lead to a rebirth of the affective ties that the exercise of discretionary powers had created between supervisors and their subordinates in the early years of the mining industry. For the first time, the supervisory personnel clearly looked to their corporate interests rather than solely to the goals of the central management. The development among supervisory personnel of an independent point of view became an important factor in the coming battle over the future of the coal industry in the Aubin Basin.

# 8. The Coal Miners' Battle

In the two decades after 1948 France underwent an unprecedented period of demographic growth and social and economic development: a new French Revolution for some observers. These changes, accompanied by the trauma of decolonization, forced the French people to make difficult decisions about the future of their country. The congeries of Socialists and republicans who governed the Fourth Republic failed the challenge. In 1958 a military coup in Algeria brought down the Fourth Republic and created the conditions for Charles de Gaulle to shape a Fifth Republic more to his liking. De Gaulle capitalized on his prestige as leader of the Free French in World War II and as embodiment of a certain idea of France to forge a new identity for the nation. Opposition to Gaullism failed to heal splits in the French left. The Communist party—the leading organization on the left—continued to operate in isolation; the union movement remained divided along political and confessional lines.

Not all the French shared equally in the fruits of the new revolution. Shopkeepers and small farmers had rallied behind Pierre Poujade's anti-tax campaign in the mid-fifties. In the early years of the Fifth Republic, large-scale agriculture and business prospered; labor and economically marginal areas like the Aubin Basin were the clear losers. Periods of depression were, of course, not new to workers in the Basin. For the first time since the Second Empire, however, Decazeville's woes were not the result of a national and international depression, as in the 1880s and the 1930s. On the contrary, they were a by-product of French economic growth.

## The Coal Industry

After the Coal Battle and the strike of 1948, sociologists evaluating the effects on workers of the dramatic economic and technological changes taking place in France gave a new gloss to Communist idealizations of the heroic miner. Much of their research was elicited by state planners who saw miners as a hindrance to building an economically progressive and socially mobile France, and wanted to know what to do about them.[1] Through interviews in the mid-fifties with underground miners and other groups of workers, Alain Touraine developed an influential sociohistorical model of class consciousness based on workers' attitudes to their work. It paired miners with construction workers as holdovers from earlier economic structures. While construction workers thought positively of their trade as the forerunner of the modern profession, miners envisaged their work negatively, in what Touraine considered the increasingly outdated discourse of productivity. In their responses to question after question miners showed themselves to be the most isolated and the most "proletarian" of workers. Touraine concluded that miners' relative isolation from society made them more work-defined than class conscious. Their conception of their work in terms of the continual demands made for greater productivity imbued them with a pessimism about the prospects for their occupation.[2] Nowhere was this truer than among the miners Touraine interviewed in the Aubin Basin and other declining southern coalfields, where an emphasis on productivity presented not only a physical and emotional strain to individual miners, but also threatened miners as a group by raising doubts about the future of their mines.

Miners' pessimism was well founded. In retrospect, the Coal Battle of the immediate postwar period appears as a transitional stage during which France sought to satisfy its immediate energy needs in order to rebuild the nation. In the late forties the Fourth Republic moved from a productionist to a more clearly productivist economic strategy. Through its industrial enterprises, including the Charbonnages, the state shaped a wage and benefits policy to limit inflation. This helped to precipitate the bitter strike of 1948. At the same time the Charbonnages began to streamline mining operations in order to limit the need for state subsidies. Between 1949 and 1955 the Charbonnages increased production from 53,048,000 tons to 57,389,000 tons, but cut the labor force in the mines by 70,000 and reduced labor costs from 75 to 60 percent of the production price.[3] The Charbonnages' decision to set the sale price of coal at the mean national production cost acted as an informal subsidy to industrial consumers, especially chemical firms which processed the coal. It crippled the long-term prospects of the coal industry, however. Such a policy forced mines with relatively high production costs, including those in the Aubin Basin, to sell at a loss, and it limited the ability of any mine to generate capital for the modernization of its installations. More important, the Charbonnages was prevented by law from moving into potentially profitable new offshoots of the coal business, as a private industrial firm would have done.[4] The restriction on the Charbonnages' ability to diversify was especially devastating at Decazeville, where the decline of chemical and metallurgical industries and other coal-consuming enterprises in the Basin raised serious doubts about the future market for the Basin's coal.[5]

A major impetus for transformation of the French coal industry was creation of the European Coal and Steel Community in 1951, which opened up France to inexpensive German coal and steel. Until World War II France's relationship to Germany had made Decazeville's location an advantage in geopolitical terms. At the end of the Third Republic, for instance, the government arranged for the transfer of a Louvroil-Montbard-Aulnoye steel tube factory from the border to Decazeville in anticipation of war with Germany. After the postwar rapprochement with Germany, state planners no longer had this incentive to decentralize industry. The new economic and political ties between France and Germany meant that distance from the German border was in fact a disadvantage.

Yet the switch to new sources of energy in France was a greater long-term threat to French mines than German coal or trade. In 1938 coal had provided 83 percent of France's energy; by 1959 this figure had fallen to 59 percent. The increased use of oil, gas, and hydro-electric power accounted for the difference. In the mid-fifties the Charbonnages projected that coal imports and exploitation of the natural gas reserves at Lacq would allow it to phase out mining operations gradually in the Aubin Basin, with closing scheduled for 1975. In anticipation, a pipeline was even built from Lacq to Decazeville; its completion in November 1961 spelled the end of the town's cokery.

## Mining in the Aubin Basin

Centralized decision-making, free from pressures by interested parties, was the basis of the Charbonnages' technocratic creed. In the first years after nationalization certain basins tried to maintain some of the freedom of action they had exercised between 1944 and 1946. However, the strikes of 1948, changes in the governing board of the Charbonnages, and formation of the European Coal and Steel Community created the conditions for the central management of the nationalized firm to impose its national strategy over individual basins.[6] In the Aubin Basin the Charbonnages invested significantly in the open-pit mines, but made fewer changes in underground mines because of the limited size and irregular nature of the Basin's coal deposits. The Charbonnages' allocation of resources accentuated existing differences between the productivity and profitability of underground pits in the Aubin Basin and mines in the Lorraine and the Nord/Pas-de-Calais.

In the 1950s the mining economy of the Aubin Basin came increasingly to depend on open-pit extraction. American power-shovels and trucks acquired under the Marshall Plan to work the consolidated open-pit mine paid off handsomely in increased productivity. Production per worker in the open-pit mines increased almost six-fold between 1946 and 1958. In 1958, 1,608 underground workers mined 558,000 tons of coal; the 153 power-shovel operators and dumptruck drivers extracted 220,000 tons, 28.3 percent of the total production.[7] Underground, the Houillères du Bassin d'Aquitaine closed down the less profitable pits of Aubin and Cransac, extended long-wall mining by groups of hewers with jackhammers, set up electric conveyor belts to reduce transportation costs, and modernized aboveground sorting and cleaning installations. Cutting machines were introduced in 1947 and 1948, but these never supplanted the use of jackhammers and explosives to extract coal.[8] In spite of this limited modernization, productivity in the underground mines of the Aubin Basin approximately doubled between 1946 and 1958, while the number of underground miners fell by almost one-half.

The Charbonnages made more dramatic changes in underground mines elsewhere by refining existing forms of long-wall mining to allow further specialization and by developing mechanized long-wall mining, in which groups of hewers used a cutting machine to attack a mine face under constant supervision. These techniques—more advanced than those used in the Aubin Basin—further reduced the ability miners had once had to regulate their own production. They fully substituted competition between specialized workers for the unity of the crew.[9] "The small crew," explained sociologists who studied this change in French mines, "is characterized not only by the small number of members, but by its functional originality as well. The rules that guide its movements are *implicit*, that is to say non-prescribed."[10] The chief miner formerly exercised a "paternal" form of authority over all operations in the particular area worked by his crew. But with the full implementation of long-wall mining the chief miner took on more supervisory functions. He directed a group of hewers or fillers in tasks clearly laid out by foremen and engineers. Researchers studying the technologically advanced mines of La Mure in the 1970s concluded that "the crews which worked under the direction of a chief, a true productivity contractor, are gone; now each miner, much more isolated, is no more than a cog in an immense machine whose operation often escapes him."[11] The introduction of mechanized coal-cutting machines made the electrician and the mechanic, more than the hewer, the crucial figures in the production process.[12] Sociologists who studied the replacement of the crew by the individual miner as the primary unit of production attributed to this change an increase in nonsyndical, nonpolitical, work-related conflicts among miners, and, less directly, a new competitiveness among their families to have the best consumer goods.[13]

The Charbonnages' decision to restrict modernization of the underground mines in the Aubin Basin permitted older modes of work organization to persist that were disappearing in other French coalfields. Researchers in the late fifties found a correlation between this situation and the attitudes of miners in the Aubin Basin, when compared to those of miners in other, more mechanized mines of southern France. Miners in the Basin were less dissatisfied with their material situation.[14] A much higher percentage of them declared that they would talk to their mine-safety delegate when they had a problem, and a much lower percentage would turn to their engineer.[15] The limited technical changes allowed elements of the miners' work culture to persist longer in the Aubin Basin than elsewhere. This enabled Decazeville's miners to mount a particularly strong defense of their livelihood and their community when these were threatened.

The miners' relationship to management in the various basins changed with the modernization of mining operations and the elaboration of a national energy policy. Technical changes brought a doubling of the number of supervisory personnel in the Aubin Basin during the first decade of nationalization, despite a decline in the size of the labor force of almost one-half. This led to some sharp confrontations, especially between the older workers and young engineers and technicians.[16] But the Miner's Statute reduced many of the antagonisms that had resulted from supervisors' exercise of discretionary powers before nationalization. Furthermore, to the extent that mechanization was introduced in French mines, engineers and master miners became less concerned with the productivity of individual miners and more with the continuous, efficient operation of the mines.[17] However, the centralization of decision-making in Paris raised a new set of problems for miners and local managers, especially as concern over the future of mining in coalfields like the Aubin Basin grew. One Decazeville underground miner described the change: "No difficulties; the engineers are quite *chics.* Yet in the past we could speak to the boss and present our point of view to him; we could discuss. Today [1956] everything is regulated, foreseen. Therefore [there is] a certain rigidity."[18] One sociologist commented that under the private companies "responsibility was clear; it could be localized. The [former] owner is perceived, in retrospect, as a remedy to the bureaucracy: he allowed a personalization of the institution and its functioning."[19] Such views were not limited to workers. A supervisor with twenty years experience in the mines explained: "In my youth there were no technocrats, but rather technicians and they were not cut off from the workers."[20] To the extent that miners in the Aubin Basin differentiated between local management and that in Paris; and that managerial personnel in the Basin perceived a divison between themselves and "technocrats" in Paris, the potential existed for cooperation between miners and supervisors against the policies of the central administration of the Charbonnages.

The 1950s saw a consolidation of the mining population in the Aubin Basin. Although the open-pit mines grew in importance, the vast majority of miners continued to work underground. In its effort to reduce the size of the labor force the Charbonnages stopped hiring adult miners in 1948 and restricted the apprenticeship program the following year.[21] As a result, miners were able to forge strong ties among themselves, unadulterated by the usual influx of new workers into the mines. The limited mechanization of mines in the Basin allowed miners to continue to develop these bonds while at work. Finally, the administrative structure of the Charbonnages created the conditions for a certain degree of cooperation between miners and supervisors, not on ideological grounds as in the postwar period, but as the result of a new division of labor and responsibility in management.

## Local Politics and the Decline of the Coal Industry

The future of the mining industry was the prime issue confronting residents of the Aubin Basin after 1948. The local population remained as dependent on mining as it had been before the war. The advantages offered miners after nationalization had attracted French workers to the mines right after the war, while stabilizing a portion of the immigrant labor which had come earlier. In the mid-fifties the proportion of the active male labor force employed in the mines remained high: Decazeville (29 percent)—but with many workers in coal-based industry; Auzits and Firmy (39 percent); Aubin (43 percent); and Cransac (63 percent); the mine labor force was 23 percent foreign-born (17 percent Spanish), but 70 percent of these immigrant workers were naturalized French citizens.[22]

All facets of mining operations, and therefore the foundation of Decazeville's economic life, were clearly controlled from Paris. In such an environment the town's political life centered on the debate over national economic policy. During the Fourth Republic Communists and Socialists in Decazeville took opposing positions on the national and international economic developments that threatened the future of mining in the Aubin Basin. The conflict was especially bitter because Ramadier had presided over the national government that ousted the Communists in 1947. Municipal council meetings often erupted into heated shouting matches between Mayor Ramadier's Socialists and the Communist minority.[23] The seriousness of the situation in the Aubin Coal Basin accentuated differences in the national economic policies of the two parties. The Communists argued that European trade organizations benefited only state monopoly capitalism and multinational corporations and would hasten divestment of private and public firms in areas like the Aubin Basin. They contended that the policies pursued by the Fourth Republic were leading to the impoverishment of the French working class. The imminent decline of industry in Decazeville seemed to prove their point. Communists in Decazeville sought to rally the town's residents in support of a national economic strategy that responded to the needs of French workers rather than to the interests of capitalist investors.

Ramadier, never a Marxist, rejected the Communist economic analysis. Following his leadership, Decazeville's Socialists embraced a strategy based on national industrial planning, a mixed economy in which the private sector played a leading role, and greater European economic cooperation. In fact, Prime Minister Pierre Mendès-France named Ramadier the French head of the European Coal and Steel Community in 1954 (although Mendès-France's successor rescinded the appointment before Ramadier could assume office). Far from repudiating political and economic cooperation with the United States and the Western European democracies, Ramadier taunted the Communists that one of Decazeville's best hopes for the future was as a potential armaments manufacturing center beyond the lines of defense in the event of a Soviet attack.[24]

Ramadier and his followers had difficulty convincing workers in Decazeville that they would have to learn to live with the economic changes that threatened their town. In 1953 he opposed the Communists' plans to modernize Decazeville's outmoded Usine Claude, a fertilizer factory that had been built after World War I and was a major customer for the town's ailing cokery; it was trying "to make something work that could not work . . . We are dying at Decazeville because we want to cling with a death grip to old machines and old methods. We have twenty-five years of coal before us. If we do not decide to abandon these old machines we will continue to live in slow motion. We risk not going as far as [we could with] the resources nature has provided us."[25] Ramadier bluntly informed the town that not enough industry would locate in the Basin to absorb workers laid off at the mines or to provide jobs for the Basin's youth. His answer was migration to more prosperous regions. Indeed, he personally arranged for thirty-six of the workers laid off at the Usine Claude to be transferred to a more modern factory in the Lorraine.

For most of the townspeople however, Ramadier was not primarily a Cassandra, but the next in a line of local leaders who had fought in Paris for Decazeville's interests in the tradition of Decazes and Deseilligny. Although Ramadier had little luck in bringing new industry—in particular the new steel plant he favored—to Decazeville, he exercised his political power to keep the Basin's mines economically viable for as long as possible. As Minister of Finance Ramadier exerted his influence to have Marshall Plan funds used for construction of a coal-burning thermal power plant in nearby Penchot. This provided a reliable and profitable market for a good portion of the less marketable coal extracted in the Basin.[26]

Despite such palliatives, the Charbonnages pursued its plan of incrementally reducing production and the size of the labor force in the Aubin Basin. This was traumatic for residents of the Basin because it appeared to contradict the spirit, if not the letter, of the Miner's Statute, as well as the Charbonnages' recent efforts to build up Decazeville's infrastructure. In the early fifties the Charbonnages launched a program to transfer young miners to other coal basins. While this measure—like the previous restrictions on hiring and apprenticeship—increased the cohesiveness of the mining population that remained, it further skewed the age distribution of the mining population in favor of older, less productive miners. In October 1959 the average age of an employee of the Charbonnages in the Basin was forty; the average underground miner was thirty-eight. A survey taken in 1960 revealed that almost half of the miners had already suffered some partially disabling injury that not only affected their productivity, but severely restricted their chances of gaining employment outside of the mines.[27]

The transfer of miners out of the Aubin Basin, which accompanied the closing of pits in the Basin during the 1950s, presented a clear threat to the future of Decazeville. Although the Socialists, the FO, and the CFTC supported the transfers, the Communists and the CGT rallied the first popular opposition to deindustrialization of the Basin around this issue.[28] In 1953 the stockpile of unsold coal in the Basin reached 116,000 tons, and the following year the mines were closed four working days per month to reduce losses. Late that year, the Charbonnages, following a program involving several declining southern coal basins, ordered the transfer of 176 North African and immigrant miners from the Aubin Basin to understaffed mines in the Lorraine. While this operation allowed miners to work toward their pension and to continue to benefit from the other provisions of the Miner's Statute, it raised an outcry from local syndicalist, political, and religious leaders. The transfer revealed for the first time to miners in the Basin what power the Charbonnages—as opposed to the Houillères du Bassin d'Aquitaine—had over their mines:

> To the authoritarian character of these measures was added the
> fact that the transfer may have taken on for the miners the

aspect of a measure of expulsion from the enterprise. In effect, each basin is organized as a unit and the miners do not see its direct dependence on a single enterprise covering all of France. The centralizing intervention appeared to contradict the autonomous structure of the basin.[29]

The CGT accused the Charbonnages of purposely selecting a northern director to carry out the dismantling of the mining industry in the Aubin Basin.[30]

In response to protests in the Basin and in other southern coalfields, the Charbonnages, in cooperation with the European Coal and Steel Community, worked out a plan of compensations for miners who voluntarily transferred to the Lorraine. In 1954–55 about fifty miners from the Aubin Basin, the majority single and of foreign ancestry, selected this option. Although many learned to adapt to their new surroundings, the program as a whole received a bad name in the Aubin Basin.[31] Miners from the Basin had difficulty adjusting to the mores of the Lorraine and responded by drawing on their national and regional identity. The use in the mines of German and of Lorraine dialects resembling German encouraged comparisons of transfers with "deportations" during the war. "The southerners," observers remarked, "reacted like a national minority frustrated in the use of its language."[32]

The transfer of workers from the mines of southern and central France to the Lorraine was the one large-scale resettlement of labor attempted in France during the 1950s. Its failure profoundly discouraged national economic planners, convincing them that such efforts would face the stiff resistance of workers who demanded a local solution to the economic problems of their region.[33] The European Coal and Steel Community then hired J. F. Gravier, famous for having identified France's economic "desert" after World War II, to analyze the situation.[34] Gravier argued that the Basin should not build its future around coal or heavy industry, or even around Decazeville and Aubin. The only hope for the area was to forsake these decaying urban centers. Efforts should be devoted instead to attracting light industry to the semirural environs and to finding jobs for miners in the nearby prosperous towns of Villefranche-de-Rouergue and Rodez.[35] Such a scenario had little appeal to miners in the Aubin Basin.

Although Belgium and Germany had already begun to close marginal mines in the 1950s, similar plans in France had been kept in check during the Fourth Republic by the moderating influence of parliamentary politics. The establishment of the Fifth Republic in 1958 tipped the scale in favor of the centralizing, modernizing, and authoritarian aspects of economic planning in France. It was no longer likely that an individual politician—even a Ramadier—would be able to use his position as deputy to help a community like Decazeville weather its economic crisis. "As political decisions have shifted in the modern welfare state from parliamentary arenas of power into technocratic arenas," Suzanne Berger contends, "the backward regions have lost much of their power to protect themselves against the effects of decisions made solely on the basis of profitability."[36] Elimination of the left from office and the redistribution of power in the state administration of the Fifth Republic placed Decazeville in a position analogous to Brittany and other disinherited parts of France.

De Gaulle's triumph reinforced the effects of a contemporaneous transformation of political life in the Basin. Although religious observance had long been lax—only 6 percent of all mine employees and only 1 percent of the underground miners attended mass regularly[37]—Decazeville and the rest of France saw the development of a politically active and committed Catholic laity in the 1950s. This orientation was strongest in the growing ranks of the supervisory personnel of Decazeville's mines. Unlike the Socialists, these Catholic *militants* were not adverse to cooperating with the Communists to achieve specific goals. All through his career Ramadier had defended an anticlerical Radical/Socialist alliance. His lifelong opposition to state aid for parochial schools alienated Catholics in the Basin. In the elections for deputy in 1958, and a year later for the town council, the Catholic Mouvement Républicain Populaire worked tacitly with the Communists and succeeded in ousting Ramadier. However, neither party could rally sufficient support to win control of Decazeville town hall. All across France the Algerian War and the inglorious end of the Fourth Republic had crippled the Socialist party and created the conditions for new alternatives on the French left. The Parti Socialiste Unifié attracted bright young leftists like Serge Mallet, and discontented Socialists, including Ramadier's long-time ally and successor as mayor of Decazeville, René Rouquette. Ramadier's defeat was a turning point in the history of the Basin, which has never again supplied the deputy for the district. The more prosperous and conservative Villefranche-de-Rouergue to the south has taken its place as the political center of the area. This further diminished the political weight that the Basin could muster in Paris.

Political divisions in Decazeville helped make unions rather than political parties the most effective force in organizing the defense of the community in the early years of the Fifth Republic.[38] The grave outlook for industry at Decazeville prompted the Catholic CFTC and the Communist CGT, representing the forces which had just upset the town's political balance, to form an Intersyndical Committee in 1959–60 to defend the miners' interests. Despite the bitter legacy of 1948, the FO and the supervisors' Confédération Générale des Cadres joined the Committee.[39] The threat to the mines produced a rapprochement between competing workers' unions and between workers and their supervisors. While the CGT remained the dominant union in the Basin, especially among the underground miners, it did not force the Communist analysis of the Basin's difficulties on its partners in order to maintain the unity of the Intersyndical Committee.[40] In fact, one bond uniting the majority on the Committee was a shared Catholic discourse. Each organization on the Committee had two delegates; aside from the two CGT Communists, of the remaining six, four were active in Catholic lay organizations and a fifth was a practicing Catholic.[41]

The prime aim of Gaullist economic policy was to open up France to the world market. To improve the competitiveness of French industry, the government looked for ways to reduce energy costs. Oil companies, investors in shipping to bring inexpensive American coal to French ports, and metallurgical firms which planned to use this coal argued for a reduction in French coal production.[42] In 1960 the Charbonnages unveiled a nationwide program to reduce coal production, repudiating earlier plans for the gradual reduction of production in the Aubin Basin. All underground pits in the Basin were to close by 1965, leaving only the open-pit mine in operation.[43] The labor force in the Basin's mines would drop from 2,747 miners and supervisory personnel in 1959 to 350 in 1965; less than 30 percent of the almost 2,400 employees to be laid off would by 1965 be eligible to receive a full pension. The great majority of miners would receive reduced retirement benefits, complete their mining careers elsewhere, or work in new private sector light industries set up in the area with financial assistance from the Charbonnages.

In its efforts to develop public support for the mine closings, the government lost no opportunity to evoke now anachronistic *Germinal*-like conditions that had once won the miners the special solicitude of the state.[44] The Minister of Industry Jean-Marcel Jean-neney rejected claims that after years of service miners deserved better treatment. He justified the immediate termination of the un-profitable mines of the Aubin Basin as a humanitarian act of national solidarity: "It would be neither reasonable nor humane to make men continue to carry out, at several hundred meters underground, the rough and often dangerous work of the mine to produce a fuel which is practically useless and can, in any case, be easily replaced by others which cost French miners less effort."[45]

The miners rejected the state's plan as an abrogation of their right to live where they had made their home and to work until they had earned a full pension. They did not seek to protect an investment in property—only one in five owned the house in which he lived—but an investment in a way of life. More than half of the miners under the age of forty-five—and therefore those most affected—were sons of miners, had married daughters of miners, and had been born in the commune in which they lived. Only 12 percent of the total labor force in the Basin's mines were sons of peasants (compared to 29 percent in the Tarn). "When you move a man like me," explained one miner, "you take everything he has away from him."[46] The miners' immediate response to the new coal plan was to organize a town-wide general strike of workers and shopkeepers, a *ville morte*, to show what would happen to Decazeville were the mines to be closed.

## The Strike of 1961–62

In November 1961 the Charbonnages began to lay off workers in preparation for closing the underground mines. It offered them a sum amounting to three month's salary and a guarantee that for their first two years in new jobs their wages would be supplemented to reach 90 percent of the pay they received in the mines. The Intersyndical Committee responded with an amalgam of demands: the CGT's call for the underground mines to stay open and for a new coal-burning power plant to be built; the CFTC's demand for social justice; and the Socialist-inspired FO's desire to see Decaze-ville develop a new economic foundation.[47] Although the CGT fought hard to undercut the other unions by arguing that their acceptance of industrial conversion and the European Coal and Steel Com-munity limited their ability to support the miners, the Intersyndical Committee maintained its unity through the strike.[48] The Committee claimed that underground mining was still viable in the Basin and that pits should remain in operation according to the schedule set by the Charbonnages in the mid-fifties. If the Charbonnages refused, miners should receive either the immediate allocation of their pension, such as was given retiring members of the state police (CRS), or the continuance of their social security plan, whatever a miner might do after being dismissed. This plan gave miners more comprehensive medical benefits and a higher pension than the general population received, and also provided access to special scholarships for their children. Such concessions would make up for the loss of rights to coal, housing, and other perquisites accorded a miner with more than fifteen years service who ended his career in the mines; more generally, they would compensate for the long-term effects of years in the mines on his health.

Finally, the Committee voiced a more general grievance about the future of the Basin. It feared that firms with government subsidies to set up factories in the Basin would leave or go bankrupt when the aid was withdrawn, or, at best, pay retrained miners at minimum wage once the state stopped supplementing wages.[49] The troubled economic history of industry at Decazeville had left an infrastructure with little appeal to outside investors: in the late 1950s half of the private housing dated from before the founding of the Third Republic; only one-fifth of the town's dwellings had running water, and only one-tenth had indoor toilets.[50] The miners felt that the job of rebuilding the region should not be left to private enterprise, but should be the responsibility of the Houillères du Bassin d'Aquitaine. The Charbonnages' obligations to individuals extended to the mining community as well.

In making these demands Decazeville miners were not acting from some romantic love of their trade. The elements of their craft the miners defended were the rights, legal and customary, which they had acquired over the past century, and particularly since nationalization of the mines. Special compensation for the difficulties of the miners' work was as much a part of the miners' self-identity as the physical aspects of the job itself. The demand that the Charbonnages take charge of assuring the economic future of the Basin had roots in the earlier hiring systems in the mines and in the relatively secure employment the industrial towns had offered.

On 19 December 1961 the miners of Decazeville went on strike to protest the layoffs announced the previous month. The Charbonnages found the Intersyndical Committee's demands unacceptable and refused to negotiate. To dramatize their struggle, the miners and their supervisors spent the duration of the strike at their workplaces—the underground pits, the open-pit mine, and the offices.[51] The miners—who had generally worked together for a dozen years or more—willingly undertook this dramatic form of solidarity to save their jobs and their community. Local managerial personnel supported the strike. The self-legitimating ideology of the engineers made them fundamentally devoted to preservation of the means of production, just as in 1948 it made them vehemently oppose the strikers' refusal to staff the safety crews. This time the engineers sided with the miners rather than with the planners in Paris, whose interests they saw as primarily financial rather than technical. In the late 1930s engineers at Decazeville had resented the introduction of timekeeping as an invasion of their prerogatives; a quarter of a century later they expressed similar doubts about what Paris planners had to say concerning the possibilities for future development of mines in the Basin. The engineers' union agreed with the miners' projection of the amount of coal which could be profitably mined in the Basin in 1965, not with that of the Charbonnages.[52] A representative of the managerial personnel on the Intersyndical Committee summed up the alliance: "When the shed burns, we don't have to know if some people wear a tie."[53]

The popular enemy were not local supervisors, but Parisian "technocrats"—decision-makers who did not take human factors into account. Although the CGT would have felt more comfortable speaking of exploitation by international capitalism, even it joined the chorus. A local CGT leader told a huge crowd of perhaps 20,000 at the beginning of the strike that technocrats "have a slide-rule in place of a heart."[54] And the Intersyndical Committee announced that in staging a sit-in strike the miners "wanted to cut themselves off voluntarily from the world without soul and without ideals that is called technocracy."[55] Roger Joulie, CGT representative on the Intersyndical Committee, suggested that the technocrats' actions were at once anachronistic and anti-French: "in the twentieth century, in the era of technical progress, in the era of voyages in space and of rockets to the moon, there is in France, in the country that everyone in the world wants as a second homeland, a government which dares to let men rot in their mine galleries."[56] The repeated attacks on technocracy reflected a rejection of explicitly political discourse that characterized other early Fifth Republic social protests like those of Breton farmers. After the ignominious collapse of the Fourth Republic, political rhetoric no longer seemed capable of expressing truly popular movements. Although the issues involved in the Decazeville strike were evidently political, "the word 'politics,' wrote one observer, "is unacceptable to the mass, which finds itself, in part thanks to that [rejection], united, conscious, and combative."[57]

The general thrust of the strikers' attack on technocracy struck a receptive chord in the Church, which had long ago identified rootlessness and alienation as major problems of modern society and had promoted a greater responsibility of employers to their employees as one solution. The Catholic hierarchy wholeheartedly endorsed the miners' position.[58] Although this made the CGT queasy, the predominantly Catholic Intersyndical Committee drew on religious discourse to counter the tenets of technocracy. In a prepared statement given to the press on 3 January 1962, the Committee asked government officials, "Have you made your examination of conscience? Have you spoken with the miners?"[59] The same religious sensibility informed the Committee's anticapitalist celebration of coal production: "And who will claim that in our country and in the world there is too much energy? In the world there are hundreds of millions of human beings who lack energy, who suffer from the cold and the dark . . . And when one knows the state of misery and of suffering which exists in a whole range of countries of Africa, Asia and of Latin America, does one have the right to say that there is no market for our coal?"[60]

The strikers went to great lengths to communicate to other Frenchmen the threat that the closing of the mines represented for their community, hoping that they would empathize and could help the miners to force the Charbonnages to open substantive discussions. In a strike like that at the mines of the Aubin Basin—just one small part of a large nationalized enterprise—the strikers could only exert political, rather than financial, pressure on the state. That the state could easily absorb the losses involved in the strike was painfully clear: Jeanneney claimed that the Charbonnages saved half a million francs each month of the strike.[61]

Unable to sway the Charbonnages by depriving it of their services, the strikers brought popular pressure to bear on the state by depriving themselves. They sought to make their condition, not that of the mines, the central issue. The absence of a clearly defined enemy in the Basin encouraged this strategy; only by forcing the state to abandon its aloofness could the workers triumph. In dramatic fashion the strikers turned the most basic condition of their occupa-tion—the need to work in the cramped underground mines and freezing open pits—against themselves. For the first ten days of the strike the underground miners refused to surface. Only on the in-sistence of the attending physicians did they agree to come up every forty-eight hours, to shower, to smoke, and to breathe fresh air. To add to their pain and sacrifice, the miners refrained from seeing their families during the strike. They did so in spite—or, it could be said, because—of the closeness of family ties in the area.[62] The lengthy sit-in strike was, by its very nature, a familial form of protest: min-ers' wives and children took a far more active role in organizing the strike of 1961–62 than any previous strike.[63] The strikers themselves were fighting as much to give their children a future in the area as to win personal benefits. Early in the strike the miners celebrated Christmas in the pits away from their families in an emotional gesture which they hoped would build nationwide public sympathy for their cause.

At the end of January 250 strikers volunteered to embark on a hunger strike to step up pressure on the Charbonnages to negotiate. Doctors selected twenty miners and ten alternates. The men, weak-ened by more than one month underground as well as by ailments resulting from years of mining, pursued the hunger strike heroically. Several refused to break their fast despite doctors' warnings: one was taken to the hospital comatose. Well before Marx it had been traditional to read the effects of capitalist industrial labor in the worker's body. By subjecting themselves to debilitating sit-in and hunger strikes, the miners of Decazeville asked the French people to see in their bodies the effects of deindustrialization.

To make their case effectively, the miners required the full nature of their suffering and the reasons for it to reach a wide audience. In a broadside prepared for the fifty-sixth day of the strike, the miners wrote that by sleeping on hay in the dark, humid galleries, deprived of their families, they "desired to show France and the world that their abnegation was the symbol of the sacrifice that would prepare a better future for all."[64] But state control of radio and television and the often unsympathetic coverage in national magazines and newspapers frustrated the strikers and prompted the only "violent" episode of the strike.[65] A group of teen-agers, many of them sons of strikers, collected copies of an issue of *Paris-Match* that denigrated the strike and burned them in a large bonfire. (A photographer for the magazine had taken pictures of the family of one of the strikers on New Year's Eve, with a bottle of champagne as a prop beside the wife, thus giving the impression that she was celebrating rather than suffering.) This angry gesture was not aimed at persons or even primarily against property: it was directed at false media images of the town's struggle.

Postwar economic modernization threatened not only the coal industry, but also the regional economics of large parts of France. Disparities between the prosperous north and east and the poorer south and west grew. Stanley Hoffmann spoke of the social and political divisions of the "stalemate society" of the Third Republic giving way to a "new fragmentation based on geographic unevenness."[66] The deindustrialization of the Aubin Coal Basin, one of the few centers of heavy industry in southwestern France, mirrored the economic decline of other sectors in the region. The number of farms in Aveyron fell by a quarter in the decade after 1953.[67] (In fact, it was from their appraisal of the Decazeville strike that agricultural syndicalists came up with the idea of a compensation annuity for peasants forced off their farms.)[68] The regional implications of the strike raised crucial strategic issues for the strikers. The majority CGT naturally favored pursuing the traditional tactic of extending the strike to its strongholds in other coal basins. But the CFTC opposed this approach and promoted a regional strategy of cooperation with farmers and other inhabitants of southwestern France to secure state aid for the area's economy.[69] The latter tactic proved more fruitful; northern miners gave money, but showed reluctance to strike in support of their colleagues in Decazeville.

Since the end of the nineteenth century miners had waged their strikes with little external support. The miners of Decazeville were pleasantly surprised therefore to receive significant assistance from labor and other organizations in southwestern France and extensive sympathetic coverage in major regional newspapers. At the end of December 1961 all 307 mayors in Aveyron resigned to avoid dealing with the national state during the strike. Peasants blocked highways as they had seen their Breton counterparts do in recent protests over agricultural prices.[70] Residents of Aveyron staged a highly successful general strike on 9 January 1962. A few weeks later, at the height of the miners' strike, some three hundred representatives of unions and economic organizations in southwestern France met in Rodez, the capital of Aveyron, to voice their grievances against the state's economic policy in the area. A representative of the Intersyndical Committee told the gathering that the regional "day of action" which it had planned for the following week would be

> the departure point of a coming to consciousness of abandoned populations, as well as the departure point . . . for the elaboration of a regional economy assuring the development and the economic expansion of a whole region [which was] doomed [to become] what is already called a French desert. . . .
>
> It will be the merit of the 2,200 miners of the Decazeville Coal Basin to have been the catalyst in this coming to consciousness.[71]

On 26 January, strikes, work stoppages, and other forms of protest took place in the seventeen departments of southwestern France, broadly known as Occitania.

Deindustrialization helped to heal the cultural breach between Decazeville and the surrounding rural regions that industrialization and the formation of a working class had created. The strikers' frequent use of *langue d'oc* contrasted sharply with the language of the technocrats whom they opposed.[72] It reinforced the idea that the violation of the economy and the culture of their community was an element of the damage being done by the French state to the region as a whole.[73] The popular Occitan slogan "Volem viure al païs" was born of the struggles of miners in Decazeville and other southern coal basins.[74]

Yet the miners' display of regional slogans, symbols, and flags did not reveal a rejection of the French nation. Instead, the strikers drew a parallel between the state of contemporary regional culture and the future—hopeful or dire—of their community. The Occitan culture of Languedoc, Nico Kielstra remarked, "has . . . become negatively defined, not as the self-evident context of people's life which may be endangered by outside influences, but as a symbolic expression of all the wrong that has been done to the people of the region in the course of history."[75] The strikers found ideological support in regionalism because it underscored and explained their second-class status as Frenchmen. One of the hunger strikers compared the miners' position to that of the Algerian rebels, not to make a connection between the Algerians' anti-colonialism and the Decazeville miners' struggle, but to underscore the treatment which he and his comrades expected to receive as Frenchmen: "I know that we have nothing to expect from an inhuman government. But the French people prevented Ben Bella from dying of hunger in prison. I am sure that the people will not allow French workers, fighting for their just rights, to destroy their health and their future by a prolonged strike."[76] Throughout the strike, the miners of Decazeville dramatized their belief that certain "national" virtues like family, community, and work were best preserved outside of Paris.[77] The strikers elaborated the integrated national and class identity developed a generation earlier in the Resistance and Coal Battle.[78] In so doing, they implicitly contrasted their vision of France to that of Gaullism, the other great popular political tradition to come out of the war.

Shortly after the strike ended, the leader of the Decazeville CGT union explained that the movement had been "a living demonstration of the themes of the CGT on the [European Coal and Steel] Community and the Common Market."[79] While the majority of strikers accepted this explanation of their plight, they were as concerned with national identity as with international economics. Instead of posing the question of the "Americanization" of the French economy as the CGT and the Communists acting on their own would have, the Intersyndical Committee concentrated on the "Americanization" of French society implied in demands that Frenchmen be geographically mobile. Defense of the region, like defense of the means of production, was inseparable in the strike discourse from defense of an image of France at odds with the vision of the technocratic planners in Paris.

Decazeville's struggle reflected the town's particular economic situation, but the strikers' success in generating regional and national support revealed that many other Frenchmen considered Gaullist modernization policies unjust and threatening.[80] Unfortunately for Decazeville, however, France's eyes were still focused in the winter of 1961–62 on the war in Algeria and terrorist bombings at home.[81] And as the strike dragged on, lassitude developed among the local and regional groups which had strongly supported the miners earlier.[82] The strike began to "rot" and after 64 days the strikers left the mines. Even then the majority of miners refused to assent to the Intersyndical Committee's resolution to end the strike. Instead, they voted only to affirm their confidence in the Committee and left the decision to give the order to go back to work up to it.[83]

Although the Charbonnages agreed to grant higher severance pay based on the length of time a miner had worked, and to award a partial pension to miners who retired between the ages of fifty and fifty-five, it refused to concede any ground on the broader demands of keeping the underground mines open, of maintaining the miners' social security benefits, or of granting pensions on the same terms as those given the state police. The Charbonnages closed the last underground mines in the Aubin Basin in 1966. As the strikers had predicted, the industries that relocated into the Basin provided few jobs and encountered severe financial difficulties once state subsidies ran out. The Basin's isolation prevented it from following the pattern of some deindustrializing areas and turning into a source of inexpensive labor for a more prosperous nearby urban center.[84] While several hundred of the younger miners reluctantly moved to other basins to finish their careers, most of the older miners had to retire early with partial or full benefits.[85] With state aid promised after the strike, Creusot-Loire renovated Decazeville's metallurgical plant in the late 1960s, but a decade later this factory was crippled by Creusot-Loire's redeployment of its capital in the face of the worldwide steel recession.[86] Only the oil crisis of 1973, which found France dependent on petroleum for two-thirds of its energy (versus less than one-third in 1960 and less than one-sixth in 1949),[87] led the Charbonnages to postpone the projected 1975 closing date for Decazeville's open-pit mines and to consider the possibility of opening other open-pit mines in the Basin. In 1983 the Charbonnages announced that some open-pit mining would continue in the Basin until at least 1989–90.[88]

Between 1962 and 1968 the population of Decazeville declined by 12.6 percent; that of Aubin, 15.2 percent; Cransac, 20.9 percent; and Viviez 13.1 percent. The number of underground miners fell from 1,522 in 1959 to zero seven years later; the total workforce employed by the Charbonnages declined from 2,747 to 443. Yet these figures mask the true dimensions of the demographic change. Between 1962 and 1968, 26 percent of the population of the Basin left; an in-migration equivalent to 12.3 percent of the population filled some of the gap. Partly in response to the strike the state helped to create a number of new administrative jobs in Decazeville: at Electricité de France, hospitals, banks, and regional schools. Small merchants were forced to close their shops because of the departure of their worker clientele; larger businesses expanded to provide services for the surrounding rural areas. "After having been a city of miners, Decazeville is becoming more and more a center of services, of commerce and of administration."[89] With the closing of the mines at Cransac the *fumeroles* reappeared, and by 1966 a thousand *curistes* were coming to Cransac annually.[90] Neither administrative posts nor jobs serving *curistes* came close to replacing the Basin's industry. In the end the region did take on some of the administrative and tourist functions that Occitan militants feared were the fate northern France had in store for the Midi.

The strike of 1961–62 failed in its primary goals, but the emblematic nature of the town's plight made the struggle an inspiration for important regionalist and labor movements in the Fifth Republic. At the time of the Decazeville strike the Occitan cause was restricted for the most part to literati and intellectuals in Montpellier and Toulouse. They were engaged in a losing battle to preserve Occitan culture against the French linguistic juggernaut.[91] The strike at Decazeville suggested to Occitan intellectuals that their real strength lay not with the poetasters, but with the workers, peasants, and tradesmen of southwestern France. The Occitan poet Joan Bodon wrote a poem in homage to the Basin's miners that began "Los carbonièrs de La Sala, / Occitans, sens o saber" (Miners of Decazeville / Occitans without knowing it).[92] As a direct result of the strike, an important group headed by Robert Lafont seceded from the leading Occitan cultural organization, the Institut d'Etudes Occitanes, to form the Comité Occitan d'Etudes et Action. Lafont, the leading theoretician of Occitan regionalism, explained that the Decazeville strike "really ended for [Occitanists] the Félibrige [the literary society founded by the nineteenth-century Occitan writer Frédéric Mistral] and the series of ideological failures recorded by Occitanism."[93] The history of Decazeville became a prime example in the Occitanists' argument that southwestern France was the victim of "internal colonialism" by northern France. The Aubin Basin had provided raw materials for the benefit of capitalism and the French state; when its natural resources ran low, the state abandoned the population.[94] Occitan regionalists agreed with *autogestionnaires* like Serge Mallet that the centralized direction of the Charbonnages had deprived the individual basins of the autonomous leadership which "would have looked for long-term solutions allowing reconversion of the [Basin's] installations and personnel."[95] The proto- (and now post-) *gauchiste* André Gorz concurred. The lesson of Decazeville was that the Communist program of keeping "decrepit mines" open was no solution; workers would have to take the offensive in reconversion battles, promoting direct state investment in profitable sectors of the economy to create industry for disinherited regions.[96] Although Occitan intellectuals were first attracted by the strikers' *patois* slogans, their support for the miners' cause was a step away from the doomed literary perspective to an interpretation of Occitanism as the cultural expression of all those dispossessed by the central state.[97]

The Decazeville strike of 1961–62 had an even greater impact on the French labor movement than on the development of Occitan politics. In his 1962 New Year's Day speech, which coincided with the end of the second week of the strike, de Gaulle noted the precipitous drop in the number of days lost to strikes under the Fifth Republic and concluded that "quite often the strike appears useless, even anachronistic."[98] The duration of the Decazeville strike revealed a continuing combativity on the part of labor. Moreover, it was the direct forerunner of the victorious nationwide miners' strike in the spring of 1963 that signaled, in the words of George Ross, "the 'rediscovery' of social conflict as a normal occurrence in French society."[99] For de Gaulle the connection between the Decazeville strike of 1961–62 and the nationwide miners' strike of March–April 1963 was clear: in his memoirs he incorrectly explained that the Decazeville strike began in September 1962, lasted more than five months, and was nearing settlement when the miners' unions launched a nationwide strike.[100] Like the Decazeville strike, the 1963 conflict drew on cooperation among the major unions and solidarity between mining engineers and miners. And like the Decazeville miners, strikers in 1963 sought to disseminate their position widely and won significant support from the public and from the Church.[101]

The strike at Decazeville was also a prototype for a number of struggles against decisions the state made about restructuring of industry in economically depressed regions of France.[102] The coal industry has always had a special relationship with the state in France, but most French industries in economic decline eventually became wards of the state. Pit closings and factory shutdowns, which in a more laissez-faire economy would remain in the realm of the private sector, became political issues in France.[103] Some of these protests took the same form as the Decazeville strike, like the 79-day underground sit-in strike of iron-ore miners at Trieux in the Lorraine in 1963.[104] A second generation of strikes against deindustrialization began with the recession of the late 1970s. These have included major conflicts in the steel-producing towns of the Lorraine[105] and a successful year-long struggle in 1980–81 by the miners of (Alès) in the Gard to open the Ladrecht (Destivals) pit. The CGT took a more militant stand in these strikes. At Alais it consciously re-jected the strategy pursued at Decazeville and refused to subordinate its actions to those of a broader coalition of interests, arguing that more moderate groups were too willing to accept social palliatives instead of fighting to keep the mines open. In the tradition of the nineteenth-century *mine aux mineurs,* the miners of Alais even mined and sold coal to dramatize their contention that the mine was profitable. In order to develop their sense of community and to communicate their interpretation of the issues, the miners of Alais also launched a "free radio," an illegal station unlicensed by the state.[106]

The fate of such movements clearly depended on the political situation. The miners at Alais held out until the election of François Mitterand as president in the spring of 1981. In the flush of victory Mitterand's Socialist government announced that it would exploit Ladrecht. It appointed a CGT militant and member of the Bureau Politique of the Communist party to head the Charbonnages and vowed first to expand, and then more cautiously to maintain the existing level of national coal production. Such promises proved hard to keep. In February 1983 the miners of Carmaux went on strike to demand the exploitation of a new open-pit mine so that production would reach a high enough level to allow Carmaux's underground mines to remain open. Most important, the strikers demanded the hiring of at least 100 young men from the waiting list of 3,000 applicants for jobs at Carmaux. The strikers held three Charbon-nages administrators hostage for part of the strike[107] and refused to accept the Charbonnages' offer to negotiate in Saint-Etienne instead of the concerned region. After twenty-two days, and shortly before the crucial nationwide municipal elections, the Charbonnages ended the strike with major concessions to Carmaux's miners on the issues of both the open-pit mine and hiring of youths for the mines.[108] The victory was short-lived, however. As a step toward balancing the budget of the Charbonnages, the state decided soon after to close more underground mines (including Ladrecht) and to invest instead in open-pit mines which required few workers. Miners responded by joining in the protests of government civil servants against the austerity measures of the Mitterand government in the spring of 1984.[109]

During the 1950s the Charbonnages undertook only limited mod-ernization of the underground pits in the Aubin Basin in anticipation of their eventual closing. While this probably helped to foster solidarity among miners, it did little to prepare towns in the Basin for the end of the mining industry. Although Ramadier exercised his influence in government to shelter Decazeville from the full effects of the postwar economic revolution, his hope of finding a place for the town in the economy of the new France was largely thwarted. After 1958 the Fifth Republic reduced the power of deputies to influence national economic decision-making. The addition of administrative centralization to the economic modernization begun under the Fourth Republic boded ill for a peripheral economic area like the Aubin Basin. Gaullist planners prided themselves on doing what was best for France without regard for the special interests of individual groups. In this spirit the Fifth Republic moved to restructure the national economy by closing down marginal enterprises. The Aubin Basin was far from the only area to suffer, but in few places were the effects as dramatic.

Miners in the Aubin Basin responded to the Fifth Republic's decision to terminate underground mining operations with a fundamentally new kind of strike. The threat to the mines brought together the miners and the local managerial staff, once the miners' most hated foes, but now opponents of the same industrial policies. The specter of deindustrialization also bridged the gap that had developed in the nineteenth century between the industrial Aubin Basin and the surrounding rural countryside of southwestern France. In fact, the ways in which the strikers analyzed their plight and justified their position reiterated the history of Decazeville's place within the national and international economy. Strikers drew on their identity as miners and as producers, as southerners and as Frenchmen, to create a broad alliance against the policies of the Fifth Republic. The miners of Decazeville, like their predecessors who had fought the company town during the first decades of the Third Republic, became convinced that defense of their community was a defense of national and republican values. Through their strike the miners of Decazeville sought to transcend the geographical and social isolation and the productivist identity Touraine found among miners. In one of the most influential analyses of mid-twentieth century miners, the sociologists Clark Kerr and Abraham Siegel argued that miners do hard work and live in separate communities; therefore they "do not aim to be more considerate of the general community than they think the general community is of them."[110] The Decazeville strikers did not try to affront society, but to inform and involve it by developing means to make the public understand what their community was experiencing and what this meant to the French people.[111] Although the strike was unsuccessful, their struggle suggested new possibilities to those who share their insecurity as workers and as residents of dispossessed areas.

# Conclusion

After residents of the Aubin Basin rebelled against outside mine entrepreneurs in 1769, one of the king's ministers took it upon himself
to ensure that the state acted forcefully to back up the concessionaires.
First, he described Aubin and its environs as deserted wastelands.
Then, to convince the king to punish the rebels, he claimed that ten
thousand men had confronted the royal forces. "An area that puts ten
thousand men under arms," replied the king, "is not so deserted. Speak
to me no more of this affair."                          —L. C. P. Bosc, *Mémoires*

Hostile observers were quick to draw a connection between the
strike of 1961–62 and the actions of English Luddites and the *canuts*
of nineteenth-century Lyon.[1] Although the goal of these critics was
to show the backward mentality of Decazeville's miners in the face
of progress, the comparison suggests structural and ideological sim-
ilarities between the experiences of workers today and in the past.
Broadly speaking, in the last two centuries mineworkers in the Aubin
Basin have undergone three periods of proletarianization—understood as a loss of power in the economic sphere rather than a loss
of property as such. In each period a popular consensus developed
in the Basin as to the proper exercise of economic and political
power. Transformation of the population and the political economy
of industry in the basin generated new forms of this ideological
opposition to proletarianization.

In the eighteenth century peasant-miners defended a conception
of private property and community rights at odds with the idea of
royal mining concessions. Their loss of the right to organize the
extraction and the sale of coal in the early nineteenth century was
related to the withdrawal of common rights elsewhere; with the
support of the state the mine concessionaire played the role of the
capitalist landlord.

The second period of industrial development in the Aubin Basin spans from the nineteenth into the twentieth century. Firms in the Basin built their investment strategies on the relationship of the state to industry; they were particularly susceptible to changes in the national political economy. Each period of growth required formation of a labor force to staff the factories and mines. Workers who came to the Basin initially developed a community and political identity through their relationship to management. But they also created their own culture and organizations, drawing on their background, their experiences at work and in the community, and increasingly on outside political guidance and support. Over the course of the nineteenth century workers in the Basin formulated a popular consensus about their right to organize work independently of strict company supervision, to have a say in local and national government, and to spend their wages how and where they pleased. When operators attempted to compensate for a drop in profits by reducing labor costs, workers mobilized the community ties they had formed during the previous period of industrial development in defense of their position. The resolution of the conflict between labor and capital came with the appearance of a new owner—1868; 1892; (and 1944)—which took advantage of an upturn in the market to make new investments. Having reinforced its position in the local economy, the new firm instituted changes in management and the nature of the labor force. This second form of proletarianization—a loss of control over the labor process—weakened workers' social networks and led them to develop new sources of support in and out of the community.

Workers' struggles to defend their position in the workplace and the community launched the third period in the Basin's history, one in which the role of the state has been paramount. In the nineteenth century the state promoted a rationalization of all levels of mine management; in the first decades of the Third Republic it established special legislation which allowed miners to compensate in part for their loss of autonomy in the organization of work. During these same years the residents of Decazeville came to associate the struggle for the independence of their community with creation of a truly "social"—even workers'—republic in France. Their actions and those of workers across France helped convince the state to withdraw its tacit support for the company town. These developments became the basis in the twentieth century of a shift within the Basin from an ideology rooted directly in the community and the labor process, to one based on parity in the treatment of workers in different regions and on the legitimacy of benefits which had been secured through national political action. Between the wars reformist *confédéré* and radical *unitaire* strategies were aimed at securing a new relationship between labor and the state. One vision of this relationship was embodied in the nationalization of the mining industry after World War II and the Miner's Statute granted during the Coal Battle; another vision underlay the bitter strike of 1948.

The third period reached a climax in the confrontation with the state over a new form of proletarianization based on the loss of employment and the consequent decline of the community, rather than on a change in property rights or in the labor process. In the strike of 1961–62 miners in the Aubin Basin drew together the threads of their past history to rally support for their cause. At the workplace they allied with the engineers—once their enemies—against the "technocratic" decision makers. In southwestern France, miners turned their regional cultural identity from a form of opposition to managers into a means to appeal to the public for justice. On a national scale, they capitalized on the role miners had played in the Resistance and the Coal Battle to articulate a view of themselves not as pure producers enjoying special privileges—an image inherited from the Third Republic—but as an embodiment of national values threatened by international capitalism.

The importance of coal mining to the economies of industrialized nations over the past century and a half permits the chronicler of a coal town to take a comprehensive view of labor history. The first two periods in the history of industry in the Aubin Basin were marked by the cooperation of state and capital in ending preindustrial modes of production and by the emergence of new industrial communities that took shape in the context of national economic growth and local struggles over political independence and job control. These developments set the stage for a third period in which the role of the state in the economy and in labor relations increased greatly. The issues of employment security and deindustrialization which characterized much of this era were descendants of earlier conflicts over property rights, political freedom, the organization of work, and the nature of the state. Constructing a genealogy of deindustrialization helps explain strikes like that of the miners of Decazeville in 1961–62, a prototype for some of the most important recent labor disputes in Europe and the United States. These movements are of such significance because they involve workers' communities that came into existence with an industrial economy and developed their identities with the consolidation of the modern democratic state. The way their fate is decided poses a particular challenge to organized labor, governments, and the public as they seek to define their vision of the society of the future.

Appendix

Abbreviations

Primary Sources

Notes

Index

# Appendix: A Social Portrait of Industrial Workers in Nineteenth-Century Decazeville

To account for the appearance of new forms of social conflict, nineteenth-century social critics posed the question: how does an individual's membership in a group affect his or her desire and ability to undertake collective action? A widespread response, clearly articulated by Gustave LeBon, was that industrialization had displaced men and women and destroyed their traditional way life. These individuals, unintegrated into the new social structure and bereft of social values, had no restraints on the passions and were the source of social turbulence. Karl Marx offered an alternative explanation for the increased social strife of the nineteenth century. He agreed that people who were uprooted and made propertyless by the development of capitalism would be forced to forsake the "rural idiocy" and corporate privileges of their preindustrial forbearers. But he did not think that this led to anarchy. The new proletarians would organize and develop a critique of capitalism that would reveal the fundamental unity of interests of all workers.

In the last quarter-century social historians have made major contributions to this debate. The great French demographer Louis Chevalier offered a new interpretation of the social breakdown argument by explaining uprisings in Paris in the first half of the nineteenth century in terms of the degradation of urban life and of a certain related biological consciousness on the part of both the bourgeoisie and the lower classes.[1] However, most social history research has been devoted to rethinking the concept of class consciousness and the social bases of collective action. E. P. Thompson and William Sewell have shown that artisans did not immediately abandon their values and conceptions of social relations, but used them to develop a radical critique of capitalism that provided one of the foundations for socialist thought in the nineteenth century.[2] Historians who have studied geographic mobility, social origins, residence patterns, and forms of sociability have emphasized the importance of shared social bonds—whether based on preindustrial experience or craft, inter-class community or inter-occupational class relations—as prerequisites for sustained social and political action. Historians who seek to understand why workers from different occupations take joint action in some situations, but not others, have focused on two poles. One argument—most fully developed by Michael Hanagan—is that skilled occupational groups sufficiently closed to prevent dilution may provide a worker vanguard by tying their fight to preserve their craft to the struggles of less skilled workers. The alternate model, more strictly Marxist in orientation, argues that a population of workers deprived of a particular job identity will be most receptive to united class action.[3]

Decazeville—a town created by the development of industry—is a good arena in which to study occupational groups and the relations between them in nineteenth-century France. Because towns in the Aubin Basin were especially susceptible to changes in the industrial economy, they experienced periods of unusual demographic growth and decline.[4]

The population of Decazeville frequently rose or fell more than 10 percent in the interval between censuses: 1833–1836; 1836–1841; 1841–1846; 1851–1856; 1861–1866; 1866–1872; 1881–1886; 1886–1891; 1896–1901; 1901–1906; 1906–1911; 1931–1936; 1962–1968. A study of Aubin during the first decades of industrialization suggests the extent of geographic mobility. A comparison of natural growth rates (births minus deaths) with census figures gives minimum migration rates: in 1851–1855 natural growth was −35 and migration 3,670; 1856–1860, 331 and −523; 1861–1865, 507 and 500; 1866–1871, 462 and −457; 1872–1875, 384 and 648; 1876–1880, 402 and −959.[5] Furthermore, these figures exclude individuals who came and left between censuses. Each period of industrial expansion brought large numbers of young male workers without family ties to towns in the Basin. In 1861, for instance, Decazeville had 2,646 unmarried males (including children), 1,816 married men, and 142 widowers; and only 1,932 unmarried females, 1,770 married women, and 314 widows.[6] The young men were the first to leave in times of crisis. Officials reported in June 1865, the month the Houillères et Fonderies declared bankruptcy, that Decazeville had lost three thousand inhabitants in the previous eight months, leaving only

**Table 1.** Population of towns in the Aubin Basin

| Year | Decazeville | Aubin | Cransac | Firmy | Viviez |
|------|-------------|-------|---------|-------|--------|
| 1806 | — | 2,954 | 607 | 1,175 | 746 |
| 1820 | — | 2,364 | 489 | 1,005 | 735 |
| 1831 | — | 3,392 | 590 | 1,524 | 754 |
| 1833 | 1,123 | — | — | — | — |
| 1836 | 2,715 | 3,017 | 565 | 1,627 | 912 |
| 1841 | 4,154 | 3,078 | 563 | 1,572 | 852 |
| 1846 | 6,323 | 3,321 | 579 | 1,586 | 1,014 |
| 1851 | 5,938 | 4,413 | 801 | 2,171 | 1,149 |
| 1856 | 8,842 | 8,048 | 942 | 2,400 | 1,557 |
| 1861 | 8,620 | 7,856 | 1,967 | 2,615 | 2,104 |
| 1866 | 7,106 | 8,863 | 3,540 | 2,580 | 2,062 |
| 1872 | 8,710 | 8,832 | 3,655 | 2,781 | 2,200 |
| 1876 | 9,547 | 9,864 | 4,468 | 2,970 | 1,754 |
| 1881 | 9,625 | 9,317 | 4,504 | 2,807 | 1,361 |
| 1886 | 10,702 | 9,054 | 4,773 | 2,723 | 1,524 |
| 1891 | 8,871 | 9,052 | 5,653 | 2,530 | 1,521 |
| 1896 | 9,361 | 9,419 | 5,955 | 2,390 | 1,766 |
| 1901 | 11,536 | 9,973 | 6,715 | 2,469 | 2,040 |
| 1906 | 12,961 | 9,986 | 6,953 | 2,581 | 2,231 |
| 1911 | 14,144 | 9,574 | 6,654 | 2,575 | 3,334 |
| 1921 | 14,089 | 9,740 | 6,441 | 2,554 | 3,309 |
| 1926 | 14,261 | 9,387 | 6,307 | 2,487 | 3,614 |
| 1931 | 15,210 | 8,322 | 5,087 | 2,387 | 3,385 |
| 1936 | 12,365 | 7,495 | 4,502 | 2,352 | 2,917 |
| 1946 | 12,138 | 7,982 | 4,821 | 2,371 | 2,961 |
| 1954 | 11,510 | 8,275 | 4,765 | 2,932 | 3,165 |
| 1962 | 11,855 | 7,821 | 4,132 | 3,323 | 2,974 |
| 1968 | 10,524 | 6,635 | 3,244 | 3,611 | 2,650 |

*Source:* Booklet compiled by J. M. Tisseyre, archivist at the Archives Départementales de l'Aveyron, except the figure for Decazeville (Lassalle) in 1833, which is
drawn from ADA 28M2 77, "Etat indiquant l'organisation proposée par le Préfet pour
la commune d'Aubin" [1833].

1,500 "fathers of families" with strong roots in the community at
work in the mines and factories.[7] The arrival and departure of large
numbers of immigrant workers before and after World War I produced a similar effect.

Towns in the Aubin Basin experienced extensive in- and outmi-
gration, but there was an underlying stability in the industrial labor

force as well. During the nineteenth century significant movement took place between towns in the Basin (which is why a complete study of geographical persistence would have to be done on a Basin-wide basis). In the 1850s workers often switched residences within the Basin in response to the competition for labor between companies at Aubin and Decazeville. In the early 1860s many workers left Decazeville for the more prosperous Aubin. A few years later workers from Aubin went in turn to the rejuvenated Decazeville. By the 1860s, however, there are also signs that workers were beginning to establish more stable communities. At the end of that decade the majority of Aubin workers did not leave for Decazeville. Instead they proclaimed the independence of their section of the town of Aubin from company control and struck against their employers.[8] For the period after 1890, electoral lists for mine-safety delegates—which include the date of hiring for all adult French miners—testify to the presence of a large community of geographically stable miners.[9] In fact, it was characteristic of Decazeville and other industrial towns in the Aubin Basin to have both a stable population of miners and metalworkers and a very mobile group of workers who came and went with changes in the economy.[10]

One way to find out more about the core population of industrial workers is through analysis of data contained in marriage registers. This source does not provide a statistical portrait of the town population as a whole; it clearly overrepresents those born and raised in the Aubin Basin and who made their life and career there. For instance, between 1837 and 1846 only one of the large contingent of British metalworkers married at Decazeville. Viewed from another angle, however, marriage records provide an invaluable statistical portrait of the element of Decazeville's population which was on the whole most committed to participation in community life.

Examination of marriage records at selected intervals (1837–1846; 1860–1864; 1881–1885; 1902–1905) can help identify the extent to which occupational groups in Decazeville constituted separate communities; the degree to which individuals in one group formed social relationships with members of their own and other occupations and classes; and how these relationships changed over the nineteenth century. Industrial workers at Decazeville fall into three primary categories: miners, metalworkers (a wide range of occupations ranging from the skilled *lamineurs, chauffeurs,* and *puddleurs,* through mechanics and the less skilled *dégrossisseurs* and *cokeurs*); and laborers (*manoeuvres* who worked in the mines and more often the factories—and who may have been past or future miners or metal-workers). (The identification of significant differences among these groups confirms that they are more than statistical artifacts of contemporary occupational categories.) The rest of the population can be divided into five other categories: other manual workers (construction and haulage workers, often employed by the company, as well as the few mine machinists); tradesmen; white-collar/officials (primarily *employés* and teachers); professionals/bourgeois (doctors, engineers, lawyers, pharmacists, *rentiers*); and peasants/farmers (primarily *cultivateurs* and *propriétaire-cultivateurs* with a very few *domestiques* and *vignerons*).[11] In the tabulations below, "total manual worker" comprises miners, metalworkers, laborers, and other manual workers; "other" refers to tradesmen, white-collar/officials, and professional/bourgeois. In the occasional case where an individual was listed as having two occupations, both were weighted equally. While the status of individual occupational groups may have altered over the course of the century, there is no evidence that the meaning of any occupational classification changed significantly.

Any categorization like this based on occupational designations without data on property holdings is problematic. For instance, an examination of the *inventaires après décès* in late nineteenth-century Decazeville reveals great disparities in the wealth of individual metalworkers.[12] Identification of individuals at a single point in their career presents a second difficulty. There was some movement from one occupational category to another as a consequence of career advancement, injury, age, or the accumulation of property. During periods of crisis in the 1870s, metalworkers with ties to the community sometimes went to work temporarily in the mines rather than leaving for work elsewhere.[13] One can find evidence of these changes by using the bride or groom's birthdate to check in the birth registers for the father's occupation at that time and comparing it with his occupation at the time of the wedding (or, if he died before the marriage, his occupation at the time of his death). When such cross-checking revealed a career change, equal weight was given to each occupation in tabulations of the father's occupation. This raises a related problem encountered by all researchers who use marriage records: the absence of occupational data for the parents of individuals who were illegitimate or whose parents had died or whose whereabouts were unknown. This can be remedied for individuals who were born in Decazeville or whose fathers died there, by looking at occupational data in the relevant birth and death records. However, this supplementary data are clearly skewed in favor of the portion of the marriage sample most firmly rooted in the town. In tabulations involving fathers of grooms and brides a differentiation has been made between material collected directly from the marriage registers and that which includes data garnered from tracking leads within the registers.

Analysis of marriage records permits us to identify the characteristics of occupational groups in terms of geographic origins, ability to sign the marriage certificate, age of marriage, social origins, and occupational inheritance. Examination of marriage partners and wedding witnesses allows us to situate these groups in the networks of sociability in the community.

Table 2 shows that over the course of the nineteenth century, the Aubin Basin ("within 5 kms.") provided an increasingly large per-

**Table 2.**　Distance from place of birth of grooms (in percentages)

| Occupation | 1837–1846 | 1860–1864 | 1881–1885 | 1902–1905 |
|---|---|---|---|---|
| Miners | N = 74 | N = 70 | N = 110 | N = 65 |
| within 5 kms. | 24.3 | 38.8 | 50.9 | 46.2 |
| 5–15 kms. | 39.2 | 52.9 | 71.8 | 61.5 |
| 15–25 kms. | 50.0 | 62.9 | 85.5 | 73.0 |
| 25–50 kms. | 70.3 | 82.9 | 91.8 | 92.3 |
| Laborers | N = 77 | N = 81 | N = 50 | N = 79 |
| within 5 kms. | 3.9 | 11.1 | 28.0 | 29.1 |
| 5–15 kms. | 18.2 | 25.9 | 50.0 | 43.0 |
| 15–25 kms. | 35.1 | 38.3 | 68.0 | 67.1 |
| 25–50 kms. | 61.0 | 64.2 | 84.0 | 92.4 |
| Metalworkers | N = 122 | N = 104 | N = 75 | N = 72 |
| within 5 kms. | 18.0 | 30.8 | 66.7 | 58.3 |
| 5–15 kms. | 27.0 | 41.3 | 77.3 | 69.4 |
| 15–25 kms. | 38.5 | 53.8 | 81.3 | 79.2 |
| 25–50 kms. | 59.0 | 79.1 | 89.3 | 88.9 |
| All grooms | N = 396 | N = 397 | N = 402 | N = 365 |
| within 5 kms. | 18.9 | 24.2 | 41.8 | 44.4 |
| 5–15 kms. | 31.6 | 35.8 | 60.7 | 59.2 |
| 15–25 kms. | 42.7 | 47.6 | 72.9 | 71.8 |
| 25–50 kms. | 66.2 | 71.5 | 85.3 | 88.8 |

centage of all Decazeville grooms. The growth leveled off after 1881–1885, as a result of the out-migration and subsequent in-migration during the last years of the Société Nouvelle and the first years of Comambault. The gradual rise in the percentage of Aubin Basin natives between 1860–1864 and 1881–1885 suggests the formation of a labor force that obviated the need to employ contractors in the 1860s and 1870s, and created the conditions for the battle between the residents and the company during the 1880s. Perhaps the most significant finding, however, is the clear difference in geographical origins between laborers on the one hand, and miners and metalworkers on the other. Although the percentage of laborers from within the Basin and its environs grew over the course of the century, it remained consistently less than that for other industrial workers. This suggests that as a stable community of industrial workers took shape at Decazeville, the more skilled and better paying jobs of miner and metalworker were more likely to be filled by natives. Recent migrants to Decazeville formed a pool of poorly paid unskilled labor.[14]

An examination of marriage partners' ability to sign their marriage certificates suggests a further division by occupation owing in part to geographical origins. The ability to sign differentiated miners and metalworkers from laborers until the end of the century, when the educational reforms of the Third Republic had fully taken effect.[15] To a large extent the differences between occupational groups in this realm can be related to geographical origins. Company-funded schools in the Aubin Basin (and in other industrial centers that sent metalworkers to Decazeville in its early years) provided a better education to children than was available in much of the countryside. The laborers' lower signing rate correlates with non-Basin and (as we shall see) peasant backgrounds. It may also indicate that migrants who worked as laborers had come to Decazeville at a later age than

**Table 3.** Marriage partners who could sign marriage certificates (in percentages)

|  | 1837–1846 | 1860–1864 | 1881–1885 | 1902–1905 |
|---|---|---|---|---|
| Miners | 26.4 | 47.8 | 88.5 | 96.0 |
| Laborers | 23.4 | 28.0 | 63.0 | 97.0 |
| Metalworkers | 49.6 | 56.1 | 89.4 | 100 |
| Total grooms | 43.4 | 51.3 | 86.8 | 98.9 |
| Total brides | 20.3 | 28.2 | 69.5 | 98.9 |

non-native miners and metalworkers, who had more likely had the opportunity to go to the town's schools as children.

Age of marriage also differentiated groups of industrial workers. More metalworkers married young—before age twenty-five—than did laborers or miners, presumably because they were most likely to have been born and raised in Decazeville and to hold down jobs that allowed them to support a family. In contrast, miners and laborers came more often from the countryside and perhaps had some form of rural property settlement to make which delayed their decision to marry. The most interesting figures in Table 4 are the ones for miners. What explains the dramatic rise in the percentage of marriages by young miners in 1881–1885? In 1860–1864 miners pursued a behavior like that of laborers, probably based on an effort to balance agricultural and industrial concerns. In the following period, however, miners' early marriages suggest that there was a large population of miners at Decazeville who had grown up in the Basin, gone to work in the mines at an early age, and become full-fledged hewers in their early twenties. In 1902–1905 elements of the previous marriage-age structure returned. Military conscription and changes introduced by Comambault in the organization of mine work forced miners to wait until their late twenties to marry.

These measures of differentiation by occupation suggest that there was probably a degree of internal recruitment within the industrial population at Decazeville. Marriage records provide us with two sources of information on this issue. First, we can examine the occupations of grooms' parents for whom we have data (Table 5).

**Table 4.**  Age of grooms at first marriage by profession (in percentages)

| Age | 1837–1846 | 1860–1864 | 1881–1885 | 1902–1905 |
|---|---|---|---|---|
| | | Miners | | |
| 15–24 | 21.1 | 23.0 | 41.7 | 20.3 |
| 15–29 | 66.2 | 62.2 | 82.7 | 80.0 |
| | | Laborers | | |
| 15–24 | 9.2 | 22.1 | 20.0 | 19.3 |
| 15–29 | 46.1 | 58.9 | 71.1 | 94.1 |
| | | Metalworkers | | |
| 15–24 | 29.0 | 39.6 | 39.5 | 31.4 |
| 15–29 | 69.4 | 76.2 | 84.0 | 92.9 |

Next, we can isolate industrial worker fathers and see whether their sons held the same jobs (Table 6).

Table 5 shows that the first miners were predominantly sons of peasant families, and a little less than half the miners continued to come from this background in the course of the century. Beginning in the 1860s, however, one can also discern a fair degree of occupational inheritance among miners. By the same token, miners were almost never sons of metalworkers. Laborers came largely from a peasant background; relatively few were sons of miners and metalworkers. Metalworkers came least often from a peasant background and were most often the sons of industrial workers, especially metalworkers. This trend peaked in the 1880s; in the 1902–1905 sample, one notes a moderate increase in metalworkers whose fathers were peasants.

If we isolate the grooms' fathers, we can get a better idea of the degree of occupational inheritance among industrial workers. Given the small number of cases, one must use the figures in Table 6 with circumspection. In general, they confirm the data on the social origins of grooms. Miners displayed a considerable degree of occupational inheritance. While their sons frequently became metalworkers, they almost never became laborers. The sons of laborers, as one would expect, worked in all areas of manual labor. While many laborers' sons became metalworkers in each period, there was also a significant movement of laborers' sons into the mining profession during the Société Nouvelle's first decades at Decazeville (reflected in the 1881–1885 sample).

Metalworkers displayed the clearest signs of occupational inheritance: the son of a metalworker rarely went to work as a miner or a laborer. At the beginning of the twentieth century, however, when changes in the metalworks—marked by a long strike in 1902—reduced the pay of skilled metalworkers, one finds 8 of the 18 sons of metalworkers whose fathers were alive at the time of the wedding had gone into commerce or, more often, into a white-collar occupation (but 0 of 16 whose fathers had died). Metalworkers whose fathers had died presumably did not have a springboard into some other occupation and went to work in the factory. The underground mines, where changes in the organization of work were restricting recruitment and advancement, present a different story. There one finds that 6 of the 14 sons of miners deceased at the time of the wedding had gone into white-collar work, or, more often, trade (but 1 of 20 whose fathers were alive). While it is risky to draw conclu-

**Table 5.**   Social background of grooms by occupation (in percentages)

### Miner

| Occupation of father | 1837–1846 N = 74 (31)[a] | 1860–1864 N = 70 (35, 42) | 1881–1885 N = 110 (49, 75) | | 1902–1905 N = 65 (34, 46) | |
|---|---|---|---|---|---|---|
| Miner | 12.9 | 31.4 | 24.5 | 30.7 | 35.3 | 37.0 |
| Laborer | 3.2 | 2.8 | 17.3 | 22.0 | 11.8 | 9.8 |
| Metalworker | 3.2 | 0 | 2.0 | 4.0 | 0 | 5.4 |
| Other manual worker | 0 | 2.8 | 4.0 | 6.7 | 1.5 | 9.8 |
| *Total manual worker* | 19.3 | 37.1 | 48.0 | 63.3 | 48.6 | 62.0 |
| Peasant/farmer | 80.6 | 51.4 | 42.8 | 28.7 | 45.5 | 33.7 |
| Other | 0 | 11.4 | 9.2 | 8.0 | 5.9 | 4.4 |

### Laborer

| Occupation of father | 1837–1846 N = 77 (35) | 1860–1864 N = 81 (24, 32) | 1881–1885 N = 50 (21, 30) | | 1902–1905 N = 79 (51, 59) | |
|---|---|---|---|---|---|---|
| Miner | 0 | 0 | 10.9 | 0 | 10.0 | 3.4 |
| Laborer | 11.4 | 16.7 | 25.0 | 9.5 | 20.0 | 18.6 |
| Metalworker | 2.8 | 0 | 0 | 7.1 | 6.7 | 4.2 |
| Other manual worker | 0 | 0 | 1.6 | 4.8 | 5.0 | 7.6 |
| *Total manual worker* | 14.3 | 16.7 | 37.5 | 21.4 | 41.7 | 33.9 |
| Peasant/farmer | 65.7 | 79.2 | 59.3 | 76.2 | 56.7 | 59.3 |
| Other | 20.0 | 4.2 | 3.1 | 2.4 | 1.7 | 6.8 |

### Metalworker

| Occupation of father | 1837–1846 N = 122 (78) | 1860–1864 N = 104 (51, 64) | | 1881–1885 N = 75 (37, 60) | | 1902–1905 N = 72 (43, 57) | |
|---|---|---|---|---|---|---|---|
| Miner | 6.8 | 8.8 | 10.2 | 5.4 | 13.3 | 11.6 | 12.2 |
| Laborer | 2.7 | 14.7 | 17.2 | 27.0 | 24.2 | 15.1 | 14.9 |
| Metalworker | 12.3 | 13.7 | 14.8 | 35.1 | 36.7 | 18.6 | 35.1 |
| Other manual worker | 5.5 | 9.8 | 9.4 | 12.2 | 10.8 | 11.6 | 9.6 |
| *Total manual worker* | 27.4 | 47.1 | 51.6 | 79.7 | 85.0 | 57.0 | 71.9 |
| Peasant/farmer | 49.3 | 39.2 | 34.4 | 8.1 | 5.8 | 23.2 | 17.5 |
| Other | 23.3 | 13.7 | 14.1 | 12.2 | 9.2 | 19.8 | 11.6 |

a. N is the total number of marriages. The first figure in parentheses gives cases with sufficient data in marriage records; the second includes additional cases completed with data from birth and death records. The percentages are calculated from the cases in parentheses.

**Table 6.** Occupational and manual worker inheritance (in percentages)

| Occupation of son | 1837–1846 | 1860–1864 | | 1881–1885 | | 1902–1905 | |
|---|---|---|---|---|---|---|---|
| | N = 9[a] | N = 15 (27) | | N = 15 (37) | | N = 20 (34) | |
| **Miner father** | | | | | | | |
| Miner | 44.4 | 73.3 | 55.6 | 80.0 | 59.4 | 60.0 | 50.0 |
| Laborer | 0 | 0 | 11.1 | 0 | 8.1 | 7.5 | 7.3 |
| Metalworker | 55.5 | 26.7 | 25.9 | 13.3 | 21.6 | 25.0 | 20.6 |
| Other manual worker | 0 | 0 | 3.7 | 6.7 | 8.2 | 2.5 | 1.5 |
| *Total manual worker* | 100 | 100 | 96.3 | 100 | 97.3 | 95.0 | 79.4 |
| | N = 7 | N = 17 (28) | | N = 29 (40) | | N = 20 (30) | |
| **Laborer father** | | | | | | | |
| Miner | 14.3 | 5.9 | 8.9 | 46.1 | 38.4 | 20.0 | 15.0 |
| Laborer | 57.1 | 23.5 | 28.6 | 7.7 | 14.0 | 30.0 | 36.7 |
| Metalworker | 28.6 | 41.2 | 39.3 | 38.5 | 33.7 | 37.5 | 28.3 |
| Other manual worker | 0 | 23.5 | 19.6 | 3.9 | 9.2 | 12.5 | 16.7 |
| *Total manual worker* | 100 | 94.1 | 96.4 | 96.2 | 95.3 | 100 | 96.7 |
| | N = 11 | N = 8 (11) | | N = 20 (33) | | N = 18 (34) | |
| **Metal-worker father** | | | | | | | |
| Miner | 9.1 | 0 | 0 | 5.0 | 11.1 | 0 | 7.4 |
| Laborer | 9.1 | 0 | 0 | 7.5 | 6.1 | 2.8 | 7.4 |
| Metalworker | 81.8 | 100 | 90.1 | 65.0 | 66.7 | 44.4 | 58.8 |
| Other manual worker | 0 | 0 | 0 | 17.5 | 6.1 | 8.4 | 2.9 |
| *Total manual worker* | 100 | 100 | 90.1 | 95.0 | 90.1 | 55.6 | 76.5 |

a. N is the number of cases found in marriage records; the figure in parentheses includes additional cases completed with data from birth and death records. The percentages are calculated from these two sets of cases.

sions from such limited data, it appears that occupational inheritance and the occupational community on which it was based were stronger among miners than metalworkers in the early twentieth century.

In any case, as the size of the tradesman/white-collar sector grew, so did the number of sons of manual workers in it. In 1837–1846, 1 of 12 tradesmen/white-collar grooms whose parentage can be traced was the son of a manual worker; in 1860–1864, 1 of 19; in 1881–1885, 8 of 44; in 1902–1905, 24 of 59. Over the course of the century, however, the move from tradesman/white collar to manual worker became less common: in 1837–1846, 25 of 29 grooms from tradesmen/white-collar backgrounds were manual workers; in 1860–1864, 19 of 29; in 1881–1885, 14 of 33; and in 1902–1905, 15 of 38. While more sons of manual workers entered the tradesman/white-collar sector at the end of the nineteenth century, fewer sons from this category became manual workers. This suggests the formation of a tradesman/white-collar sector, which, although open to the recruitment of manual workers, formed a somewhat more separate sphere than in the past.

To what extent were the social networks formed by industrial workers at Decazeville intra- and interoccupational and to what extent did they extend outside of the population of manual workers? The marriage registers provide us with two sorts of material to answer this question. First, we can proceed in a manner analogous to our study of occupational inheritance to tabulate occupational and social endogamy based on the occupations of the groom and the father-in-law. Then we can examine the occupations of the witnesses at each wedding.

Analysis of marriage partners echoes—though more faintly—conclusions drawn from the study of occupational inheritance. Miners chose fewer brides from the peasantry and more from miners' families as the century drew to a close. Laborers selected their mates more often from the peasantry than other industrial workers. The marriage of laborers' daughters to miners peaked in the 1881–1885 sample, the same period in which the entry of laborers' sons into mining reached its apex. In contrast, the early twentieth century saw an increase in the percentage of marriages between laborers and laborers' daughters. As one would expect, metalworkers married peasants' daughters less frequently than other industrial workers; however, the relative decline in marriages between metalworkers

**Table 7.** Social background of brides (in percentages)

| Bride's father | 1837–1846 | 1860–1864 | | 1881–1885 | | 1902–1905 | |
|---|---|---|---|---|---|---|---|
| **Miner groom** | N = 74 (47)ᵃ | N = 70 (39, 43) | | N = 110 (71, 90) | | N = 65 (31, 51) | |
| Miner | 6.4 | 15.3 | 23.2 | 23.9 | 23.3 | 35.5 | 37.3 |
| Laborer | 8.5 | 15.3 | 16.3 | 19.7 | 21.1 | 12.9 | 16.7 |
| Metalworker | 6.4 | 7.7 | 5.8 | 7.0 | 11.1 | 5.7 | 7.8 |
| Other manual worker | 8.5 | 12.8 | 11.6 | 9.9 | 11.1 | 5.7 | 13.7 |
| *Total manual worker* | 29.8 | 51.3 | 57.0 | 60.6 | 66.7 | 67.7 | 75.5 |
| Peasant/farmer | 63.8 | 35.9 | 31.4 | 18.3 | 18.9 | 21.0 | 17.6 |
| Other | 6.4 | 12.8 | 11.6 | 21.1 | 14.4 | 11.3 | 6.9 |
| **Laborer groom** | N = 77 (43) | N = 81 (35, 45) | | N = 50 (25, 34) | | N = 79 (49, 61) | |
| Miner | 13.9 | 0 | 1.1 | 24.0 | 14.7 | 15.3 | 17.2 |
| Laborer | 9.3 | 31.4 | 33.3 | 12.0 | 17.6 | 36.7 | 34.4 |
| Metalworker | 0 | 7.1 | 7.8 | 0 | 2.9 | 4.1 | 4.9 |
| Other manual worker | 4.7 | 2.8 | 5.6 | 16.0 | 13.2 | 6.1 | 7.3 |
| *Total manual worker* | 27.9 | 41.4 | 47.8 | 52.0 | 48.5 | 62.2 | 63.9 |
| Peasant/farmer | 62.7 | 50.0 | 43.3 | 44.0 | 45.6 | 28.6 | 24.6 |
| Other | 9.3 | 9.7 | 8.9 | 4.0 | 5.9 | 9.2 | 11.5 |
| **Metalworker groom** | N = 122 (94) | N = 104 (64, 77) | | N = 75 (45, 60) | | N = 72 (44, 63) | |
| Miner | 7.4 | 7.8 | 10.4 | 20.0 | 16.7 | 26.1 | 30.1 |
| Laborer | 5.4 | 17.2 | 16.9 | 13.3 | 10.0 | 31.8 | 26.2 |
| Metalworker | 14.9 | 21.9 | 22.1 | 22.2 | 23.3 | 6.8 | 14.3 |
| Other manual worker | 9.0 | 18.8 | 19.5 | 3.3 | 5.0 | 9.1 | 12.9 |
| *Total manual worker* | 37.7 | 65.6 | 68.8 | 58.9 | 65.0 | 73.9 | 84.4 |
| Peasant/farmer | 40.9 | 23.4 | 20.8 | 25.6 | 21.7 | 15.9 | 9.5 |
| Other | 21.5 | 10.9 | 10.4 | 15.6 | 13.3 | 10.2 | 6.2 |

a. N is the total number of marriages. The first figure in parentheses gives cases with sufficient data in marriage records; the second includes additional cases completed with data from birth and death records. The percentages are calculated from the cases in parentheses.

**Table 8.**  Occupational and manual worker endogamy (in percentages)

| Occupation of groom | 1837–1846 | 1860–1864 | | 1881–1885 | | 1902–1905 | |
|---|---|---|---|---|---|---|---|
| | N = 20ᵃ | N = 16 (30) | | N = 49 (58) | | N = 51 (76) | |
| **Miner father-in-law** | | | | | | | |
| Miner | 15.0 | 37.5 | 33.3 | 39.5 | 36.2 | 25.0 | 37.3 |
| Laborer | 30.0 | 0 | 1.7 | 14.0 | 8.6 | 15.5 | 18.8 |
| Metalworker | 35.0 | 31.2 | 26.7 | 20.9 | 17.2 | 22.5 | 25.0 |
| Other manual worker | 15.0 | 18.8 | 25.0 | 18.6 | 20.8 | 15.5 | 10.5 |
| *Total manual worker* | 95.0 | 87.5 | 86.7 | 93.0 | 82.8 | 78.4 | 91.6 |
| | N = 17 | N = 39 (49) | | N = 35 (45) | | N = 41 (52) | |
| **Laborer father-in-law** | | | | | | | |
| Miner | 23.5 | 15.4 | 13.3 | 40.0 | 41.1 | 9.6 | 16.3 |
| Laborer | 23.5 | 28.2 | 30.6 | 8.6 | 13.3 | 43.9 | 40.4 |
| Metalworker | 35.3 | 28.2 | 26.5 | 17.1 | 13.3 | 34.1 | 31.7 |
| Other manual worker | 11.8 | 2.6 | 15.3 | 11.4 | 16.7 | 2.4 | 1.9 |
| *Total manual worker* | 94.1 | 74.4 | 85.7 | 77.1 | 84.4 | 90.2 | 90.1 |
| | N = 18 | N = 25 (30) | | N = 24 (40) | | N = 15 (30) | |
| **Metalworker father-in-law** | | | | | | | |
| Miner | 16.7 | 10.0 | 8.3 | 20.8 | 25.0 | 20.0 | 13.3 |
| Laborer | 0 | 10.0 | 11.7 | 0 | 2.5 | 13.3 | 10.0 |
| Metalworker | 77.8 | 56.0 | 56.7 | 41.7 | 35.0 | 20.0 | 30.0 |
| Other manual worker | 5.5 | 20.0 | 13.3 | 20.8 | 7.5 | 13.3 | 20.0 |
| *Total manual worker* | 100 | 96.0 | 90.0 | 83.3 | 70.0 | 66.7 | 73.3 |

a. N is the number of cases found in marriage records; the figure in parentheses includes additional cases completed with data from birth and death records. The percentages are calculated from these two sets of cases.

and metalworkers' daughters in the final sample suggests the beginning of a breakdown in the metalworkers' occupational community in the early twentieth century.

The law required that four witnesses be present at the wedding ceremony. If the reasons for the choice of witnesses remained the same over the century, then analysis of their occupations provides another way to assess the development of social networks.[16] Examination of the occupations of marriage witnesses points to a growing solidarity among metalworkers during the heyday of the metallurgical industry, and among miners at the end of the century. The increase in the percentage of industrial worker witnesses at the marriages of all industrial workers over the course of the century also points to both the development of interoccupational working-class sociability and a declining, although still quite significant, level of social relations between industrial workers and tradesmen (who accounted for most of the nonindustrial witnesses).

How does this welter of figures enhance the account of Decazeville miners presented in the body of this work? Each set of marriage records presents us with a snapshot of the less geographically mobile element of the town's population. In the late 1830s and 1840s the new town of Decazeville was primarily a city of recent rural immigrants. There was relatively little difference between the social profile of the miners and the laborers who married in Decazeville during this period. Both groups were predominately of rural agricultural origins with the educational handicaps this created. The metalworkers—the largest body of workers in Decazeville—presented somewhat different characteristics. Fewer came from rural agricultural backgrounds; more displayed a certain degree of literacy. While the son of a miner or a laborer rarely held the same job as his father at the time he married, the sons of metalworkers became metalworkers and metalworkers' daughters married metalworkers. Although metalworkers formed the strongest occupational community in the town, they seldom acted as a group or made common cause with the miners and laborers, even those who worked at their side in the factory. They preferred instead to protect their prerogatives through subtle and not so subtle guerilla tactics on the shopfloor.[17]

The 1860s marked an important turning point in the economic history of the Aubin Basin. The ironworks gave way to the mines as the basis of the local economy. While the metalworkers remained the leading element of the town's industrial working population,

**Table 9.** Marriage witnesses (a) who were from the same occupation as the grooms; (b) who were industrial workers (in percentages)

| Grooms | 1837–1846 | | 1860–1864 | | 1881–1885 | | 1902–1905 | |
|---|---|---|---|---|---|---|---|---|
| | (a) | (b) | (a) | (b) | (a) | (b) | (a) | (b) |
| Miners | 7.7 | 25.6 | 10.8 | 36.3 | 36.9 | 55.2 | 38.8 | 72.3 |
| Laborers | 11.0 | 22.7 | 15.6 | 37.5 | 12.0 | 44.4 | 25.1 | 67.3 |
| Metalworkers | 16.8 | 24.4 | 34.3 | 46.4 | 25.5 | 49.4 | 24.9 | 62.6 |
| Industrial workers | | 24.3 | | 40.7 | | 50.4 | | 67.2 |
| Nonindustrial workers | | 14.0 | | 23.2 | | 31.6 | | 35.7 |

Town officials, who often served as fourth witnesses, were not included in this table.

the miners began to develop the characteristics of an occupational community during this period. They became differentiated from the laborers, a larger proportion of whom were recent rural migrants. Higher percentages of miners than in the past were the sons of miners, could sign their marriage certificates, and married the daughters of miners. The growing community of miners helped convince companies to eliminate the use of contractors and provided the basis for the solidarity miners showed in defending their wages and their community in 1867.

By the early 1880s mining had clearly replaced metalworking as the dominant sector of the economy: the weddings of miners as a proportion of industrial worker weddings went from one-quarter (1837–1846: 27.1 percent; 1860–1864: 27.4 percent) to almost one-half (1881–1885: 46.8 percent). Tabulations of occupational inheritance and intermarriage suggest that in the absence of jobs in the metalworks during the metallurgical crisis of the 1870s and 1880s miners incorporated laborers into their social network more than at any other time. Yet miners continued to constitute a group bound by common experiences: they came increasingly from the Basin, maintained a relatively high degree of occupational inheritance, drew more than other occupational groups on their fellow miners for wedding witnesses, and married earlier—presumably a reflection for many of them of a career in the mines which had begun in their youth. It was this strong miners' occupational community which confronted the Société Nouvelle in the strike of 1886.

The early twentieth century was a period of rapid expansion in the population of Decazeville. (The large number of new arrivals are greatly underrepresented in the marriage records.) Although the individual occupational communities retained much the same characteristics as in the 1880s, there are signs that the metalworkers' community was disintegrating. Information on residential neighborhoods drawn from the 1911 census provides corroborating evidence. As one would expect, the maximum concentration of metalworkers lived in areas with the smallest concentration of miners and *vice versa*. Equally important, however, is the finding that metalworkers were much less concentrated in certain districts than miners; they often lived in areas with large numbers of shopkeepers and other non-manual workers.[18] Laborers showed most clearly the effects of the massive immigration. In the 1880s laborers and their sons who worked in the mines and factories were relatively easily integrated into the population of miners and metalworkers. The rapid demographic growth and changes in the organization of work in the mines and metalworks two decades later made laborers' integration into the occupational communities of miners and metalworkers more difficult; this was reflected in a higher incidence of laborer intermarriage. This same period witnessed the growth of a tradesman/white-collar sector which, although increasingly open to manual workers, sent fewer of its sons to work in industry. By the same token, while more industrial workers served as witnesses at tradesman/white-collar weddings, fewer individuals from this sector were witnesses to industrial worker weddings. In this situation it is perhaps not surprising that the miners' union took the lead in trying to organize an *ouvrieriste* politics in Decazeville, nor that it ultimately failed in the face not only of opposition from other social classes, but also of a fragmentation of the population of industrial workers.

In fact, one does not see a group of skilled industrial workers providing guidance and support to another group of workers, to nearly the extent Hanagan has shown took place in some industrial towns in the Loire. (This is different from the incorporation of unskilled workers into an occupational community, as in the case of laborers and miners; on the contrary, it is predicated on the alliance of separate bodies of workers.) Nor, however, did the workers of Decazeville ever fully constitute a homogeneous mass potentially receptive to united class action. There were several reasons for this. First, metalworkers did not form a single craft, but rather a wide collection of workers with different skills.[19] Nor were recruitment, advancement, and intermarriage of metalworkers as closed as in most artisanal or skilled industrial trades or as open as in unskilled labor. Metalworkers from Decazeville may very likely have worked at firms elsewhere in France as youths,[20] but they were not part of a regular national network, like glassworkers and many other skilled industrial workers in the nineteenth century. In sum, metalworkers did not possess the cohesion necessary to transform their experience at work into the basis of a skilled workers' socialism which could in turn be presented as the basis of a political movement uniting all workers. This was true for miners as well. Although less divided by skill, they were less closed in recruitment and had little control over advancement. Furthermore, because of the relationship of mining to the state, miners were pulled in the direction of a corporate-based reformism rather than a skilled workers' socialism.[21] In an integrated mining and metallurgical center like Decazeville a second factor came into play. The metalworks were dependent on the availability of low cost coal from the mines. Metalworkers were reluctant to support striking miners in 1867, 1878, and 1886 because they saw the miners' success as an indirect threat to their livelihood. The decade of cooperation between the miners' and metalworkers' unions which ended after the 1902 strike provided only a brief respite in the generally cool relations between miners' and metalworkers' organizations. In 1917–1919, when the metalworkers' union next resurfaced as a potent force in Decazeville, it no longer drew its strength from skilled workers, but instead from the new unskilled industrial labor force. This revolutionary syndicalist metalworkers' union could find little ground for cooperation with the miners' union, which continued to favor the strategy of working to influence state authorities it had developed in the decade before the war.[22]

Neither the social structure nor the strength of social bonds determines the nature and timing of collective action, no more than do exploitation or ideology. But study of the characteristics of groups of workers at Decazeville can help us understand how its industrial population came into existence in the nineteenth century, what social resources workers in the community drew on in times of crisis, and what the potential limitations to labor and community solidarity were. As such, this portrait of Decazeville's population helps fulfill the aim of this book: to contribute to a political, economic, and social history of France written from the bottom up.

# Abbreviations Used in Sources and Notes

| | |
|---|---|
| ABHAD | Archives of the Bassin Houiller d'Aquitaine |
| ACFTC | Archives of the Confédération française des Travailleurs Chrétiens |
| ACGTD | Archives of the Confédération Générale du Travail (Decazeville) |
| ACGTFSS | Archives of the Confédération Générale du Travail—Fédération du Sous-sol (Paris) |
| ACHDGM | Archives of the Comité d'Histoire de la Deuxième Guerre Mondiale |
| ADA | Archives Départementales de l'Aveyron |
| ADL | Archives Départementales du Lot |
| AEM | Archives of the Ecole des Mines (Paris) |
| AER | Archives of the Evêché de Rodez |
| AF | Archives Foucras |
| AG | Assemblée Générale |
| AMG | Archives of the Ministère de la Guerre (Vincennes) |
| AN | Archives Nationales |
| APD | Archives of the Paroisse de Decazeville |
| APP | Archives of the Préfecture de Police (Paris) |
| APR | Archives of Paul Ramadier |
| CA | Conseil d'Administration |
| CCHF | Comité Central des Houillères Françaises |
| CFTC | Confédération Française des Travailleurs Chrétiens |
| CGT | Confédération Générale du Travail |
| CGTU | Confédération Générale du Travail Unitaire |
| CPA | Commissaire de Police d'Aubin |
| CPD | Commissaire de Police de Decazeville |
| CS | Conseil Syndical (of CGT unless specified otherwise) |
| CSD | Commissaire Spécial de Decazeville |

| | |
|---|---|
| DA | Direction d'Aubin |
| DCMD | Deliberations of the Conseil Municipal de Decazeville |
| DD | Direction de Decazeville |
| DG | Direction Générale (Comambault) |
| DGA | Direction Générale (Aubin) |
| FO | Force Ouvrière |
| FSS | Fédération des Travailleurs du Sous-sol (CGT) |
| GG | Garde Générale (Comambault) |
| IISG | Internationaal Instituut voor Sociale Geschiedenis |
| MI | Ministère de l'Intérieur |
| MTP | Ministère des Travaux Publics |
| PA | Préfet de l'Aveyron |
| PO | Paul Oustry |
| POSR | Parti Ouvrier Socialiste Révolutionnaire |
| PR | Paul Ramadier |
| SAF | Société Anonyme des Aciéries de France |
| SCF | Société Anonyme de Commentry—Fourchambault |
| SCFD | Société Anonyme de Commentry—Fourchambault et Decazeville |
| SHFA | Société Anonyme des Houillères et Fonderies de l'Aveyron |
| SLSAA | Société des Lettres, Sciences et Arts de l'Aveyron |
| SNHFA | Société Nouvelle des Houillères et Fonderies de l'Aveyron |
| SpVf | Sous-préfet de Villefranche-de-Rouergue |
| VM | Victor Mazars |

# Primary Sources

**Archives of the Central State**

1. Archives Nationales (AN)
   - AQ   Business Records
     - 59AQ: SHFA, SNHFA, SCF
     - 60AQ: Compagnie d'Orléans
     - 84AQ: SHFA
     - 110AQ: SCF
     - 111AQ: SAF; Société de Châtillon, Commentry et Neuves-Maisons
   - BB   Justice
     - BB18; BB30
   - C   National Assembly
   - F   Personnel, Police, and Administration
     - F 1C III: Public opinion and elections
     - F 7: Police
     - F 12: Commerce and industry
     - F 14: Public works, including mines
     - F 17: Education
     - F 22: Labor
2. Archives du Ministère de la Guerre (AMG)
   MR1274: "Mémoire sur les départements de la Lozère et de l'Aveyron par M. de Caulincourt, lt. d'état major attaché à la géodesie" (1836)
3. Archives of the Préfecture de Police (APP) in Paris
   BA186; BA187: Decazeville strikes of 1878 and 1886
4. Archives of the Service des Mines (Rodez)

**Departmental Archives**

1. Archives Départementales du Lot (ADL)
   C385; IIIE 101/6 f°131–145: Mining in the Aubin Basin during the *ancien régime*

2. Archives Départementales de l'Aveyron (ADA)
   E: 2E 12 27: "Histoire des compagnies des usines d'Aubin (jusqu'à 1882)"—anonymous manuscript (1882)
   J: Miscellaneous acquisitions
   M: Personnel, police, and administration
   R: Military
   S: Public works, including mines
   T: Education
   U: Justice
   V: Religion

## Municipal Archives

1. Aubin: "Délibérations du conseil municipal"
2. Cransac: "Délibérations du conseil municipal"
3. Decazeville: "Délibérations du conseil municipal" (DCMD); birth, marriage, and death registers; *inventaires après décès*
4. Firmy: "Délibérations du conseil municipal"

## Archives of Public and Private Institutions

1. Employers
   a. Charbonnages de France (Paris)
   b. Comité Central des Houillères Françaises: formerly held by the Charbonnages de France; now AN 40AS
   c. Houillères du Bassin d'Aquitaine at Decazeville (ABHAD)
2. Unions
   a. Confédération Française des Travailleurs Chrétiens at Decazeville (ACFTCD): important documentation on the strike of 1961–62. At Rodez, records of the departmental federation.
   b. Confédération Générale du Travail at Decazeville (ACGTD): records of the miners' and metalworkers' unions in the Aubin Basin and of the Union départementale des syndicats de l'Aveyron (1885–1966).
   c. Confédération Générale du Travail. Federation du Sous-Sol in Paris (ACGTFSS): important documentation on the strike of 1961–1962.
3. The Catholic Church
   a. Evêché de Rodez (AER)
   b. Paroisse de Decazeville (APD)
   c. Paroisse de Combes
4. Other
   a. Comité d'Histoire de la Deuxième Guerre Mondiale (ACHDGM): material on the Resistance in the Aubin Basin
   b. Ecole des Mines (AEM): reports by student engineers

　　c.　Parti Socialiste. Fédération de l'Aveyron (Rodez)
　　d.　Société des Sciences, Lettres, et Arts de l'Aveyron (SLSAA) in Rodez: includes Fonds Daudibertières, papers collected by local historian Gaston Daudibertières
　　e.　Société des Secours Minières at Decazeville: records since implementation of 1894 legislation

## Archives of Individuals

1. François Cabrol: held by Féligande and Huntziger families
2. Cabrolière, Coursières, Estrella: papers held by individuals in the Basin
3. Henri Fayol: held by Michel Brun
4. Abbé Foucras (AF): material on the Resistance in the Aubin Basin held by Abbé Foucras
5. Jules Guesde: at International Instituut voor Sociale Geschiedenis in Amsterdam (IISG)
6. Paul Ramadier: previously held by Ramadier family; now largely in ADA
7. René Rouquette: held by René Rouquette
8. René Waldeck-Rousseau: at Institut de France in Paris

## Interviews

André Cayrol; Marceau Coursières; and individual and group conversations with miners and their families

　　Complete listings of the materials in company archives are contained in Bertrand Gille, "Les Archives de la Compagnie des Houillères et Fonderies de l'Aveyron," *Revue d'histoire de la sidérurgie,* 1 (1960): 53–56; Gille, *Etat sommaire des archives d'entreprise conservées aux Archives nationales (Série 1AQ–64AQ)* (Paris: Imprimerie nationale, 1957); Isabelle Guérin-Brot, "Les Archives des houillères du bassin d'Aquitaine, groupe de l'Aveyron," *Revue d'histoire des mines et de la métallurgie,* 2 (1970): 227–242; and Guérin-Brot, *Etat sommaire ... (Série 65AQ–119AQ)* (Paris: Imprimerie nationale, 1977). See also Chantal Leroy-Devaux, "Les Sources d'archives de l'histoire des mines en France," *Bulletin d'histoire moderne et contemporaine,* 10 (1977): 73–133. For a list of the reports by student engineers, consult Gerd Hardach, *Der soziale Status des Arbeiters in der Frühindustrialisierung* (Berlin: Duncker & Humblot, 1969), pp. 197–205.

## Periodicals

*L'Appel* (1937)
*L'Aveyron* (1936–1939)

*L'Aveyron républicain* (1886)
*Le Bassin houiller de l'Aveyron* (1887–1889)
*Le Capdençois socialiste* (1934–1935)
*Le Centre-Presse* (1961–1962; 1977–1978) (regional edition)
*Le Cri du peuple* (1886)
*La Dépêche* (1886; 1898–1914; 1940–1944; 1947–1948; 1961–1962; 1977–
   1978) (regional edition)
*L'Eclaireur* (1911–1914; 1916–1922)
*L' Eveil de Livinhac-le-Haut* (1907–1916)
*Le Figaro* (1961–1962)
*La Gazette des tribunaux* (1869; 1886)
*L'Humanité* (1961–1962)
*L'Indépendent du bassin houiller de l'Aveyron* (1902–1904)
*L'Intransigeant* (1886)
*Le Journal de l'Aveyron* (1848; 1886)
*Le Journal des débats* (1886)
*La Justice* (1886)
*Le Lien de Combes* (1940–1948)
*Masses ouvrières* (1962)
*Le Matin* (1886)
*Le Midi libre* (1961–1962) (regional edition)
*Le Monde* (1961–1963; 1983–1984)
*Le Moniteur d'Aubin et du canton* (1889)
*Le Pays noir* (1888–1892)
*Le Petit méridional* (1886)
*Le Progrès de l'Aveyron* (1930–1935)
*Le Progrès de l'Aveyron, du Tarn et du Lot* (1935–1936)
*Le Progrès de Villefranche-de-Rouergue* (1886)
*Le Prolétaire de l'Aveyron* (1883)
*Le Rappel* (1886)
*La Résistance en Rouergue* (1970–1978)
*La Revue religieuse de Rodez et de Mende* (1886; 1895)
*Le Rouergue républicain* (1948)
*Le Socialiste* (1886)
*Le Socialiste aveyronnais* (1937–1939)
*Le Socialiste de l'Aveyron* (1905–1906)
*Le Soir* (1886)
*Le Syndicaliste* (1919)
*Le Temps* (1886)
*L'Union des gauches* (1921)
*La Voix des travailleurs* (1889–1898)
*La Voix de peuple* (1945–1948)

A useful guide to the periodicals published in Aveyron is Danielle Le Nan and Jean-Louis Malaviale, *Bibliographie de la presse française politique et d'information générale 1865–1944: Aveyron* (Paris: Bibliothèque nationale, 1966).

For a bibliography of printed primary and secondary sources, see my "Labor, Management, and the State in an Industrial Town, 1826–1914" (Ph.D. diss., Stanford University, 1981), pp. 338–373.

# Notes

**Introduction**

1. A phenomenon similar to deindustrialization may occur in regions dependent on market agriculture: wine production provides a good case in France.

2. See Charles Tilly, "Flows of Capital and Forms of Industry in Europe, 1500–1900," *Theory and Society*, 12 (1983): 123–142. From the general concept of "urbanization" in *The Vendée* (Cambridge: Harvard University Press, 1964), Tilly developed a fruitful connection of work organization to working-class protest, and the effects of centralization of state power and the development of capitalism to community life. See especially Edward Shorter and Charles Tilly, *Strikes in France 1830–1968* (Cambridge: Cambridge University Press, 1974); and Charles Tilly, "Did the Cake of Custom Break?" in *Consciousness and Class Experience in Nineteenth-Century Europe*, ed. John Merriman (New York: Holmes & Meier, 1979), pp. 17–44. My book is one answer to Tilly's call for specific historical studies of these processes. See, for instance, his criticism of "theories of work-discipline that deduce the forms of control over producers in setting after setting from the logic of production itself, without systematic variation by place and time" in "Two Callings of Social History," *Theory and Society*, 9 (1980): 680.

3. See Tessie Liu, "From De-industrialization to Cottage Industries: The Historical Record" (paper presented at the North American Labor History Conference, October 1984).

4. A valuable study of the effects of an earlier period of deindustrialization and related phenomena on the political orientation of the Var and France as a whole is Tony Judt, *Socialism in Provence 1871–1914: A Study in the Origins of the Modern French Left* (Cambridge: Cambridge University Press, 1979).

5. In the Appendix (A Social Portrait of Industrial Workers in Nineteenth-Century Decazeville) I examine relations between miners and met-

alworkers. For my other work on Decazeville's metalworkers, see "The Origins of Industrial Labor Management in France: The Case of the Decazeville Ironworks During the July Monarchy," *Business History Review,* 57 (Spring 1983): 1–19; "L'Industrie métallurgique et les ouvriers métallurgistes de Decazeville, 1892–1914" (forthcoming in *Procès-verbaux des séances de la SLSAA*); and "Guillaume Verdier et le syndicalisme révolutionnaire aux usines de Decazeville (1917–1920)," *Annales du Midi,* 96 (1984): 171–198. For a comparison of managerial practices in mining and metallurgy in France during the nineteenth century, see my "The Lamb and the Tiger: Paternalist Discourse and Practice in the Management of Labor in Nineteenth-Century French Mining and Metallurgy" (forthcoming in *Comparative Studies in Society and History*).

When used as shorthand for the major firm in the town, "Decazeville" includes other company operations in the Basin.

6. Bertrand Gille, "Les plus grandes compagnies houillères françaises en 1840," in *Charbon et sciences humaines,* ed. Louis Trénard (Paris: Mouton, 1966), pp. 153–171.

7. Maurice Lévy-Leboyer, "The Large Corporation in Modern France," in *Managerial Hierarchies: Comparative Perspectives on the Rise of the Modern Industrial Enterprise,* ed. Alfred D. Chandler, Jr. and Herman Daems (Cambridge, Mass.: Harvard University Press, 1980), pp. 127–129.

8. Pierre Sorlin, *La Société française,* 2 vols. (Paris: B. Arthaud, 1969), I, 163.

9. Shorter and Tilly, *Strikes in France,* p. 115.

10. See Leon Fink, "Looking Backward: Reflections on Workers' Culture and the Conceptual Dilemmas of the New Labor History" (paper presented at the research conference on the Future of American Labor History research conference, October 1984). For an overview of some recent approaches to French labor history, see my "The Night of the Proletarians: Deconstruction and Social History," *Radical History Review,* 28–30 (1984): 444–463.

11. For artisanal workers, see Ronald Aminzade, *Class, Politics, and Early Industrial Capitalism: A Study of Mid-Nineteenth Century Toulouse* (Albany: State University of New York Press, 1981); Robert Bezucha, *The Lyon Uprising of 1834: Social and Political Conflict in the Early July Monarchy* (Cambridge, Mass.: Harvard University Press, 1974); Christopher Johnson, *Utopian Communism in France: Cabet and the Icarians 1839–1857* (Ithaca: Cornell University Press, 1974); and William Sewell, *Work and Revolution in France: The Language of Labor from the Old Regime to 1848* (Cambridge: Cambridge University Press, 1980). On skilled industrial workers see Michael Hanagan, *The Logic of Solidarity: Artisans and Industrial Workers in Three French Towns 1871–1914* (Urbana: University of Illinois Press, 1980) and Joan W. Scott, *The Glassworkers of Carmaux* (Cambridge, Mass.: Harvard University Press, 1974). On the ideological

continuities between the outlooks of the two groups, see Bernard Moss, *The Origins of the French Labor Movement: The Socialism of Skilled Workers* (Berkeley: University of California Press, 1976).

12. Dick Geary, *European Labour Protest 1848–1939* (New York: St. Martin's Press, 1981) provides a good interpretive summary of recent research.

13. See the Appendix (A Social Portrait); and Yves Lequin, *Les Ouvriers de la région lyonnaise (1848–1914)*, 2 vols. (Lyon: Presses universitaires de Lyon, 1977), vol. I, for an analysis of the geographic and social origins of industrial workers during the nineteenth century. On miners and their ties to the land in France, see Rolande Trempé's extraordinary *Les Mineurs de Carmaux 1848–1914*, 2 vols. (Paris: Editions ouvrières, 1971).

14. Pierre Guillaume, "La Situation économique et sociale du département de la Loire d'après l'Enquête sur le travail agricole et industriel du 25 mai 1848," *Revue d'histoire moderne et contemporaine*, 10 (1963): 32.

15. Michael Hanagan emphasizes this aspect of artisanal and skilled industrial labor in "Artisan and Skilled Worker: The Problem of Definition," *International Labor and Working Class History*, 12 (November 1977): 28–31.

16. Shorter and Tilly, *Strikes in France*, pp. 13, 127.

17. Charles Tilly, Louise Tilly, and Richard Tilly, *The Rebellious Century 1830–1930* (Cambridge, Mass.: Harvard University Press, 1975), p. 42. For the difficulties in categorizing miners, see Hanagan, *The Logic of Solidarity*, pp. 220–221.

18. In studying French miners one can draw on a number of excellent local studies, including Jean-Michel Gaillard, "Un Exemple de 'Ville-Usine': La Grand-Combe (Gard) et sa 'Compagnie des Mines' (1835–1921)" (Troisième cycle, Université de Paris X-Nanterre, 1974); Reed Geiger, *The Anzin Coal Company 1800–1833* (Newark: University of Delaware Press, 1974); Marcel Gillet, *Les Charbonnages du nord de la France au XIXᵉ siècle* (Paris: Mouton, 1973); Pierre Guillaume, *La Compagnie des Mines de la Loire 1846–1854* (Paris: Presses universitaires de France, 1966); Odette Hardy-Hémery, *De la Croissance à la désindustrialisation. Un Siècle dans le Valenciennois* (Paris: Presses de la Fondation nationale des sciences politiques, 1984); and Trempé, *Les Mineurs*. Michelle Perrot's *Les Ouvriers en grève. France 1871–1890*, 2 vols. (Paris: Mouton, 1974) provides a wealth of information and insights on miners' strikes.

19. My analysis of the relation of labor management to business structures has been particularly influenced by Sidney Pollard, *The Genesis of Modern Management: A Study of the Industrial Revolution in Great Britain* (Cambridge: Harvard University Press, 1965) and by Alfred Chandler, *Strategy and Structure. Chapters in the History of Industrial Enterprise* (Cambridge: M.I.T. Press, 1962). I have found work on the history of labor management from several perspectives quite helpful. Important Marxist

works on the history of the labor process include Harry Braverman, *Labor and Monopoly Capital* (New York: Monthly Review Press, 1974); Dan Clawson, *Bureaucracy and the Labor Process: The Transformation of U.S. Industry, 1860–1920* (New York: Monthly Review Press, 1980); and Stephen Marglin, "What Do Bosses Do? The Origins and Functions of Hierarchy in Capitalist Production," *The Review of Radical Political Economics*, 6 (Summer 1974): 60–112. For an important corrective to these "objective" accounts of de-skilling (especially Braverman's), see David Stark, "Class Struggle and the Transformation of the Labor Process," *Theory and Society*, 9 (1980): 89–130. For Marxist-influenced analyses of workers' control over production, see E. P. Thompson, "Time, Work-Discipline, and Industrial Capitalism," *Past and Present*, 50 (February 1971): 76–136; Eric Hobsbawm, "Custom, Wages, and Work-Load," in *Labouring Men* (New York: Basic Books, 1964), pp. 344–370; David Montgomery, *Workers' Control in America* (Cambridge: Cambridge University Press, 1979); Katherine Stone, "The Origins of Job Structures in the Steel Industry," *The Review of Radical Political Economics*, 6 (Summer 1974): 113–173; and Patrick Fridenson, "France, Etats-Unis: Genèse de l'usine nouvelle," in *Le Soldat du travail*, ed. Lion Murard and Patrick Zylberman (Paris: *Recherches*, 1978), pp. 375–388. Michelle Perrot, drawing as much on Michel Foucault as on Marx, offers a helpful framework for examining developments in labor management since the seventeenth century in "The Three Ages of Industrial Discipline in Nineteenth-Century France," in *Consciousness and Class Experience in Nineteenth-Century Europe*, ed. John Merriman (New York: Holmes & Meier, 1979), pp. 149–168. From a related perspective, see Alberto Melucci, "Action patronale, pouvoir, organisation: Règlements d'usine et contrôle de la main d'oeuvre au XIX$^e$ siècle," *Mouvement social*, 97 (October-December 1976): 139–159.

20. There is an extensive literature on the importance of labor costs in the economics of coal mining in France. Early in this century François Simiand determined that in France, which has depended on the importation of coal to satisfy a significant portion of its domestic energy needs, the quantity and price of imported coal had a determining effect on the price at which French companies sold their coal. His analysis of government statistics on the French coal industry during the nineteenth century showed that as the sale price of coal rose, the production cost of coal also rose, but more slowly; productivity declined; and the miner's average wage rose. When the sale price of coal first began to fall these trends initially continued, but as the sale price continued to drop the production cost of coal fell, productivity rose, and the miner's average salary stagnated or dropped slightly. Studies of individual firms reveal that their aim in periods of rising prices was to keep the rate of wage increase below that of the increase in profits; in periods of declining profits the company's goal was to prevent profits from declining to the level they had reached in the previous period of falling

prices. Because miners had a great deal of success in defending their average wage—which increased during each period of rising sale price of coal—the trend over time was for the percentage of the sale price of coal spent on labor to increase. This forced mine managers to look to new ways to administer the miners' work in order to raise productivity. François Simiand, *Le Salaire des ouvriers des mines de charbon en France* (Paris: Edouard Cornély, 1907); Jean Bouvier, François Furet, and Marcel Gillet, *Le Mouvement du profit en France au 19ᵉ siècle* (Paris: Mouton, 1965); Geiger, *The Anzin Coal Company;* Gillet, *Les Charbonnages;* and Trempé, *Les Mineurs.* For the twentieth century, see Maurice Borgeaud, *Le Salaire des ouvriers des mines de charbon en France depuis 1900* (Paris: Presses universitaires de France, 1938). The best synthesis of this research is by Marc Simard, "Situation économique de l'entreprise et rapports de production: le cas de la Compagnie des Mines d'Anzin (1860–1894)," *Revue du Nord,* 65 (July-September 1983): 586–588, which I followed above. The crucial work in the field is Trempé, *Les Mineurs,* vol. I, to which I refer the reader for an excellent analysis—not attempted here—of the labor economics of the coal industry.

For statistics on wages in different basins and on national coal production, I have depended on the annual *Statistique de l'industrie minérale* (Paris: Imprimerie nationale), published by several different ministries over the years. I have supplemented this with statistical compilations in *Coal Mine Labor in Europe: Twelfth Report of the Commissioner of Labor* (Washington: Government Printing Office, 1905); and B. R. Mitchell, *European Historical Statistics 1750–1970* (London: Macmillan Press, 1975).

21. See my "The Lamb and the Tiger" and "The Origins and Development of *Fayolisme*" (forthcoming in *Sociologie du travail*).

22. In contrast to the usage of many sociologists, my use of "community" is historical and relative. Community is a historical concept because it is continually created, lost, and recreated over time as the result of individuals' actions in the face of changing circumstances. Community is not a phenomenon limited to the preindustrial period that necessarily dissolves into individualism, class allegiance, or nationalism with modernization, industrialization, or consolidation of the nation-state. Community is a relative concept because it exists to some degree in a wide variety of circumstances. In any given situation it may draw more or less of its cultural and organizational coherence from relationships based on the family, the household, the workplace, the market, or the settlement.

22. See Shorter and Tilly, *Strikes in France,* and Geary, *European Labour Protest.* For the mining industry in France, see Rolande Trempé's excellent "Le Réformisme des mineurs français à la fin du XIXᵉ siècle," *Mouvement social,* 65 (October-December 1968): 93–107.

23. See my "The Role of Mine Safety in the Development of Working-Class Consciousness and Organization: The Case of the Aubin Coal Basin,

1867–1914," *French Historical Studies,* 11 (Spring 1981): 98–119; and more generally my "The Implementation of Social Reform: Labor Inspectors in France, 1892–1914" (paper presented at the French Historical Studies Conference, March 1985).

24. Decazeville differs from the archetypal Occitan community. The town is located in the northern half of the department of Aveyron, an area that some Occitanists consider too far north to form part of Occitania. Since the early nineteenth century most of Decazeville's residents have earned their living in heavy industry rather than grape-growing, husbandry, or other activities generally associated with Occitan life. Yet neither of these factors disqualifies Decazeville as a community in which to study the confrontation of the culture of southwestern France with that of northern France. In a perverse way, Decazeville may be the ideal choice. Gérard Cholvy argues that during the nineteenth century many natives of lower Languedoc rejected their degraded Occitan culture in favor of the language and mores promoted by the national French state because they offered the best opportunities for upward social mobility through such jobs as teachers and civil servants. Two categories of inhabitants in Languedoc did not follow this pattern: residents of the mountainous north and industrial workers. The miners of Decazeville belong to both of these groups. See Cholvy, "Histoires contemporaines en pays d'Oc," *Annales: E.S.C.,* 33 (1978): 863–879.

## 1. The Triumph of Industrial Capitalism

1. AN F 14 7631, "Mémoire sur la mine de fontaïne pour être remis au conseil des mines" (Flauguergues), 20 Floréal VI. L. C. P. Bosc, *Mémoires pour servir à l'histoire du Rouergue,* 3 vols. (Rodez, 1797), I, 43–46 and III, 122–123. Amans-Alexis Monteils, *Description du département de l'Aveiron,* 2 vols. (Rodez, Year X), I, 58–59, 62–65. J. F. Henry de Richeprey, *Journal des voyages en Haute-Guienne* [1775], 2 vols., ed. H. Guilhamon (Rodez: Commission des Archives Historiques du Rouergue, 1952 and 1957), I, 11–12, 14 (note by Guilhamon). Jean Tisseyre, "Les Mines d'alun de Fontaynes," *Revue du Rouergue,* 23 (1969): 367–375. Lucien Mazars, *Cransac (Aveyron): Ville thermale* (Rodez: P. Carrère, n.d.).

2. Louis Lempereur, *Etat du diocèse de Rodez en 1771* (Rodez: Imprimerie Louis Loup, 1906), pp. 15–17. Monteils, *Description,* I, 62.

3. Lempereur, *Etat,* pp. 4–8. Priests were trying to get assistance for their parishioners and had little interest in presenting a bright picture of the local economy.

4. Monteils, *Description,* I, 62–63.

5. AN F 14 7626, "Rapport de l'agent des mines à la commission des armes de la République" [Year II?]; report on the mines of Aubin by the national agent for the district of Aubin, 24 Messidor II. AN F 14 7627, "Note

pour servir au mémoire de Morand sur les mines embrasés du Rouergue lu à l'Académie des sciences," Floréal V. SLSAA Fonds Daudibertières, carton 2, "Mémoire du Citoyen Crêtes, conseiller d'Etat, "Notice sur les houillères . . . ," 12 Pluviôse IX. G. Daudibertières, "L'Etat civil de Vialarels (ancienne paroisse de Decazeville)," *Revue du Rouergue,* 19 (1965): 294. Lucien Mazars, *Aubin: Son histoire des origines à la Révolution de 1789* (Rodez: Imprimerie Carrère, n.d.), p. 45. ADL C385 no. 16, report of König, 28 October 1755 (quoted).

6. Marcel Rouff, an enthusiastic admirer of the edict of 1744, emphasizes this. *Les Mines de charbon en France au XVIIIᵉ siècle* (Paris: F. Rieder, 1922), pp. 76–77.

7. Bosc, *Mémoires,* III, 123–124. Mazars, *Aubin,* pp. 46–47.

8. Rouff, *Les Mines,* pp. 145 (n. 1), 281.

9. ADL C385 no. 12, petition by Tullier and Douin, 1 December 1753; no. 15, Intendant of Montauban, 30 January 1754; no. 27, Roux to Intendant of Montauban, 30 June 1760. AN F 14 7627 (21), untitled report [1759], and "Mémoire" [1763].

On the period between 1763 and 1768 see Mazars, *Aubin,* pp. 48–50. ADL C385 no. 53, "Mémoire de l'état actuel de la procédure faite à la requête de procureur du Roy, contre les rébellionnaires de Livignac," [n.d.]; no. 43, Tubeuf to Douin, 16 August 1763; no. 14, Tubeuf to Intendant of Montauban, 25 May 1764; no. 59, report [to Intendant of Montauban?], 15 November 1766; no. 68, letter by Bournazel [n.d.]. Marcel Rouff, *Tubeuf, un grand industriel français au XVIIIᵉ siècle d'après ses papiers personnels* (Paris: Société nouvelle, n.d.).

For the events of 1769 see AN F 14 7626, covering note to "26 Septembre 1782 procès-verbal de l'assemblée de la haute Guyenne," 22 May 1783, and "Conclusion" to the dossier on the concession granted Tullier and Douin. AN F 14 7627 (21), report of the Intendant of Montauban, 3 May 1769. Rouff, *Les Mines,* pp. 144–145. Bosc, *Mémoires,* III, 125–128. Mazars, *Aubin,* pp. 52–56.

On the abortive attempt to reopen the mines in 1779 see L. d'Alauzier, "Un Document sur la première concession des mines d'Aubin-Decazeville," in *11ᵉ Congrès d'études de la fédération des sociétés académiques et savantes Languedoc-Pyrénées-Gascogne, Albi 11–13 juin 1955* (Albi: Imprimerie reliure des orphelins-apprentis, 1956), pp. 124–127, and ADL IIIE 101/6 fᵒ 131–145, statement by Vassal, 25 October 1779.

10. AN F 14 7626, Besson to Boulloye, 22 June 1783.

11. Ibid., 11 August 1783.

12. Ibid., 17 August 1783. On state supervision of the mines before the Revolution, see Bertrand Gille, "L'Administration des mines en France sous l'ancien régime," *Revue d'histoire des mines et de la métallurgie,* 1 (1969): 3–35.

13. AN F 14 7626, "Rapport du bureau du bien public: Extrait du

procès-verbal de l'assemblée provinciale de la haute Guyenne," 26 September 1782.

14. France, Chambre des députés, *Rapport fait au nom de la Commission des mines chargée d'examiner le projet et les propositions de loi sur le régime des mines par M. Alexandre Zévaès* (Paris: Imprimerie de la Chambre des députés, 1909), p. 10.

15. Emmanuel Le Roy Ladurie argues that in the eighteenth century antiseigneurial revolts were less common in Auvergne and Languedoc than in Bourgogne. See "Révoltes et contestations rurales en France de 1675 à 1788," *Annales: E.S.C.*, 29 (1974): 6–22. Certainly in the Aubin Basin the primary sociopolitical conflicts before the Revolution were between the peasantry and state-supported capitalist entrepreneurs, not local lords.

16. Marcel Gillet, *Les Charbonnages du nord de la France au XIX^e siècle* (Paris: Mouton, 1973), p. 28. Philippe Guignet, *Mines, manufactures et ouvriers du Valençiennois au XVIII^e siècle* (New York: Arno Press, 1977).

17. Monteils, *Description*, II, 9–10.

18. Ibid., I, 67–68. Mazars, *Aubin*, p. 58. For a history of the Revolution in the Aubin Basin, see Lucien Mazars, *La Révolution en Rouergue: District d'Aubin 1789–1795*, 2 vols. (Villefranche-de-Rouergue: Imprimerie Salingardes, 1976 and 1978). Conflicts over coal mining were related to a wider crisis over wood rights which was a contributing factor to the prerevolutionary crisis in the Languedoc. Edward A. Allen, "Deforestation and Fuel Crisis in Pre-Revolutionary Languedoc, 1720–1789," *French Historical Studies*, 13 (1984): 455–473.

19. See Rouff, *Les Mines*, pp. 589–590. Rouff's work is the standard history of mining in France during the eighteenth century. It is also an important intellectual document of the early twentieth century. The book is essentially a *solidariste* attack on small property-owners who were unable to provide the same social services and safe mining conditions for their miners as Anzin. Rouff argues not the merits of capitalism but the beneficial effects of larger social organizations for the individual. Rouff's argumentation helped provide a historical basis for reformers' projects to nationalize French mines between the wars.

20. Pierre Guillaume, "La Propriété minière en France jusqu' à la première guerre mondiale," *L'Information historique*, 21 (1959): 195–199. See also his "La Redevance tréfoncière et les propriétaires tréfonciers dans le bassin houiller de la Loire," in *Actes du 88^e congrès national des sociétés savantes Clermont-Ferrand 1963: Section d'histoire moderne et contemporaine* (Paris: Imprimerie nationale, 1964), pp. 489–503, and his *La Compagnie des mines de la Loire 1846–1854* (Paris: Presses universitaires de France, 1966), p. 117.

21. ADA J465, engineer Gardien to chief engineer d'Aubuisson, 25 February 1815; 1 May 1815. On mining in the Aubin Basin during the Napoleonic period, see G. Daudibertières, "La Première concession des mines

de houille accordée par Napoléon I$^{er}$ dans le département de l'Aveyron,"
*Procès-verbaux des séances de la SLSAA*, 37 (1954–1958): 104–108. For
material on the more advanced operations at Carmaux, see Rolande Trempé,
"Contribution à l'histoire des mineurs sous la Révolution et l'Empire: Le
Journal d'exploitation tenu par le directeur des mines de Carmaux de 1787
à 1816," in *Actes du 83$^e$ congrès national des sociétés savantes Aix-Mar-
seille 1958. Section d'histoire moderne et contemporaine* (Paris: Imprimerie
nationale, 1959), pp. 513–526.

22. Marie Christine Cartayrade, "Ils étaient paysans les sont-ils restés?
Evolution d'une commune en Rouergue: Aubin 1825–1870" (Mémoire,
Université de Paris I, 1971), p. 27; and R. Beteille, *Les Aveyronnais: Essai
géographique sur l'espace humain* (Poitiers: Imprimerie l'Union, 1974), pp.
27–50.

23. On the subject of French industrialists and British industry, see
Peter Stearns, "British Industry through the Eyes of French Industrialists,
1820–1848," *Journal of Modern History*, 37 (1965): 50–61.

24. J. B. Silly, "La Concentration dans l'industrie sidérurgique en France
sous le Second Empire," *Revue d'histoire de la sidérurgie*, 3 (1962): 22–24.

25. Louis Cassiat, "La Naissance de Decazeville," *Cahiers rouergats*,
2 (June 1970): 22–37. G. Daudibertières, "Le Duc Decazes et l'industrie du
fer dans l'Aveyron. Ses premiers projets en 1825," *Procès-verbaux des séances de la SLSAA*, 37 (1954–1958): 390–394, and his "La Société des
Houillères et Fonderies de l'Aveyron et le premier développement industriel
de Decazeville," *Mémoires de la SLSAA*, 28 (1964): 479–495. Alex Gromb,
"La Société des Houillères et Fonderies de l'Aveyron (1826–1865)" (D.E.S.,
Université de Paris, 1963).

26. Arthur Louis Dunham, *The Industrial Revolution in France 1815–
1848* (New York: Exposition Press, 1955), p. 142. [Bertrand Gille], "Le Fi-
nancement de l'industrie sidérurgique française au XIX$^e$ siècle," *Revue d'histoire de la sidérurgie*, 2 (1961): 282–285. In "Le Mouvement du profit au
XIX$^e$ siècle," *Revue d'histoire de la sidérurgie*, 7 (1966): 42, Gille discusses
self financing at Decazeville in light of Jean Bouvier, François Furet, and
Marcel Gillet, *Le Mouvement du profit en France au 19$^e$ siècle* (Paris: Mouton, 1965).

27. Louis Bergeron, *Les Capitalistes en France (1780–1914)* (Paris: Gallimard, 1978), p. 29.

28. François Crouzet, "Les Origines du sous-développement économique du sud-ouest," *Annales du midi*, 71 (1959): 71–79. André Armengaud, "A Propos des origines du sous-développement industriel dans le sud-
ouest," *Annales du Midi*, 72 (1960): 75–82. Jean-Michel Gaillard, "La Naissance d'une entreprise industrielle au XIX$^e$ siècle: la Compagnie des Mines
de la Grand-Combe," in *Mines et mineurs en Languedoc-Roussillon et régions voisines de l'antiquité à nos jours* (Montpellier: Fédération historique
du Languedoc méditerranéen et du Roussillon, 1977), p. 193.

29. André-Jean Tudesq, *Les Grands notables en France (1840–1849): Etude historique d'une psychologie sociale,* 2 vols. (Paris, Presses universitaires de France, 1964), I, 428.

30. Félix Ponteil, *Un Type de grand bourgeois sous la monarchie parlementaire: Georges Humann 1780–1842* (Paris: Editions Ophrys, 1977), pp. 46–50.

31. François Cabrol et al., "Extinction de la mendicité," *Mémoires de la SLSAA,* I, part 2 (1838): 213–258.

32. Louis Puech and P. Soulié, *François Cabrol* (Rodez: Imprimerie Ratéry-Virenque, 1882), pp. 29–30.

33. AN 84AQ17, DD to CA, 18 April 1827.

34. Bertrand Gille, "Les Débuts de la Compagnie des Mines, Fonderies et Forges de l'Aveyron (Decazeville)," *Revue d'histoire de la sidérurgie,* 9 (1968): 66. These articles are transcripts of the minutes of the firm's first board meetings and general assemblies, located in the series AN 84AQ.

35. Daudibertières, "La Société des Houillères et Fonderies," 494.

36. AN 59AQ544, DD to CA, 13 February 1829. AN 84AQ31, CA to DD, 30 September 1829.

37. G. Daudibertières, "La Formation du nom de la ville de Decazeville," *Procès-verbaux des séances de la SLSAA,* 40 (1967–1970): 325–329.

38. SLSAA, Fonds Daudibertières, carton 16, DD to PA, 30 June 1832.

39. Ibid., carton 10, petition [October 1832].

40. ADA 28M2 77, "Etat indiquant l'organisation proposée par le Préfet pour la commune d'Aubin" [1833].

41. *Le Bassin houiller de l'Aveyron illustré* (Decazeville: F. Chirac, n.d.), p. 43.

42. Mazars Archives, mine report, 1 January 1838. See also AN 84AQ30, DD to CA, 27 May 1839.

43. ADA 93S1, DD to PA, 28 February 1838. For an interesting account of the Houillères et Fonderies' manipulation of the national press in its campaign against vestigial local mining interests, see Paul Dropy, "Drame de la mine," *Procès-verbaux des séances de la SLSAA,* 42 (1975): 39–48.

44. AN F 14 7634 (36), SHFA to PA, 23 March 1844.

45. AN F 14 4311 (3), statement by the Conseil général des mines in granting the iron ore concession of Lagrange in 1828.

46. AN 84AQ2, CA of SHFA, 5 January 1834; 7 January 1834. ADA 84S1, MTP to PA, 3 April 1840. Jean Vial, *L'Industrialisation de la sidérurgie française 1814–1864,* 2 vols. (Paris: Mouton, 1967), I, 131. L. Lévêque, *Histoire des forges de Decazeville* (Saint-Etienne: Société de l'Industrie Minérale, [1916]), p. 71.

47. In 1857 Emile Trautmann, state engineer in Rodez since 1848, received an annual salary of 2,500 francs. He was paid an additional 2,100 francs for four consultations by Grand Central, owner of the mines of Aubin. ADA 84S1, *fiche indicative* for Emile Trautmann, 1857.

48. AN F 14 3827, report of state engineer [1846].

49. AN 84AQ20, DD to CA, 1 February 1837.

50. AN 84AQ21, DD to CA, 5 July 1838. Maurice Lévy-Leboyer, *Les Banques européennes et l'industrialisation internationale dans la première moitie du XIX^e siècle* (Paris: Presses universitaires de France, 1964), p. 657.

51. J. B. Silly, "La Reprise du Creusot 1836–1848," *Revue d'histoire des mines et de la métallurgie*, 1 (1969): 255–256.

52. Lévêque, *Histoire*, p. 57. G. Daudibertières, "Un Centenaire industriel: La Grande activité des Forges de Decazeville," *Procès-verbaux des séances de la SLSAA*, 37 (1954–1958): 200–201.

53. Jacques Wolff, "Decazeville: Expansion et déclin d'un pôle de croissance," *Revue économique*, 23 (September 1972): 767.

54. AN F 14 7692 (67), Cabrol to Galtyric, 15 June 1865.

55. APD, "Livre de paroisse" of Decazeville, pp. 1–2. ADA 20 V2, a contract drawn up by Vialarels' principal residents agreeing to support a priest at the suppressed parish, 4 January 1809. SLSAA, Fond Daudibertières, carton 21, copy of "Livre de raison de Jean Balthazar Joulia de Lassalle" containing two letters to the Bishop of Cahors, dated 1821 and 17 March 1831. The miners to whom Lassalle referred worked for a small firm which extracted alum before the establishment of the Houillères et Fonderies. J.-M. Tisseyre, "Les Mines d'alun de Fontaynes," *Revue du Rouergue*, 23 (1969): 367–375.

56. APD, "Livre de paroisse" of Decazeville, p. 7. See also the description in AER, Crozier, "Visites," [1843], p. 37.

57. Cabrol Archives, A. Farnaud to Cabrol, 17 March 1846. The young Gustave Moreau later graced the Church with a striking series of paintings. Gabriel Bou, *14 Tableaux de Gustave Moreau: Le Chemin de croix de l'église Notre-Dame de Decazeville (Aveyron)* (Rodez: Editions Subervie, 1964).

58. Ardouin-Dumazet, *Voyages en France*, 35^e série (Paris: Berger-Levrault, 1904), p. 23.

59. AER, *visite pastorale* to Gua, 8 April 1872.

60. AN 84AQ34, CA to DD, 1 February 1840. The Houillères et Fonderies quickly learned to use its position in the local economy to punish those who opposed its plans. When the landowner Galtier won 60 francs from the firm in 1837 in recompense for smoke damage to his chestnut trees, it retaliated immediately. The director wrote to the board: "To make Galtier repent for this unseemly hostility, I forbade haulage to his tenant-farmer, whose name he had used in making his claims. Moreover, M. Galtier has two houses near the factory . . . fully occupied by our workers. These bring him one hundred francs per month. I prohibited, on threat of dismissal, any individual working for the company to live in M. Galtier's houses." The tenant-farmer then threatened to bring Galtier to court for using his

name without permission unless Galtier dropped charges against the company. AN 84AQ20, DD to CA, 31 October 1837.

61. AN 84AQ23, DD to CA, 6 July 1840.

62. René Garmy, La *"Mine aux mineurs" de Rancié*, 2nd ed. (Paris: Editions Montchrestien, 1970). John Merriman, "The Demoiselles of the Ariège, 1829–1831," in *1830 in France*, ed. John Merriman (New York: Franklin Watts, 1975), pp. 87–118. Maurice Agulhon, *La République au village* (Paris: Librairie Plon, 1970), pp. 42–92.

63. Aubin Municipal Archives, "Délibérations du conseil municipal," 3 July 1853.

64. Cransac Municipal Archives, "Délibérations du conseil municipal," 16 May 1891. *Le Bassin houiller*, p. 61. Mazars, *Cransac, passim*.

65. Charles Tilly, "Flows of Capital and Forms of Industry in Europe, 1500–1900," *Theory and Society*, 12 (1983): 123–142.

66. Sidney Pollard, ed., "Introduction" to *Region und Industrialisierung* (Göttingen: Vandenhoeck & Ruprecht, 1980), pp. 22–23.

## 2. Work in the Mines

1. Recent reviews of the literature on the French economy in the nineteenth century include Rondo Cameron and Charles Freedeman, "French Economic Growth: A Radical Revision," *Social Science History*, 7 (Winter 1983): 3–30, which stresses the dynamism of French agriculture; and William Sewell, *Work and Revolution in France. The Language of Labor from the Old Regime to 1848* (Cambridge: Cambridge University Press, 1980), pp. 143–161, which focuses on artisanal production.

2. Sewell, *Work and Revolution*.

3. See François Crouzet, "Le Charbon en France au XIX^e siècle," in *Charbon et sciences humaines*, ed. Louis Trénard (Paris: Mouton, 1966), pp. 173–206.

4. AN 84AQ20, DD to CA, 17 October 1837.

5. SLSAA, Fonds Daudibertières, carton 9, state engineer, 4 August 1854.

6. Guy Thuillier, *Aspects de l'économie nivernaise au XIX^e siècle* (Paris: Armand Colin, 1966), p. 336.

7. With 4.74 percent of French miners in its employ in 1840, the Houillères et Fonderies mined only 2.32 percent of the nation's coal. Bertrand Gille, "Les plus grandes compagnies houillères françaises en 1840," in *Charbon et sciences humaines*, pp. 154, 156. Elsewhere I have criticized Jacques Wolff for using Gille's statistics to argue that the company was an extraordinarily inefficient employer of labor in the ironworks: see my "The Origins of Industrial Labor Management in France: The Case of the Decazeville Ironworks During the July Monarchy," *Business History Review,*

57 (Spring 1983): 5, n. 12. In fact, what the figures reveal is that the Houillères et Fonderies was an inefficient employer of labor in the mines.

8. Maurice Lévy-Leboyer, *Les Banques européennes et l'industrialisation internationale dans la première moitié du XIX<sup>e</sup> siècle* (Paris: Presses universitaires de France, 1964), p. 339, n. 80.

9. André Garcia, "Le Bassin houiller de l'Aveyron: Etude de développement industriel," *Revue géographique des Pyrénées et du Sud-Ouest,* 30 (1959): 374.

10. SLSAA, Fonds Daudibertières, carton no. 5, production figures provided by the Charbonnages de France. AN F 14 3827, state engineer [1846].

11. Ibid. AN F 14 3828, state chief engineer, 10 January 1855.

12. See my "The Origins of Industrial Labor Management"; Gerd Hardach, "Les Problèmes de main d'oeuvre à Decazeville," *Revue d'histoire de la sidérurgie,* 8 (1967): 51–68; and his *Der soziale Status des Arbeiters in der Frühindustrialisierung* (Berlin: Duncker & Humblot, 1969).

13. See Appendix: A Social Portrait of Industrial Workers in Nineteenth-Century Decazeville.

14. AN 84AQ27, DD to CA, 10 July 1856. Mass departures raised costs (AN 84AQ21, DD to CA, 19 July 1838) and disrupted production in the ironworks (AN 84AQ20, DD to CA, 12 October 1837).

15. ADA 93S5, report of state engineer, 9 March 1870.

16. Mazars Archives, Carron to DD, 15 August 1837.

17. In his study of Silesian workers, Lawrence Schofer also concludes that "labor market conditions suffice to explain a good deal of [the] presumably 'anti-industrial' behavior" of workers who did not devote themselves fully to industrial work; *The Formation of a Modern Labor Force: Upper Silesia, 1865–1914* (Berkeley: University of California Press, 1975), p. 52.

18. See AN 84AQ7, CA to AG, 30 May 1849.

19. ADA 7M24, "Situation du colonage partiaire" (Perception de Decazeville) [1853].

20. For a good example, see ADA 93S1, mine guard, 12 March 1856.

21. AN 84AQ17, DD to CA, 25 January 1827. Mazars Archives, mine report, May 1828.

22. See Rolande Trempé, *Les Mineurs de Carmaux 1848–1914* (Paris: Editions ouvrières, 1971), pp. 107–116.

23. George Jared Lamb, "Coal Mining in France, 1873 to 1895" (Ph.D. diss., University of Illinois at Urbana-Champaign, 1976), pp. 159–160.

24. Lucien Mazars, "Travail, moeurs et coutumes pendant les toutes premières années du bassin industriel de Decazeville (période 1827–1842) à travers quelques lettres adressées à François Cabrol, Directeur des 'Houillères et Fonderies de l'Aveyron,' " *Revue du Rouergue,* 13 (1959): 193.

25. Roger Cornu and Bernard Picon, *Analyse contextuelle de la mobilité. II-Mineurs cévenols et provençaux face à la crise des charbonnages*

(Aix-en-Provence: Laboratoire d'économie et de sociologie du travail, 1975), pp. 45, 118–119.

26. Mazars Archives, mine report, March 1828.

27. AN 84AQ20, DD to CA, 25 February 1837.

28. Mazars Archives, mine report, February 1830, "Règlement de Tramont."

29. A. T. Ponson, *Traité de l'exploitation des mines de houille,* 4 vols. (Liège: E. Noblet, 1855), IV, 283.

30. Bertrand Gille, "Les Débuts de la Compagnie des Mines, Fonderies et Forges de l'Aveyron (Decazeville)," *Revue d'histoire de la sidérurgie française,* 9 (1969): 69 [CA of SHFA, 23 April 1831].

31. AN 84AQ14, AG, 24 May 1853.

32. SLSAA Fonds Daudibertières, carton 9, report of state engineer, 26 July 1856. AN 84AQ8, report of CA of SHFA to AG, 20 May 1856. AN F 14 3828, inspector of Division des mines, 8 June 1857.

33. AMG MR1274, "Mémoire . . . Caulincourt" [1836].

34. Mazars, "Travail, moeurs et coutumes," 190.

35. AN F 14 7629(32), state engineer to Directeur général des mines, 20 January 1838.

36. AN 84AQ30, DD to CA, 15 April 1840.

37. The Decazeville management commented in 1839 that "a whole crowd of new mining companies has provided a multitude of jobs to student-engineers": "Even now [these new companies] ask for them daily while they are still in school. Those who have any bit of experience at all immediately acquire a certain worth, which makes them cocky. They are sure not to go jobless; they are offered jobs from all sides. This fever cannot last however, because the majority of these companies are only stock-market speculations." AN 84AQ30, DD to CA, 27 June 1839.

38. AN 84AQ34, CA to DD, 12 July 1839.

39. According to Pierre Guillaume, the Compagnie des Mines de la Loire felt that the engineer "should renounce all independence and fade into the general organization of the enterprise, just as the worker should be a docile instrument obeying more and more rigid rules." *La Compagnie des Mines de la Loire 1846–1854* (Paris: Presses universitaires de France, 1966), p. 119. See also his "Notes sur les ingénieurs des charbonnages de la Loire au XIX$^e$ siècle," in *Charbon et sciences humaines,* pp. 221–232.

40. Mazars Archives, mine reports, July 1827; August 1827; December 1829; July 1833.

41. For one example, see my "Labor, Management and the State in an Industrial Town: Decazeville, 1826–1914" (Ph.D. diss., Stanford University, 1981), pp. 76–77.

42. Ibid., pp. 68–69.

43. On the advantages and disadvantages of contracting, see Bernard

Mottez, *Systèmes de salaire et politiques patronales* (Paris: Editions du C.N.R.S., 1966), ch. 1.

44. However, in the Aubin Basin one does not find the hiring of miners by the year, in the fashion of the peasant *louée*, in which the peasant pledged to be at the disposition of the company for a year, although the company did not promise to engage him for the full year. Cornu and Pichon, *Analyse contextuelle*, p. 36.

45. AEM M1854/558, Valton and Lemonnier, "Voyage," p. 492. The authors go on to contrast the situation in the Aubin Basin with that in the Pas-de-Calais, where the operators "are trying little by little to create a population of miners." C. Ledoux, *L'Organisation du travail dans les mines et particulièrement dans les houillères tant en France qu'à l'étranger* (Paris: Imprimerie Chaix, 1890), pp. 44–45, sharply criticized the use of contractors in the Aubin Basin.

46. Daudibertières, "Un Centenaire industriel. La Grande activité des forges de Decazeville," *Procès-verbaux des séances de la SLSAA*, 37 (1954–1958): 195–196.

47. Cabrol contrasted the mines of Paleyrets no. 3, 5, and 6, which were operated under *entreprise générale*, to Lagrange no. 9, mined by *chantiers séparés*. AN 84AQ23, DD to CA, 30 June 1843.

48. The board advocated the use of the contract system to provision the blast furnaces—"if all were done by contract, we would know what to expect." AN 84AQ32, CA to DD, 25 November 1833. Commenting on a recent contract made with a local contractor Tinel, the board wrote to the management: "As the rate paid for coal in this contract is lower than that in other *chantiers*, you will undoubtedly push production there to its maximum. Contracts which engage us in the future must also be avoided, so that if the forge suffers an accident or stops due to unforeseeable circumstances, we will not have contracts on our hands. I think you could avail yourself of the expression used in earlier contracts with the same Tinel: 'The coal which the Company will need up to 12,000 tons in such a time, the Company committing itself not to obtain it elsewhere, etc.' " AN 84AQ33, DD to CA, 3 September 1835.

49. Mazars Archives, mine report, January 1832.

50. Ibid., 13 March 1839.

51. Reid, "Labor, Management, and the State," pp. 79–83.

52. AEM, M1854/558, Valton and Lemonnier, "Voyage," p. 389. AN F 14 3828, state engineer, June 1856.

53. AN 84AQ31, CA to DD, 22 December 1829. AN 84AQ1, CA of SHFA, 12 October 1830; 19 October 1830. AN 59AQ544, DD to CA, 29 December 1829.

54. AN 84AQ32, CA to DD, 18 September 1833.

55. AN C947, *Extrait du règlement de la caisse de secours de la Com-*

*pagnie des Houillères et Fonderies de l'Aveyron* (Villefranche-de-Rouergue: H. Castan, n.d.).

56. On the economics of coal mining in the nineteenth century, see the Introduction, n. 20.

## 3. The Company Town and the State

1. AMG MR1274, "Mémoire . . . Caulincourt."

2. AN 59AQ545, clipping of an article in *Le Mot d'ordre* (14 April 1886).

3. Peter Stearns, *European Society in Upheaval*, 2nd ed. (New York: Macmillan, 1975), pp. 158–159.

4. Walter Isard, "Some Locational Factors in the Iron and Steel Industry Since the Early Nineteenth Century," *Journal of Political Economy*, 56 (1948): 203–217. Norman Pounds, "Historical Geography of the Iron and Steel Industry of France," *Annals of the Association of American Geographers*, 47 (1957): 3–14.

5. Peter Stearns makes this point in *Paths to Authority* (Urbana: University of Illinois Press, 1978).

6. On Grand-Combe, see Jean-Michel Gaillard, "Un Exemple de 'Ville-Usine': La Grand-Combe (Gard) et sa 'Compagnie des Mines' (1835–1921)" (Troisième cycle, Université de Paris X-Nanterre, 1974); Gaillard, "La Naissance d'une entreprise industrielle au XIX$^e$ siècle: 'la Compagnie de la Grand-Combe',￼" in *Mines et mineurs en Languedoc-Roussillon et régions voisines de l'antiquité à nos jours* (Montpellier: Fédération historique du Languedoc méditerranéen et du Roussillon, 1977), pp. 191–200; and Isabelle Roger, "L'Apport de la compagnie minière au développement de Grand-Combe, 1830–1946," in ibid., pp. 281–288. On Montceau-les-Mines, see R. Beaubernard, *Un "Laboratoire sociale" au XIX$^e$ siècle* (Paris: Editions du Civry, 1981); Léon Laroche, *Montceau-les-Mines: Quelques aperçus sur l'histoire de la ville et de son exploitation houillère* (Montceau-les-Mines: Imprimerie ouvrière, 1924); and Lucien Peyronnard, *Le Charbon de Blanzy. La famille Chagot et Montceau-les-Mines. Histoire économique, politique et sociale du pays montcellien de 1769 à 1927*, 2 vols. (Le Creusot: Ecomusée de la Communauté Le Creusot/Montceau-les-Mines, 1981). On Le Creusot, see Christian Devillers and Bernard Huet, *Le Creusot: Naissance et développement d'une ville industrielle 1782–1914* (Seyssel: Champ Vallon, 1981). On industrial towns in the Lorraine, see Serge Bonnet and Roger Humbert, *La Ligne rouge des hauts fourneaux* (Paris: Editions Denoël, 1981) and Serge Bonnet, with Etienne Kagan and Michel Maigret, *L'Homme du fer. Mineurs de fer et ouvriers sidérurgistes lorrains 1889–1960*, 2 vols. (Nancy: Centre Lorrain d'Etudes Sociologiques, 1976–77).

For a provocative analysis of French industrial towns in terms of Michel Foucault's disciplinary strategies, see Lion Murard and Patrick Zylberman,

"Le Petit travailleur infatigable ou le prolétaire régénéré," *Recherches*, 25 (1976): 7–287. Such studies of repressive structures have encouraged a number of complementary analyses of workers' resistance to them. See F. Portet, "Le Creusot: la 'société-machine'," *Milieux*, 0 (January 1980): 23–32, and "Le Creusot: la ville technique," *Milieux*, 1 (April 1980): 34–49.

7. See Philippe Ariès, *Histoire des populations françaises et de leurs attitudes devant la vie depuis le XVIIIᵉ siècle* (Paris: Seuil, 1976), pp. 69–118; Daniel Bertaux, *Destins personnels et structure de classe* (Paris: Presses universitaires de France, 1976); and my "The Lamb and the Tiger: Paternalist Discourse and Practice in the Management of Labor in Nineteenth-Century French Mining and Metallurgy" (forthcoming in *Comparative Studies in Society and History*).

8. Louise Tilly, "Structure de l'emploi, travail des femmes et changement démographique dans deux villes industrielles: Anzin et Roubaix, 1872–1914," *Mouvement social*, 105 (October-December 1978): 33–58.

9. For a comparison of the managerial systems at the Le Creusot metallurgical factory and the Anzin coal mines, see my "The Lamb and the Tiger."

10. Pierre Guillaume, "Grèves et organisations ouvrieres chez les mineurs de la Loire au milieu du XIXᵉ siècle," *Mouvement social*, 43 (April-June 1963): 5–18. E. Tarlé, "La Grande coalition des mineurs de Rive-de-Gier en 1844," *Revue historique*, 177 (1936): 249–278.

11. See Christopher Johnson, "The Revolution of 1830 in French Economic History," in *1830 in France*, ed. John Merriman (New York: Franklin Watts, 1975), pp. 139–189.

12. See the Appendix.

13. Louis Reybaud, "L'Etablissement de Decazeville," *Journal des économistes*, 3rd ser. 39 (September 1875): 335.

14. Michel Chevalier, *Visite de Mgr. le Duc de Montpensier* (Paris: Imprimerie le Normant, [1843], p. 19. See also DCMD, 10 February 1855. The expansion of mining operations in the final decades of the nineteenth century made town planning in the Aubin Basin even less structured, if possible, than before. In 1882 the Cransac municipal council voted to erect one school rather than three distributed throughout the commune, in part because "the center of population in the different parts of the commune is not stable, as in towns; it is subordinated to the opening or the closing of galleries, mine shafts and pits, and as a consequence a schoolhouse useful now in a particular section could ultimately become deserted." Cransac Municipal Archives. "Délibérations du conseil municipal," 8 October 1882.

15. AMG MR1274, "Mémoire . . . Caulincourt." AN 84AQ18, DD to CA, 23 August 1833. AN 84AQ32, CA to DD, 4 October 1833. AN F 1C III Aveyron 7, PA, 1 April 1857. I disagree with Peter Stearns' description of Decazeville's housing program as "truly impressive" (*Paths to Authority*, p. 97). For the poor conditions in company housing during the 1830s, see

G. Daudibertières, "De l'influence qu'exerça la grande industrie sur la santé des premiers habitants de Decazeville," *Procès-verbaux des séances de la SLSAA*, 39 (1963–1966): 280.

16. AN F 1C III Aveyron 7, PA, 1 April 1857. Vauquesal-Papin, "L'Association créatrice de l'industrie de fer dans l'Aveyron," *La Vie du rail*, 1233 (1 March 1970): 16–17.

17. AN 84AQ32, CA to DD, 14 April 1830.

18. AN 84AQ24, DD to CA, 6 July 1840; 9 January 1841.

19. AEM M1838/224, Mousse, "Mémoire sur l'usine de Decazeville."

20. AN 84AQ24, DD to CA, 18 January 1841.

21. AN 84AQ11, AG of SHFA, 30 May 1854.

22. AN F 1C III Aveyron 7, SpVf, 25 November 1853; PA, 18 March 1854.

23. ADA 2 E 12 27, "Histoire des compagnies des usines d'Aubin (jusqu'à 1882)," pp. 38–39.

24. AN 84AQ36, CA to DD, 15 December 1855.

25. AN 84AQ26, DD to CA, 7 July 1849; 20 July 1849.

26. AN F 1C III Aveyron 7, PA, 6 January 1854.

27. This analysis turns ultimately on the extent to which the capital invested in a company town derived from profits made on the labor done by workers in that town, or from other sources. At Decazeville the workers' financing of the town's social life was more direct than at Grand-Combe or Le Creusot, where the language of company largesse dominated.

28. SLSAA, Fonds Daudibertières, carton 16, DD to PA, 30 June 1832. I discuss Cabrol's similar argument for a national guard unit at Decazeville in "Decazeville: Company Town and Working-Class Community" in *French Cities in the Nineteenth Century*, ed. John Merriman (London: Hutchinson, 1982), p. 195.

29. DCMD, 11 May 1873.

30. AN 84AQ5, CA of SHFA, 22 March 1853. See Bertrand Gille, "Esquisse d'une histoire du syndicalisme patronal dans l'industrie sidérurgique française," *Revue d'histoire de la sidérurgie*, 5 (1964): 209–249.

31. François Cabrol and Michael Chevalier, *Polémique* (Rodez, 1846), p. 11.

32. Cabrol Archives, Cabrol to Chevalier, 30 June 1846.

33. Cabrol and Chevalier, *Polémique*, p. 5.

34. Cabrol Archives, list of expenses for celebration, 16 August 1846; Amans to Cabrol (1846); *Journal de l'Aveyron*, 4 December 1901.

35. AN 59AQ544, DD to CA, 24 July 1843; 25 July 1843; 8 August 1843. *La Dépêche*, 3 August 1943.

36. For an analysis of management in the ironworks see my "The Origins of Industrial Labor Management in France: The Case of the Decazeville Ironworks During the July Monarchy," *Business History Review*, 57 (Spring 1983): 1–19.

37. Cabrol Archives, Amans to Cabrol, 28 March 1848.

38. AN 84AQ26, DD to CA, 18 April 1848.

39. Ibid., 5 April 1848; 28 April 1848.

40. *Journal de l'Aveyron*, 11 March 1848; 22 March 1848. AN 84AQ26, DD to CA, letters no. 232 and 233 (March 1848); 28 March 1848; 10 April 1848; 18 April 1848; 5 May 1848; 25 August 1848.

41. AN 84AQ27, report of CA of SHFA to AG, 16 May 1848. The February Revolution had scared stockholders. Cibiel, deputy and member of the board of the Houillères et Fonderies, wrote to Cabrol in the spring of 1848 that he saw no way to prevent the provisional government from fully applying Louis Blanc's ideas. After delivering the railroads and mines to the workers, the government would certainly turn to firms that manufactured rails: "We are therefore threatened with the loss of Decazeville." The best that could be done was to make sure that workers at Decazeville did not get wind of such plans. Cabrol Archives, Cibiel to Cabrol, 1848.

42. AN 84AQ26, DD to CA, 7 July 1849; 20 July 1849.

43. Paul Ramadier, "Decazeville (1829–1949)," *Revue du Rouergue*, 3 (January-March 1949): 135.

44. ADA 4 MI 16bis, testimony of J. Series, Aubin miner, 13 December 1851; "Marche des insurgés de l'arrondissement de Villefranche (Aveyron)" by Bartine, 30 January 1852; justice of the peace (Aubin) to state prosecutor, 9 January 1852. AN BB 30 401, reports of Commission mixte (Rodez) [February 1852]. For events in the rest of the department, see F. Mazenc, *Coup d'état du 2 décembre 1851 dans l'Aveyron* (Albi: Imprimerie Nouguies, 1872).

45. Cabrol Archives, Cabrol to Decazes, 16 November 1848.

46. Cabrol Archives, Cabrol to Amans, 20 December 1851.

47. This bore some relationship to the expressions of political loyalty to leading families that characterized mid-nineteenth-century rural Aveyron. P. M. Jones, "Political Commitment and Rural Society in the Southern Massif Central," *European Studies Review*, 10 (1980): 337–356.

48. Cabrol Archives, F. Guizot to Cabrol, 26 April 1852.

49. In 1850 Cabrol charged that the local state mining engineer ("full-blooded red and socialist") favored the Aubin company with which his superior was associated; AN 84AQ26, DD to CA, 23 November 1850. Three years later he claimed that heads of the Aubin company with ties to the government had masterminded the dismissal of the prefect of Aveyron and his replacement by one of their allies; ibid., 26 November 1853.

50. Ramadier, "Decazeville," 136. DCMD, 29 October 1855. On this general issue, see Louis Girard, *La Politique des travaux publics du Second Empire* (Paris: Armand Colin, 1952).

51. AN 84AQ26, DD to CA, 26 December 1855.

52. AN F 1C III Aveyron 7, PA to MI, 6 January 1854.

53. AN F 1C III Aveyron 5, PA to MI, 26 July 1853.

54. ADA 3M, SpVf to PA, 8 August 1853; CPD to PA, 4 September 1853.

55. ADA 3M, SpVf to PA, 19 June 1857; SpVf to DD, 21 June 1857 (quoted); SpVf to PA, 21 June 1857. Although the prefect saw in the massive abstentions proof that many of Decazeville's workers were socialists, and Theodore Zeldin, a century later, that they were republicans, the company's influence appears to provide a more consistent explanation. ADA 3M, PA to MI, 2 July 1857. Theodore Zeldin, *The Political System of Napoleon III* (New York: Norton, 1971), p. 73.

56. Although Stearns (*Paths to Authority*) and Murard and Zylberman ("Le Petit travailleur infatigable") evaluate the company town very differently, none sees a political component at work in it.

**4. Community in Crisis**

1. M. R. Guglielmo, "*Facteurs et formes de l'évolution urbaine à Decazeville,*" *Bulletin de l'Association de géographes français*, 249–250 (March-April 1955): 84. For more on the demographic effects of the crisis, see Appendix: A Social Portrait of Industrial Workers in Nineteenth-Century Decazeville.

2. Computed from statistics in "La Croissance des grandes firmes," *Revue d'histoire de la sidérurgie*, 4 (1963): 129.

3. Arthur Louis Dunham, *The Anglo-French Treaty of Commerce of 1860 and the Progress of the Industrial Revolution in France* (Ann Arbor: University of Michigan Press, 1930), p. 151.

4. AN 59AQ489, AG of SNHFA, 27 February 1869.

5. Ministère de l'Agriculture, du Commerce, et des Travaux Publics, *Statistique de l'industrie minérale* (Paris: Imprimerie nationale) for the years 1853, 1876, and 1909.

6. The Second Empire broke up the monopolistic Compagnie des Mines de la Loire, and divided the new Pas-de-Calais coalfield into some twenty concessions.

7. J. M. Gaillard makes this point with respect to the mines of Grand-Combe. "La Naissance d'une entreprise industrielle au XIXᵉ siècle: 'la Compagnie de la Grand-Combe'," in *Mines et mineurs en Languedoc-Roussillon et régions voisines de l'antiquité à nos jours* (Montpellier: Fédération historique du Languedoc méditerranéen et du Roussillon, 1977), pp. 191–200.

8. Michael Stephen Smith, *Tariff Reform in France 1860–1900: The Politics of Economic Interest* (Ithaca: Cornell University Press, 1980), pp. 93–94.

9. Ibid., p. 92. Between 1851 and 1869 French coal production tripled to 13,464,000 tons, while coal imports rose 283 percent to 8,304,000 tons.

10. L. Michaux-Bellaire, *Mémoire en défense pour la Compagnie des Houillères et Fonderies de l'Aveyron contre s. Exc. M. le Ministre des Fi-*

*nances, représentant d'Etat* (Paris: Imprimerie le Normant, n.d.), p. 3 (contained in AN 65AQ886). AN 84AQ11, report of CA to AG, 21 May 1861. SLSAA, Fonds Daudibertières, carton 9, state engineer, 20 July 1861; 10 July 1862. ADA 93S3, state engineer, 15 July 1868.

11. Gaillard, "La Naissance," pp. 194–197.

12. Philippe Guignet, "L'Emeute des quatre sous ou les voies de la protestation sociale à Anzin (mai 1833)," *Revue du nord,* 219 (October-December 1973): 347–364. Pierre Guillaume, "Grèves et organisations ouvrières chez les mineurs de la Loire au milieu du XIX$^e$ siècle," *Mouvement social,* 43 (April-June 1963): 5–18. E. Tarlé, "La Grande coalition des mineurs de Rive-de-Gier en 1844," *Revue historique,* 177 (1936): 249–278.

13. Joan Scott, *The Glassworkers of Carmaux* (Cambridge, Mass.: Harvard University Press, 1974), p. 66.

14. On the beginnings of the substitution of company control for that of contractors in the Aubin Basin, see AN F 14 3828, state engineer, 31 January 1858. For a similar transition in the mines of the Bouches-du-Rhône during the 1860s, see Lucien Gaillard, "Les Grèves dans le bassin minier de Bouches-du-Rhône sous le Second Empire," in *Actes du 91$^e$ congrès national des sociétés savantes Rennes 1966* (Paris: Bibliothèque nationale, 1969), III, 281–306. Carmaux extended the use of production rates during the Second Empire. Rolande Trempé, *Les Mineurs de Carmaux 1848–1914* (Paris: Editions ouvrières, 1971), pp. 223–238.

15. AN 84AQ36, CA to DD, 22 January 1861.

16. See the Appendix: A Social Portrait.

17. ADA 52M3, justice of the peace (Aubin), 31 October 1867.

18. ADA 52M3, CPA to PA, 21 October 1867; 22 October 1867; Jausions to PA, 22 October 1867; gendarmerie (Decazeville), 22 October 1867; PA to MI, 22 October 1867; SpVf to PA, 23 October 1867. AN BB 18 1757, attorney general to Garde des Sceaux, 3 November 1867 (quoted).

19. AN BB 18 1544, attorney general to Garde des Sceaux, 3 July 1855. ADA 52M2, SpVf to PA, 23 October 1857. ADA 93S5, CPA to PA, 22 July 1868.

20. ADA 11 M2 25, SpVf to PA, 3 December 1874.

21. The beginning of the change in the role of the state mining engineers dates from the 1838 legislation on mine floods. For the first time state engineers, acting through the prefect, were able to make companies take steps to improve safety. George Jared Lamb, "Coal Mining in France, 1873 to 1895" (Ph.D. diss., University of Illinois at Urbana-Champaign, 1976), pp. 246–247.

22. AN 84AQ36, CA to DD, 17 November 1856. See also Jean Riche, *L'Evolution sociale des mineurs de Ronchamp aux XIX$^e$ et XX$^e$ siècles* (Besançon: Jacques et Demontrand, 1964), pp. 79–86, for a similar incident at Ronchamp in 1857; and more generally, Alberto Melucci, "Action patronale, pouvoir, organisation. Règlements d'usine et contrôle de la main

d'oeuvre au XIX<sup>e</sup> siècle," *Mouvement social*, 97 (October-December 1976): 149–150.

23. ADA 93S2, MTP to PA, 3 February 1856.

24. ADA 93S2, chief engineer to PA, 16 February 1866. See also ADA 93S5, state chief engineer, 14 February 1870; mine guard, 27 November 1870. AN 59AQ487, CA of SNHFA, 10 August 1871.

25. AEM J1862/c/cl. 269, Paul Hébert, "Notes sur . . . l'usine d'Aubin (Aveyron)."

26. See my "The Origins of Industrial Labor Management in France: The Case of the Decazeville Ironworks During the July Monarchy," *Business History Review*, 57 (Spring 1983): 1–19.

27. Jean Vial, *L'Industrialisation de la sidérurgie française 1814–1864*, 2 vols. (Paris: Mouton, 1967), I, 396. Reed Geiger, *The Anzin Coal Company 1800–1833* (Newark: University of Delaware Press, 1974). Marcel Gillet, *Les Charbonnages du nord de la France au XIX<sup>e</sup> siècle* (Paris: Mouton, 1973), p. 315. Pierre Guillaume, *La Compagnie des mines de la Loire 1846–1854* (Paris: Presses universitaires de France, 1966).

28. ADA 52M3, SpVf to PA, 12 December 1864; state engineer, 12 December 1864; Cabrol to Galtayric, 15 June 1865. ADA 58M1 3, SpVf to PA, 10 January 1865.

29. AN 84AQ6, CA of SHFA, 28 July 1863.

30. ADA J492, Bernard to Carbonel, 11 April 1863.

31. ADA J492, Achille Wallace to Carbonel, 19 September 1865. The managerial crisis of the late sixties was a nationwide phenomenon. For other cases in heavy industry, see Eugène Jolant, *Usines de Torteron. Histoire de la métallurgie en Berry* (Bourges: Imprimerie des Orphelins du Centre, n.d.), p. 10; Robert R. Locke, *Les Fonderies et forges d'Alais à l'époque des premiers chemins de fer 1829–1874*, trans. Elisabeth-Anne Benoist-d'Azy (Paris: Marcel Rivière, 1978); Guy Thuillier, *Aspects de l'économie nivernaise au XIX<sup>e</sup> siècle* (Paris: Mouton, 1966), pp. 201, 302; and Rolande Trempé, "Analyse du comportement des administrateurs de la Société des mines de Carmaux vis à vis des mineurs," *Mouvement social*, 43 (April-June 1963): 53–91.

32. Guillaume, *La Compagnie*, pp. 55, 61, 65.

33. Lamb, "Coal Mining in France," pp. 132–133, 349–350. Trempé, "Analyse du comportement."

34. On the strike of 1869 at Aubin, see Lucien Mazars, "La Grève sanglante de 1869 à Aubin," *Procès-verbaux des séances de la SLSAA*, 43 (1979): 107–117; and my "Labor, Management, and the State in an Industrial Town: Decazeville 1826–1914" (Ph.D. diss., Stanford University, 1981), pp. 142–153.

35. AN 84AQ6, CA of SHFA, 7 December 1861.

36. ADA 5M10, dossier on the election of 1863.

37. ADA 52M3, justice of the peace (Aubin) to PA, 15 February 1865.

38. L. Lévêque, *Histoire des forges de Decazeville* (Saint-Etienne: Société de l'Industrie Minérale, [1916]), pp. 75–76. AN BB 18 1757, district attorney to attorney general, 4 October 1867. ADA 93S3, state engineer, 10 January 1868.

39. ADA 3M, mayor of Decazeville to PA, 30 July 1865.

40. ADA 52M3, mayor of Decazeville to SpVf, 27 January 1867; SpVf to PA, 30 January 1867.

41. ADA 52M3, mayor of Decazeville to SpVf, 29 January 1867; justice of the peace (Aubin), 7 February 1867. Logis de gendarmerie (Decazeville) to justice of the peace (Aubin), 7 February 1867. ADA 68S2, justice of the peace (Aubin) to PA, 26 January 1867; PA to MI, 30 January 1867. AN BB 18 1757, district attorney to attorney general, 4 October 1867.

42. ADA 52M3; mayor of Decazeville to PA, 2 October 1867; gendarmerie (Decazeville), 2 October 1867; CPD, 3 October 1867; SpVf to PA, 4 October 1867. AN BB 18 1757, district attorney to attorney general, 4 October 1867; PA to MI, 5 October 1867.

43. AN BB 18 1757, district attorney to attorney general, 4 October 1867. A similar effort to set work hours precipitated a strike at Anzin in 1866. A. Fortin, "Les Conflits sociaux dans les houillères du Pas-de-Calais sous le Second Empire," *Revue du nord*, 43 (April-June 1961): 349–355. See also Trempé, *Les Mineurs*, pp. 210–217.

44. Rémi Gossez, "Une Grève de mineurs à l'événement de Napoléon III," in *Actes du 78ᵉ congrès national des sociétés savantes Toulouse 1953* (Paris: Imprimerie nationale, 1954), pp. 365–390.

45. Pierre Guillaume, "Grèves et organisations ouvrières," 18, comments that the Loire miners' leader, Michel Rondet, made a brilliant move by launching a struggle with the owners over an issue—enforcement of the 1813 decree on company obligations to injured miners—which the state could not ignore.

46. Pétrus Faure, *Histoire du mouvement ouvrier dans le département de la Loire* (Saint-Etienne. Imprimerie Dumas, 1956), p. 165–167. Thuillier, *Aspects de l'économie nivernaise*, pp. 288–289. Jean-Baptiste Dumay, *Mémoires d'un militant ouvrier du Creusot 1841–1905* (Paris: François Maspéro, 1976), pp. 121–122.

47. ADA 52M3, workers' demands attached to SpVf to PA, 4 October 1867; mayor of Decazeville to PA, 4 October 1867.

48. For a recent reappraisal of working-class "traditionalism," see Peter Stearns, "The Effort at Continuity in Working-Class Culture," *Journal of Modern History*, 52 (1980): 626–655.

49. AN BB 18 1757, district attorney to attorney general, 4 October 1867. ADA 52M3, Rouquayrol to PA, 2 October 1867; SpVf to PA, 4 October 1867; 6 October 1867. ADA 11 M2 25, mayor of Decazeville to SpVf, 5 October 1867.

50. ADA 52M3, petition included with Trille to Jausions, 9 October 1867.

51. ADA 52M3, Trille to Jausions, 9 October 1867; mayor of Decazeville to PA, 9 October 1867. ADA 11 M2 25, mayor of Decazeville to SpVf, 5 October 1867.

52. ADA 52M3, Trille to Jausions, 9 October 1867.

53. ADA 93S3, state engineer, 10 January 1868.

54. ADA 52M3, PA to MTP, 18 October 1867.

55. For a similar experience a decade earlier at Montceau-les-Mines, see Lamb, "Coal Mining in France," p. 361. Such incidents were the prelude to companies' more regular recruitment of state mining engineers. André Thépot, "Les Ingénieurs du corps des mines" in *Le Patronat de la seconde industrialisation,* ed. Maurice Lévy-Leboyer (Paris: Editions ouvrières, 1979), pp. 237–246.

56. AN BB 18 1757, Minister of Justice to MTP (?), 2 November 1867; MTP to Minister of Justice, 21 November 1867.

57. Auguste Chirac, "Correspondance," *La Revue socialiste,* 3 (1886): 165–167. In 1878, when a senior master miner or a junior engineer might expect to earn about 3,000 francs a year, each member of the board took home 15,000 francs for his services; the chief executive officer received 39,000 francs annually. AN 59AQ488, CA of SNHFA, 13 March 1878. Over the life span of the Société Nouvelle, its board members received remuneration for their services totaling about one-tenth of the sum paid out in dividends to all stockholders, including those on the board.

58. On Deseilligny, see ADA 5M11, "M. Deseilligny" (1869); Joseph-Antoine Roy, *Histoire de la famille Schneider et du Creusot* (Paris: Marcel Rivière, 1962), pp. 42–43; and Jean Bouvier, "Aux origines de la Troisième République. Les Réflexes sociaux des milieux d'affaires," *Revue historique,* 210 (1953): 277, 283.

59. Rozy, "Excursion à Decazeville," in *Congrès scientifique de France. 40ᵉ session tenue à Rodez le 21 septembre 1874,* I, 108 (Rodez: Imprimerie Vᶜ E. Carrère, 1874).

60. On the favorable coal market of the early Third Republic, see Alain Lemenorel, "La Crise houillère en France: 1870–1875. Crise des structures ou crise conjoncturelle?," *Revue historique,* 540 (October-December 1981): 411–445.

61. AN 59AQ487, AG of SNHFA, 28 February 1873; 26 February 1876. See the hagiographic account of Deseilligny's achievements at Decazeville given by his associate D. Vigue: *De l'origine de Decazeville et de la Compagnie des Houillères et Fonderies de l'Aveyron jusqu' à nos jours* (Decazeville: F. Chirac, 1891).

62. Smith, *Tariff Reform in France,* p. 111.

63. Louis Reybaud, "L'Etablissement de Decazeville," *Journal des économistes,* 3rd ser., 39 (September 1875): 330. Rozy, "Excursion," 101.

For women workers' protests, see ADA 52M5, mayor of Decazeville to SpVf, 2 September 1872. ADA 11 M5 4, CSD to PA, 17 March 1890.

64. Ministère des Travaux publics, *Notice sur le nombre, les salaires et la durée du travail des ouvriers de mines, en 1890* (Paris: Imprimerie nationale, 1891).

65. Initially, the move to direct company control of mining operations was more a matter of redistributing administrative responsibilities than changing personnel. Deseilligny recruited many of his supervisors from among former contractors. ADA 52M3, SpVf to PA, 2 July 1868. For more on the demise of contractors at Decazeville and their replacement by company personnel, see AN 59AQ487, CA of SNHFA, 29 October 1878. ABHAD, SNHFA "Fiches des agents," Jean Pierre Auguste Bezamet to Petitjean, 29 November 1880.

Similar changes took place in other French mines at this time. The *chef de poste* first appears in mine regulations at Montceau-les-Mines in 1872. Lucien Peyronnard, *Le Charbon de Blanzy. La Famille Chagot et Montceau-les-Mines. Histoire économique, politique et sociale du pays montcellian de 1769 à 1927*, 2 vols. (Le Creusot: Ecomusée de la Communauté Le Creusot/Montceau-les-Mines, 1981), I, 230–231.

66. ADA 68S1, "Etat général des mines concédées du département de l'Aveyron pendant l'année 1883," 6 March 1884. Within each category of supervisory personnel there was a wide variation in salaries. In the mid-nineties the highest paid mineworkers at Campagnac, *boiseurs* and miners who dug in rock, received an average daily wage of 5.75 francs when working at piece-rates; *chefs de poste* received annual salaries of from 1,862 francs to 2,172 francs; master miners' annual salaries, including bonuses and lodging, went from 2,100 francs to 3,120 francs; annual salaries for engineers ranged from 2,440 francs to 11,406 francs. ADA J494, "Tableau du personnel général de la Compagnie et administration de Paris" (circa. 1896).

67. A. P. Deseilligny, *De l'influence de l'éducation sur la moralité et le bien-être des classes laborieuses* (Paris, 1868), pp. 245–246.

68. Ibid., p. 263. On this same subject, see the comments by J. Euverte, former director of Terrenoire and Le Creusot: "De l'organisation de la main-d'oeuvre dans la grande industrie," *Journal des économistes*, 3rd ser. 19 (1870): 372.

69. Deseilligny, *De l'influence*, pp. 223–224.

70. Rozy, "Excursion à Decazeville," 114.

71. Deseilligny, *De l'influence*, pp. 265–266. Deseilligny reiterated this position in 1874 when he told the Chamber that the education given workers' children at Le Creusot was good enough to allow them to become engineers. Chambre des députés, *Annales de la Chambre des députés. Débats parlementaires* (Paris: Imprimerie du *Journal officiel*, 1874) 21 (19 May 1874): 64. See also my "The Lamb and the Tiger: Paternalist Discourse and Practice in the Management of Labor in Nineteenth-Century French Mining

and Metallurgy" (forthcoming in *Comparative Studies in Society and History*).

72. Sanford Elwitt points out the connection between Deseilligny's philosophy of education and that of early Third Republic educational reformers, *The Making of the Third Republic: Class and Politics in France, 1868–1884* (Baton Rouge: Louisiana State University Press, 1975), pp. 201–202.

73. ADA 3M, mayor of Decazeville to PA, 18 December 1868.

74. ADA 3M, Deseilligny to SpVf, 20 May 1869.

75. René Izac, "Péripéties électorales en Aveyron à la fin du Second Empire," *Revue du Rouergue,* 36 (1982): 209.

76. ADA 5M11, variety of reports of local officials; A. Cibiel, *Protestation contre l'élection de la troisième circonscription électorale de l'Aveyron adressée à MM. les membres du Corps Législatif* (Villefranche-de-Rouergue, 1869). This was probably one of the last political charivaris in France. Eugen Weber found no political charivaris after the Second Republic; *Peasants into Frenchmen: The Modernization of Rural France 1870–1914* (Stanford: Stanford University Press, 1976), p. 493. Charles Tilly notes that the political charivari "faded fast" after the beginning of the Second Empire. "Charivaris, Repertoires and Urban Politics" in *French Cities in the Nineteenth Century,* ed. John M. Merriman (London: Hutchinson, 1982), p. 79.

77. However, there were certainly instances of pressure put on workers at Decazeville to vote for Deseilligny. See, for instance, the statement of Jean Paul Labougle in AN C1362, 12 June 1869.

78. See Fernand L'Huillier, *La Lutte ouvrière à la fin du Second Empire* (Paris: Librairie Armand Colin, 1957); Trempé, *Les Mineurs,* pp. 544–551 and *passim;* and Gaillard, "Les Grèves dans le bassin minier des Bouches-du-Rhône."

79. AN 110AQ152, DD to DG, 16 July 1908 ("Renseignements concernant l'établissement de Decazeville pendant la guerre de 1870"). Lévêque, *Histoire,* p. 80.

80. ADA 3M, mayor of Decazeville to PA, 28 July 1870. *Le Bassin houiller illustré* (Decazeville: F. Chirac, n.d.), p. 19.

81. Reybaud, "L'Etablissement," 336–339. DCMD, 11 May 1873.

82. See Daniel Puymeges, "L'Hôpital et la politique sociale patronale au XIX^e siècle. L'Exemple du Creusot," *Milieux,* 9 (February-March 1982): 46–53.

83. Reybaud, "L'Etablissement," 336. See also AN 59AQ11, CA of SCFD, "Annexe," 9 June 1902. For similar developments elsewhere, Dominique Sauvageot, "Les Cités ouvrières du Creusot et de Montceau-les-Mines du collectif au pavillionnaire," *Milieux,* 2 (June 1980): 27–33; Javier Figueroa, "La Politique du logement de la société des houillères de Blanzy de 1833 à 1900," *Milieux,* 2 (June 1980): 34–39; and Christian Devillers and

Bernard Huet, *Le Creusot. Naissance et développement d'une ville indus-trielle 1782–1914* (Seyssel: Champ Vallon, 1981).

84. AN 59AQ489, AG of SNHFA, 28 February 1880. See also AN 59AQ10, CA of SCFD, 4 October 1899.

85. See my "Labor, Management and the State," pp. 154–156.

86. See my "The Lamb and the Tiger."

## 5. The Long Depression

1. ADA U Watrin V, no. 6, interrogation of Petitjean, 12 March 1886.

2. Statement of SNHFA board member Paul Schneider speaking on behalf of the SNHFA and other coal companies, 21 June 1878. Chambre des députés, *Procès-verbaux des séances de la Commission du tarif des douanes,* in *Annales du Sénat et de la Chambre des députés. Session ordinaire de 1878* (Paris: Imprimerie et Librairie du *Journal officiel,* 1879), 12:422.

3. Michelle Perrot, *Les Ouvriers en grève. France 1871–1890* (Paris: Mouton, 1974), p. 151. Between 1868 and 1891 the SNHFA earned an average annual profit of 1.5 percent. APD, clipping from *La Dépêche,* 26 August 1929, p. 7.

4. Michael Stephen Smith, *Tariff Reform in France 1860–1900: The Politics of Economic Interest* (Ithaca: Cornell University Press, 1980), pp. 61, 91, 95–96. Smith does not point out the split on the board of the Société Nouvelle, although it could be used to support his argument that a spirit of compromise developed in tariff politics during the 1870s and 1880s.

5. Charles Peyrouty, "L'Implantation de la main d'oeuvre dans le bas-sin houiller aveyronnais" (Mémoire, Université de Toulouse, 1970), p. 62. Many miners employed by the Société Nouvelle lived in Combes, a section of Aubin which adjoined Decazeville.

6. See Appendix: A Social Portrait of Industrial Workers in Nineteenth-Century Decazeville.

7. AN C3022, Enquête parlementaire (Société de la Vieille Montagne). Charles Peyrouty, "La Mutation foncière a Decazeville (Aveyron) 1880–1905" (Mémoire, Université de Toulouse, n.d.).

8. Patrick Couffin, "Aspects de la vie ouvrière à Decazeville au début du XX^e siècle (1892–1914)" (Mémoire, Université de Paul Valéry [Mont-pellier III], 1975), p. 115.

9. G., "Decazeville," *La Science sociale,* 2 (August 1886): 98.

10. See the Appendix: A Social Portrait.

11. On the relationship between the ability to sign and literacy, see François Furet and Jacques Ozouf, *Reading and Writing: Literacy in France from Calvin to Jules Ferry* (Cambridge: Cambridge University Press, 1982), pp. 16–17.

12. See the Appendix. As early as 1843, the secretary to the Bishop of Rodez reported that the youths receiving confirmation at Decazeville "are

generally educated and speak French, which is a pleasure." AER, Crozier, "Visites," p. 38.

13. G., "Decazeville," 96. Odette Hardy-Hémery is more explicit. She notes that in the late nineteenth-century mining towns of the Valenciennes "patois was the language of people who wanted to maintain their identity in opposition to the managers." *De la Croissance à la désindustrialisation. Un Siècle dans le Valenciennois* (Paris: Presses de la Fondation nationale des sciences politiques, 1984), p. 45.

14. *Le Cri du peuple,* 28 April 1886, p. 1.

15. Some variant of the theory of resource mobilization underlies most social histories of protest. See Charles Tilly, *From Mobilization to Revolution* (Reading, Mass.: Addison-Wesley, 1978); and Craig Calhoun, *The Question of Class Struggle* (Chicago: University of Chicago Press, 1982).

16. Other studies of the relationship between religious practice and republicanism in southern France include Rolande Trempé, *Les Mineurs de Carmaux 1848–1914* (Paris: Editions ouvrières, 1971); Raymond Huard, *Le Mouvement républicain en Bas-Languedoc 1848–1881* (Paris: Presses de la Fondation nationale des sciences politiques, 1982); and Jean Faury, *Cléricalisme et anticléricalisme dans le Tarn (1848–1900)* (Toulouse: Publications de l'Université de Toulouse-le-Mirail, 1980). For the north, see Yves-Marie Hilaire, *Une Chrétienté au XIXᵉ siècle. La Vie religieuse du diocèse d'Arras (1840–1914),* 2 vols. (Villeneuve-d'Ascq: Publications de l'Université de Lille III, 1977).

17. Donald Reid, "Labor, Management and the State in an Industrial Town: Decazeville, 1826–1914" (Ph.D. diss., Stanford University, 1981), pp. 169–173, and Marie-Christine Cartayrade, "Aux frontières de la paysannerie: l'église et les ouvriers d'Aubin (1815–1870)," in *Christianisme et monde ouvrier,* ed. François Bédarida and Jean Maitron (Paris: Editions ouvrières, 1975), pp. 273–287.

18. AER, procès-verbal (Firmy), 1 June 1857; procès-verbal (Cransac), 12 December 1856; procès-verbal (Viviez), 17 January 1858; visite pastorale, (Aubin), 6 April 1872; visite pastorale (Firmy), 10 April 1872; visite pastorale (Decazeville), 11 April 1872.

19. G. Christopher Davies and Mrs. Broughall, *Our Home in Aveyron with Studies of Peasant Life and Customs in Aveyron and the Lot* (London: William Blackwood and Sons, 1891), p. 95. G., "Decazeville," 96. Monique Bornes-Vernet, "Les Saints guérisseurs en Bas-Rouergue," (Thèse, Université de Montpellier, 1969).

20. Gérard Cholvy, "Le Catholicisme en Rouergue au XIXᵉ et XXᵉ siècles, première approche," in *Etudes sur le Rouergue* (Rodez: Imprimerie P. Carrère, 1974), pp. 250–251. See also Françoise Géraldini, "Cléricalisme et anticléricalisme dans le bassin de Decazeville, 1872–1908" (Mémoire, Université de Toulouse-le-Mirail, 1976).

21. ADA 5M11, PA to mayor of Decazeville, 21 May 1869. The pre-

vious republican proselytizer in Decazeville, Cadiat, had also been a renegade company employee.

22. DCMD, 31 May 1854; 10 November 1856. AN F 17 9322, report of school inspector, 18 March 1856. AN F 17 9336, report of school inspector, 10 March 1860. ADA 2E 12 27, "Histoire," pp. 61–62. Cartayrade, "Aux frontières," p. 279.

23. Aubin Municipal Archives, "Délibérations du conseil municipal," 8 February 1878.

24. DCMD, 18 May 1878; 29 August 1878; / January 1879; 16 February 1880. As these gestures make clear, Cayrade and his supporters were quite moderate republicans. While in the Chamber between 1881 and 1885, Cayrade voted against separation of Church and state and against direct election of the Senate.

25. AN 59AQ487, CA of SNHFA, 12 November 1868; 6 April 1870; 13 April 1870; 24 August 1871; 29 October 1873.

26. Ibid., 2–4 October 1872; 26 March 1873. "Règlement de la caisse de secours de la Société Nouvelle des Houillères et Fonderies de l'Aveyron" (1878).

27. APP BA186, "Greve de Decazeville Mars 1878," no. 17. *L'Estafette* clipping, 26 March 1878. According to some reports, the contractors dismissed by the Société Nouvelle in the early 1870s were active in fomenting discontent against the firm during the next decade. Léon Renault and Aubin, *Cour d'assises de l'Aveyron. Affaire Watrin. Audiences des 15, 16, 17, 18, 19, 20 juin 1886. Plaidoiries de M. Léon Renault et de M. Aubin pour Mlle. Watrin, partie civile* (Paris: Imprimerie et librairie centrales des chemins de fer, 1886), p. 21; and G., "Decazeville," 106.

28. AN 59AQ488, CA of SNHFA, 15–31 March 1878 and 1–8 April 1878.

29. ADA J495, Levainville to Carbonnel, 17 March 1878.

30. APP BA 186, "Grève de Decazeville Mars 1878," reports by Lombard, police officer, no. 21, 26 March 1878; no. 23, 30 March 1878. *Le Journal de l'Aveyron*, 26 March 1878, p. 3.

31. *Le Journal de l'Aveyron*, 30 March 1878, p. 3. See also APP BA 186, "Grève de Decazeville Mars 1878," no. 37, 17 March 1878.

32. APP BA 186, "Grève de Decazeville Mars 1878," no. 10 and no. 18 (quoted), Lombard, police officer.

33. ABHAD, SNHFA, "Fiches des agents," Colrat to Petitjean, 18 November 1878, details the number of gendarmes housed, the duration of their stay and contains a request for reimbursement of expenses incurred by the engineers who lodged them.

34. Perrot, *Les Ouvriers*, pp. 91, 368. Perrot presents a rich and stimulating panorama of strikes, including those at Decazeville, during the first two decades of the Third Republic. See especially pp. 366–376 for miners' strikes.

35. ABHAD, SNHFA, "Fiches des agents," Colrat to Petitjean, 21 December 1880.

36. Ibid., 22 October 1881.

37. L. Lévêque, *Histoire des forges de Decazeville* (Saint-Etienne: Société de l'Industrie Minérale, [1916l]), pp. 82–84. Gérard Laffont reiterates this criticism in "Une Crise sociale sous la III<sup>e</sup> République: la grève de Decazeville (janvier-juin 1886)" (Mémoire, Université de Montpellier, 1964).

38. Lévêque, *Histoire*, pp. 79–81. See the perceptive comments on coal company management in Perrot, *Les Ouvriers*, pp. 671–672.

39. ADA U Watrin VI, no. 155, interrogation of Petitjean, 2 February 1886.

40. *Gazette des tribunaux*, 18 June 1886, p. 576 (testimony of Laur). See also ADA U Watrin V, no. 8, interrogation of Petitjean, 12 March 1886.

41. ADA U Watrin VI, no. 338, interrogation of Jules Grès, 1 March 1886.

42. ADA U Watrin VI, no. 310, interrogation of Pierre Galtié, 1 March 1886.

43. ADA U Watrin VI, no. 130, interrogation of Léon Gaston, 26 March 1886. Renault and Aubin, *Cour d'assises*, p. 51.

44. *Le Journal de l'Aveyron*, 30 January 1886, p. 1.

45. ABHAD, SNHFA, "Fiches des agents," Jules Watrin to chief executive officer [1882].

46. AN 110AQ41(2), Société Anonyme des Houillères de Saint-Etienne to SNHFA, 2 January 1882; 18 January 1882. Lucien Gaillard has discovered the same phenomenon in the mines of the Bouches-du-Rhône; "Les Grèves dans le bassin minier des Bouches-du-Rhône sous le Second Empire," in *Actes du 91<sup>e</sup> congrès national des sociétés savantes Rennes 1966* (Paris: Bibliothèque nationale, 1969), III, 281. So do Guy Thuillier in the forges of the Nièvre (*Aspects de l'économie nivernaise au XIX<sup>e</sup> siècle* (Paris: Armand Colin, 1966), pp. 280–281) and Christopher H. Johnson in the mines of Le Bousquet ("Union-Busting in Graissessac: Deindustrialization, the Strike of 1894, and the Changing Labor Force in the Hérault Coal Basin," paper presented at the Social Science History Association Meeting, October 1983). See also Marcel Gillet, *Les Charbonnages du nord de la France* (Paris: Mouton, 1973), p. 324.

This practice persisted into the twentieth century in the Aubin Basin. In 1919 the chief mining engineer at Decazeville commented that a new engineer was needed at the Campagnac mine: the current one lacked "the energy, the spirit and the independence of a young engineer from outside of the region." AN 110AQ155, chief engineer to DD, 10 March 1919.

47. Perrot points out that strikes over supervisory personnel occurred more often in economically marginal areas and industries, like the mines of Aveyron, where a "certain semi-colonial style" of management based on

brute exploitation of a labor force with close ties to the land persisted (*Les Ouvriers*, p. 299).

48. See Michael Z. Brooke, *Le Play: Engineer and Social Scientist* (London: Longman, 1978); Sanford Elwitt, "Social Reform and Social Order in Late Nineteenth-Century France: The Musée Social and Its Friends," *French Historical Studies*, 11 (1980): 431–451; and my "The Lamb and the Tiger: Paternalist Discourse and Practice in the Management of Labor in Nineteenth-Century French Mining and Metallurgy" (forthcoming in *Comparative Studies in Society and History*).

49. ADA U Watrin V, no. 185, interrogation of Petitjean. See also ADA U Watrin VI, no. 147, interrogation of Jean-Louis Erra.

50. The nature of the "debts" owed Watrin came out clearly in the questioning of those accused of his murder. Typical was the case of Lescure who had been fired after serving a forty-day prison sentence. Lescure had gone to see Watrin to ask for his job back. Watrin rehired him with the advice, "Travaille et sois sage." Company operation of a small restaurant provided Watrin with a further means of making individuals in the town dependent on him. A woman named Pendariès, another of those accused in Watrin's murder, received fifty-eight chits for meals on his special recommendation.

51. *L'Aveyron républicain*, 3 February 1886, p. 3. See also Renault and Aubin, *Cour d'assises*, p. 51. ADA U Watrin VI, no. 175, interrogation of François Soubrié, 5 February 1886; VI, no. 184, interrogation of Jean-Louis Soubrié, 5 February 1886.

52. AN 110AQ7(4), "Notes de M. Watrin sur une visite faite à Longwy" [1885].

53. AN 59AQ488, CA of SNHFA, 5 March 1879.

54. ADA U Watrin VI, no. 381, interrogation of Louis Rouquette, 4 April 1886.

55. AN 59AQ487, CA of SNHFA, 6 February 1868; 13 February 1868; 21 May 1873; 25 February 1874; 24 November 1875; 2 February 1876.

56. ADA 58B9, La Fraternelle . . . *Statuts* (Figeac: Imprimerie Veuve Lacroix et Louis Mules, 1880). ADA U Watrin V, nos. 23–24, information provided by vice-president of La Fraternelle, 21 February 1886.

57. ADA U Watrin VI, no. 184, interrogation of Jean-Louis Soubrié, 5 February 1886.

58. ADA U Watrin VI, no. 175, interrogation of François Soubrié, 5 February 1886; VI, no. 184, interrogation of Jean-Louis Soubrié, 5 February 1886; VI, no. 292, interrogation of Blazy, 18 February 1886.

59. On the "Bande Noire," see R. Beaubernard, *Un "Laboratoire sociale" au XIX^e siècle* (Paris: Editions de Civry, 1981).

60. One of the first leaders of the Decazeville miners' union, Jean-Pierre Blanc, was a former miner turned shopkeeper. Because of his relative independence, he was chosen to head the strike delegation in January 1886.

61. ADA U Watrin VII, no. 582, Cayrade to president of SNHFA, 7 December 1885; VII, no. 580, Petitjean to chief executive officer, 23 November 1885. (At this time the Société Nouvelle had two chief executive officers.) See Arthur Borghese, "Industrialist Paternalism and Lower-Class Agitation: The Case of Mulhouse, 1848–1851," *Histoire sociale-Social History*, 13 (1980): 55–84, for another example of an alliance of workers and merchants against company interference in commerce.

62. *La Gazette des tribunaux*, testimony of Cayrade, 19 June 1886, p. 579. ADA U Watrin VI, no. 91, interrogation of Cayrade, 20 February 1886. In January 1886 workers owed the Société Nouvelle approximately 120,000 francs or about 60 francs per worker—two-thirds of a hewer's monthly wages. *Le Temps*, 10 June 1886, p. 2.

63. APP BA186, "Grève de Decazeville Février 1886," no. 101, agent "26," 5 February 1886.

64. ADA U Watrin VI, no. 139, interrogation of Jean François Rouzet, 20 March 1886.

65. AN 59AQ488, CA of SNHFA, 22 October 1880; 14 April 1884; 21 April 1884.

66. In 1881 the company had thrown its weight behind the republican Mandagot in an unsuccessful effort to prevent the election of Cayrade to the Chamber. ADA 3M440, Mayor of Firmy to PA, 23 September 1881.

67. *La Gazette des tribunaux*, 19 June 1886, p. 580. ADA U Watrin VI, no. 29, interrogation of Bedel, 7 February 1886; VI, no. 176, interrogation of François Soubrié, 20 March 1886.

68. ADA U Watrin VI, no. 117, interrogation of Henri Juillard, 20 March 1886.

69. ADA U Watrin VI, no. 379, interrogation of Auguste Glazier, 3 April 1886. ADA 5M18, CPD to SpVf, 23 October 1885. On these elections in Aveyron, see René Izac, "Les Elections législatives de 1885 dans l'Aveyron," *Revue du Rouergue*, 37 (Winter 1983): 316–333.

70. Georges Stell, *Les Cahiers de doléances des mineurs français* (Paris: Bureaux du *Capitaliste*, 1883), p. 6.

71. Ibid., pp. 44, 52–53.

72. ADA 52M3, CPA to SpVf, 11 March 1884; 12 March 1884; 15 March 1884; CPD to SpVf, 12 March 1884; 13 March 1884.

73. C. Ledoux, *L'Organisation du travail dans les mines et particulièrement dans les houillères tant en France qu'à l'étranger* (Paris: Imprimerie Chaix, 1890), p. 21.

74. ADA 52M6, CSD to PA, 29 April 1890. ADA J495, Seibel to president of Campagnac, 21 July 1890.

75. ADA 11 M5 6, CSD to PA, 13 September 1887; 17 September 1887; 13 October 1887.

76. ADA 55M1, Brajou and Lacombe, leaders of the Decazeville miners' union, to PA, 29 September 1887; PA to mayor of Decazeville, 17

November 1887. ACGTD, AG (Decazeville), 9 July 1887; 6 November 1887.

77. ACGTD, AG (Decazeville), 3 October 1885.

78. ADA 55 M1, Costes, general secretary of the Decazeville miners' union, 7 February 1885. ACGTD, AG (Decazeville), 2 August 1885; 6 September 1885; CS (Decazeville), 19 April 1885. APP BA186, agent "26," 31 January 1886. *L'Eclaireur,* 27 September 1913, p. 1 (VM).

79. Accident compensation was a subject of increasing concern to firms in the Aubin Basin. ADA J492, "Rapport de la Compagnie des Mines de Campagnac" (June 1865). AN 60AQ355, Commission d'Aubin, 13 August 1868. AN 60AQ322, "Audiences et jugements," Tribunal de Villefranche-de-Rouergue, 7 April 1872. Whenever possible, companies punished accident victims who sought legal redress. In 1880 a miner who had been injured while employed by the Société Nouvelle and had then been given a position as supervisor, was fired when he sought further compensation in the courts (AN 59AQ488, CA of SNHFA, 8 December 1880). In a similar case, the Société Nouvelle gave a miner who had lost his leg in an accident in 1877 a monthly pension of ten francs and assigned him temporarily to a supervisory position. He sued the firm for a life-time guarantee of either a supplementary pension or a job. He lost the case and was fired. Only when the Société Nouvelle was in desperate need of workers during the strike of 1886 was he rehired (ADA 53M1, MTP to PA, 5 August 1885. *L'Intransigeant,* 9 March 1886, p. 2).

80. G., "Decazeville," 105. ADA 11 M5 6, CPD to PA, 2 October 1887.

81. ADA U Watrin VI, no. 120, interrogation of Jean-Pierre Blanc, 20 February 1886

82. See Marc Simard, "Situation économique de l'entreprise et rapports de production: le cas de la Compagnie des Mines d'Anzin (1860–1894)," *Revue du nord,* 65 (July-September 1983): 581–602.

83. See my "The Lamb and the Tiger" and my unpublished "A New Look at Zola's *Germinal.*"

84. Georges Clemenceau, *La Mêlée sociale* (Paris: Bibliothèque Charpentier, 1895), *passim,* esp. pp. 284–286.

85. Georges Clemenceau, *Rapport présenté à la Commission d'enquête parlementaire sur la situation des ouvriers de l'agriculture et de l'industrie en France (Grève d'Anzin)* (Paris: Imprimerie de la Chambre des députés, 1885). On the Radicals' interest in coal miners, see Leo Loubère, "The French Left-Wing Radicals: Their Economic and Social Program Since 1870," *The American Journal of Economics and Sociology,* 26 (1967): 191–192.

86. AN 59AQ545, essay on the SNHFA (1892).

87. Chambre des députés, *Procès-verbaux de la Commission des mines déposés par M. Gustave Drou, président de la Commission,* no. 878, 4 vols. (Paris: Imprimerie de la Chambre des députés, 1903), IV, 377–378. *La Voix des travailleurs,* 30 January 1896, p. 3 (VM). ADA U Watrin VI, no. 163,

interrogation of Pierre Gieysse, master miner, 19 February 1886; VI, no. 362, interrogation of Verneuil, engineer, 7 March 1886. *Le Cri du peuple,* 19 February 1886, p. 1.

88. *Le Temps,* 11 June 1886, p. 2.

89. AN 59AQ488, CA of SNHFA, 14 March 1883; 16 May 1883; 10 October 1883; 7–9 September 1884. The firm also began to refuse to hire new workers over thirty-five years of age. ACGTD, AG (Decazeville), 3 May 1885. See Rolande Trempé, "Travail à la mine et vieillissement des mineurs au XIXᵉ siècle," *Mouvement social,* 124 (July-September 1983): 133.

90. During the late nineteenth century companies throughout France made the crew responsible for more timbering. For Anzin, see my "The Lamb and the Tiger." For Commentry, see AN 59AQ26, "Boisage" by Henri Fayol (1878).

91. See Louise A. Tilly and Joan W. Scott, *Women, Work, and Family* (New York: Holt, Rinehart and Winston, 1978).

92. ADA U Watrin, no. 34, interrogation of Petitjean, 7 March 1886; VI, no. 362, interrogation of engineer Verneuil, 7 March 1886; V, no. 358, interrogation of Hippolyte Delagnes, 5 March 1886; VI, no. 363, interrogation of the state mining engineer Vidal, 7 March 1886; VI, no. 96, interrogation of Louis Baldos, 3 March 1886; VI, no. 124, interrogation of Elie Montferrand, 3 March 1886; VI, no. 163, interrogation of Pierre Gieysse, master miner, 19 February 1886; VI, no. 164, interrogation of Gieysse, 5 March 1886.

93. *Le Matin,* 28 January 1886, p. 1.

94. ADA U Watrin V, no. 95, interrogation of Jean Baldet, 29 January 1886; VI, no. 130, interrogation of Léon Peyrot, CPD, 30 January 1886; VI, no. 123, interrogation of Elie Montferrand, 29 January 1886; VI, no. 125, interrogation of Montferrand, 30 March 1886; VI, no. 348, interrogation of Frédéric Puechgarric, 20 March 1886; VI, no. 175, interrogation of François Soubrié, 5 February 1886. APP BA186, "Grève de Decazeville 1886," agent "26," 31 January 1886 and 15 February 1886.

95. ADA U Watrin VI, no. 118, interrogation of Jean-Pierre Blanc, 29 January 1886.

96. ADA U Watrin VI, no. 121, interrogation of Jean-Baptiste Carrié, 29 January 1886.

97. ADA U Watrin VI, no. 118, interrogation of Jean-Pierre Blanc, 29 January 1886. More than four years after the *watrinade,* the Decazeville union secretary Lacombe wrote: "I can guarantee that if Watrin was assassinated, it is the company supervisory personnel that should bear the responsibility, since it was these employees who named him as the perpetrator of all the injustices committed against the workers." *La Voix des travailleurs,* 7 September 1890, p. 3.

98. The case of Marcellin Entraygues, a miner at Paleyrets, illustrates the dilemma of working-class leaders in a company-controlled town. Once

in contact with the company administration, they found it very difficult to maintain their independence. Entraygues was popular among his peers and had been chosen by them to serve on the board of the mutual aid fund. He quit work with the other miners at his pit on the morning of 26 January, but because of his status as a fund commissioner, he did not want to be "remarked" and returned home rather than joining his comrades when they went to convince miners at other pits to join the strike. After strikers chose Entraygues as a delegate that afternoon, they had to go to his house to bring him to town hall. ADA U Watrin VI, no. 97, interrogation of Marcellin Entraygues, 29 January 1886.

99. APP BA186, "Grève de Decazeville," no. 88, agent "26," 1 February 1886.

100. At the end of 1883 the mines of the Société Nouvelle employed 1 director, 10 engineers, 14 master miners, 75 *chefs de poste*, 981 adult underground workers; aboveground there were 604 adult men, 345 women and 22 children. ADA 68S1, "Etat général des mines concédées du département de l'Aveyron pendant l'année 1883," 6 March 1884.

101. APP BA186, "Grève de Decazeville," no. 48, "Boisglory," 28 January 1886; no. 66, telegram to *Le Gaulois*, 30 January 1886; no. 47, Léon Say to Petitjean (undated). *Le Cri du peuple*, 1 February 1886, p. 1 (DQ). *Le Matin*, 31 January 1886, p. 1. AN 59AQ488, CA of SNHFA, 29 January 1886; 30 January 1886.

102. AN 59AQ488, CA of SNHFA, 15 February 1886, 22 February 1886.

103. AN 59AQ489, AG of SNHFA, 27 February 1886.

104. The workers later decided to ask for 1.15 francs for all wagons of coal, lump and fine, and 1.05 francs per completed brace, thirty centimes more than the company offered.

105. AN 59AQ489, AG of SNHFA, 27 February 1886.

106. *Le Temps*, 5 March 1886, p. 2. Radical republican reformers like Clemenceau felt that the 1810 law should be rewritten to deny mining firms the right to provoke strikes which were advantageous to them. Clemenceau, *La Mêlée sociale*, p. 294. On the government's role in strikes during this period, see Jacques Néré, "Aspects du déroulement des grèves en France durant la période 1883–89," *Revue d'histoire économique et sociale*, 34 (1956): 286–302.

107. The departure of board members from Decazeville in early March significantly improved relations between the company, represented by Petitjean, and the government. *Le Temps*, 7 March 1886, p. 2.

108. AN 59AQ488, CA of SNHFA, 30 March 1886. The miners of Firmy waited a month to join the strike because, unlike their comrades at Decazeville, a majority were small landholders for whom managerial abuses and wage reductions were less central to their personal lives and economic situation. *L'Intransigeant*, 14 March 1886, p. 1. *Le Cri du Peuple*, 7 June 1886, p. 1.

109. AN 110AQ52(4), procès-verbal of SNHFA Société de Secours, 15 March 1886. During the strike at least one fund commissioner was suspected of trying to get miners to return to work. His house was seriously damaged by a dynamite charge placed on his doorstep. *La Justice,* 23 May 1886, p. 2.

110. ADA U Watrin VI, no. 87, interrogation of Cayrade, 28 January 1886; VI, no. 99, interrogation of Alexandre Bos, 29 January 1886; VI, no. 102, interrogation of Nègre, 29 January 1886; VI, no. 106, interrogation of Chaveau, 4 February 1886. The municipal officials' statement also reveals their distance from the workplace experiences of Decazeville's industrial workers.

111. For the cooperative, see *Le Cri du peuple,* 7 March 1886, p. 1; 25 April 1886, p. 1. For the civil burials, see *Le Matin,* 8 May 1886, p. 1; and *Le Cri du peuple,* 10 May 1886.

112. *Le Cri du peuple,* 25 May 1886, p. 1. Robert Erales, "La Grève des mineurs de Decazeville, 26 janvier-12 juin 1886" (Mémoire, Université de Toulouse-le-Mirail, 1971), pp. 220–221.

113. *Le Cri du peuple,* 21 April 1886, p. 1; 23 April 1886, p. 1. *L'Aveyron républicain,* 24 April 1886. Cayrade died of apoplexy shortly after the strike ended.

114. The outpouring of support for Decazeville's strikers (and for those at Vierzon later in the year) inspired Paul Lafargue to write Friedrich Engels that the politicization of the French public could allow French workers to bypass the accumulation of strike funds that was a fundamental aspect of British craftworkers' organization: "The French with their public subscriptions prove to English trade-unionists that they have no need for funds prepared in advance to find money." Friedrich Engels and Paul and Laura Lafargue, *Correspondance,* 3 vols. (Paris: Editions sociales, 1956–1959), I, 383 (letter of 18 September 1886).

115. Perrot, *Les Ouvriers,* p. 527.

116. See Henri Feller, "Physionomie d'un quotidien: *Le Cri du peuple* (1883–1889)," *Mouvement social,* 53 (October-December 1965): 69–87. Clemenceau lamented that the Graissessac miners' strike of 1894 suffered because the miners' moderation made it bad copy for the national press, *La Mêlée sociale,* p. 340.

117. Perrot, *Les Ouvriers,* p. 195. *Le Cri du peuple,* 8 April 1886, p. 1.

118. See my "The Role of Mine Safety in the Development of Working-Class Consciousness and Organization: The Case of the Aubin Coal Basin, 1867–1914," *French Historical Studies,* 12 (Spring 1981): 108–110.

119. *La Dépêche,* 9 March 1886, pp. 2–3. During the final weeks of the strike the Chamber of Deputies began considering revisions of the law of 1810, but these debates led to no substantive changes. George Jared Lamb, "Coal Mining in France, 1873 to 1895" (Ph.D. diss., University of Illinois at Urbana-Champaign, 1976), p. 260.

120. AN F 12 4656, attorney general to Garde des Sceaux, 18 March 1886.

121. *La Dépêche*, 8 March 1886, p. 2.

122. *Le Cri du peuple*, 21 May 1886, p. 1.

123. My interest in this problem stems from Eugen Weber's pathbreaking *Peasants into Frenchmen: The Modernization of Rural France 1870–1914* (Stanford: Stanford University Press, 1976). Weber is concerned with the nonindustrial population of the French countryside, however.

124. ADA 11 M5 6, CSD to PA, 27 November 1886. "Kroumir" was a common epitaph for scabs throughout France; Perrot, *Les Ouvriers*, p. 519.

125. Chambre des députés, *Annales de la Chambre des députés. Débats parlementaires*, 17 (13 March 1886): 1, 508. Such tales of fraternization had little basis in fact, however, for the general at Decazeville posted a warning to his men not to socialize with residents of the town. *Le Temps*, 18 March 1886, p. 2. See Leo A. Loubère, "Left-Wing Radicals, Strikes, and the Military 1880–1907," *French Historical Studies*, 3 (1963): 93–105.

126. *Le Cri du peuple*, 10 April 1886, p. 1.

127. Engels and Lafargue, *Correspondance*, 1, 361 (letter of 25 May 1886).

128. Socialist unity in the electoral campaign was marred by the Possibilists' decision to run their own candidate, a Decazeville miner.

129. Engels and Lafargue, *Correspondance*, I, 342–343 (letter of 15 March 1886). See Jacques Néré, "La Crise industrielle de 1882 et le mouvement boulangiste," 2 vols. (Thèse de doctorat, Université de Paris, 1958), I, 136–180; and Alexandre Zévaès, *La Grève de Decazeville (janvier-juin 1886)* (Paris: Bureau d'Editions, 1938), pp. 29–32.

130. For Laur's picaresque life, see his articles in the newspaper *La Guerre aux abus* (1890–1892) and his *L'Epoque boulangiste*, 2 vols. (Paris: Le Livre à l'auteur, 1914).

131. SLSAA, Fonds Daudibertières, carton no. 23, report to G. Paul, 14 May 1886. For the conversation between the Minister and representatives of the board, see AN 59AQ488, CA of SNHFA, 16 May 1886.

132. *La Dépêche*, 7 June 1886, p. 2. *Le Journal de L'Aveyron*, 8 June 1886, p. 1. *La Justice*, 7 June 1886, p. 2.

133. *Le Cri du peuple*, 2 June 1886, p. 1.

134. *L'Intransigeant*, 8 June 1886, p. 1.

135. Francis Laur, *Essai de socialisme expérimental. La Mine aux mineurs* (Paris: E. Dentu, 1887), p. 106.

136. Ibid., pp. 138–139.

137. Ibid., p. 6.

138. Ibid., pp. 17–18.

139. The need to obtain a state mine concession made the establishment of a *mine aux mineurs* far more difficult than contemporaneous efforts

among skilled industrial workers to create cooperatives, such as the glass-works formed by Carmaux glassworkers at Albi.

140. The different viewpoints of Laur and Jean Jaurès on mine-safety delegates provide a good example of the two options for republican social policy. See my "The Role of Mine Safety," 106. Following the Decazeville strike Laur became an enthusiastic partisan of Boulanger. After 1889 he embraced the worst of Michelet, combining attacks on the *accaparement* of commodities by cartels with a virulent anti-Semitism. On Laur the anti-Semite, see Zeev Sternhall, *La Droite révolutionnaire: les origines françaises du fascisme 1885–1914* (Paris: Seuil, 1978), *passim*. Through all of this, Laur continued to maintain that the *mine aux mineurs* provided the best alternative to cartels. *L'Accaparement* (Paris: Société anonyme des publications scientifiques et industrielles, 1900), 4 vols.

141. Pierre Sorlin, *Waldeck-Rousseau* (Paris: Armand Colin, 1966), pp. 332–333.

142. AN 59AQ488, CA of SNHFA, 8 June 1886.

143. AN 59AQ488, CA to SNHFA, 12 July 1886; 19 July 1886. SLSAA, Fonds Daudibertières, carton no. 23, note to chief executive officer, 7 June 1886 (quoted); chief executive officer to Petitjean, 9 June 1886. Petitjean pointed out that the rate hike would "cost nothing, if the inspection of the wagons of lump coal is exercised with great vigilance at the central sorting center."

144. SLSAA, Fonds Daudibertières, carton no. 23, report by Petitjean, 8 June 1886. Even Basly "recognized that Petitjean had undertaken praise-worthy efforts to get the company to make concessions." AN F 12 4656, CSD to MI, 12 June 1886.

145. Chambre des députés, *Commission . . . Drou*, IV, 377–378. The miners' demand for Blazy's removal helped clarify what Carter Goodrich called the "frontiers of control." A businessman named Remès, who had attempted unsuccessfully to mediate the strike, explained to strikers that "it was contradictory that [chief miners] wanted the right to choose, to pay, and to fire their helpers while they in turn wanted to impose on the company this or that individual [Blazy]." *Le Temps*, 11 June 1886, p. 2. The strike forced the Société Nouvelle to recognize the reverse of this argument.

146. Renault and Aubin, *Cour d'assises*, pp. 53–55. There is no evidence that anyone planned the murder. André Marc Vial is wrong to argue that those who killed Watrin "were under the influence of anarchist leaders"; *Germinal et le 'socialisme' de Zola* (Paris: Editions sociales, 1975), p. 58.

147. *La Justice*, 20 June 1886, p. 3.

148. AN 59AQ488, CA of SNHFA, 21 June 1886. On "Les Incorrigibles," see ADA 11 M5 5, CSD to PA, 4 November 1886. ADA 11 M5 6, CSD to PA, 21 September 1886; 5 October 1886; 26 October 1886; 27

October 1886; 28 November 1886; 10 December 1886; 18 April 1887; 2 May 1887. ADA 55M1, PA, 10 March 1888.

149. AN 59AQ489, AG of SNHFA, 28 February 1887. AN 59AQ545, essay on the SNHFA [1892].

150. The cancellation of profits on coal sales by losses on the forges is starkly illustrated in *Compte-rendu de l'assemblée générale de la Société des Houillères et Fonderies de l'Aveyron du 4 février 1892* (Decazeville: F. Chirac, 1892).

151. Lévêque, *Histoire,* p. 89.

152. *Le Matin,* 28 January 1886, p. 1.

153. *Le Bassin houiller de l'Aveyron,* 14 July 1889, p. 3; 1 September 1889, p. 1. ADA 11 M5 4, CSD to PA, 15 December 1890. ADA 5M18, SpVf to PA, 5 October 1889; PA, 7 October 1889. An 111AQ223, DA to DGA, 22 November 1890. ADA 5M18, chief state engineer, 3 April 1889 (quoted).

154. AN 110AQ(1), C. Péguet, principal mine engineer of SCF at Decazeville (1892). ADA 67S1bis, state engineer, 3 July 1891. ADA 68S6, CSD to PA, 3 February 1892. ADA 11 M5 4, CSD to PA, 20 August 1891; 22 August 1891; 24 August 1891.

155. AN 59AQ545, report by Lasserre to Fayol, 4 March 1892.

156. AN 110AQ1(7), company note, 10 May 1888. ADA 5M18, PA, 7 October 1889. ADA 55M1, Brajou to PA, 31 May 1888; PA to justice of the peace (Decazeville), 4 June 1888. ADA 3M, PA to MI, 12 September 1889.

157. ADA 5M18, CSD to PA, 26 September 1889; 12 October 1889; 21 October 1889; CPD to PA, 8 October 1889. *Le Pays noir,* 6 October 1889, p. 3. *Le Bassin houiller de l'Aveyron,* 27 October 1889, p. 2. *Le Temps,* 25 October 1889, p. 4. The Minister of Public Works put pressure on leading members of the Société Nouvelle's board to have Gastambide and Blazy dismissed. ADA 11 M4 7, MI to PA, 8 November 1889.

158. ADA 11M5 6, CSD to PA, 5 October 1886. ADA 11M5 4, CSD to PA, 14 June 1889; 28 June 1889; 26 May 1890; 9 June 1890; 4 June 1891; 10 June 1891; 12 April 1892; report of gendarmerie (Decazeville), 3 June 1891. *Le Pays noir,* 15 January 1888; 20 January 1889; 27 January 1889.

159. *Le Bassin houiller de l'Aveyron,* 1 September 1889, p. 2 (quoted); 15 September 1889, p. 1.

160. AN 110AQ23(1), "Note sur un projet d'extinction d'un haut fourneau" by Jules Héliot, 26 July 1890. ADA J495, Seibel to President of Campagnac, 2 August 1890 (quoted). AN BB 18 1823, attorney general to Garde des Sceaux, 6 August 1890. ADA 11 M5 4, CPD to PA, 2 September 1890. Gastambide also raised managers' salaries without the requisite approval of the board. AN 59AQ9, CA of SCF, 24 March 1892.

161. Lévêque, *Histoire,* p. 93.

162. AN 59AQ489, AG of SNHFA, 27 February 1889. AN 59AQ9, CA of SCF, 12 April 1892. Stockholders were beginning to oppose explicitly political managerial strategies in other enterprises as well. See Rolande

Trempé, "Une Campagne électorale étudiée d'après les archives privées. La Campagne électorale de 1898 dans la deuxième circonscription d'Albi, d'après les archives privées du Marquis Ludovic de Solages, candidat contre Jean Jaurès" in *Actes du 82ᵉ congrès national des sociétés savantes 1957. Section d'histoire moderne et contemporaine* (Paris: Imprimerie nationale, 1958), p. 489, n. 2.

163. APD, "Livre de paroisse." DCMD, 23 September 1888; 1 October 1888; 7 October 1888; 20 October 1888; 31 October 1888. ADA 11 M5 4, CSD to PA, 31 October 1888; CPD to PA, 2 September 1888.

164. AN 59AQ488, CA of SNHFA, 10 April 1878.

165. The town financed its share of the costs with a 50 percent increase in the local property tax: "this tax increase, far from burdening the workers, will affect only the landowners, those who are, after all, most interested in the establishment of a garrison." DCMD, 26 September 1886 (quoted). ADA 11 M5 6, CSD to PA, 27 September 1886; 3 December 1886. *La Justice*, 2 May 1886, p. 2.

166. I discuss the *commissaire spécial's* attack on Gastambide in "The Role of Mine Safety," 105, n. 14.

167. *Le Pays Noir*, 5 November 1888, p. 1.

168. ADA 23 M3 2bis, PA to MI, 9 November 1888.

169. AN 110AQ39(3), "Tragique cinquantenaire. Une Explosion du grisou à Cransac le 2 Novembre 1888 amena une terrible catastrophe et tua près de 50 ouvriers" [November 1938].

170. See Perrot, *Les Ouvriers*, p. 46; and Pierre Reboul, "La Mine dans la littérature du XIXᵉ siècle" in *Charbon et sciences humaines*, ed. Louis Trénard, pp. 427–442 (Paris: Mouton, 1966).

171. See Susanna Barrows' excellent analysis of the contemporary sociological interpretation of crowd events like the murder of Watrin in *Distorting Mirrors: Visions of the Crowd in Late Nineteenth-Century France* (New Haven: Yale University Press, 1981).

172. Engels and Lafargue, *Correspondance*, I, 343 (letter of 15 March 1886).

173. Jacques Julliard, "Jeune et vieux syndicat chez les mineurs du Pas-de-Calais (à travers les papiers de Pierre Monatte)," *Mouvement social*, 47 (April-June 1964): 7–30.

## 6. The Second Industrial Revolution

1. See David Landes, *Prometheus Unbound* (Cambridge: Cambridge University Press, 1969), chs. 5 and 6.

2. Herman Lebovics, "The Great Depression and New Conservatism, 1880–1896" (paper presented at the French Historical Studies Conference, April 1984).

3. Peter Stearns, *Revolutionary Syndicalism and French Labor: A Cause*

*Without Rebels* (New Brunswick, N. J.: Rutgers University Press, 1971); and Jacques Julliard, "Théorie syndicaliste révolutionnaire et pratique gréviste," *Mouvement social*, 65 (October-December 1968): 55–69.

4. Guy Thuillier, *Aspects de l'économie nivernaise au XIX^e siècle* (Paris: Mouton, 1966), p. 113.

5. Fayol Archives, Fayol, "Observations et expériences personnelles," pp. 86–87.

6. See my "L'Industrie métallurgique et les ouvriers métallurgistes de Decazeville, 1892–1914" (forthcoming in *Procès-verbaux des séances de la SLSAA*).

7. ADA 11 M5 7ser, CSD to PA, 15 June 1914.

8. J. M. Gaillard, "La Crise économique et sociale dans le bassin houiller d'Alès à la fin du XIX^e siècle" in *Mines et mineurs en Languedoc-Roussillon et régions voisines de l'antiquité à nos jours* (Montpellier: Fédération historique du Languedoc méditerranéen et du Roussillon, 1977), pp. 211–221.

9. France; Chambre des députés, *Rapport fait au nom de la Commission du travail et de la sécurité dans les mines par M. Louis Lacombe, député* (Paris: Imprimerie de la Chambre des députés, 1896), p. 116.

10. AN 110AQ56, "Rapport annuel, Mines, 1899–1900." AN 110AQ57, "Rapport annuel, Mines, 1900–01." AN 110AQ61, "Rapport annuel, Mines, 1911–12." AN 110AQ62, "Rapport annuel, Mines, 1912–13."

11. AN59AQ14bis, Fayol, "Note pour le Conseil d'administration," p. 34, 9 January 1908.

12. AN110AQ55, "Rapport annuel, Mines, 1895–96."

13. AN 59AQ14bis, Fayol, "Note pour le Conseil d'administration," pp. 25–26, 9 January 1908.

14. SCFD, *Procès-verbal de l'Assemblée générale ordinaire des actionnaires. Rapport du Conseil d'administration. Rapport des commissaires* (Paris: Imprimerie Paul Dupont, 1900–1914). ADA 86S5, mine controller, 16 January 1913. AN 110AQ152, DD to DG, 7 January 1909.

15. On the high fertility of miners see Michael Haines, *Fertility and Occupation: Population Patterns in Industry* (New York: Academic Press, 1979) and E. A. Wrigley, *Industrial Growth and Population Change: A Regional Study of the Coalfield Areas of North-west Europe in the Later Nineteenth Century* (Cambridge: Cambridge University Press, 1961). On the decline in births in Montceau-les-Mines and Le Creusot after strikes at the turn of the century as both a rational response to economic insecurity and the ultimate antipaternalist gesture, see my "The Lamb and the Tiger: Paternalist Discourse and Practice in Nineteenth-Century Mining and Metallurgy (forthcoming in *Comparative Studies in Society and History*). Patrick Couffin draws figures from the 1896 census to argue that in Decazeville younger workers' families were limiting family size in comparison with earlier generations; "Aspects de la vie ouvrière à Decazeville au début du

XXᵉ siècle (1892–1914)" (Mémoire, Université de Paul Valéry (Montpellier III), 1975), pp. 25–26.

16. Couffin, "Aspects," pp. 29–35.

17. Chambre des députés, *Rapport . . . Lacombe*, p. 121.

18. AN 110AQ43(3), DD to DG, 7 February 1900. For similar trends at Carmaux, see Rolande Trempé, *Les Mineurs de Carmaux 1848–1914* (Paris: Editions ouvrières, 1971), pp. 152–153; and in the Valenciennes, see Odette Hardy-Hémery, *De la Croissance à la désindustrialisation. Un siècle dans le Valenciennois* (Paris: Presses de la Fondation nationale des sciences politiques, 1984), pp. 32–33. On the mobility of workers at the Decazeville steelworks before the war, see Rolande Trempé, "Pour une meilleure connaissance de la classe ouvrière. L'Utilisation des archives d'entreprise: le fichier du personnel," in *Mélanges d'histoire sociale offerts à Jean Maitron* (Paris: Editions ouvrières, 1976), pp. 249–263.

19. AN 110AQ241, DA to DD, 14 September 1905. Some employees left Decazeville for better pay and promotions in the new iron-ore mines of the Lorraine. Louis Köll, *Auboué en Lorraine du fer. Du Village rural à la cité minière* (Paris: Karthala, 1982), p. 81.

20. France. Ministère du Commerce, de l'Industrie, des Postes et des Télégraphes. Office du travail. *Salaires et durée du travail dans l'industrie française*, 4 vols. (Paris: Imprimerie nationale, 1894), II, 32–33. ADA 67S10, statistics compiled for the state assessment of the *redevance*, 1900–01; 1910–11.

21. *Premier congrès de l'hygiène des travailleurs et des ateliers* (Paris: L'Emancipatrice, 1905), p. 116. Mazars and a co-author lifted this passage word-for-word from Georges Stell! *Les Cahiers de doléances des mineurs français* (Paris: Bureaux de *Capitaliste*, 1883), pp. 26–27.

22. AN 110AQ41(4), "Rapport de M. Latapie, maître-mineur à Decazeville, au sujet de sa tournée dans le département du Lot pour le recrutement d'ouvriers," 28 June 1909. See also Gabriel Boscary, *Evolution agricole et condition des cultivateurs de l'Aveyron pendant le XIXᵉ siècle* (Montpellier: Imprimerie Gustave Firmin, Montane et Sicardi, 1909). There was no system of seasonal rural labor at Decazeville such as one finds in the Gard before the war. Henri Pin, *Les Mines de houille dans le Gard. La condition du mineur* (Montpellier: Imprimerie générale du Midi, 1914), pp. 45–46.

23. AN 110AQ152, DD to DG, 5 February 1908.

24. On the rise in the cost of living at Decazeville before the war, see Couffin, "Aspects," pp. 105–107.

25. ADA 33 M1 6, CSD to PA, [1914].

26. 110AQ61, "Rapport annuel, Mines, 1911–12."

27. ADA 11M5 7ser, CSD to PA, 7 May 1913. M.R. Guglielmo, "Facteurs et formes de l'évolution urbaine à Decazeville," *Bulletin de l'Association de géographes français*, 249–250 (March-April 1955): 84.

28. Rolande Trempé, "La Main d'oeuvre étrangère aux mines de Carmaux entre les deux guerres," *Revue du Tarn*, 64 (December 1971): 453–460.

29. In addition, peasant-miners saw foreign immigrants, who had nothing but their labor power, as "the true proletarians." See the comments of the Carmaux peasant-miner Edouard Roy in *Une Fumée sur le toit. Charlou, mineur et paysan* (Paris: Editions universitaires, 1982), pp. 122–123.

30. *L'Eclaireur*, 31 January 1914, p. 2.

31. See M. R. Brodie, *Fayol on Administration* (London: Lyon, Grant and Green, n.d.) and my "The Genesis and Development of the Thought of Henry Fayol" (forthcoming in *Sociologie du travail*).

32. AN 59AQ11, CA to SCFD, 6 September 1902.

33. AN 59AQ9, CA of SCF, 8 March 1892. ADA 68S6, CSD to PA, 2 March 1892.

34. ADA 11 M5 5, CSD to PA, 3 December 1892; 5 December 1892. AN 110AQ95, "Rapport annuel, Usines, 1905–06."

35. AN 110AQ56, "Rapport annuel, Mines, 1896–97." AN 110AQ63, "Rapport annuel, Mines, 1913–14."

36. AN 110AQ56, "Rapport annuel, Mines, 1896–97." The six included white collar employees.

37. AN 59AQ10, CA of SCFD, 13 May 1901. Fayol strongly promoted school as the training ground for supervisory personnel. Fayol Archives, Fayol, "Observations et expériences personnelles," p. 17.

38. AN 110AQ43(3), "Note," Direction des mines (Decazeville), 12 September 1893.

39. See, for example, ADA 93S4, MTP to PA, 16 February 1882; 7 July 1882.

40. ADA 93S5, MTP to PA, 8 January 1875. AN 110AQ39(1), engineer to DD, 9 October 1891. Articles 25 through 35 of Société anonyme des Aciéries de France. Houillères d'Aubin, *Règlement pour l'exploitation des mines à grisou approuvé par arrêté préfectoral en date du 18 juillet 1889* (Rodez, n.p., 1889) (ADA 54B1–6). Lucien Mazars, "La Lampe de mine et son évolution dans le bassin d'Aubin," *Procès-verbaux de la SLSAA*, 37 (1954–1958): 70–76. AN 110AQ11(1), report of A. Marchal, 17 July 1909. For a clear example of safety regulations being used to punish miners' political actions, see Hardy-Hémery, *De la Croissance*, p. 56.

41. *Le Cri du peuple*, 25 May 1886, p. 1, and 28 May 1886, p. 1. *La Justice*, 26 May 1886, pp. 2–3. APP BA186, Havas dispatch, 26 May 1886. These explosions differed fundamentally from the anarchist *attentats* of the 1890s. The miners used one of the tools of their trade to further their strike effort; the anarchists chose dynamite because of its destructive power, both in symbolic and real terms. See Eric Hobsbawm's perceptive comments on the significance of forms of violence in miners' strikes: "Labor History and Ideology," *Journal of Social History*, 6 (1974): 378–379.

42. AN 59AQ488, 23 April 1879. ADA 93S4, MTP to PA, 2 August 1884. AN 111AQ294, DA to engineer, 15 July 1889. Houillères d'Aubin, *Règlement*, articles 14 and 16. AN 110AQ39(1), state engineer to DD, 9 October 1891.

43. Houillères d'Aubin, *Règlement*, article 2.

44. For a similar development at Carmaux during this same period, see Roy, *Une Fumée sur le toit*, p. 113.

45. AN 110AQ56, "Rapport annuel, Mines, 1897–98."

46. Fayol Archives, "Abattage," [ca. 1878–1879].

47. AN 59AQ26, Fayol, report on the mines of Commentry, 1878–79.

48. ADA 11 M4 7, PA to MI, 22 February 1888. ADA 11 M5 5, report of gendarmerie (Gua), 16 March 1890. ADA 11 M5 4, CSD to PA, 28 March 1890; 16 May 1890; 18 July 1890.

49. On the shift from collective to individual paysheets in the Loire, see Charles Benoist, *L'Organisation du travail*, 2 vols. (Paris: Plon, 1905–1913), I, 220–221; and in the Nord, Hardy-Hémery, *De la Croissance*, p. 61.

50. AN BB 18 2028, justice of the peace (Decazeville) to attorney general, 19 February 1896. ADA 11 M5 7, CSD to PA, 18 January 1902. AN 110AQ48(1), Decazeville miners' union to DD, 18 February 1900; Service des mines (Decazeville) to DG, 23 February 1900. *La Voix des travailleurs*, 10 October 1895, p. 3; 5 January 1896, p. 3; 30 January 1896, p. 3 (VM); 6 February 1896, p. 3 (VM); 22 October 1896 (quoted). SLSAA, Fonds Daudibertières, carton no. 23, chief executive officer to Petitjean, 9 June 1886 and notes on this letter by DD [1899].

51. France; Chambre des députés, *Procès-verbaux de la Commission des mines déposés par M. Gustave Drou, président de la Commission*, no. 878, 4 vols. (Paris: Imprimerie de la Chambre des députés, 1903), IV, 392.

52. ADA 68S2, state engineer to PA, 16 March 1896.

53. AN 110AQ56, "Rapport annuel, Mines, 1898–99."

54. SLSAA Fonds Daudibertières, carton no. 23, chief executive officer to Petitjean, 9 June 1886 and notes on this letter by DD [1899].

55. According to the state engineer assigned to the Aubin Basin: "Payment by production differs little from payment by the day. The irregularity of the deposits in Aveyron's mines often makes it difficult to settle on fixed rates in advance; if the *chantier* turns out to have been worse than anticipated, one gives the worker the agreed-upon rate, but for the following pay period the fixed rates are reduced by as much. Since it is difficult to determine in what proportion greater or lesser productivity in a *chantier* comes from the quality of the *chantier* or the activity of the worker, one is evidently led to set the rates in such a way as to make everyone earn about the same daily wage." Chambre des députés, *Procès-verbaux . . . Drou*, IV, 360–362.

56. Ibid., 377–378.

57. ADA 11 M5 5, state engineer, 30 January 1887; 18 July 1887.

58. Despite these changes, the miner retained much more autonomy

than the semiskilled factory worker. Georges Lefranc goes too far when he writes of miners at the turn of the century: "At a time when Taylorism had not yet strongly affected French industry . . . work in the mines is already close to what workers' labor will become with the scientific organization of work and the proliferation of non-specialist labor." *Le Mouvement syndical sous la Troisième République* (Paris: Payot, 1967), p. 75.

59. AN 110AQ294, DA to state engineer, 2 March 1888. AN 111AQ300, DA to mine controller, 9 February 1914.

60. AN 40AS34, "Réponse au questionnaire de la Commission parlementaire des mines" (SCFD to CCHF, 15 March 1903). In 1903 there were 1,361 underground miners at Decazeville, including 375 hewers (average daily wage: 5.40 francs); 374 assistant hewers (4.28 francs); 176 timbermen (4.97 francs); 154 assistant timbermen (3.62 francs). Of the 704 workers in the open-pit mines, 380 were directly involved in extraction (3.56 francs); the others, who were less well paid, were employed primarily in transport. For related developments in the Valenciennes, see Hardy-Hémery, *De la Croissance*, p. 50.

61. See my "Labor, Management and the State in an Industrial Town: Decazeville, 1826–1914" (Ph.D. diss., Stanford University, 1981), Appendix 7. The labor force in the Carmaux mines was also aging; Trempé, *Les Mineurs*, pp. 141–147, 513–518. On the eve of World War I miners at Montceau-les-Mines expressed a reluctance to having their sons become miners, in part because of the prospects of slow advancement: "instead of becoming a miner at twenty, you remain a poorly paid *manoeuvre* until you are thirty." Lucien Peyronnard, *Le Charbon de Blanzy, La Famille Chagot et Montceau-les-Mines. Histoire économique, politique et sociale du pays montcellien de 1769 à 1927*, 2 vols. (Le Creusot: Ecomusée de la Communauté Le Creusot/Montceau-les-Mines, 1981), II, 259.

62. AN 40AS34, "Réponse aux questionnaire de la Commission parlementaire des mines." ADA 11 M5 7, CSD to PA, 18 March 1900.

63. Chambre des députés, *Procès-verbaux . . . Drou*, IV, 337.

64. Chambre des députés, *Rapport . . . Lacombe*, p. 49.

65. AN 110AQ56, "Rapport annuel, Mines, 1898–99." The earlier increase in haulers at Carmaux affected union militancy there more than did the frustration of *aides* in crews at Decazeville.

66. See my analysis of the 1902 Decazeville metalworkers' strike in "L'Industrie métallurgique et les ouvriers métallurgistes" and Michael Hanagan's comments on the organization of work in the Loire steelworks in *The Logic of Solidarity: Artisans and Industrial Workers in Three French Towns 1871–1914* (Urbana: University of Illinois Press, 1980), pp. 129–136. For a detailed examination of these developments at the Anzin coal mines and the Le Creusot steelworks, see my "The Lamb and the Tiger."

67. See my "La Grève de 1913 à Aubin-Cransac" (forthcoming in *Revue du Rouergue*).

68. ACGTD, AG (Decazeville), 15 August 1897; 16 January 1898; 29 May 1898. ADA 11 M5 7ser, CSD to PA, 19 March 1912. *La Voix des travailleurs,* 29 October 1893, p. 4 (advertisement). AN F 7 12497, CSD to MI, 1 July 1902. *L'Indépendent,* 14 December 1902, p. 3.

69. AN F 7 12772, CSD to MI, 31 October 1892. The most complete profile of union membership in the Basin is provided by a list of members of the Aubin miners' union as of 1 January 1894. Of the 133 members, 89.5 percent were "miners," 3 percent were *manoeuvres,* and the remainder held auxiliary positions in the mines or were small businessmen in the town. More than two-thirds of the union members were married (68.4 percent); 29.3 percent were single; one was a widower and the status of two was unknown. At least 87.5 percent rented their housing, but only 3.6 percent of these rented from the company. Statistics computed from "Liste alphabétique des individus qui ont adhéré au Syndicat des mineurs d'Aubin, destinée à Monsieur le Préfet de L'Aveyron," in ADA 11 M4 7.

70. ADA 11 M5 7, CPD to PA, 13 March 1900. Chambre des députés, *Procès-verbaux . . . Drou,* IV, 378–380.

71. *L'Eclaireur,* 17 January 1914, pp. 1–2 (VM).

72. ADA 55M1, PA to Minister of Commerce and Industry, 16 March 1895.

73. AN 110AQ55, "Rapport annuel, Mines, 1893–94."

74. See my "The Role of Mine Safety in the Development of Working-Class Consciousness and Organization: The Case of the Aubin Basin, 1867–1914," *French Historical Studies,* 12 (Spring 1981): 115–118.

75. ACGTD, executive meeting (Decazeville), 20 May 1909.

76. *L'Eclaireur,* 24 November 1912, p. 4.

77. ACGTD, AG (Aubin), 11 April 1909.

78. ACGTD, CA (Aubin), 16 October 1910. In 1895 the Decazeville union's general assembly had decided: "in the future no member of the union should ever circulate a subscription list for a non-union comrade; by the same token, a union member should not sign any subscription list which does not bear the union seal." ACGTD, AG (Decazeville), 13 January 1895.

79. ACGTD, AG (Decazeville), 27 November 1910.

80. ADA 55 M1, "Statuts de la Chambre syndicale." See also ACGTD, AG (Decazeville), 12 November 1893.

81. ACGTD, AG (Aubin), 16 July 1911.

82. ACGTD, AG (Decazeville), 18 June 1911.

83. Ibid., 26 July 1896. At this meeting, Mazars cited the example of the miners' union at Carmaux which was fighting a mutual aid fund nicknamed "L'Etrangloir" that was organized outside of union ranks. I discuss the mutual benefits funds and funeral societies in greater detail in my "Labor, Management, and the State," ch. 9.

84. Pierre du Maroussem, "Picqueur sociétaire de la 'Mine aux mi-

neurs' de Monthieux (Loire-France)," *Les Ouvriers des deux mondes,* 2ᵉ série 5 (1899): 365–436.

85. *L'Eclaireur,* 24 November 1912, p. 4. For *mines aux mineurs* in the Aubin Basin, see especially ACGTD, AG (Aubin), 29 June 1890. ADA 11 M5 4, CSD to PA, 30 June 1890. *La Voix des travailleurs,* 22 February 1891, pp. 2–3.

86. ADA 52M6, CPD to PA, 28 April 1890.

87. Chambre des députés, *Rapport . . . Lacombe,* p. 118.

88. Reid, "The Role of Mine Safety." Arthur Fontaine, "Notes sur l'inspection du travail au moyen de délégués ouvriers en France," in *Congrès international pour la protection légale des travailleurs tenu à Paris, du 25 au 28 juillet 1900* (Paris: Arthur Rousseau, 1901), pp. 350–369.

89. CGT-FSS, *Compte-rendu officiel des travaux au 34ᵉ congrès national corporatif. 14ᵉ de la Fédération nationale des travailleurs du soussol et parties similaires tenu à Saint-Etienne les 25, 26, 27, 28, 29 et 30 juin 1920* (Paris: Imprimerie nouvelle, 1920), p. 38.

90. In 1911 the Decazeville director wrote that "with our current fund [for metalworkers] we have some control over the worker; in case of a more or less suspect illness, we can have [the suspect worker] watched by our guards and if we learn that there is a feigned illness . . . we warn the worker, [then] we terminate payments." AN 110AQ54(1), DD to DG, 31 July 1911. Even after the mutual aid fund passed to workers' control, companies in the Basin sought to use their hospitals to similar effect. In 1900 the director of the mines of Aubin reported that all miners who were seriously injured on the job were brought to the company hospital and kept there: "Hospitalization of the injured presents a double advantage: the chance for the doctor to see the patient daily, and the impossibility for the latter to prolong—as is often done by design—the time required to heal the injury." AN 111AQ297, DA to director of mines of Nontron [St. Pardoux, Dordogne], 9 August 1900. For mutual aid funds at Carmaux, see Trempé, *Les Mineurs,* pp. 586–602. For the history of social welfare programs in France, see Henri Hatzfeld, *Du Pauperisme à la sécurité sociale* (Paris: Armand Colin, 1971).

91. AN 110AQ61, "Rapport annuel, Mines, 1911–12." For a similar development in the Valenciennes, see Hardy-Hémery, *De la Croissance,* p. 53.

92. AN 59AQ9, CA of SCF, 13 December 1894. ADA 11 M5 6, CSD to PA, 29 October 1894; 5 November 1894; 26 December 1894. *La Voix des travailleurs,* 9 May 1895, p. 3; 23 May 1895, p. 3. ADA 90S1, "Sentence arbitrale," 19 November 1895. ACGTD, AG (Firmy), 25 December 1895. ADA 52M8, CPD to PA, 10 August 1896.

93. ADA 11 M5 6, CSD to PA, 27 November 1895.

94. ACGTD, meeting of union and nonunion members, 25 February 1908 [quoted]. *La Dépêche,* 23 August 1906, p. 4 (VM).

95. Archives of the Société des Secours Minières at Decazeville, Aubin (SAF), 3 August 1895; 5 October 1895; 9 October 1895.

96. ADA 11 M5 6, CSD to PA, 11 November 1894.

97. AN 111AQ295, DA to chief engineer, 1 April 1895.

98. Archives of the Société des Secours Minières at Decazeville, Aubin (SAF), 14 March 1895.

99. ADA 11 M5 7, CSD to PA, 11 February 1895; 18 March 1895. The Socialist deputy Auguste Vaillant offered an apparent solution to the Aubin fund's dilemma. He suggested that Socialist leaders could place young leftist doctors in mining centers. These physicians would not only charge less than local doctors, but would be ideologically sympathetic to the workers' cause as well. Unfortunately, this experiment ended in fiasco at Aubin. See my "Labor, Management, and the State," p. 296.

100. AN F 7 12764, CSD to MI, 16 November 1907. ADA 90S1, Ministre du Travail to PA, 10 December 1910. ACGTD, AG (Aubin), 25 August 1912.

101. AN 110AQ56, "Rapport annuel, Mines, 1898–99."

102. See Bruno Mattei, "La Normalisation des accidents du travail: L'Invention du risque professionnel," Les Temps modernes, 31 (January 1976): 988–1003. The efforts of mining companies to settle accident compensation cases amicably had provided a model for legislators. See Paul Butor, Le Risque professionnel et les accidents du travail dans les sociétés houillères (Béthune: A. David, 1902), pp. 40–47.

103. ACGTD, AG (Combes), 16 January 1898; AG (Decazeville), 26 March 1911. ADA 11 M5 7, CSD to PA, 2 July 1901.

104. ACGTD, AG (Decazeville), 19 February 1907.

105. Ibid., 27 July 1900.

106. ADA 55M3, notes on Chambre syndicale des ouvriers mineurs (1912). ACGTD, CS (Decazeville), 6 August 1911.

107. See my "The Role of Mine Safety."

108. Chambre des députés, Procès-verbaux . . . Drou, IV, 337. Ministère des Travaux Publics, Notice sur le nombre, les salaires et la durée du travail des ouvriers des mines en 1890 (Paris: Imprimerie nationale, 1891).

109. ADA 11 M5 5, report of gendarmerie (Decazeville), 24 December 1887.

110. Chambre des députés, Rapport . . . Lacombe, p. 119. Chambre des députés, Procès-verbaux . . . Drou, IV, 324. Eric Hobsbawm cites the reduction in the coal extracted per man-day in France between 1887–1895 and 1909–1914 as an example of workers learning the "rules of the game" of remuneration for production; see his Labouring Men (New York: Basic Books, 1964), pp. 350–351. Miners in the Aubin Basin began by limiting their hours of work.

111. See my "L'Industrie métallurgique et les ouvriers métallurgistes."

112. ACGTD, AG (Combes), 26 April 1891.

113. ACGTD, réunion extraordinaire (Decazeville), 12 April 1908. See réunion extraordinaire (Combes), 28 March 1909.

114. The law specified a timetable for the gradual establishment of an eight-hour work day, not eight hours of presence at the workplace.

115. AN 110AQ51(1), DG to director of the forges (Decazeville) [copy of DA's policy].

116. ACGTD, AG (Decazeville), 17 February 1907.

117. However, spurred by the dramatic growth of the union, participation in May day activities at Aubin increased in the years before the war. See my "La Grève de 1913 à Aubin-Cransac."

118. ADA 52M6, SpVf to PA, 16 April 1913.

119. *La Voix des travailleurs*, 8 June 1890, pp. 1–2.

120. Peter Stearns draws attention to the importance of collective bargaining in the French coal industry in "Against the Strike Threat: Employer Policy toward Labor Agitation in France, 1900–1914," *Journal of Modern History*, 40 (1968): 493–494. See also Yves Lequin, *Les Ouvriers de la région lyonnaise (1848–1914)*, 2 vols. (Lyon: Presses universitaires de Lyon, 1977), II, 275.

121. See the report written by Mazars early in 1907 (ADA 55M2) in which he chronicles his disappointment with efforts in 1900 and 1902 to negotiate with Comambault.

122. ADA 84S1, Cahier de revendications des mineurs (Decazeville), 15 September 1902.

123. Chambre des députés, *Procès-verbaux . . . Drou*, I, 182–183. See the annual *Statistique de l'industrie minérale* for the lower wages paid in the Aubin Basin than in Nord, Pas-de-Calais, and elsewhere; for instance, *Statistique . . . 1898*, p. 10.

124. ACGTD, meeting of Comité de défense, 4 March 1900.

125. Archives of Waldeck-Rousseau XXXI 4.590(1), telegram, Waldeck-Rousseau to PA, 7 March 1900.

126. AN 59AQ12, CA of SCFD, 7 February 1900.

127. AN 110AQ51(1), CA of SCFD, 25 April 1906 [quoted]; DG to DD, 24 April 1906. This was an element in the more general approach of Comambault to the administration of labor. The company's head office wrote in 1908: "It is quite important that all legitimate grievances raised by workers receive satisfaction without waiting for them to make a demand, because there are always drawbacks in letting them make a demand and having to give in to it." AN 110AQ47(2), DG to M. Seigle, 8 July 1908.

128. ACGTD, Aubin union to DD, DA, and Director of Campagnac, 24 October 1910.

129. AN 111AQ246, "Délibération du Conseil municipal de la Commune d'Aubin," 25 September 1910.

130. ADA 11 M5 7ser, CSD to PA, 13 November 1910; 15 November 1910. Such arrangements were incorporated on the national level as well.

After passage of the miners' pension law in 1914, the sub-prefect commented: "We don't have to fear a strike for some time: the recent law on miners' pensions imposed a certain number of days of work per year. This will make all those who would have been lightly disposed to strike or not to work think twice." ADA 44 M1 6, SpVf to PA, 9 March 1914.

131. ACGTD, AG (Decazeville), 26 March 1911; AG extraordinaire (Decazeville), 14 May 1911.

132. AN 59AQ12, CA of SCFD, 13 December 1906; 14 November 1907.

133. See Joël Michel, "Syndicalisme minier et politique dans le Nord/Pas-de-Calais: le cas Basly (1880–1914)," *Mouvement social*, 87 (April-June 1974): 9–33.

134. See Jacques Julliard, "Jeune et vieux syndicat chez les mineurs du Pas-de-Calais (à travers les papiers de Pierre Monatte)," *Mouvement social*, 47 (April-June 1964): 7–30; and Rolande Trempé, "Le Réformisme des mineurs français à la fin du XIXᵉ siècle," *Mouvement social*, 65 (October-December 1968): 93–107.

135. AN F 7 13788, clippings from *L'Humanité*, 26 April 1911; 29 April 1911.

136. Jean René Tuffou, *Les Mineurs de Graissessac. Le Bousquet d'Orb au XIXᵉᵐᵉ siècle* (Béziers: Annales du Milieu Rural, 1981), pp. 53–54.

137. ADA 52M9, CPD to PA, 16 December 1901; 17 February 1902. ADA 11 M4 7, CSD to PA, 26 December 1901. AN BB 18 2201 and 2202, CPD to district attorney, 26 December 1901. ADA 52M8, CPD to PA, 10 March 1902.

138. Chambre des députés, *Procès-verbaux . . . Drou*, IV, 367. On the strike of 1902 at Decazeville, see my "L'Industrie métallurgique et les ouvriers métallurgistes."

139. In her excellent study of the national miners' federation, Diana Cooper-Richet attributes the split to regionalism and especially to local political traditions. In accounting for Decazeville's dissident stance, she points to a revolutionary political tradition dating back to 1886; "La Fédération nationale des mineurs. Contribution à l'histoire du syndicalisme français avant 1914" (Troisième cycle, Université de Paris I, 1976), pp. 196–201. However, Decazeville had no more of a radical tradition than nearby staunchly loyalist Carmaux. The key to using local tradition as an explanatory device in the case of Decazeville is to consider the effect that the regional political economy of the Aubin Basin had on the thinking of the leadership of the miners' union. This, not the abandonment of a radical tradition, explains why the same leadership of the Decazeville union could later espouse reformist positions.

140. Unity was short-lived. The reformist unions in the Nord/Pas-de-Calais seceded in 1912.

141. ACGTD, AG (Decazeville), 12 May 1912.

142. Ibid., 26 March 1911.

143. ADA 11 M5 7ser, CSD to PA, 22 October 1911.

144. AN 110AQ47(2), clipping from *La France*, 24 October 1911.

145. ADA 11 M5 7ser, CSD to PA, 7 March 1912.

146. ACGTD, AG (Aubin), 10 March 1912. But see also my "La Grève de 1913 à Aubin-Cransac."

147. *L'Eclaireur*, 7 March 1914, p. 2 (VM).

148. AN 110AQ49(3), GG to DD, 28 February 1914. See also Trempé, *Les Mineurs*, pp. 613–616.

149. AN 110AQ49(3), DD to DG, 25 February 1914.

150. AN 110AQ49(3), *La France* clipping, 5 March 1914.

151. *L'Eclaireur*, 6 September 1913, pp. 1–2. In making this argument, Mazars echoed the contemporary transformation of the syndicalist movement. In 1909, for instance, Eugène Guérard, the reformist national leader of the railway workers' union, defended himself against his revolutionary critics by charging that the violence of the *watrinade* and the strike which followed had permanently crippled labor organization at Decazeville. Elie Fruit, *Les Syndicats dans les chemins de fer en France (1890–1910)* (Paris: Editions sociales, 1976), p. 191.

152. *L'Eclaireur*, 17 August 1913, p. 2. For a more detailed discussion of the development of Mazars' thought in the years before the war, see my "La Grève de 1913 à Aubin-Cransac."

153. ACGTD, union statement on the 1889 election, 13 September 1889.

154. For Le Creusot, see René Parize, "La Stratégie patronale au Creusot pendant les grèves de 1899–1900," *Cahiers de l'Institut Maurice Thorez*, 24 (1978): 13–46. For Montceau-les-Mines, see A. Lanfrey, "Eglise et monde ouvrier. Les Congrégationistes et leurs écoles à Montceau-les-Mines sous le Second Empire et la IIIᵉ République (1875–1903)," *Cahiers d'histoire*, 22 (1978): 51–71; Roger Marchandeau, "La Bande à Patin (1888–1899): Histoire de la police privée de la Compagnie des Mines de Blanzy," *Revue périodique de 'La Physiophile'*, 95 (December 1981). 3–30.

155. AN 110AQ55, "Rapport annuel, Mines, 1894–95; 1895–96.

156. Couffin, "Aspects," p. 176. Guglielmo, "Formes et facteurs," 84. Appendix: A Social Portrait.

157. *L'Indépendent*, 26 September 1902, p. 3.

158. ADA 35 M5 2, SpVf, January 1914. ACGTD, AG (Decazeville), 7 February 1909. For consumer actions elsewhere in France, see Jean-Marie Flonneau, "Crise de vie chère et mouvement syndical, 1910–1914," *Mouvement social*, 72 (July-September 1970): 49–81.

159. AN 110AQ1(7), [1893].

160. AN 59AQ9, CA of SCF, 15 November 1894.

161. AN 110AQ1(7), DG to DD, 13 April 1892; 20 April 1892; 16 May

1892 (quoted). ADA 8M74, CSD to PA, 16 April 1892; 18 April 1892; 27 April 1892; 6 May 1892; CPD to PA, 16 April 1892; 29 April 1892. ADA 68S6, CSD to PA, 2 February 1892; 4 February 1892. ADA 5M15, CSD to PA, 25 March 1892; 16 May 1892.

162. On socialism in the Aubin Basin before the war, see Hubert-Rouger, *La France socialiste*, 4 vols. (Paris: Aristide Quillet, 1913), II, 143–150, useful despite numerous factual errors. Jean-Michel Gaillard has identified a similar *symbiose syndicalisme-socialisme* in the Gard. "La Pénétration du socialisme dans le bassin houiller du Gard," in *Droite et Gauche en Languedoc-Roussillon* (Montpellier: Centre d'histoire contemporaine du Languedoc méditerranéen et du Roussillon, 1975), pp. 271–287.

163. ADA 5M19, CSD to PA, 7 July 1893. *La Voix des travailleurs*, 27 July 1893, p. 3.

164. Ibid., 9 August 1893; 14 August 1893; 24 August 1893; 28 August 1893. AN 59AQ9, CA of SCF, 7 September 1893.

165. Approximately 80 percent of eligible voters participated in this and most elections in Decazeville before the war.

166. ADA 11M5 6, CPD to PA, 18 April 1887; 2 May 1887. ADA 55 M1, PA, 10 March 1888.

167. ADA 5M18, CSD to PA, 23 August 1889.

168. *La Voix des travailleurs*, 17 December 1893, p. 1 (VM).

169. On *allemanisme* see Bernard Moss, *The Origins of the French Labor Movement: The Socialism of Skilled Workers* (Berkeley: University of California Press, 1976), pp. 130–135. Although the *allemanistes'* primary appeal was to Parisian artisans, Trempé and Gilbert Laval have noted the influence of *allemanisme* in Carmaux during the 1890s as well. Trempé, *Les Mineurs*, p. 899. Gilbert Laval, "Carmaux-1892: Les Ressorts du militantisme de classe," *Revue du Tarn*, 105 (Spring 1982): 41. In *France 1848–1945*, 2 vols. (Oxford: Clarendon Press, 1973), I, 259, n. 1, Theodore Zeldin observes that Allemane's "proselytizing work" in the provinces deserves more study.

Maurice Dommanget suggests in *La Chevalrie du travail française 1893–1911* (Lausanne: Editions Rencontre, 1967), pp. 363–365, that the Chevalrie du Travail, a secret Masonic organization of socialist and union militants, introduced the POSR to Decazeville, but the details are sketchy.

170. ACGTD, AG (Combes), 16 January 1898.

171. ACGTD, AG (Decazeville), 29 November 1896; 20 December 1896 (quoted).

172. *La Dépêche*, 16 April 1898, p. 3.

173. DCMD, 9 June 1901. Joan Scott describes contemporary socialist municipalities like Carmaux as "enclaves of resistance" which perpetuated "a sense of working-class non-acceptance of, if not active opposition to, bourgeois republican France." "Mayors versus Police Chiefs: Socialist Mu-

nicipalities Confront the French State" in *French Cities in the Nineteenth Century*, ed. John Merriman (New York: Holmes & Meier Publishers, 1981), p. 235. Decazeville Socialists were stymied in their effort to create such an enclave.

174. ACGTD, CS (Decazeville), 31 March 1901.

175. AN F 7 12497, Commissaire spécial de Villefranche-de-Rouergue to MI, 27 December 1903; CSD to PA, 21 December 1903; 28 September 1904; 5 December 1904; 20 December 1904; 16 January 1905.

176. ADA 52M8, CPD to PA, 17 March 1902. ACGTD, CS (Decazeville), 9 November 1902. IISG, Fonds Jules Guesde 332/45, Pierre Taillefer to Guesde, 29 March 1902.

177. See my "L'Industrie métallurgique et les ouvriers métallurgistes."

178. IISG, Fonds Jules Guesde 301/3, Duc-Quercy to Guesde, 8 May 1906.

179. Ibid. See also *Le Socialiste de l'Aveyron*, 3 December 1905, p. 3 (VM); 14 January 1906, p. 3 (VM); 21 January 1906 (VM); 28 January 1906, p. 3; 15 April 1906, p. 3. AN F 7 12544, CSD to MI, 21 August 1905; 13 October 1905; 23 October 1905; 3 November 1905; 11 November 1905; 13 November 1905; 29 November 1905; 21 December 1905; 3 February 1906; 14 March 1906; 15 March 1906; 3 April 1906; 19 June 1906. ADA 5M16, anonymous undated report on Pierre Myrens. AN F 7 12764, CSD to MI, 29 April 1906; PA to MI, 2 May 1906.

180. IISG, Fonds Jules Guesde 301/3, Duc-Quercy to Guesde, 8 May 1906.

181. See my "L'Industrie métallurgique et les ouvriers métallurgistes."

182. ADA 55M3, notes on Chambre syndicale des ouvriers mineurs de l'Aveyron [1912]. ACGTD, Dentraygues to Ramadier, 1 August 1911; AG of metalworkers' union, 26 August 1911. APR, Panissal to Ramadier, 14 February 1914.

183. *La Voix des travailleurs*, 7 December 1893, p. 3 (VM) (quoted). ADA 11 M5 6, CSD to PA, 4 December 1893; 5 December 1893.

184. ADA 11 M5 7ser, CSD to PA, 27 November 1911; 1 December 1911.

185. *La Voix des travailleurs*, 12 April 1891, p. 2 (Lacombe); 21 June 1891, p. 2 (Lacombe); 24 July 1892, p. 3 (quoted). This article was published at the height of the underground miners' opposition to company efforts to employ rural immigrants as helpers.

186. *L'Eclaireur*, 30 July 1921, p. 1. For Jaurès' view of Occitan culture, see André Armengaud, "Jean Jaurès et le fait régional," in *96ᵉ Congrès national des sociétés savantes, Toulouse, 1971 Histoire moderne* (Paris: Bibliothèque nationale, 1976) I, 249–254.

For a similar assessment of the position of Occitan culture among the miners of Carmaux, see Rolande Trempé, "Problèmes culturels autour des mineurs de Carmaux," *Revue du Tarn*, 96 (Winter 1979): 591; and among the workers in Hérault before the war, Jean Sagnes, *Le Mouvement ouvrier en Languedoc* (Toulouse: Privat, 1980), p. 34.

## 7. The Politics of Production

1. See Richard Kuisel's excellent *Capitalism and the State in Modern France* (New York: Cambridge University Press, 1981).

2. For a detailed study of labor and industry at Decazeville during and after the war, see my "Guillaume Verdier et le syndicalisme révolutionnaire aux usines de Decazeville (1917–1920)," *Annales du Midi*, 96 (1984): 171–198. On the state's policy toward the coal industry during the war, see M. Oliver, *La Politique du charbon 1914–1921* (Paris: Félix Alcan, 1922).

3. Wartime inflation, fueled by the state's financial and wage policies, increased the discrepancy in the production and sale prices between the better-endowed coalfields (Pas-de-Calais, Blanzy, Carmaux, and Albi) and their less fortunate *confrères* (Aubin, Loire and Gard). Comambault estimated in 1920 that if all restrictions were removed immediately from the French coal market, it would no longer be profitable to operate a number of France's mines. Fayol Archives, "Rapport annuel, Mines, 1919–20."

4. AN 110AQ1(5), "Enquête de la Commission des Mines du Sénat," January 1935. For specific examples of the effect of unfavorable postwar rail rates on Decazeville's sales, see APR, Comambault, "Note sur la situation des Mines et Usines de Decazeville au point de vue des transports," February 1931.

5. AN 110AQ67, "Rapport annuel, Mines, 1926–27."

6. AN 110AQ1(5), "Enquête de la Commission des Mines du Sénat," January 1935.

7. AN 111AQ313, DA to state engineer, 6 September 1922.

8. AN 110AQ97, "Rapport annuel, Forges, 1918–19." AN 110AQ99, "Rapport annuel, Forges, 1925–26." AN 110AQ100, "Rapport annuel, Forges, 1931–32." But see AN 110AQ249, Conférence D, 1 July 1925, for an attack on miners who devoted too much time to agricultural pursuits while employed at the mines.

9. Jacques Tomasi, "Le Migrant dans l'entreprise. De la Journée de travail à l'essai à la 'carrière' dans une entreprise: le migrant étranger à Decazeville 1920–1930," *Recherches régionales*, 23 (January-March 1982): 109–110.

10. ADA 54M 3bis, CSD to PA, 10 February 1921. *La Voix des travailleurs*, 26 March 1932, p. 4. The match was not perfect, however. Workers at Decazeville from farming backgrounds had worked on small family farms and then gone to Decazeville to work in industry. The large proprietors who increasingly dominated the area around Rodez and the mountainous areas north of the Aubin Basin (and who were most likely to hire agricultural

labor) doubted that unemployed workers from Decazeville could adjust to the new forms of large-scale agriculture. *Le Progrès de l'Aveyron,* 17 January 1932, p. 4.

11. There is a growing literature on immigrant miners during the interwar period. See the excellent study by Gary S. Cross, *Immigrant Workers in Industrial France: The Making of a New Laboring Class* (Philadelphia: Temple University Press, 1983); Francis Bousquet, "Les Etrangers à Aubin et Cransac en 1931" (Mémoire, Université de Toulouse-le-Mirail, 1973); Odette Hardy-Hémery, *De la Croissance à la désindustrialisation. Un Siècle dans le Valenciennes* (Paris: Presses de la Fondation nationale des sciences politiques, 1984), pp. 221–243; and my "The Limits of Paternalism: Immigrant Coal Miners' Communities in France, 1919–1945," *European History Quarterly,* 15 (1985): 98–119.

12. AN 110AQ41(3) contains a fascinating dossier on German prisoners of war employed at Decazeville.

13. For Aubin, see AN 111AQ315–317.

14. AN 110AQ11(3), "Programme d'économies à réaliser à Combes Banel" by chief engineer, 11 April 1925.

15. See Rolande Trempé, "La Main d'oeuvre étrangère aux mines de Carmaux entre les deux guerres," *Revue du Tarn,* 64 (December 1971): 453–460, for statistics on the instability of immigrant labor in the mines of Carmaux.

16. For the situation in the Aubin Basin, see my "The Limits of Paternalism," 104–105.

17. AN 110AQ188, DD to chief engineer, 11 November 1935 and "Projet de lettre" which follows.

18. Fayol Archives, SCFD, "Rapport annuel, 1919–20." This change was made somewhat earlier in the north. André Lebon, *Martin du Tiss. Mineur en 1900* (Paris: Jean-Pierre Delarge, 1979), p. 34.

19. AN 110AQ11(1), company chief engineer to DD, 12 December 1923. AN 110AQ3(1), DD to state mine engineer, 31 December 1920. AN 110AQ156, DD to DG, 15 April 1925. AN 110AQ44(5), DD to state chief mine engineer, 8 September 1928. AN 111AQ313, DA to state mine engineer, 6 September 1922. *La Voix des travailleurs,* 2 September 1935.

See also AN 110AQ45(1), "Organisation du travail dans la Loire" (1 April 1920), for the greater specialization of miners in the Loire Basin than at Decazeville; and Odette Hardy-Hémery's excellent studies of the more advanced forms of rationalization implemented at Anzin: "Rationalisation, technique et rationalisation du travail à la Compagnie des Mines d'Anzin (1927–38)," *Mouvement social,* 72 (July-September 1970): 3–48; and *De la Croissance,* pp. 178–211.

20. AN 110AQ10(1), chief engineer to DD, 28 May 1915.

21. APR, "Réalisations de la Compagnie de Châtillon-Commentry et Neuves-Maison aux Houillères d'Aubin depuis 1930" by director Jean, 18

November 1944. In the early 1930s new owners at Aubin were able to expand long-wall mining as a means to improve productivity and to reduce fire hazards.

22. AN 110AQ176, "Note pour le Conseil d'administration," 14 December 1943.

23. AN 110AQ48(1), DD to DG, 2 July 1921.

24. See my "The Limits of Paternalism," 103.

25. AN 110AQ197, DD to Mines d'Albi, 4 January 1930.

26. APR, "Réalisations de la Compagnie de Châtillon-Commentry et Neuves-Maison, 18 November 1944.

27. AN 110AQ67, "Rapport annuel, Mines, 1926–27."

28. AN 110AQ3(1), company chief engineer to DD, 3 September 1928. AN 110AQ69, "Rapport annuel, Mines," 1929–30; 1931–32; 1932–33; 1933–34. See Alain Baudant's study of a similar accident prevention program at Pont-à-Mousson: "La Protection ouvrière à Pont-à-Mousson," in *Actes du 103ᵉ Congrès national des sociétés savantes, Nancy, 11 et 12 Avril 1978* (Paris: Association pour l'étude de l'histoire de la Sécurité Sociale, 1978), pp. 29–42.

29. AN 110AQ176, "Note pour le Conseil d'administration," 14 December 1943.

30. AN 110AQ11(1), Compte-rendu du réunion du Comité régional Aveyron-Tarn, 2 December 1937. For the similar situation in the Nord and Pas-de-Calais, see my "The Lamb and the Tiger: Paternalist Discourse and Practice in Nineteenth-Century French Mining and Metallurgical Firms" (forthcoming in *Comparative Studies in Society and History*).

31. AN 110AQ11(1), DD to DG, 7 April 1938. The introduction of timing in the thirties reduced the initiative and authority of underground mining engineers throughout France. Diana Cooper-Richet, "Les Ingénieurs des houillères et des mines et leurs syndicats du Front populaire à nos jours," in *Clefs pour une histoire du syndicalisme cadre*, ed. Marc Descostes and Jean-Louis Robert (Paris: Editions ouvrières, 1984), p. 192. Hardy-Hémery, *De la Croissance*, p. 193.

32. AN 111AQ314, DA state chief engineer, 12 November 1924.

33. AN 110AQ69, "Rapport annuel, Mines," 1932–33; 1933–34. AN 110AQ70, "Rapport annuel, Mines," 1935–36. Pierre Vernet, "Une Mine à ciel ouvert," *Bibliothèque de travail*, 506 (November 1961): 9–10.

34. AN 110AQ44(4), DD to DG, 6 December 1918. AN 110AQ45(1), records of the Commissions mixtes. For a good study of the miners of the Gard during the war see Raymond Huard, "Les Mineurs du Gard pendant la guerre de 1914–1918. Guerre, syndicalisme, mentalités," in *Economie et société en Languedoc-Roussillon de 1789 à nos jours* (Montpellier: Fédération historique du Languedoc méditerranéen et du Roussillon, 1978), pp. 275–294. See also Max Gallo's comments on labor in Decazeville's mines in "Quelques aspects de la mentalité et du comportement ouvriers dans les

usines de guerre: 1914–1918," *Mouvement social*, 56 (July-September 1966): 3–33.

35. See my "Guillaume Verdier et le syndicalisme révolutionnaire."

36. The most important study of the split in the French labor movement after World War I remains Annie Kriegel, *Aux origines du communisme français*, 2 vols. (Paris: Mouton, 1964). For events in the Aubin Basin, see AN F 7 12974, CSD to MI, 8 February 1920; 21 August 1920; 1 November 1920; Roujou and Delvot of the Decazeville Communist party to Gervais (1922).

37. *Le Progrès de l'Aveyron*, 3 December 1933, p. 1; 29 July 1934, p. 1 (PR); 5 August 1934, p. 1 (PR). ADA 23 M5 1, CSD to PA, 17 November 1933. APR, PR to SpVf, 6 April 1925; Socialist electoral poster (1929); Neo-Socialist electoral poster (1935); PR to Albert Rives, 16 April 1935. For general expositions of Ramadier's ideas, see his *Le Socialisme de Léon Blum* (Paris: Librairie des Municipalités, 1951); *Socialisme, humanisme et action* (Paris: Librairie des Municipalités, 1961); and "Les grèves de 1936," *Cahiers Paul Ramadier*, 1 (1967): 7 48.

38. AN 110AQ50(1), clipping from *La Dépêche*, 10 March 1931. AN 110AQ159, DD to DG, 16 May 1933.

39. On the weakness of the Communists in Decazeville until the mid-thirties, see AN F 7 12736, CSD to MI, 2 March 1925; 1 April 1925; 2 May 1925. Rolande Trempé, "Aspects du communisme dans la région toulousaine de 1921 à 1932," in *Actes du 95ᵉ congrès national des sociétés savantes. Toulouse 1971. Section d'histoire moderne et contemporaine* (Paris: Bibliothèque nationale, 1972), II, 372. H. Assier, R. Bouer and A. Buchholz, "L'Implantation du socialisme et du communisme dans l'Aveyron de 1870 à 1958" (Mémoire, Université de Toulouse-le-Mirail, 1973).

Communists were much stronger in Aubin than in Decazeville. Four factors account for this: Ramadier's personal popularity in Decazeville; the Communist Edmund Ginestet's popularity in Aubin; the greater concentration of miners in Aubin, and the historical political animosity of the two towns, dating back to their nineteenth-century heritage as company towns.

40. ACGTD, CS (Aubin/Cransac), 6 February 1927; 10 March 1927; 15 June 1930; AG, 5 January 1930; 3 August 1930; 15 October 1933.

41. See CGT-FSS, *Compte rendu officiel des travaux du 34ᵉ congrès national corporatif. 14ᵉ de la Fédération nationale des travailleurs du sous-sol et parties similaires tenu à Saint-Etienne les 25, 26, 27, 28, 29, 30 juin 1920* (Paris: Imprimerie Nouvelle, 1920), pp. 47–90.

42. ADA 52M17, PA to MT, 10 September 1925. See also AN 110AQ45(1), DD to DG, 15 November 1926. ACGTD, PO to Vigne, 21 September 1928.

43. ACGTD, PO to Vigne, 9 February 1925. See also ACGTD, PO to Bureau Fédéral (CGT-FSS), 16 December 1924; AG (Decazeville), 23 August 1925; PO to Vigne, 12 August 1925; 31 March 1931.

44. ACGTD, PO to Vigne, 9 September 1925. On the phenomenon of

union locals in France "threatening" the national federation or confederation, see my "Guillaume Verdier et le syndicalisme révolutionnaire."

45. ACGTD, PA to Vigne, 31 January 1926; 4 February 1926.

46. ACGTD, PO to VM, 13 January 1923; AG (Decazeville), 10 July 1927. AN 110AQ48(1), GG to DD, 19 August 1927.

47. See the discussion of *unitaires'* relations with immigrant miners at Decazeville in my "The Limits of Paternalism," 106–108.

48. Georges Dumoulin, postwar *confédéré* leader, expressed the belief that workers always obtained more if they could negotiate without striking; *Carnets de route (Quarante années de vie militante)* (Lille: Editions de 'L'Avenir,' 1938), p. 259.

49. ADA 52M14, CSD to PA, 6 April 1933.

50. Ibid., 12 November 1923. The *unitaires* of the Aubin Basin were more loyal to the national strategy than was their national federation. The local *unitaires* strongly opposed their national federation's decision to call a regional strike limited to the southern coal basins of the Loire, the Gard, and the Aveyron in December 1928–January 1929. ACGTD, CS (Decazeville *unitaires*), 1 January 1929. AN 110AQ49(1(2)), CGTU, *Bulletin d'information réservé au rapport d'activité présenté au Congrès national ordinaire (Vᵉ Congres de la CGTU) Paris, 15–21 septembre 1929*, 2 (July 1929): 26–27. For a contemporary account of these strikes, see M. Cheminais, "Les grèves des mines de la Loire, du Gard, et de l'Aveyron," *Le Musée social*, 36 (June 1929): 241–267.

51. AN F 7 13903, Inspecteur principal de Decazeville, 15 November 1923.

52. See, for example, *La Voix des travailleurs*, 8 February 1930, p. 3.

53. ACGTD, CS (Decazeville *unitaires*), 7 August 1927 (quoted); AG (Decazeville *unitaires*), 20 April 1924.

54. ADA 52M16, CSD to PA, 9 February 1931; 15 February 1931; 18 July 1931; 1 August 1931; 28 September 1931; 5 October 1931; 9 November 1931.

55. ACGTD, AG (Decazeville), 13 October 1935.

56. Miners in the Gard did not strike either and benefited from accords that resulted from strikes elsewhere. Marianne Caron-Leuilliez suggests that in the Gard this was the result of union discipline and the strength of the Communist party; "Le Mouvement de grèves de juin et juillet 1936 dans le Bas Languedoc méditerranéen," in *Droite et Gauche en Languedoc-Roussillon* (Montpellier: Centre d'histoire contemporaine du Languedoc méditerranéen et du Roussillon, 1975), pp. 289–308.

57. AN 110AQ101, "Rapport annuel, Usines, 1936–37." ADA 11M5 12, Commissaire spécial d'Albi to MI, 16 December 1936. Similar developments took place in other mines.

There was no talk of coordinating unionization of workers and supervisors in the Aubin Basin. Oustry "could not imagine that . . . [supervisors], who had only scorn and disdain for workers, could find a place in our workers' organization." ACGTD, PO to Robert Tixier of St. Eloy les Mines, 27 October 1936.

58. Other factors like the introduction of the forty-hour week and paid vacations accounted for part of the reduction in productivity. ADA 51 M6 5, state chief engineer, "Baisse de production des Houillères d'Aubin," 2 September 1937. AN 110AQ1(6), Report of the Inspecteur général, Tarn-Aveyron coal production, 15 January 1938. ADA 66S2, report of state engineer, 11 May 1936. APR, "Réalisations de la Compagnie de Châtillon-Commentry et Neuves-Maisons . . . ," 18 November 1944.

59. AN 110AQ11(3), DG to DD, 16 November 1937; 18 November 1937; Syndicat des Ingénieurs . . . des Houillères du Sud-Ouest . . . , 3 December 1937, Compte-rendu du Comité Régional Aveyron-Tarn, 2 December 1937; DA to DG-SCFD, 11 December 1937. AN 110AQ179, DD to DG, 3 March 1938.

60. ADA 51 M6 5, state chief engineer, "Baisse de production des Houillères d'Aubin," 2 September 1937.

61. AN 110AQ11(1), DD to DG, 13 May 1938. ADA 51 M6 5, state chief engineer to Directeur des Mines (MTP), 12 May 1938. Albert Tournier, secretary of the Decazeville CGT miners' union, to PA, 16 May 1938. Ruling of the Commission de conciliation, 18 May 1938.

62. AN110AQ170, "Rapport annuel, Mines, 1938–39."

63. For an account of the Third Republic's round-up of Communists in the Aubin Basin, see A. Boutet, "Non, la vérité est toute autre," *Résistance en Rouergue,* 22 (May 1975): 17; 23 (September 1975): 5. ADA 13 M1 23, Inspecteur principal de police spéciale (Decazeville) to Commissaire spécial de Rodez, 29 November 1939; 30 December 1939. ADA 13 M1 24, CPD to SpVf, 28 November 1939. ADA 13 M1 25, Commissaire spécial de Rodez to PA, 20 December 1939; Inspecteur principal to Commissaire spécial de Rodez, 7 March 1940; 6 June 1940.

On Vichy labor policy, see Monique Luirard, "Les Ouvriers de la Loire et la Charte du travail," *Revue d'histoire de la deuxième guerre mondiale,* 102 (April 1976): 57–82.

64. See Roger Bourderon, "Mouvement de la main d'oeuvre et S.T.O. dans les mines du Gard pendant la guerre," *Revue d'histoire de la deuxième guerre mondiale,* 112 (October 1978): 47–66.

65. *La Dépêche,* 7 May 1943, p. 2; 29 February 1944, p. 2. AN 110AQ173, DD to DG, 1 April 1940. AN 110AQ149, DG to DD, 4 April 1940. AN 110AQ175, DD to DG, 21 January 1943; 24 March 1943; 21 July 1943; 7 October 1943. AN 110AQ195, DD to miners' union, 1 February 1941; 5 April 1941. AN 110AQ203, DD to Délégué régional aux questions ouvrières et sociales, 6 March 1943. AN 110AQ210, DD to Comité d'Organisation de l'Industrie des Combustibles Minéraux Solides, 30 July 1942; 4 November 1942. AN 110AQ238, DD to head mine engineer and head machine-shop

engineer, 19 May 1942. AN 110AQ258, Conférence D, 14 August 1940; 9 September 1940. ADA 13 M1 23, Inspecteur des Renseignements généraux (Rodez), 6 July 1943.

After securing the union's acceptance into the mines of the bourgeois "sons of archbishops" who were evading the STO, Comambault shocked the union by taking advantage of these youths' education to have them time tasks. Archives of the CCHF (formerly catalogued as 44(II) in the Archives of the Charbonnages de France), DA and DD to PA, 10 May 1943; and especially DD to DG, 21 June 1943.

66. *La Dépêche,* 4 May 1942. For an extended exposition of this idea, see the 1941 New Year's message of the general direction of Comambault; AN 110AQ258, Conférence D, 8 January 1941. On the position of engineers after the Popular Front, see Luc Boltanski, *Les Cadres* (Paris: Editions du minuit, 1982), pp. 63–153; and Ingo Kolboom, "Patronat et cadres: la contribution patronale à la formation du groupe des cadres (1936–1938)," *Mouvement social,* 121 (October-December 1982): 71–95.

67. AN 110AQ176, "Note pour le Conseil d'administration," 14 December 1943.

68. AN 110AQ174, DD to DG, 4 August 1942; 27 October 1942.

69. AN 110AQ176, "Note pour le Conseil d'administration," 14 December 1943. On such injuries, see Xavier Charpin's account of the Loire mines during the war: *L'Adieu différé. Mineur à La Chana en 41, une gueule noire raconte . . .* (Saint-Etienne: La Hénaff Editeur, 1981).

70. Alan S. Milward's conclusion that Germany was unable to exploit the French economy fully because it could not get labor to work more productively is borne out in the mines of the Aubin Basin and elsewhere; *The New Order and the French Economy* (Oxford: Clarendon Press, 1970), pp. 181–209.

71. For the situation in the Aubin Basin, see ACGTD, CS (Decazeville) for the duration of the Occupation.

72. Interview with M. and Mme. André Cayrol, July 1977.

73. ACGTD, CS extraordinaire (Decazeville), 8 October 1939; CS (Decazeville), 28 January 1940; 17 March 1940. The non-Communist union officials tried unsuccessfully to allow former Communist union delegates to maintain their offices. ADA 68S1, state engineer to PA, 15 August 1940.

74. Gérard Bouladou, *Les Maquis du Massif Central méridional* (Lille: Université de Lille III, 1975), p. 101. Interview with M. and Mme. Marceau Coursières, July 1977. ADA 13 M1 23, Inspecteur principal de Decazeville to Commissaire spécial of Rodez, 3 December 1940. ADA 13 M1 24, Commissaire principal des Renseignements généraux (Rodez), 2 April 1942; 15 July 1942. AN F 1C III 1201, Préfecture régionale de Montpellier, 7 January 1943; 5 February 1943; 9 October 1943; 6 November 1943. AF, Marceau Coursières, "Les Communistes en Aveyron de 1940 à 1945."

75. ACHDGM, "Groupe Franc Aubin-Cransac avec Maquis Bayard par

Capitaine Albanhac . . . de l'A.S. du Bassin Houiller . . ."; "Historique de l'A.S. départementale. Extrait du rapport adressé à M. le Lt. Colonel Journel . . . par M. Léon Freychet, chef de l'A.S. départementale" (March 1944); "Rapport du Lt. Colonel Journet en date du 18 Février 1947"; Roger Pages, "Historique du Groupe Franc de Firmy." Paul Gayraud, *La Guerre du brassard: Maquis du Rouergue* (Paris: Editions Jeanne Santier, 1946), pp. 59–69. For the fullest account of the military actions of the Resistance in the area, see Bouladou, *Maquis.*

76. AF, "Actes des maquis dans l'arrondissement de Villefranche-de-Rouergue." More detailed accounts of the sabotage can be found in the Comambault archives.

77. See my "The Limits of Paternalism," 110–111.

78. See AN F 1C III 1141, PA, 3 July 1942. ACHDGM, Goy dit Valzergues, "L'Organisation et l'action militaire de la Résistance dans le Bassin houiller de Decazeville-Aubin," 30 November 1944.

Mine managers in the Basin who employed STO evaders were at some risk of reprisals from Occupation authorities; SLDO (Hérault), 30 March 1944. (I would like to thank Roger Austin for passing a copy of this document on to me.) See also AN 110AQ150, DG to DD, 8 May 1943; 17 November 1943. AN 110AQ175, DD to DG, 10 June 1943; 18 June 1943; 26 June 1943. AN 110AQ238, "Compte rendu de la visite de la Commission mixte franco-allemande de désignation des ouvriers pour la relève, 11 février 1943." Archives of the CCHF (formerly catalogued as 44(II) in the Archives of the Charbonnages de France), DA and DD to PA, 10 May 1943; DA to state chief engineer, 30 September 1943; Comite d'Organisation de l'Industrie des Combustibles Minéraux Solides to Inspecteur général des mines (Paris), 6 October 1943. Archives of the Service des Mines (Rodez), state engineer, 15 March 1944.

79. Etienne Dejonghe and Daniel Laurent make this point in *Libération du Nord et du Pas-de-Calais* (Paris: Hachette Littérature, 1974), pp. 234–235.

80. ACGTD, CS (Decazeville), 25 June 1944. AF, CGT de Decazeville, "Les Représentants des travailleurs du bassin houiller aux camarades responsables des maquis," 2 July 1944; Délibérations du Comité de la Libération Nationale du Bassin Houiller, July-October 1944. AN F 1C III 1141, secrétaire général du PA, 10 July 1944. *La Voix du peuple,* 5 July 1944, p. 4. The best accounts of the period are Georges Sentis, "Les Communistes des bassins houillers de l'Aveyron et du Tarn à la Libération" (Troisième cycle, Université de Lille III, 1980) and his "Les Communistes du Tarn et de l'Aveyron à la Libération," *Cahiers d'histoire de l'Institut de recherches marxistes,* 5 (1981): 95–120.

81. AF, Marceau Coursières, "Réflexions et histoire locale," *Résistance en Rouergue,* 20 (October 1974): 5. ADA 11 M5 14, Renseignements généraux de Rodez, 14 July 1944.

82. ACGTD, AG (Decazeville), 8 October 1944. ACHDGM, "Rapport de Michel Calliau (Délégué militaire départemental de l'Aveyron), 23 août-24 september 1944." *La Voix du peuple,* 21–28 January 1945, p. 1. AF, Marceau Coursières, "Rapport sur la création du CDL de l'Aveyron" (September 1944).

83. ACHDGM, "Rapport de Michel Calliau . . ." Charles-Louis Foulon, *Le Pouvoir en province à la Libération* (Paris: Fondation nationale des sciences politiques/Armand Colin, 1975), p. 169.

84. ACGTD, AG (Decazeville), 31 December 1945. Early in 1947 the Decazeville CFTC complained of the difficulty of attracting members because the CGT controlled the distribution of food. Archives of the CFTC at Rodez, Conseil départemental, 9 February 1947.

85. ACGTD, CS (Decazeville), 27 May 1945.

86. *La Voix du peuple,* 26 April 1947, p. 3.

87. See especially "Etude sur le problème social des mines dans le Nord et le Pas-de-Calais" (May 1945), in Francis-Louis Closon, *Commissaire de la République du Général de Gaulle. Lille, septembre 1944-mars 1946* (Paris: Julliard, 1980), pp. 191–222; and Dejonghe and Laurent, *Libération du Nord,* pp. 231–246.

88. In the Aubin Basin nationalization also allowed for a more efficient exploitation of coal deposits, which had been divided up by the concessions granted to private firms during the nineteenth century. In the words of one engineer, "the administrative history of the [Aubin] Basin is very complex. A large number of firms followed one after the other; the concessions were modified on many occasions. The result was an extraordinary division of the basin into small concessions, with fanciful, overlapping boundaries . . . This situation prevented rational exploitation of the deposit under a single direction." T. Loisy, "Les Bassins houillers du Sud-Ouest," in *La Vie économique d'une région française* (Toulouse: Imprimerie Fournié, 1947), p. 126.

89. FSS, *Congrès national. Montceau-les-Mines des 12–13–14–15–16 février 1946* (Paris: CGT, 1946), p. 13.

90. Houillères du Bassin d'Aquitaine, *Modernisation. Equipement 1946–1952* (Toulouse: Imprimerie Fournié, 1952). J. F. Gravier, *Etudes régionales d'emploi. Auvergne-Aquitaine* (Luxemburg: CECA, 1957), p. 62.

91. ACGTD, CS (Decazeville), 29 June 1947.

92. See Parti communiste français, Région de l'Aveyron, V<sup>e</sup> *Conférence régionale 15 et 17 juin 1945* (Rodez: Imprimerie Carrère, 1945). For an excellent analysis of the position of the Communists in the nationalized mines, see Darryl Holter, "Mineworkers and Nationalization in France: Insights into Concepts of State Theory," *Politics and Society,* 11 (1982): 29–49.

93. ABHAD, Houillères du Bassin d'Aquitaine, "Rapport de gestion. Exercise 1947," p. 33. Holter cites data to show that after the war, "[miners']

activity far outstripped that of the metals trade, textiles, mechanical and electric industries and virtually every other industry in France." "State Intervention and the Nationalization of Coal Mining in France" (paper presented at the Social Science History Association Meeting, October 1983).

94. AN 110AQ259, Conférence D, 6 September 1944. ACGTD, CS (Decazeville), 17 September 1944.

95. See Marc Lazar, "Ouvrier, histoire et littérature de parti: L'exemple du mineur," *Revue des sciences humaines,* 190 (April-June 1983): 101–111. Thorez's inexact description of himself as a miner, and the son and grandson of a miner, fit into this cult of the miner. See Philippe Robrieux, *Maurice Thorez: vie secrète et vie politique* (Paris: Fayard, 1975), pp. 7–18. For a corrective to the Party's view of the miner, see François Ewald, "La Condition du mineur" in André Théret, *Parole d'ouvrier* (Paris: Grasset, 1978), pp. 7–60.

96. *La Voix du peuple,* 21–28 January 1945, p. 1.

97. Ibid., 17 March 1945, p. 1.

98. Ibid., 6 October 1945, p. 2. For union discussions of miners' resistance to the cult of productivity, see ACGTD, CS (Decazeville), 21 January 1945; 28 January 1945; 4 February 1945.

99. ACGTD, AG (Decazeville), 28 January 1945.

100. ACGTD, AG of Syndicat des Agents de Maîtrise et Employés des Mines de Decazeville, 21 July 1945; CS of Syndicat des Agents . . . , 15 September 1945.

101. See the comments of Louis Charly, who represented Decazeville's union of supervisory personnel and employees at the FSS congress in 1946. FSS, *Congrès national . . . 1946,* p. 94.

102. *La Voix du peuple,* 17 March 1945, p. 1.

103. Ibid., 28 June 1947, p. 3.

104. Annie Lacroix, "CGT et 'Bataille de la Production' de septembre 1944 au printemps 1946," *Cahiers d'histoire de l'Institut de recherches marxistes,* 10 (1982): 77–78.

105. Holter, "Mineworkers and Nationalization," 42–46.

106. ACGTD, CS (Decazeville), 23 March 1947; 27 August 1948.

107. ADA 89S5, Albert Tournier to PA, 7 July 1947.

108. *La Dépêche,* 27 November 1947, p. 2.

109. Ibid., 28 November 1947, p. 2.

110. Dejonghe and Laurent, *Libération du Nord,* pp. 245–46.

111. Archives of the CFTC at Rodez, Conseil départemental, 21 November 1948. ACGTD, CS (Decazeville), 8 October 1948; 16 November 1948; Bureau de l'Union départemental (Aveyron), 18 November 1948; FO broadsides (1948). *La Dépêche,* 20 October 1948, pp. 2–3; 16 November 1948, p. 2. *Le Rouergue républicain,* 28 October 1948, p. 1. Roland Passevant, *Les Communistes au quotidien* (Paris: Bernard Grasset, 1980), p. 170. Fran-

cis Cabrol, "Mines et mineurs de Decazeville 1945–1962: Histoire d'une fin" (Mémoire, Université de Toulouse-le-Mirail, 1974), pp. 34–37.

112. *La Voix du peuple,* 30 October 1948, p. 2.

113. Cabrol, "Mines et mineurs," p. 34.

114. *Le Rouergue républicain,* 7–8 November 1948, p. 2. See ACGTD, "A Tous les Mineurs" [1948].

115. ACGTD, Bureau de l'Union départemental, 18 November 1948.

116. Claude Dubar, Gérard Gayot, and Jacques Hedoux, "Sociabilité minière et changement social à Sallaumines et à Noyelles-sous-Lens (1900–1980)," *Revue du nord,* 64 (April-June 1982): 460–461. For Carmaux, see Gilbert Laval, "1944–1945–1946–1947. La Bataille du charbon à Carmaux et la nationalisation des Houillères: le sentiment d'être vaincu," *Revue du Tarn,* 99 (Autumn 1980): 392–402.

117. Serge Moscovici, "Les Mineurs jugent la nationalisation," *Sociologie du travail,* 2 (1960): 224.

118. Ibid., 222.

119. ACGTD, CS (Decazeville), 28 March 1949; 13 November 1950.

120. Roger Cornu and Bernard Picon, *Analyse contextuelle de la mobilité. II-Mineurs cévénols et provençaux face à la crise des charbonnages* (Aix-en-Provence: Laboratoire d' économie et de sociologie du travail, 1975), p. 374. Christian Personnaz, "L'Evolution d'un groupe d'entreprises publiques: Charbonnages de France et Houillères du Bassin" (Mémoire, Université de Paris, 1968).

### 8. The Coal Miners' Battle

1. However, the researchers did not necessarily share this viewpoint. Guy Barbichon, "La Perception des risques chez les mineurs," *Bulletin du C.E.R.P.,* 11 (1962): 1–11. Barbichon and Serge Moscovici, "Modernisation des mines: Conversion des mineurs," *Revue française du travail,* 16 (July-September 1962): 3–201. Philippe Cornuau and Alain Girard, "Les Attitudes des mineurs du Centre-Midi et l'évolution de l'emploi," in Institut national d'études démographiques, *Région Languedoc Roussillon. Economie et population,* (Paris: Presses universitaires de France, 1957), pp. 71–235. Guy Durand, "Intégration psychologique des travailleurs à l'entreprise dans les mines de Carmaux" (D.E.S., Université de Paris, 1971). Françoise Lantier, "Etude psychologique de la rémunération du travail dans les mines de charbon semi-mécanisées," *Bulletin du C.E.R.P.,* 10 (1961): 1–27. Serge Moscovici, "Les Mineurs jugent la nationalisation," *Sociologie du travail,* 2 (1960): 216–229. Moscovici, "La Résistance à la mobilité géographique dans les expériences de reconversion," *Sociologie du travail,* 1 (1959): 24–36. Francis Roy, "L'Adaptation en Lorraine des mineurs du Centre-Midi à la suite des opérations de transfert," in *Région Languedoc Roussillon,* pp. 235–260.

2. Alain Touraine, *La Conscience de classe* (Paris: Seuil, 1966), esp. pp. 47, 65, 68–70, 93. See also his "L'Evolution de la conscience et de l'action ouvrière dans les charbonnages," in *Le Charbon et sciences humaines*, ed. Louis Trénard (Paris: Mouton, 1964), pp. 251–264.

3. Darryl Holter, "State Intervention and the Nationalization of Coal Mining in France" (paper presented at the Social Science History Association Meeting, October 1983).

4. Henri Claude, "La Leçon de Decazeville," *Economie et politique*, 191 (February 1962): 3. Dominique Saumon and Louis Puiseux, "Actors and Decisions in French Energy Policy," in *The Energy Syndrome*, ed. Leon Lindberg (Lexington, Mass.: D. C. Heath, 1977), pp. 128, 138–139. Michel Toromanoff, *Le Drame des houillères* (Paris: Editions du Seuil, 1969), pp. 32, 116–117. In the Aubin Basin the Houillères du Bassin d'Aquitaine was allowed to take a 15 (and later 50) percent participation in the ailing Usines Chimiques et Métallurgiques de Decazeville (UCMD) because it had been attached to the mines of Decazeville before nationalization.

5. Jacques Wolff, "Decazeville: expansion et déclin d'un pôle de croissance," *Revue économique*, 23 (September 1972): 781–783. Lucien Mazars, *Terre de mine* (n.p., 1983), pp. 90–93.

6. Bernard Chenot, *Les Entreprises nationalisées* (Paris: Presses universitaires de France, 1972), pp. 41–42.

7. Pierre Renais, "Decazeville," *L'Aide américaine à la France*, 33 (December 1949): 51–56. A. Albenque, "La Modernisation des découvertes de Decazeville," *Revue du Rouergue*, 4 (1950): 40–48. Wolff, "Decazeville," 779–780.

8. Houillères du Bassin d'Aquitaine, *Modernisation: Equipement 1946–1952* (Toulouse: Imprimerie Fournié, 1952), p. 35. Francis Cabrol, "Mines et mineurs de Decazeville 1945–1962: Histoire d'une fin" (Mémoire, Université de Toulouse-le-Mirail, 1974), pp. 75–76. G. Flottes, "Le Bassin houiller aveyronnais. Modernisation et perspectives d'avenir," *Revue du Rouergue*, 6 (1952): 273–294. L. de Mijolla, "Situation actuelle du bassin houiller de Decazeville," *Revue du Rouergue*, 7 (1953): 318–325.

9. Barbichon and Moscovici, "Modernisation," 42, 68–69, 119, 125. See also the classic study by E. L. Trist and K. W. Bamforth, "Some Social and Psychological Consequences of the Longwall Method of Coal-Getting," *Human Relations*, 4 (1951): 3–38.

10. Barbichon and Moscovici, "Modernisation," 118.

11. Université des Sciences Sociales de Grenoble, *La Mure en Mathyisme. La Volonté de vivre* (n.p.: CNRS et l'Etablissement Public Régional Rhône-Alps, 1981), p. 13.

12. Roger Cornu and Bernard Picon, *Analyse contextuelle de la mobilité. II-Mineurs cévenols et provençaux face à la crise des charbonnages* (Aix-en-Provence: Laboratoire d'économie et de sociologie du travail, 1975), pp. 158–159.

13. Barbichon and Moscovici, "Modernisation," 127–129. For a different interpretation of the effects of mechanization of mine work, see Ian Rutledge, "Changes in the Mode of Production and the Growth of 'Mass Militance' in the British Mining Industry, 1954–1974," *Science and Society*, 41 (Winter 1977–78): 410–429.

14. Barbichon and Moscovici, "Modernisation," 96, 141, 145.

15. Cornuau and Girard, "Les Attitudes," pp. 148–149.

16. Ibid.

17. Université des Sciences Sociales en Grenoble, *La Mure en Mathyisme*, p. 13.

18. Barbichon and Moscovici, "Modernisation," 147.

19. Moscovici, "Les Mineurs," 221.

20. Jacques Le Bailly and Jack Chargelègue, "Decazeville. Avec les entêtés de la côte 'moins 360,' " *Paris-Match*, 13 January 1962, p. 29.

21. On the apprenticeship program at Decazeville after the war, see Jeunes Patrons, *Réalisations d'apprentissage* (Paris: Centre des Jeunes Patrons, 1945); and ADA 66S2, "Situation de l'industrie minérale dans le département de l'Aveyron en 1946," 31 October 1947.

22. J. F. Gravier, *Etudes régionales d'emploi. Auvergne-Aquitaine* (Luxemburg: CECA, 1957), pp. 59, 62.

23. DCMD, 23 January 1949; 15 February 1950; 24 April 1950; 6 October 1950; 6 January 1951.

24. Paul Ramadier, "La Situation et l'avenir du Bassin Houiller," *Revue du Rouergue*, 8 (1954): 18.

25. DCMD, 15 October 1953; 25 February 1954.

26. Mazars, *Terre de Mine*, p. 91. Ramadier also used his influence to obtain the same benefits for workers in the UCMD (see note 4) as were given miners. These were withdrawn, however, when the gas from Lacq replaced coal at the plant. Marc Dumont, "Le Bassin de Decazeville: un problème type de conversion" (Thèse, Université de Paris, 1966), p. 137, n. 1. The extension of the Miner's Statute to the non-miners at UCMD became the basis of striking miners' demand in 1961–62 that they retain the Statute in their new jobs. Archives of the Charbonnages de France 1.21841 (27), clipping from *La Voix du Nord*, 2 March 1962 (article by José Hanu).

27. Pierre Combal, "La Reconversion à Decazeville et ses problèmes" (D.E.S., Université de Toulouse, 1967), pp. 37–40.

28. Roy, "L'Adaptation," pp. 235–236.

29. Barbichon and Moscovici, "Modernisation," 158.

30. ACGTD, press clipping on the tenth congress of the Aveyron Union départementale (CGT), 12–13 June 1954.

31. Combal, "La Reconversion" p. 37. Roy, "L'Adaptation," p. 245.

32. Barbichon and Moscovici, "Modernisation," 163–164.

33. Moscovici pointed out that the transfers were carried out ineptly;

sociologists should have been called in before, not after the operation. Like all the sociologists who studied miners during the 1950s, he suggested that the Charbonnages had done an inadequate job of breaking the insularity of the mining community. A widespread formal and informal information network that would stress the advantages of moving, together with better preparation at the receiving areas, would have made the transfers more successful. See "La Résistance à la mobilité géographique," 14–26.

34. J. F. Gravier, *Paris et le désert français* (Paris: Le Portulan, 1947).

35. Gravier, *Etudes régionales*, pp. 66–68.

36. Suzanne Berger, "Bretons, Basques, Scots and Other European Nations," *Journal of Interdisciplinary History*, 3 (1972): 174.

37. APD, Livre de paroisse, October 1955. Monique Bornes-Vernet, "Les Saints guérisseurs en Bas-Rouergue" (Thèse, Université de Montpellier, 1969), pp. 210–213.

38. When Decazeville's miners struck to protest the closing of the town's mines in 1961, many local Socialists saw their decision as a rejection of the measured approach taken by Ramadier to reindustrialize the Basin. Colette Rabary, a Socialist leader and long-time friend of Ramadier, wrote in anguish on Christmas Eve of 1961: "At Decazeville there is nothing more. Rouquette is outstripped by this strike. The void is complete. I am heartbroken to observe this. I had thought him more stable." Archives of the Parti Socialiste, Fédération de l'Aveyron.

39. ACFTC, "Comité intersyndical de défense du Centre-Midi," 23 August 1960; 11 September 1960; 23 September 1960. The CGT-FSS held several conferences for their unions in the threatened coalfields of southern and central France. The representatives from the Aubin Basin were always the most pessimistic participants at these meetings; in April 1961 a *cri d'alarme* at Decazeville forced the CGT-FSS to dispatch its ailing leader Léon Delfosse to the Aubin Basin. ACGTFSS, "La Grève de Decazeville." Report to the Bureau Politique du Parti Communiste Français, 18 January 1962.

40. ACGTD, Bureau syndical (Decazeville), 24 August 1961. André Quintard, "Les Mineurs de Decazeville contre l'Europe des monopoles et le pouvoir personnel," *Cahiers du communisme*, 38 (May 1962): 114–115. At the outbreak of the strike the CGT represented 44 percent of the miners, the CFTC 25 percent. Micheline Colin, "Le Conflit de Decazeville (décembre 1961-février 1962)," *Esprit*, 306 (May 1962): 853.

41. *Masses ouvrières*, 186 (June 1962): 25. After the 1961–62 strike the CGT privately accused Action Catholique of having served as an "occult direction" of the strike with the goal of "evangelizing the working class." ACGTFSS, speech by official of the CGT-FSS at Decazeville, 6 January 1963.

42. Saumon and Puiseux, "Actors and Decisions," pp. 139–140.

43. On the unfolding of the strike, see Michel Daynac, "Decazeville: autopsie d'une grève, décembre 1961-février 1962," *Cahiers d'histoire de*

*l'Institut de recherches marxistes*, 9 (1962): 95–122. Louis Erignac, *Trois siècles de luttes populaires en Bas-Rouergue. 1643–1962. De la révolte des Croquants à la grève de Decazeville* (Villefranche-de-Rouergue: Fédération de l'Aveyron et la Section de Villefranche-de-Rouergue du Parti Communiste Français, 1977), pp. 253–278. Roger Lajoie-Mazenc, *Colère au fond des puits* (Villefranche-de-Rouergue: Editions Salingardes, 1964). Rolande Trempé, "Un Combat d'avant-garde: La Grève des mineurs de Decazeville," in *Economie et société en Languedoc-Roussillon de 1789 à nos jours* (Montpellier: Fédération historique du Languedoc méditerranéen et du Roussillon, 1978), pp. 295–319.

44. When the state moved later to close more technologically advanced pits, it deliberately obscured the extraordinary transformation of the miners' work brought by mechanization of underground extraction, preferring instead to confirm popular stereotypes of the miner derived from accounts of the pick-and-shovel period. Claude Mazauric and Jacques Dartigue, *Ladrecht* (Paris: Editions sociales, 1982), p. 71.

45. ACTFC, "Exposé de M. Jeannenay, Ministre de l'Industrie devant . . . l'Assemblée national," 9 February 1962. See also France; Secrétariat d'Etat auprès du Premier Ministre chargé de l'Information, "Le Problème de Decazeville" (1962).

46. Cornuau and Girard, "Les Attitudes," pp. 120, 123–124, 203 (quoted), 213–214, 218. Gravier, *Etude régional*, p. 62.

47. The CGT felt that the strike initially focused more on the other unions' concerns with reconversion than with defense of the coal industry. The CGT worked hard to make its program dominate. See especially ACGTFSS, "La Grève de Decazeville." Report to Bureau politique of the Communist party.

48. The CGT opposed the CFTC and the FO throughout the strike. Two days after it began the CGT-FSS leader Achille Blondeau told a private meeting of Decazeville CGT members not to underestimate the enemy, which he identified as the Gaullists, the Church, and the Socialists. In the first period of the strike the CGT felt that the CFTC was setting the agenda. The CGT strategy was to reclaim the leading role by prolonging the strike in expectation that the CFTC (and the FO) would eventually want to end the movement. This, Blondeau pointed out to the Decazeville CGT, put local militants from other unions between the "hammer and the anvil": their constituencies in Decazeville and their more cautious national federations. ACGTFSS, "Cahier" kept by Blondeau during the strike.

In a situation reminiscent of the one faced by the *confédérés* between the wars, the national FO miners' federation proved reluctant to act during the strike. This prompted the FO in the Basin to write an anguished letter to its national federation which pointed out that national FO support was a matter of life or death for the local organization. ACGTFSS, Union locale des syndicats Force Ouvrière du Bassin houiller to Fédération nationale du

Sous-Sol CGT-FO, 29 December 1961. The FO was also almost totally absent from the 21 January meeting to plan the massive 26 January demonstration in support of the strike. Serge Mallet suggests that this was because the FO was primarily a union of civil servants with guaranteed employment. "Les Oubliés de Decazeville," *France Observateur*, 613 (1 February 1962): 15.

49. The Communists used the fate of the retrained miner as an example of the "pauperization" of the working class which Thorez preached in the 1950s. Claude, "La Leçon," 8.

50. SLSAA Fonds Daudibertières, "Divers B, no. 7," Houillères du Bassin d'Aquitaine . . . ; "Enquête sur les logements du personnel ouvrier . . ."

51. There had been several sit-in strikes in French mines in the past. During the three-week strike in the Cévennes in 1952, the management refused to allow the miners to provision the strikers and had the CRS do the job. The Charbonnages fired 269 miners (2.5 percent of the underground labor force) at the end of the strike. Cornu and Picon, *Analyse contextuelle*, pp. 373–374.

52. ACGTD, "La Position des ingénieurs des H.B.A. (Groupe Aveyron) face à la crise charbonnière . . . ," 19 December 1961; statement by Syndicat des Ingénieurs de l'Aveyron, 22 December 1961. See also Cornu and Picon's comments about the reaction of supervisory personnel to mechanization and pit closings in the Cévennes; *Analyse contextuelle*, pp. 162–164, 272–273.

In a superb paper Etienne Dejonghe analyzes how the mechanization of mining in the Nord/Pas-de-Calais reduced the autonomy of mine engineers and created resentment among them; "Ingénieurs et sociétés dans les Houillères du Nord/Pas-de-Calais de la Belle Epoque à nos jours" (paper presented at the conference "Ingénieurs et Société," Le Creusot, October 1980).

53. *Centre-Presse*, 22 January 1962, p. 3. This political alliance of workers and *cadres* is not among the kind of alliances that Serge Mallet and other theorists of the "new working class" saw developing in technologically advanced industries. For Mallet, following Touraine, the miners were the rearguard of the French working class. See especially the 1968 edition of Mallet's *La Nouvelle classe ouvrière* (Paris: Editions du Seuil, 1968).

54. Bex Soulhac, "La Grève des mineurs de Decazeville du 19 décembre 1961 au 21 février 1962 vue à travers *La Dépêche du Midi* (édition de Toulouse), *La Dépêche du Midi* (édition de l'Aveyron) et *Le Sud-Ouest* " (Mémoire, Université de Toulouse-le-Mirail, 1975), p. 10.

55. ACFTC, "Rapport du Comité intersyndical des mineurs à la Réunion des organisations syndicales et professionnelles de 16 départements du Sud-ouest à Rodez le 21 janvier 1962."

56. ACFTC, "Discours de clôture prononcé par M. Joulie," 21 January 1962.

57. Colin, "Le Conflict," 850.

58. *Centre-Presse,* 5 February 1962, p. 2. Although the CGT was suspicious of the Church's involvement in the strike, it recognized its power. The CGT-FSS leader Achille Blondeau even copied a portion of the papal encyclical "Mater et Magistra" into the notebook he kept during the strike. (ACGTFSS, "Cahier Blondeau.") The passage explained that it was the Church's obligation to intervene in public policy issues which concerned moral principles and, equally important, that when ecclesiastical authorities pronounced on such issues, it was the duty of Catholics to obey.

59. *Masses ouvrières,* 186: 19.

60. ACFTC, "Conférence de presse du Comité intersyndical des mineurs," 23 December 1961. One CGT official could not refrain from commenting on the margin of a CFTC handout which began "Before closing a factory one must open another . . .": "Quel idéologue quel rêveur." ACGTFSS, comments on "Information des cadres sur la grève des mineurs de Decazeville."

61. ACFTC, "Exposé de M. Jeanneney . . . ," 9 February 1962.

62. This feeling that family values were best preserved in workers' communities is clear in the strikers' contrast of their sons to the insolent leather-jacketed sons of the rich. ACGTFSS, *Bulletin du Comité Intersyndical,* no. 4, 27–28 December 1961.

63. ACFTC, "Rapport du Comité intersyndical . . . le 21 janvier 1962." *Masses ouvrières,* 186: 97–101.

64. ACGTD, draft of broadside, February 1962.

65. ACFTC, "Rapport du Comité intersyndical . . . le 21 janvier 1962." The government was equally interested in publicizing its point of view. See the detailed analysis of the coverage given the strike in the regional press of 30 December 1961. Archives of the Charbonnages de France 1.21841, "Communication téléphonique de M. Mauger—Samedi 30 décembre 1961 8 h 30."

66. Stanley Hoffmann, "Paradoxes of the French Political Community," in *In Search of France* (New York: Harper Torchbooks, 1965), p. 66.

67. Roger Beteille, *Les Aveyronnais. Essai géographique sur l'espace humain* (Poitiers: Imprimerie l'Union, 1974), p. 157.

68. Roger Lajoie-Mazenc, *Marcel Bruel et le défi agricole* (Villefranche-de-Rouergue: Guibert, 1976), p. 122.

69. Colin, "Le Conflit," 853.

70. The peasants' support of Decazeville's miners later became an important building block in Maoist interpretations of the revolutionary potential of French society. Michel Le Bris, *Occitanie: Volem viure!* (Paris: Gallimard, 1974), pp. 230, 239, 259, 324–325.

71. ACFTC, "Discours de clôture prononcé par M. Joulie," 21 January 1962. Ironically, the term "French desert" had been coined by J. F. Gravier,

who laid the groundwork for the Charbonnages' plan which prompted the strike.

72. A young engineer in the Lorraine commented ten years later: "The fact that the workers have to speak French and not Lorraine [to the engineer] appears good to me. Unable to express themselves as easily, they argue much less and the meetings go much better; they find themselves facing a recognized authority." Jean-Pierre Barou, *Gilda, je t'aime à bas le travail!* (Paris: Les Presses d'aujourd'hui, 1973), p. 66.

73. The *chtimi* spoken in northern coal mines separated miners from the rest of society. Henri Roussel, "Le parler du mineur," in *Charbon et sciences humaines,* ed. Louis Trénard (Paris: Mouton, 1966), pp. 289–296. The economy of southwestern France limited the isolation of miners from rural life, however, and made language a source of regional unity in a time of crisis.

74. Alain Berger and Jacques Rouzier, *Vivre et produire en Languedoc-Roussillon. Approche économique et humaine* (Toulouse: Privat, 1981), p. 241.

75. Nico Kielstra, "The Languedoc: Positive and Negative Definitions of a Region and a Culture" (paper presented at the Conference of Europeanists in Washington, D.C., October 1980). See also Rolande Trempé, "Problèmes culturels autour des mineurs de Carmaux," *Revue du Tarn,* 96 (Winter 1979): 587–593.

76. Bex Soulhac, "La Grève," p. 151.

77. A miner from the Aubin Basin expressed this sentiment clearly in 1956: "Lorraine breaks *'l'amitié familiale.'* France is composed of hamlets and hamlets of families. To destroy the family is to destroy France and work in the same stroke." Cornuau and Girard, "Les Attitudes," p. 203. See also Claude Dubar, Gérard Gayot, and Jacques Hedoux, "Sociabilité minière et changement social à Sallaumines et à Noyelles-sous-Lens (1900–1950)," *Revue du nord,* 64 (April–June 1982): 460–461, for a similar identification of national and communal values in the declining coal-mining community of Sallaumines.

78. In contrast, Poujadist peasants and shopkeepers had earlier drawn on neo-Vichyite discourse to justify their opposition to state economic policies.

79. Archives Cabrolière, "Intervention du Camarade Labrune au Conseil National," 26 March 1962. Yet, as Trempé points out, the relation of Gaullist economic plans and European economic integration to the fate of Decazeville was rarely raised directly during the strike for fear of breaking political and syndical unity; "Un combat," p. 315.

80. Laurence Wylie has argued that the miners of Decazeville received widespread support because they symbolized each Frenchman's desire to preserve his *droits acquis:* "Every group tried to identify itself with them; it was just as though Frenchmen, by sponsoring the cause of the miners,

were strengthening their own claims to one right or another." ("Social Change at the Grass Roots," in *In Search of France,* p. 226.)

81. Although the Communist Party provided the prime political support for the strikers, it too was preoccupied by the OAS terrorist attacks. Daynac, "Decazeville," 107–108; 117–118.

82. On declining support for the strike from local and regional groups, see ACGTFSS, "Cahier Blondeau"; "Réunion militants le 14 février (Decazeville)," comments on Labrune.

83. The CGT let it be known that its partners on the Intersyndical Committee had forced it to agree to end the strike. *Centre-Presse,* 21 February 1962, p. 2. The material in Blondeau's notebooks testifies to the emotional problems which ending a traumatic strike like that at Decazeville presented when there was no clear-cut victory. ACGTFSS, "Notes discours Blondeau. Assemblée des Syndiqués le 19 février 1961"; and an account of a meeting of Decazeville CGT militants, 17 February 1962, in "Cahier Blondeau."

84. This has been done in some parts of the Nord/Pas-de-Calais. Bernard Convert, Pierre Jakubowski, and Michel Pinet, "Mobilité professionnelle, mobilité spatiale et restructuration économique. Le cas Bassin minier Nord/Pas-de-Calais," *La vie urbaine,* 52, 53, 54 (1976): 115–123.

85. Case studies in the Archives Rouquette show a fall in salary to 50 percent of a miner's wages from 90 percent once the state wage guarantee was withdrawn. See also ACFTC, "Memorandum à M. Le Préfet de L'Aveyron (remis par les travailleurs des usines de reconversion) le 9 mai 1964"; Houillères du Bassin d'Aquitaine, "Note au sujet de la reconversion en Aveyron," 15 March 1966. ACGTD, Comité Intersyndical des Mineurs, "Document sur les problèmes du Bassin de l'Aveyron. Revendications intéressant l'ensemble du personnel," 18 February 1965. Jean-Michel Guillou, "Problèmes de reconversion à Decazeville" (Mémoire de stage, Ecole Nationale d'Administration, 1966). Roger Lajoie-Mazenc, *Déracinés et proscrits* (Villefranche-de-Rouergue: Editions Salingardes, 1966). José Cubéro, "Une Ville moyenne: Decazeville" in *Les Transformations du cadre de vie* (Paris: La Documentation française et l'Institut national de recherches et de documentation pédagogique, n.d.), pp. 30–52. For the difficulties of conversion in the Cévennes, see Cornu and Picon, *Analyse contextuelle,* pp. 220–275.

86. On the effects of Creusot-Loire's investment strategies on French industry and the industrial town of Rive-de-Gier in particular, see P. Gaume, "Comment une société multinationale déstabilise une région: Creusot-Loire dans la région stéphanoise," *Economie et Humanisme,* 263 (January-March 1982): 29–39.

87. Saumon and Puiseux, "Actors and Decisions," p. 119.

88. Mazars, *Terre de mine,* pp. 119–120.

89. Beteille, *Les Aveyronnais,* pp. 215–216.

90. Lucien Mazars, *Cransac. Ville thermale* (Rodez: F. Carrère, n.d.). The defunct mine itself became a tourist attraction with the opening of a Musée de la Mine in Aubin.

91. For an overview of the history of regionalist movements in France, see Christian Gras, "Le Mouvement régionaliste français et l'histoire sociale: éléments de problématique et de bibliographie," *Mouvement social*, 92 (July-September 1975): 103–117.

92. Joan Bodon, "Los Carbonièrs de La Sala," in *Los Carbonièrs de La Sala*, ed. Ives Roqueta (Nîmes: Edicions "vent terral," 1975), p. 155.

93. Robert Lafont, *La Revendication occitane* (Paris: Flammarion, 1974), pp. 271–272.

94. Robert Lafont, *Clefs pour l'Occitanie* (Paris: Seghers, 1971), p. 220.

95. Serge Mallet, "La Révolte des colonisés de l'intérieur," *France Observateur*, 610 (11 January 1962): 13.

96. André Gorz, *Strategy for Labor: A Radical Proposal*, trans. Martin A. Nicolaus and Victoria Ortiz (Boston: Beacon Press, 1967), pp. 173–174.

97. See James Jacobs, "Ethnic Mobilization and the Pursuit of Post-Industrial Values," *The Tocqueville Review*, II, 2–3 (Spring-Summer 1980): 52–85.

98. Charles de Gaulle, *Discours et messages. Avec le renouveau 1958–1962* (Paris: Plon, 1970), p. 374.

99. George Ross, "Anatomy of a Strike in a Manager State," *New Politics*, II (Autumn 1963) 3:101. Philippe Bauchard and Maurice Bruzek, *Le Syndicalisme à l'épreuve* (Paris: Laffont, 1968), ch. 1. Pierre Belleville, *Une Nouvelle classe ouvrière* (Paris: Julliard, 1963), pp. 236–272. Serge Mallet, "Le Deuxième âge du gaullisme," *Esprit*, 318 (June 1963): 1041–1057.

100. Charles de Gaulle, *Mémoires d'espoir. L'Effort 1962–...* (Paris: Plon, 1971), pp. 138–139.

101. Ironically, one reason for the public's support of the miners was that during the mild winter of 1963 the strike did not result in any fuel shortages. The miners' triumph was based clearly on their success in the public and political arena and not on the economic pressure they generated. Saumon and Puiseux argue that the nature of the miners' victory created a malaise, especially in the larger basins. Miners quit what they saw as a dying industry and their sons left to work elsewhere. Increasingly the Charbonnages in the Nord/Pas-de-Calais and the Lorraine came to depend on short-term immigrant labor for underground miners ("Actors and Decisions," p. 140). This was less true in the southern coal basins where miners had lived for almost a generation with the spectre of pit closings.

102. Pierre Dubois, in a study of strikes in the private sector in the early 1970s—before *la crise*—points out the importance and the uniqueness of strikes against mass firings. In 1971, 10.6 percent of all labor conflicts in France were over the dismissal of more than twenty employees. And whereas the general tendency of strikes in France has been to become shorter

in duration, 30.5 percent of all strikes over employment in France in 1973 lasted more than a month. Pierre Dubois, "Les Grèves et le droit à l'emploi," *Revue française des affaires sociales*, 28 (1974): 119–153.

103. See Stephen S. Cohen's comments in "Informed Bewilderment: French Economic Strategy and the Crisis," *The Tocqueville Review*, III, 1 (Fall 1980–Winter 1981): 78–113.

104. Jacques Jeandin, *Trieux, 79 Jours au fond pour la Lorraine* (Paris: Editions sociales, 1977). Roger Biard, *Les Mines de fer de Lorraine. Une Richesse nationale en péril* (Paris: Editions sociales, 1966).

105. The political economy of the steel industry gave government more leeway in dismantling the steelworks than had been the case in the nationalized coal industry. While the steel company heads were the butt of widespread antagonism for their unpopular decisions to lay off workers and to close factories, the state (which indirectly controlled the companies) was able to step in as the "arbiter" and offer solace in the form of early retirement benefits and inducements for new industries to settle in the area. Gérard Noirel, *Vivre à Longwy* (Paris: Editions sociales, 1981), p. 72. See also Claude Durand, *Chômage et violence* (Paris: Editions Galilée, 1981).

106. *Options Quinzaine*, 49 (7 May 1980): 4–5. Christian Arguel, "La Bataille du charbon dans les Cévennes," *Cahiers du communisme*, 57 (April 1981): 22–27. Mazauric and Dartigue, *Ladrecht*.

107. This type of action has become a common means of forcing a distant administration to enter into some form of discussion in strikes against deindustrialization. See Durand, *Chômage et violence*, ch. 2.

108. *Le Monde*, 1 March 1983, p. 44; 3 March 1983, p. 28; 6 March 1983, p. 14.

109. *Le Monde*, 2 March 1984, pp. 28–29.

110. Clark Kerr and Abraham Siegel, "The Interindustry Propensity to Strike: An International Comparison," in Clark Kerr, *Labor and Management in Industrial Society* (Garden City, N.Y.: Doubleday, 1964), p. 112.

111. In recent years historians of French labor have closely examined how craftsmen and early industrial workers used the values and symbols of their work and social community to effect social protest. These actions, although filled with meaning for the participants, often appeared senseless to outside observers. See, for instance, William Reddy, "The *Batteurs* and the Informer's Eye: A Labour Dispute Under the French Second Empire," *History Workshop*, 7 (Spring 1979): 30–44. The Decazeville strikers reversed this approach. Because they depended on generating public support, they used their work experiences to develop a symbolic discourse to enable others to understand what was happening to their community.

**Conclusion**

1. Raymond Aron made the reference to Luddites (*Le Figaro*, 29 December 1961, p. 1); Jacques Le Bailly and Jack Charlelègue wrote of the strikers as *canuts* ("Decazeville: Avec les entêtés de la côte 'moins 360,' " *Paris-Match*, 13 January 1962, p. 29).

**Appendix**

1. Louis Chevalier, *Laboring Classes and Dangerous Classes in Paris During the First Half of the Nineteenth Century*, trans. Frank Jellinek (New York: Howard Fertig, 1973). See also Philippe Ariès, *Histoire des populations françaises et de leurs attitudes devant la vie depuis le XVIIIᵉ siècle* (Paris: Seuil, 1976).

2. E. P. Thompson, *The Making of the English Working Class* (New York: Pantheon Books, 1963). William Sewell, *Work and Revolution in France: The Language of Labor from the Old Régime to 1848* (Cambridge: Cambridge University Press, 1980).

3. Many social historians have shown that community and craft cohesion provided important bases for collective action, and conversely, that breakdown impeded such activity. Examples include Charles Tilly's pathbreaking *The Vendée* (Cambridge, Mass.: Harvard University Press, 1964); Craig Calhoun, *The Question of Class Struggle* (Chicago: University of Chicago Press, 1982); Joan Scott, *The Glassworkers of Carmaux* (Cambridge, Mass.: Harvard University Press, 1974); Elinor Accampo, "Industrialization and the Working-Class Family: Saint-Chamond 1815–1880" (Ph.D. diss., University of California at Berkeley, 1984); David Crew, *Town in the Ruhr: A Social History of Bochum, 1860–1914* (New York: Columbia University Press, 1979); Yves Lequin, *Les Ouvriers de la région lyonnaise (1848–1914)*, 2 vols. (Lyon: Presses universitaires de Lyon, 1977), 1; and Michael Hanagan's excellent *The Logic of Solidarity* (Urbana: University of Illinois Press, 1980). For a more strictly Marxist argument that the breakdown of craft communities created—at least briefly—a radical working class, see John Foster, *Class Struggle and the Industrial Revolution* (New York: St. Martin's Press, 1974), and Christopher Johnson's excellent "Patterns of Proletarianization: Parisian Tailors and Lodève Woolens Workers," in *Consciousness and Class Experience*, ed. John Merriman (New York: Holmes and Meier, 1979), pp. 65–84.

4. Several historians have used population lists to demonstrate the high degree of geographic mobility of workers in nineteenth-century cities. For an example, see Crew, *Town in the Ruhr*. Two French researchers have analyzed extant census lists from pre-1914 Decazeville, although not to determine levels of persistence: Patrick Couffin, "Aspects de la vie ouvrière à Decazeville au début du XXᵉ siècle (1892–1914)" (Mémoire, Université

de Paul Valéry (Montpellier III), 1975); and Charles Peyrouty, "L'Implantation de la main d'oeuvre dans le bassin houiller aveyronnais" (Mémoire, Université de Toulouse, 1970).

5. Anne-Marie Girbal and Jacques Derruau, "Etude démographique de la commune d'Aubin, Aveyron 1850–1880" (D.E.S., Université de Toulouse-le-Mirail, n.d.), p. 24.

6. DCMD, 10 May 1862.

7. ADA 52M3, state engineer, 15 June 1865; SpVf to PA, 19 June 1865.

8. For events at Aubin, see my "Labor, Management, and the State in an Industrial Town: Decazeville, 1826–1914" (Ph.D. diss., Stanford University, 1981), pp. 142–153.

9. These lists are in ADA series S. For an analysis of their content, see ibid., p. 325.

10. For a look at the increasing mobility of the labor force in the Decazeville metallurgical factory, see Rolande Trempé, "Pour une meilleure connaissance de la classe ouvrière. L'Utilisation des archives d'entreprise: le fichier du personnel," in *Mélanges d'histoire sociale offerts à Jean Maitron* (Paris: Editions ouvrières, 1976), pp. 249–263.

11. I have not included an analysis of the brides by occupation because the majority were listed as "sans profession."

12. Unfortunately the surviving *inventaires après décès* for pre-1914 Decazeville are not particularly suitable for systematic analysis.

13. ADA 44M1 5, DD to SpVf, 6 December 1875; DD to PA, 7 December 1875.

14. Lequin came to similar conclusions about miners, metalworkers, and laborers in his *Les Ouvriers,* esp. I, 237–238, 258, 262–264, 266–267.

15. On the ability to sign as an indicator of literacy, see François Furet and Jacques Ozouf, *Reading and Writing: Literacy in France from Calvin to Jules Ferry* (Cambridge: Cambridge University Press, 1982), pp. 16–17.

16. Because witnesses were asked to sign the marriage register it is possible that industrial workers in the first samples were reluctant to select other industrial workers who could not sign as witnesses. I have found no indication of this, however; many witnesses testified that they could not sign and made a mark.

17. See my "The Origins of Industrial Labor Management in France: The Case of the Decazeville Ironworks during the July Monarchy," *Business History Review,* 58 (Spring 1983): 1–19.

18. Couffin, "Aspects," pp. 24–26.

19. See Jean-Paul Courtheoux, "Privilèges et misères d'un métier sidérurgique au XIX<sup>e</sup> siècle: le puddleur," *Revue d'histoire économique et sociale,* 37 (1959): 161–184.

20. For a Decazeville metalworker's account of his travels, see ABHAD, SNHFA "Fiche des agents," Georges Vayssière, a smith who left the Decazeville forges in 1867 at age nineteen "to travel as is the custom." Right

through the end of the nineteenth century metalworkers favored the national costume of velvet pants and silk caps rather than the broad-brimmed hats and blue blouses of the region's peasantry which miners wore.

21. Rolande Trempé, "Le Réformisme des mineurs français à la fin du XIX$^e$ siècle," *Mouvement social,* 65 (October-December 1968): 3–13.

22. See my "L'Industrie métallurgique et les ouvriers métallurgistes de Decazeville, 1892–1914" (forthcoming in *Procès-verbaux des séances de la SLSAA*) and "Guillaume Verdier et le syndicalisme révolutionnaire aux usines de Decazeville (1917–1920)," *Annales du Midi,* 96 (1984): 171–198.

# Index

Agriculture, miners' ties to, 5, 26–27, 33, 40, 74, 161, 228, 229, 232, 259n14,17, 261n44, 300n8, 300–301n10, 323n20; and strikes, 57, 61, 74, 97, 281n108

Algerian War, 188, 198, 206–207, 318n81

Allemane, Jean, and *allemanisme*, 144, 151–153, 154, 298n169

Anzin, 2, 13–14, 18, 25, 27, 51, 88, 89, 254n19, 269n43, 280n90; strike of *1884*, 90, 99

Artisans and skilled workers, 5–6, 24, 52, 72, 115, 298n169, 320n111

Association de l'Industrie Française, 74

Aubin, 9–10, 18; population, 16, 194, 208, 222, 224; politics, 22, 47, 48, 58, 68, 142, 303n81; housing, 40, 180, 292n69; commerce, 41; mine management, 47, 65, 162, 164–165, 191

Aubin Basin: resources, 9–10, 16; economics, 43, 51, 61, 70, 74, 89, 159–160, 161, 162, 163, 164, 169, 173, 188, 189, 190, 212, 300n3; labor, 142, 170–173, 179, 180, 185. *See also* Agriculture; Region

Auzits, 194

Bartuel, Casimir, 145

Basly, Emile: and *1886* strike, 99, 103, 105, 284n144; Pas-de-Calais deputy, 143, 154

Batère, 115

Ben Bella, Ahmed, 207

Berger, Suzanne, 198

Besson, Alexandre Charles, 12–13

Blanc, Jean-Pierre, 93, 277n60

Blanc, Louis, 265n41

Blanzy. *See* Montceau-les-Mines

Blazy, Camille, 80, 122, 285n157; and cooperative store, 83, 84, 85, 95; and *1886* strike, 92, 93, 96, 105, 284n145

Blondeau, Achille, 314n48, 316n58

Board of directors, 56–57, 61
   SHFA, 17, 30, 32, 41, 45, 55, 56–57
   SNHFA, 84; structure of, 63–64, 73–74, 79, 80, 109, 270n57, 274n4, 285n160; in *1878* strike, 77, 78; in *1886* strike, 95, 96, 102–103, 105, 106, 112, 281n107
   SCFD, 121

Bodon, Joan, 209

Bordeaux, 16, 51, 95

Bos, Alexandre, 76, 98

Bos, Philippe, 141

Boulanger, General Georges, 72, 101, 112, 114, 284n140; and *boulangisme* at Decazeville, 109–110, 153

de Bournazel, Count, 11

Bouvari, Emile, 154

Bouyssi, 100

Britanny, 198, 205

Bureau d'Etudes (Decazeville), 164–166

Cabrol, François: as manager, 17–18, 22, 25, 32, 56, 83; as political leader, 41–48, 67, 107, 110, 168, 265nn41,49

Cabrol, Jules, 154

Cadiat, 44, 45, 275n21

Cahors, 16, 21

Campagnac, 18, 22, 109, 271n66, 276n46; safety at, 54, 55–56, 57. *See also* Cransac

Carmaux, 14, 178, 211, 267n14, 284n139, 292nn83,90, 298nn169,173, 299n186, 300n3; comparison to the Aubin Basin, 51, 65, 120, 128, 179, 290n44, 291nn61,65, 296n139

Carnot, Sadi, 110

Carrié, Jean-Baptiste, 93, 99, 100, 103

Catholic Church: during the Old Regime, 10, 252n3; and companies, 20–21, 42, 75–76; observance, 76–77, 111, 198; and *1886* strike, 98; and *1961–62* strike, 199, 203, 313n41, 314n48, 316n58; and *1963* strike, 210. *See also* Confédération Française des Travailleurs Chrétiens

Cayrade, Jules, 76, 154, 275n24, 278n66, 282n113; and *1878* strike, 78, 79; and cooperative, 84–85, 90; and *1886* strike, 93, 94, 98

Chagot, 55. *See also* Montceau-les-Mines

Chamber of Deputies, 90, 112, 282n119; and *1886* strike, 98, 100, 101, 102, 103, 105

Chaneau, Commandant, 110

Charbonnages de France, 182, 315n51; structure of, 178–179, 184, 189–190, 193, 194, 209, 211; in Aubin Basin, 191, 192, 196, 197, 199, 208, 313n33, 317n71; and *1961–62* strike, 200, 201, 203, 204. *See also* Houillères du Bassin d'Aquitaine

Chevalier, Auguste, 48, 58

Chevalier, Louis, 221

Chevalier, Michel, 40, 43, 48, 50

Cibiel, Alfred, 67–68, 76, 86

Clemenceau, Georges, 90, 101, 158, 281n106, 282n116

Coal industry, 2, 3, 190, 199, 208, 216
by nation: Great Britain, 1, 2, 24, 28, 50, 51, 73, 95, 145; Belgium, 2, 24, 197; Germany, 2, 24, 52, 115, 190, 197
by mine (outside of the Aubin Basin): Rive-de-Gier, 14, 60, 104, 318n86; Commentry, 25, 51, 115, 124, 150, 280n90; Grand-Combe, 25, 27, 42, 51, 264n27; Ricamarie, 49; Graissessac, 51, 282n116; Brassac, 115; Lens, 115, 143; Montvicq, 115; Pont-à-Vendin, 115, 143; Albi, 178, 179, 300n3; Waziers, 181; La Mure, 192; Ronchamp, 267n22; Sallaumines, 317n77. *See also* Anzin; Carmaux; Montceau-les-Mines
by department: Gard, 90, 116, 288n22, 300n3, 304nn50,56; Hérault, 116, 300n186; Tarn, 116, 178, 200; Bouches-du-Rhône, 267n14. *See also* Loire; Nord; Pas-de-Calais

Coal Battle, 4, 7, 160, 183, 184, 186, 187, 189; in the Aubin Basin, 180–181; legacy, 185, 207, 216

Colamet, 61

Combes, 74, 129, 138, 153, 273n5

Comité Central des Houillères Françaises, 143, 147, 170

Commerce in Decazeville, 178, 208; company involvement in, 40–41, 42, 54, 58, 81–85, 95, 106, 108, 148–149, 277n50, 278n61,62; and independent cooperatives, 98, 149, 168

Communists, 159, 168, 188, 189, 211; and *unitaires*, 158, 173; at Decazeville, 169, 184, 196, 198, 199; and Nazi-Soviet pact, 175, 176; and Resistance, 178; and Coal Battle, 180, 181, 182, 185, 186, 187; and *1961–62* strike, 207, 209, 318n81; at Aubin, 303n81

Community, 251n22

Compagnie des Mines de la Loire, 57, 132, 266n6

Compagnie d'Orléans, 20, 21, 47

Compagnie du Nord, 20

Company town: creation of, 7, 37–39, 264n27; and Third Republic, 73, 75, 79, 86, 90; demise of, 100, 107, 109, 215. *See also* individual towns.

Confédération Française des Travailleurs Chrétiens, 176; and *1948* strike, 182, 183; and CGT, 196, 199, 200, 308n84, 313n40; and *1961–62* strike, 205, 314n48, 316n60.

Confédération Générale des Cadres, 199

Confédération Générale du Travail, 115, 154, 159, 211; and miners, 129, 144; post-*1944*, 180, 182, 183, 185, 186

Confédération Générale du Travail (*cont.*)
  *Confédérés*, 158, 168, 169–173, 179,
    185, 216, 314n48
  Aubin Basin (post-*1944*), 178, 180,
    308n84, 313n40; and *1948* strike,
    182–183; and transfers, 196–197;
    in Intersyndical Committee, 199–
    200; and *1961–62* strike, 202, 203,
    207, 314n48, 318n83
  Fédération du Sous-Sol: post-*1944*,
    179, 180, 183, 184, 210–211; and
    *1961–62* strike, 205, 313n39,41,
    314nn47,48, 316nn58,60. *See also*
    Unions (miners'); Strike strategies;
    Supervisors and supervision
Confédération Générale du Travail
  Unitaire (*unitaires*), 158, 168, 169,
  171–173, 179, 185–186, 216,
  304n50
Contractors: need for, 26, 33–34, 35,
  40, 119, 261n48; criticism of, 52, 53
  55, 91; demise of, 65, 66, 70, 86, 111,
  227, 237, 271n65; and *1878* strike,
  77, 78; and *1886* strike, 275n27
Courtinade, 11
Cransac, 263n14; *fumeroles*, 9, 22,
  208–209; population, 16, 194, 208;
  mining, 18, 22, 40, 65, 110, 115, 191.
  *See also* Campagnac
Le Creusot, 25, 42, 60, 63, 64, 68, 69, 109,
  116, 121, 140, 264n27, 271n71, 287n15
Creusot-Loire, 208
Crew in mines, 29–31, 35–36, 91–92,
  105, 111, 124–127, 137–138, 147,
  155, 175, 192, 284n145, 299n185. *See*
  *also* Occupations (mining)

Decazes, Elie, 16, 43, 46, 195
Decazeville: competition with Aubin,
  18, 47–48, 68, 108, 265n49, 303n39;
  population, 18, 39, 50, 52, 53, 74,
  106, 117–118, 119–120, 194, 208,
  222–239; housing, 35, 39, 40, 69–70,
  74, 118, 161, 180, 201, 257–258n60,
  263–264n15; tradesmen/white collar,
  39, 46, 78, 79, 149, 232, 235, 238;
  municipal services, 41, 42, 69, 168;
  tolls, 41, 69, 82, 168; police, 42, 48,
  89, 109–110, 264n28, 286n165;
  neighborhoods, 149, 237; sociability,
  224. *See also* Commerce; Politics.

Decazeville Liberation Committee, 178
Delfosse, Léon, 313n39
Deindustrialization: defined, 1–2,
  247n1; and coal mining, 3, 4; at De-
  cazeville, 50, 196, 200, 212, 216
Delaitre, Michel, 32
Delon, Eugène, 86
Deseilligny, Alfred: as manager, 64–67,
  73, 74, 79, 80, 82, 83, 116, 121, 122,
  271n65; and education, 65–67, 77,
  271n71, 272n72; as politician, 67–70,
  75, 76, 85, 110, 155, 168, 272nn76,
  77; and Gastambide, 107, 108; and
  Ramadier, 168, 195
Doctors, 35, 60, 76, 77, 294n99. *See*
  *also* Mutual aid funds; Safety and
  hazards
Douzeich, Auguste, 154
Duc-Quercy, Albert, 151, 153
Dunham, Arthur Louis, 17

Education: and management, 42, 66–
  67, 122, 227–228; and the Third Republic, 72, 77–78, 103–104, 109; and
  literacy, 235, 237
Engels, Friedrich, 102, 112, 282n114
Engineers, 31–33, 46, 93–94, 166, 174,
  176, 185, 192–193, 216, 260nn37,39
Entraygues, 94, 280–281n98
European Coal and Steel Community,
  190, 191, 195, 197, 200, 207

Fayol, Henri, 6, 121–122, 123, 124, 164
Félibrige, 209
Firmy: population, 9, 16, 194; industry,
  17, 18, 19, 33, 35, 79; politics, 68;
  and *1886* strike, 281n108
Force Ouvrière: and *1948* strike, 182–
  183; and transfers, 196, 199; and
  *1961–62* strike, 200, 314–315n48
La Fraternelle, 82–85; 278n62
Freycinet, Charles, 50, 101, 102

Galtié, Pierre, 80
Gambetta, Léon, 102
Gastambide, Jules, 92, 107–109, 147,
  150, 285nn157,160
de Gaulle, Charles, and Gaullism, 159,
  178, 188, 198, 207, 210, 212, 314n48,
  317n79
Ginestet, Edmund, 303n39

Gorz, André, 209
Grand Central, 47
Gravier, J. F., 197, 316–317n71
Great Depression, 158, 159; at Decaze-
    ville, 160, 161, 162, 167, 174
Grès, Jules, 80
Guérard, Eugene, 297n151
Guesde, Jules, and *guesdisme,* 153, 154
Guglielmo, M. R., 50

Hanagan, Michael, 222, 238
Héliot, Jules, 108–109
Hoffmann, Stanley, 205
Houillères du Bassin d'Aquitaine, 178,
    180, 184, 191, 196, 201
Humann, Jean-Georges, 17

Immigrant labor, 223, 289n29; prewar,
    119–121, 130; interwar, 161–163,
    164, 166, 167, 175, 185, 186; and
    unions, 169, 172, 173; in the Resis-
    tance, 177, 178; post-*1945,* 194, 196,
    319n101
Institut d'Etudes Occitanes, 209
Intersyndical Committee, 199, 200,
    201, 202, 203, 206, 207, 318n83

Jaurès, Jean, 154, 156–157, 284n140
Jausions, 62
Jeanneney, Jean-Marcel, 200, 203
Joly de Bammeville, Arthur, 73
Joulie, Roger, 202
Julliard, Jacques, 112

Kerr, Clark, 212
Kielstra, Nico, 206

Laborers, 225–238
Lacoste, Robert, 182
Lacq, 190, 312n26
Lafargue, Laura, 102, 112
Lafargue, Paul, 101, 103, 282n114
Lafont, Robert, 209
Lamendin, Arthur, 154
de Lassalle, 21
Laur, Francis, 102–104, 112, 132,
    284n140
Laur, Joseph Paul, 80
Lebon, Gustave, 221
Le Chapelier law, 49

Lecoeur, Auguste, 180, 182
Ledoux, C., 88
Loire: coal mining, 13, 14, 24, 25, 37,
    116, 170, 300n3; strikes, 39, 52; labor
    and unions, 60, 87, 88, 140, 144, 238,
    290n49, 304n50
Long Depression, 4, 72, 103, 114; at
    Decazeville, 73, 74, 75, 86, 111
Lorraine: steel, 1, 50, 73, 115, 117, 159,
    210, 288n19, 317n72; coal, 191,
    319n101; and transfers from the
    Aubin Basin, 195, 196, 317n77,
    319n101
Lot River, 9, 10, 16, 19, 69
Louis XVIII, 16
Louvroil-Montbard-Aulnoye, 190

Mallet, Serge, 198, 209, 315n53
Management. *See* Board of directors;
    Bureau d'Etudes; Contractors; Fran-
    çois Cabrol; Alfred Deseilligny;
    Henri Fayol; Paternalism; Receiver-
    ship; Region, and managerial person-
    nel; Supervisors and supervision;
    individual firms
Mandagot, 86, 278n66
Maoism, 316n70
Marriage age of Decazeville residents,
    228, 237
Marriage, birth and death registers as
    sources, 224–225, 228–229, 232, 235,
    237, 322n11
Marriage witnesses, 235, 238, 322n16
Marshall Plan, 191, 195
Martin, 83, 96
Marty, Louis, 183
Maruéjouls, Emile, 107, 149, 151, 153,
    154, 155
Marx, Karl, 101, 102, 204, 221
Master miners, foremen, and *chefs de
    poste,* 32–33, 61, 65, 93–95, 122–
    123, 164–166, 174, 271n65
Mazars, Victor: union leader, 119, 129,
    131, 132, 133, 134, 136–137, 139,
    142–143, 145–147, 170, 173, 288n21,
    292n83, 297n151; Socialist, 151–152,
    153, 154
Méline Tariff, 114, 119
Mendès-France, Pierre, 195
Merrheim, Alphonse, 142–143

Metalworks at Decazeville: SHFA, 16, 19–20, 50; SNHFA, 73, 79, 108–109; SCFD, 116, 117, 159, 185; Creusot-Loire, 208

Metalworks elsewhere: Longwy, 1, 81; Alais, 16; Châtillon, 16; Fourchambault, 16, 25, 60, 115; Terrenoire, 16; Saint-Etienne, 18, 23, 81, 87, 211; Mont St.-Martin, 82; Imphy, 115, Joudreville, 115; Montluçon, 115; Pamiers, 115; Vierzon, 282n114. *See also* Le Creusot; Lorraine

Metalworkers at Decazeville, 322–323n20, British, 26, 35, 44, 224; SHFA, 26, 44; SNHFA, 66, 77, 80, 96; SCFD, 128, 133–134, 293n90; social characteristics of, 224–239

Metalworkers' union at Decazeville, 138, 141, 149, 150, 152, 153, 239

Michelet, Jules, 24, 102, 104, 284n140

Millerand, Alexandre, 153

*Mine aux mineurs*, 103–104, 211, 284n140; in Aubin Basin, 104, 132

Miners (Aubin Basin): number, 3, 25, 30, 116, 117, 118–119, 125, 160, 161, 189, 191, 208, 258–259n7, 281n100, 291n60; public image, 3, 99, 180, 181, 184, 185, 186, 189, 212–213, 216, 315n53; geographic origins, 26–27, 75, 92, 117–119, 162, 200, 227, 235, 299n185; social background, 26–27, 65, 67, 200, 229, 232, 235, 237, 238; property ownership, 27, 74, 200; absenteeism, 28, 161, 165, 168, 174; explosives, 28, 124, 289n41; apprenticeship, 28–29, 92, 126–127, 130, 162, 175–176, 193, 196; lamp and tools, 29, 123–124, 163, 301n18; pay-sheet, 29, 105, 125, 130, 290n49; advancement, 32, 66–67, 122; wives, 38, 204; social relationships, 39, 74, 149, 200, 232, 235, 237; age of marriage, 74, 228; fertility, 117–118, 287n15; recruitment of, 118–120, 161, 175, 194, 215; age, 127, 196; transfers, 196–197, 208, 312–313n33. *See also* Agriculture; Contractors; Crew; Immigrant workers; Laborers; Mines and mining; Open-pit mining; Safety and health; Strikes; Supervi-sors and supervision; Unions (min-ers')

Miner's Statute, 179, 182, 193, 196, 216, 312n26

Mine-safety delegates, 165, 169, 174, 179, 184, 192; demand for, 87–88, 93, 284n140; as union leaders, 129, 132–133, 137, 152, 155; qualifications of, 129–130

Mines and mining (Aubin Basin): pro-duction figures, 3, 14, 20, 24, 25, 30, 51–52, 70, 91, 113, 116, 159, 160, 167, 189, 266n9; concessions, 10–16, 96, 99, 105, 214, 281n106, 282n119, 306n88; preindustrial, 10–16; depos-its and coal quality, 20, 51, 161, 163–164; and iron industry, 25–26, 27, 30, 31, 34, 50, 51, 56, 91, 106, 159, 261n48; grades of coal, 28, 30, 53, 91, 92, 96, 124, 281n104; work day, 29, 59–60, 88, 130, 138–139, 161, 167, 175, 179, 180, 294n110, 295n114, 305n58; long-wall mining, 30, 163, 191–192; commercial ententes, 51, 115; productivity, 71, 127–128, 165, 167, 174–175, 180, 189–190, 191, 294n110, 305n58, 308–309n93; mechanization, rationalization and timing of tasks, 116–117, 163, 166–167, 172, 175, 177, 179, 186, 191–194, 306n65, 314n44; markets, 159, 160, 166, 190; and chemical industry, 160, 182, 190, 195, 311n4, 312n26. *See also* Bureau d'Etudes; Contrac-tors; Miners; Management; National-ization; Open-pit mining; Safety and health; State and industry; Supervi-sors and supervision; Wages

de Mirabeau, Honoré-Gabriel, 14

Mistral, Frédéric, 209

Mitterand, François, 211

Montauban, 12, 47

Montbazens, 76, 86

Montceau-les-Mines: mining, 25, 55, 270n55, 271n65; 291n61; 300n3; labor and unions, 84, 90, 109, 140, 144, 287n15

Monteils, Amans-Alexis, 9–10, 14

Montpellier, 9, 209

de Montpensier, Duke, 43

Moreau, Gustave, 257n57
de Morny, Duke, 47
Mouvement Républicain Populaire, 198
Mutual aid funds, 5; SHFA, 34–35, 36, 38, 41–42; conflicts over administration, 59–61, 77–78, 88–89, 93, 96–97, 281n98, 282n109; post-*1894*, 133–135, 141, 152, 155, 165, 169, 182, 184, 292n83, 293n90, 294n99

Napoléon, 14–15, 24
Napoléon III (Louis Napoléon), 46, 49, 60, 132
Nationalization of mining industry, 2, 7, 15; demanded by unions, 99–100, 146–147, 160, 169–170; in practice, 178–180, 184, 186, 187, 193, 308n88. *See also* Charbonnages de France
Neo-Socialists, 168, 179
Nord: coal mining, 24, 25, 37, 52, 87, 118, 170, 191, 315n52, 318n84; labor and unions, 140, 143, 162, 173, 177, 179, 274n13, 290n49, 291n60, 293n91, 296n140, 319n101

Occitania, 8, 206, 209–210, 252n24. *See also* Region
Occupations (mining): helpers, 27–29, 35, 92, 93, 95, 125, 129, 161, 164, 175, 185; hewers, 27–30, 35, 65, 74, 92, 93, 98, 128, 129, 130, 137, 161, 162, 163, 164, 175, 228; timbermen, 28, 93, 93, 129, 130, 133, 137, 161, 162, 280n90; open-pit workers, 30–31, 91, 130; female, 64–65, 66, 116–117, 130; *boute-feux*, 66, 124; electricians, 161, 163, 192; mechanics, 161, 163, 192. *See also* Crew, Laborers
Open-pit mining: labor, 25, 29, 30–31, 34, 120, 128, 161, 162; investments, 30, 35, 51, 64, 91–92, 116, 166–167, 185, 191, 193, 208
Opportunists, 87, 104
Organization of work in the mines. *See* Crew; Contractors; Engineers; Miners; Mines and mining; Occupations; Open-pit mining; Supervisors and supervision; Wages
Orleanism, 44, 103
Oustry, Paul, 170, 171, 304n57

Parlement of Toulouse, 13
Parti Socialiste Unifié, 198
Pas-de-Calais: coal mining, 51, 87, 90, 118, 170, 191, 266n6, 300n3, 315n52, 318n84; labor and unions, 140, 143, 144, 162, 173, 177, 179, 184, 261n45, 295n123, 296n140, 319n101
Paternalism, 6, 45, 70, 90, 122, 161
Paul, Marcel, 179, 180, 182
Penchot, 196
Pensions: pre-*1894*, 92, 93; post-*1894*, 125, 130, 144–145, 169, 179, 196, 295–296n130
Perrot, Michelle, 73, 276–277n47
Petit, Eugène, 135
Petitjean, Jules, 78, 80, 81, 84, 106; and *1886* strike, 94, 96–97, 103, 105, 281n107, 284nn143,144
Politics in Decazeville: under SHFA, 42–48, 58, 266n55; under Deseilligny, 67–69, 272n77; in *1878*, 76–77, 78–79; under SNHFA, 85–86, 98, 107–109, 111, 278n66, 282n110; prewar, 148–154, 298n165, 299n173; interwar, 168–169; postwar, 178, 194, 198. *See also* Republicanism at Decazeville; Socialism
Popular Front, 159, 175, 176, 177, 179; and mining, 160, 165, 167, 169, 174; strikes during, 173, 186, 304n56
Poujade, Pierre, and Poujadism, 188, 317n78
Proletarianization, 120, 214–216
Protoindustry, 23
Provincial Assembly of Haute-Guyenne, 13

Rabary, Colette, 313n38
Radicals, 114, 115, 159; and *1886* strike, 96, 101, 102, 104; in Decazeville, 152–153, 154, 168, 198
Railways, 37, 72, 110; consumer of Basin products, 20, 50, 64; transportation of Basin products, 47, 51, 160, 168–169
Ramadier, Paul: and Decazeville politics 154, 168–169, 194–196, 198, 212, 303n39; and national politics, 169, 175, 182, 185, 194–196, 198–199, 312n26, 313n38

Rancié, 22, 103
Raoul-Duval, Fernand, 73
Rebellions during the Old Regime, 11–12, 214, 254n15
Receivership, 56, 58–63
Region (southwestern France): culture of, 7–8, 74–75, 100–101, 151, 156, 197, 216, 273–274n12, 317n73; and managerial personnel, 11–12, 17, 80–81, 94, 197, 274n13, 276n46, 276–277n47, 317n72; cooperation within, 13, 205–206; economics of, 17, 73, 89–90, 116, 149, 205; and miners' unions, 143–144, 170–172, 180, 205, 296n139. *See also* Aubin Basin; Occitania
Republicanism at Decazeville, 44–45, 67, 75–76, 79
Resistance, 4, 7, 159, 176–178, 183, 186, 207, 216
Revolution of 1789, 14–15, 20, 68, 104
Reybaud, Louis, 40, 69
Riant brothers, 18
Rieupeyroux, 76
Rieux, Albert, 173
Rodez, 46, 47, 160, 197, 205, 300n10; Bishop of, 21, 273n11
Rolland, 48
Rondet, Michel, 87–88, 269n45
Rothschilds, 102
Rouquayrol, B., 58–62, 68, 69
Rouquette, René, 198, 313n38
Ross, George, 210
Rouzet, Jean-François, 85

Safety and health, 27, 34, 59–60, 124, 179, 289n40; accidents, 10, 54–56, 110, 133, 134, 135–137, 154; and the state, 11, 15, 70; fires, 31, 32, 62, 64, 94, 107, 116; company liability, 55, 89, 123, 279n79; medical care of injured, 69, 134, 165, 169, 181, 196, 293n90; and 1898 law, 149, 294n102. *See also* Contractors; Doctors; Mine-safety delegates; Mutual aid fund; State and industry
Saar, 160
Sainte Barbe, 46, 70, 157; Saint Eloi, 70; SCF withdrawal from celebration, 122

Sand, Georges, 102
Say, Léon, 73, 96, 102, 103
Schneider, Eugène, 64
Schneider, Paul, 73, 109
Scott, Joan, 53
Second Industrial Revolution, 114
Second Republic, 44–47, 101, 103–104
*Seize mai* crisis, 72, 75, 79
Service du Travail Obligatoire, 175–176, 177, 306n65, 307n78
Sewell, William Jr., 221
Shorter, Edward, 6
Siegel, Abraham, 212
Simiand, François, 250–251n20
Socialism and Socialists, 5, 114, 115, 159, 182, 188, 211; and 1886 strike, 90, 101, 102, 104, 112, 283n128; in Aubin Basin, 110, 149, 150–154, 168, 169, 194–196, 198, 200; and 1961–62 strike, 313n38, 314n48. *See also* Jean Allemane; Paul Ramadier
Société Anonyme de Commentry-Fourchambault (et Decazeville) (Comambault), 107, 115–177, 185, 186, 228, 295n127
Société Anonyme des Houillères et Fonderies de l'Aveyron, 16–22, 24–36, 39–48, 50, 51, 52, 55, 56, 58, 71, 76, 83, 86, 222. *See also* Board of directors
Société de la Vieille Montagne, 74
Société des Aciéries de France, 22, 129
Société Nouvelle des Houillères et Fonderies de l'Aveyron, 51, 63–71, 73–113, 116, 121, 122, 124–125, 150, 154, 227, 237. *See also* Board of directors
de Solages, Marquis, 14
*Solidarisme*, 67, 254n19
Soubrié, Jean-Louis, 83
State and industry
Supervision of mining, 3–4, 6–7, 123–124, 133, 141, 265n49, 270n55, 285n158; and safety, 11, 12–13, 14, 15, 19, 267n21, 269n45; and accidents, 52, 53, 54–56, 62, 63, 70; and 1886 strike, 94, 97; and Gastambide, 109, 285n158; and labor recruitment, 162, and productivity, 174–175

State and industry (cont.)
  Strikes, 6, 49, 53, 141; 1867, 62–63;
    1878, 78–79; 1886, 96, 105; 1919–
    1920, 168; 1948, 182–183; 1961–
    62, 199–208
  Economic policy, 19–20, 49–51, 72–
    73, 160, 168, 169, 173, 175–176,
    189–190, 196–200, 210–211, 215;
    tariff policy, 16, 17, 24, 43, 51, 53,
    63, 64, 73–74, 168. See also Na-
    tionalization; Safety and health;
    Strikes; Technocracy and techno-
    crats
Stell, Georges, 87, 143, 288n21
Strikes: legalization of, 49, 53, 63; of
  miners, 52–53, 72, 75, 181, 281n106,
  295–296n130, 315n51; supervision of
  pits during strikes, 62–63, 94, 99,
  145–146, 183, 184, 202; troops, 78,
  95, 101, 183, 275n33, 283n125; national sentiment, 79, 100–101, 206–
  207, 212, 215, 283n123, 317n77; public support, 79, 205–206, 282n114;
  press coverage, 90, 98–101, 204–205,
  316n65; May day, 138–140; strike insurance, 143; and job security, 210–
  211, 319–320n107; 1867, 56–63, 67,
  69, 70, 88, 237, 239; 1869 (Aubin),
  49, 57, 69, 224; 1878, 77–79, 88, 93,
  111, 149, 239; 1886, 4, 93–106, 111–
  112, 124, 125, 140, 146, 149, 151,
  237, 239, 277n60, 297n151; 1902,
  144, 149, 150–151, 153, 229, 239;
  1912, 145; 1913 (Aubin), 129; 1914,
  145–146; 1919, 168; 1920, 168; 1927
  (Sacco and Vanzetti), 172–173; 1929,
  304n50; 1933, 172; 1947, 182, 184;
  1948, 182–185, 187, 189, 199, 202,
  216; 1961–62, 5, 8, 200–208, 209,
  210, 211, 212–213, 214, 216, 312n26,
  313n38, 314n47, 314–315n48,
  317n79, 317–318n80, 318n83,
  320n111; 1963, 210, 319n101. See
  also Agriculture; Anzin; State and industry; Strike strategies of unions
Strike strategies of unions: pre-1914,
  140–141; confédérés, 172; unitaires,
  172–173; 1961–62, 203–204, 314n48
Supervisors and supervision: SHFA, 29,
  31–34; SNHFA, 52, 69, 79–80,
  270n57, 271n66; SCFD, 122–123,

124, 163–167, 172, 175; nationalization and Coal Battle, 177, 178, 179,
  181, 185, 187, 192–194, 202, 210,
  212, 315n52; and discipline, 31, 122–
  123, 168, 174–176, 181, 193; and
  unions, 174, 181, 182, 183, 184, 187,
  304–305n57. See also Bureau
  d'Etudes; Contractors; Engineers;
  Master miners, foremen and chefs de
  poste

Taylor, F. W. and Taylorism, 163, 290–
  291n58
Technocracy and technocrats, 191,
  202–203, 206, 207, 216
Thompson, E. P., 8, 221
Thorez, Maurice, 181, 309n95, 315n49
Tilly, Charles, 6, 247n2
Tilly, Louise, 6
Tilly, Richard, 6
Toulouse, 9, 160, 209
Touraine, Alain, 189, 212, 315n53
Tournier, Albert, 172, 181
Tubeuf, 11
Trieux, 210

Unions (miners'): legal status, 49, 87;
  pre-1914, 86–89, 93, 98, 106, 110,
  128–148, 149, 155–156, 238, 239,
  292n78; membership of, 88, 98, 129–
  132, 169, 173, 178, 292n69; and republicanism, 88, 107, 147; social services, 132, 169; pre-1914 relations
  with national federation, 140, 142,
  143–45, 296n139, 296n140; and
  Union Fédérale, 144; and socialism,
  150–154; World War I, 168; and productivity, 174–175, 180–181, 185,
  186; Vichy period, 175, 176, 177, 186,
  306n73; in Aubin, 292n69, 295n117.
  See also Intersyndical Committee;
  Nationalization; Victor Mazars; Region, and miners' unions; individual
  confederations
Usine Claude, 195
d'Uzès, Duchess, 11

Vaillant, Auguste, 294n99
Vial, Jean, 56
Vichy regime, 159, 317n78; and min-
  ing, 160, 175–176, 179, 186, 306n70

Villefranche-de-Rouergue, 12, 17, 67, 68, 197, 198
Viviez, 18, 40, 74, 159, 208

Wages of miners, 250–251n20; pre-*1886*, 29, 33–34, 35, 59–60, 64, 77–78, 89, 271n66; and *1886* strike, 92, 93–95, 97, 105, 281n104, 284n143; pre-*1914*, 125–128, 140, 141–142, 147, 290n55; interwar period, 164, 169, 170, 172, 173, 177, 179, 180, 182; post-*1944*, 189. *See also* Miners, paysheet

Waldeck-Rousseau, René, 87, 102, 104–105, 114, 141
Watrin, Jules, 80–81, 93; and commerce, 82–85, 108, 277n58; murder of, 94–95, 96, 97, 98, 100, 280n97, 284n146; trial of murderers, 105–106
World War I: economic effects of, 158, 159, 162, 164, 167–168, 300n3

Zola, Emile: *Germinal,* 51, 90, 107, 112, 181, 199